Convention on Contracts for the International Sale of Goods (CISG)

Convention on Contracts for the International Sale of Goods (CISG)

Fourth Edition

Joseph Lookofsky

This book was originally published as a monograph in the International Encyclopaedia of Laws/Contracts.

Founding Editor: Roger Blanpain
General Editor: Frank Hendrickx
Volume Editor: Jacques Herbots

Wolters Kluwer

Published by:
Kluwer Law International B.V.
PO Box 316
2400 AH Alphen aan den Rijn
The Netherlands
E-mail: international-sales@wolterskluwer.com
Website: www.wolterskluwer.com/en/solutions/kluwerlawinternational

Sold and distributed by:
Wolters Kluwer Legal & Regulatory U.S.
7201 McKinney Circle
Frederick, MD 21704
United States of America
E-mail: customer.service@wolterskluwer.com

Printed on acid-free paper

ISBN 978-94-035-4072-6

e-Book: ISBN 978-94-035-4073-3
web-PDF: ISBN 978-94-035-4074-0

Printed in the United Kingdom.

The Author

Joseph Lookofsky is Professor Emeritus of Law at the University of Copenhagen in Denmark.

Professor Lookofsky was born in New York, USA. He received his BA in Economics from Lehigh University in 1967 and his J.D. from New York University School of Law in 1971. He became a member of the New York State Bar that year and worked as an attorney for United Artists Corporation, specializing in contract and copyright law.

In 1973, Lookofsky married a Dane and moved to Denmark where he became a consultant to Danish Advocates. In 1981, upon completion of the regular five-year law programme at the University of Copenhagen, he received the *cand.jur.* degree.

In 1981, Lookofsky became a Fellow (*stipendiat*) at the University of Copenhagen Law Faculty; he became a full-time member of the Law Faculty in 1982. In 1989 – upon publication and defence of his doctoral thesis 'Consequential Damages in Comparative Context' – he was awarded the *dr jur.* degree. In 1992, he was appointed to a chair in Private and Commercial Law (*Formueret*). He has taught and led BA-level courses in European & International Commercial Law as well as related upper-level (MA) elective courses. In 1998, Professor Lookofsky was named Teacher of the Year (*Årets Underviser*) at the Copenhagen Law Faculty.

Professor Lookofsky has lectured on the Convention on Contracts for the International Sale of Goods (CISG) and other international commercial topics for the Danish Bar Association (*Advokatsamfund*), the Duke University Law School in North Carolina, the University of Bologna (Facoltá di Giurisprudenza), the Albert-Ludwigs-Universität in Freiburg (Institut für Ausländisches und Internationales Privatrecht), the Duke University Summer Institute in Transnational Law, and the Cornell-Paris I (Sorbonne) Summer Institute of International & Comparative Law.

Lookofsky's more than hundred published works (in Danish and English) cover such topics as Danish contracts and sales law, international contracts and sales, private international law, comparative commercial law and international commercial arbitration.

The Author

Professor Lookofsky serves as United Nations (UNCITRAL) National Reporter for Denmark of cases relating to the CISG and international arbitration. He is a Titular Member of the International Association of Comparative Law (*Académie internationale de droit comparé*). He also serves as an arbitrator in international commercial disputes.

Table of Contents

List of Abbreviations

BGH	Bundesgerichtshof
C&F	Cost and Freight
CIF	Cost, Insurance and Freight
CIP	Carriage and Insurance Paid To
CISG	Convention on Contracts for the International Sale of Goods
CISG AC16	CISG Advisory Council
CISG-Online	CISG Database available at cisg-online.org
CISGW3	Pace University Electronic Library on CISG, available at www.cisg.law.pace.edu/
CLOUT	Case Law on UNCITRAL Texts, available at www.uncitral.org
CPT	Carriage Paid To
EU	European Union
FAS	Free Alongside Ship
FOB	Free on Board
ICC	International Chamber of Commerce
LG	Landesgericht
LPISG	United Nations Limitations Convention
OLG	Oberlandesgericht
PIL	Private International Law
TP	Third Person
UCC	Uniform Commercial Code
ULF	Uniform Law on the Formation of Contracts for the International Sale of Goods
ULIS	Uniform Law for the International Sale of Goods
UNCITRAL	United Nations Commission on International Trade Law

List of Abbreviations

UNCITRAL Case Digest	UNCITRAL Digest of Case Law on the United Nations Convention on Contracts for the International Sales of Goods, available at https://uncitral.un.org/en/case_law/digests
UNILEX	International Case Law & Bibliography on the UNIDROIT Principles and the 1980 UN Convention (CISG), available at www.unilex.info/

Chapter 1. Introduction

§1. International Sales and the CISG

I. The Law of Sales under Domestic Law

A. *Sales Law as Contract Law*

1. The law of Sales is often treated as a distinct legal discipline, but it is also seen as a subset of the more general law of Contracts (and Obligations).[1] Even within this larger context, the contract for the sale of goods is universally acknowledged to be the single most important contract type, and the law of sales is rightly regarded as the cornerstone of commercial law.[2]

B. *Domestic Sales Law Applied to Domestic and International Sales*

2. Sales contracts between parties residing in a single State (and capable of being performed within the borders of that State) are governed by the domestic sales law of the State concerned.[3] Prior to the development of an international sales law acceptable to a broad range of States in the international commercial community, most contract draftsmen – as well as national courts and international arbitrators – were also obliged to apply domestic sales law to international contracts of sale, i.e., contracts between parties residing in different States.[4]

II. International Sales Law: The CISG

3. The United Nations Convention on Contracts for the International Sale of Goods (hereinafter 'the Convention' and/or 'the CISG') is the first international sales law to be accepted by the international community of nations.[5]

---

1. In those legal systems where the general law of obligations is not codified, the influence of a codified sales statute on general contract doctrine can be considerable; *see*, for example, as regards Danish law, Lookofsky & Ulfbeck, *Køb (Law of Sales)* 5th ed. (2020) and Bryde Andersen & Lookofsky, *Lærebog i Obligationsret* vol. I, 4th ed. (2015), Chs 1 and 5; *compare*, for example, regarding American sales and contract law, E.A. Farnsworth, *Contracts* (2004), para. 1.7.
2. *See*, for example, Lookofsky & Ulfbeck, *ibid.*
3. In the present (international sales) context, it seems more appropriate to refer to local law as 'domestic' (rather than 'national') law, in that the 1980 Convention on Contracts for the Sale of goods (CISG) has become *part* of the legal system of each CISG Contracting State.
4. *See infra*, Nos 9 et seq.
5. Regarding the 1964 ULIS Conventions, which were not widely accepted, *see infra*, Nos 11 et seq.

III. Convention Preamble: Objectives of Signatory States

4. The CISG Convention was signed on 11 April 1980, at a diplomatic conference attended by sixty-two States. As documented by its Preamble,[6] the States who signed the treaty did so in light of the broad objectives in the resolutions adopted by the sixth special session of the General Assembly of the United Nations on the establishment of a new International Economic Order. The signatories also considered that the development of international trade on the basis of equality and mutual benefit is an important element in promoting friendly relations among States. The signatory States were also of the opinion that the adoption of uniform rules which govern international sales and take into account the different social, economic and legal systems would contribute to the removal of legal barriers in international trade and promote the development of international trade.

IV. Entry into Force: Initial Ratifications

5. The Convention entered into force on 1 January 1988 (twelve months after the date of deposit of the tenth instrument of ratification).[7] As of that date, international sales (as defined in CISG Part I)[8] became subject to the Convention regime in the following States: Argentina, China, Egypt, France, Hungary, Italy, Lesotho, Syria, United States (US), Yugoslavia and Zambia.

V. Subsequent Ratifications: Three-Fourths of World Trade

6. By 2021, instruments of ratification had been deposited by more than ninety States, collectively representing more than three-fourths of total world trade. A list of CISG adherences, including effective dates, is provided in an Appendix to this monograph.

---

6. Professors Honnold and Flechtner observed that the CISG Preamble was first considered and prepared two days before the adjournment of the Vienna Conference: *see* Honnold/Flechtner, *Uniform Law for International Sales under the 1980 United Nations Convention* 4th ed. (2009), 704–705. Although the CISG Preamble might sometimes lend some 'make-weight' support to the 'international' treaty *interpretation* mandated by Art. 7(1), *see infra*, Nos 27 et seq., Professor Flechtner (*ibid.*) sees no significant role for the Preamble as regards resolving specific challenging issues under the Convention.
7. *See* Art. 99(1).
8. For a more precise indication of the Convention's sphere of application, *see infra*, Nos 51 et seq.

VI. Major Significance

7. On the basis of this impressive and steadily growing list of ratifications, the CISG Convention must be regarded as the most significant piece of substantive contract legislation in effect at the international level. Given the fact that the international contract of sale is the single most important international contract type,[9] coupled with the fact that the parties to most such contracts do not (as sometimes elsewhere alleged) 'contract out' of this well-balanced rule-set,[10] on the contrary,[11] the Convention has clearly earned its place in the contractual segment of the *International Encyclopaedia of Laws*.

8. Before proceeding in this monograph with a more detailed examination of the substance of the CISG Convention and its component parts, the Convention will be considered in historical perspective and in relation to certain fundamental aspects of Private International Law (PIL).

§2. Historical Perspective: The Hague Sales Conventions and the Conflict of Laws

I. Purely Domestic Sale Subject to Local Law

9. In the case of a purely domestic contract of sale – for example, a contract between A and B, both residents of State X, for the sale and delivery of goods located in that State – the domestic sales law of State X will most likely be well suited to the parties' local needs. So, if a dispute should later arise between the parties to such a sale, it would seem appropriate for a court in State X to apply the domestic law of X to resolve the problem, in that all connecting links point to the (law of the) locality concerned.

9. *See supra*, No. 1.
10. Well-positioned Chinese sellers, for example, would hardly agree to the regulation of their contracts with non-Chinese buyers by foreign (domestic) rules of law: *see* Lookofsky, *Understanding the CISG* 5th Worldwide ed. (2017), §1.2. On the contrary: Chinese parties often expressly 'contract in' to the Convention, *see* (e.g.) China International Economic and Trade Arbitration Commission, People's Republic of China, 9 Jan. 2008, available at http://cisgw3.law.pace.edu/cases/080109c1.html; *accord* J. Coyle, 'The Role of the CISG in U.S. Contract Practice: An Empirical Study', *University of Pennsylvania Journal of International Law* 38 (2016) 195 at 233 (regarding enthusiasm for CISG among Chinese merchants). *Compare* Coyle at 236 (CISG-sceptical U.S. companies, often unaware that selection of U.S. state law will result in CISG application, unknowingly fail to opt out); regarding the narrow interpretation of clauses which might otherwise suggest intent to 'contract out', *see infra*, No. 71.
11. *Accord* F. Ferrari & M. Torsello, *International Sales Law – CISG in a Nutshell* 2nd ed. (2018), at V-VI (operators with sufficient negotiating power to impose choice of their domestic law are indifferent to CISG; in practice, however, highly unlikely that many operators are in that position).

II. International Sale: Problem of Selecting Applicable Law

10. In cases involving an international contract of sale – for example, a contract for the sale of goods (perhaps located in State Z) between merchants A and B doing business in different States (X and Y) – the situation is clearly more complex. Quite apart from the important procedural issue of identifying the court(s) competent to decide disputes between A and B,[12] there is also the issue of the applicable substantive law, that is, the selection of the rules which regulate the process of sales contract formation, the rules which determine the obligations of the respective parties, their remedies for breach, etc.

III. Pre-CISG: Choosing the Applicable Law

A. *Limited Acceptance of ULIS/ULF*

11. Prior to the advent of the CISG Convention, very few States had made treaty commitments to apply international sales law rules to international contracts of sale, in that the Uniform Law for the International Sale of Goods (ULIS) and the Uniform Law on the Formation of Contracts for the International Sale of Goods (ULF), both done at the Hague in 1964, had been ratified by only a very small number of States.[13]

B. *Choice-of-Law Rules Determine Applicable Domestic Law*

12. Given this limited ULIS/ULF adherence, and prior to the advent of the CISG, most States had no choice but to resolve international sales contract disputes by the application of domestic sales law rules, and to decide which domestic rules of law to apply – that is, whether to apply the law of the seller's State, the buyer's State or that of some third State – the competent forum court had to make use of its own (national) choice-of-law rules, also known as rules of 'private international law' (PIL) or 'conflict of laws'.[14]

C. *Concrete Illustration*

13. Suppose, for example, that in 1987 – that is, prior to the entry into effect of the CISG Convention in France and the US – a contract for the sale of goods (wine)

---

12. This competency (jurisdictional) issue, while generally outside the scope of the present study, will be referred to below in a few specific CISG Convention contexts: *see*, for example, *infra*, Nos 140 et seq. regarding Art. 28, No. 158 regarding Art. 31, and No. 244 regarding Art. 57(1). For a comparison of the extraterritorial jurisdiction of American and European courts, *see* J. Lookofsky & K. Hertz, *Transnational Litigation and Commercial Arbitration* 4th ed. (2017), Ch. 2.
13. The Hague Conventions were ratified by the following States: Belgium, Gambia, FR Germany, Israel (ULIS only), Italy, the Netherlands, San Marino and the United Kingdom (UK).
14. *See* J. Lookofsky, *Understanding the CISG* 5th Worldwide ed. (2017), §1.2.

was entered into between a French seller and an American buyer. Suppose further that in 1988, the buyer brought an action in a French court alleging a breach of that contract (delivery of 'watered-down' wine).

Assuming the contract did not itself contain a valid choice-of-law clause, the French court – acting in 1988 – would first need to determine whether French or American (or some other) domestic sales law should govern the sale. In other words, before proceeding to resolve the merits of the case (on the basis of domestic rules of substantive law), the French court was required to resort to its own PIL (choice-of-law) rules to determine which domestic sales law to apply.[15]

D. The 1955 Hague Convention

14. Continue to consider the foregoing illustration. Though not an adherent to the 1964 Hague Conventions (ULIS/ULF), France has long been a party to the 1955 Hague Convention on the Law Applicable to International Sales of Goods. And since the main default choice-of-law (PIL) rule under this 1955 Convention is that the 'seller's law' applies,[16] the French court would most likely have applied French sales law to decide the merits of the case concerned, even though this would represent a domestic (French) and perhaps also parochial solution to an international problem. And although an American court, confronted with a similar pre-CISG situation, would probably have applied a more flexible conflict-of-laws (PIL) rule to select the applicable substantive law,[17] the end result would surely have been an equally provincial solution, that is, the application of domestic law to an international sales dispute.[18]

---

15. Note that France never adhered to the 1964 ULIS/ULF Conventions. *See* text *supra*, No. 11. Note also that if the parties in this example, exercising their contractual freedom, had designated the law applicable to their contract – for example, 'This contract is governed by English law' – the validity of this designation would also depend upon the (domestic) law which the forum court designated as the applicable law; under the 1955 Hague Convention (*infra*, No. 14), ratified by France, but not by the US, the validity of the parties' determination would depend upon the 'putative law', that is, in the example just provided, English law.
16. Absent express agreement regarding the applicable law, a sale shall be governed by the domestic law of the country in which the vendor has his or her habitual residence at the time when he or she receives the order. *See* Art. 3 of the 1955 Hague Convention.
17. *See* generally J. Lookofsky & K. Hertz, *Transnational Litigation and Commercial Arbitration* 4th ed. (2017), Ch. 3.3.
18. The US is not a party to the 1955 Hague Convention on the Law Applicable to International Sales. The currently (2016) applicable sales conflicts rule in most American states is found in §1-105(1) of the Uniform Commercial Code (in some States replaced by a similarly worded §1-301). Absent agreement, an American court will apply the UCC 'to transactions bearing an appropriate relation to the [particular American] state'. The application of this rule varies considerably from State to State. *See* J. Lookofsky & K. Hertz, *ibid.*, Ch. 3.3.2(A).

IV. After 1 January 1988: New CISG Regime Applies in Courts and Arbitral Tribunals

15. These days – and as regards all international sales contracts entered on or after 1 January 1988 (when the CISG became effective in France and the US) – both French and American courts are bound to resolve international sales problems by more appropriate, international means.

16. The Convention is, of course, binding upon all CISG Contracting States, and the (competent) courts of these States are therefore bound to apply the CISG as the default rule-set in all sales cases which lie within the Convention scope.[19] In those instances where the parties to an international sales contract have agreed to arbitrate such disputes as may arise under that contract, the arbitrators selected will, in all likelihood, consider themselves bound to do the very same thing.[20]

17. The significance of the Convention as the applicable substantive law is more fully explained in the overview provided in Chapter 2 below.

---

19. *See infra*, Nos 19 et seq. CISG Art. 6 governs cases where the parties have contracted out (*infra*, No. 26).
20. Arbitrators may apply the CISG by virtue of Art. 1 (*infra*, Nos 21–22 and 51 et seq.) or by virtue of the parties' express agreement to 'contract in' (*infra*, No. 73). *See*, for example, Arbitral award No. SCH-4366, decided 15 Jun. 1994 by Internationales Schiedsgericht der Bundeskammer der gewerblichen Wirtschaft – Wien, RIW 1995, 590, 591, CLOUT Case 93, also in UNILEX and CISGW3 (CISG applied pursuant to Art. 1(1)(b) since the parties had chosen Austrian law and since the CISG is the international sales law of Austria). *See* generally Janssen & Spilker, 'The Application of the CISG in the World of International Commercial Arbitration', *Rabels Zeitschrift fuer auslaendisches und internationales Privatrecht* 77(1) (2013) 131–157; F. Ferrari & M. Torsello, *International Sales Law – CISG in a Nutshell* 2nd ed. (2018), at 111 (arbitration tribunals generally apply CISG as if they were courts in Contracting States, although there also may be other justifications).

Chapter 2. Convention Overview

§1. Convention Consists of 101 Articles: Parts I–IV

18. The CISG Convention contains a total of 101 separate articles. These individual provisions have been organized within the Convention's four main Parts (I–IV). The purpose of this chapter is to provide an overview of these four Parts.

§2. Sphere of Application and General Provisions

I. Sphere of Application

19. Part I of the Convention contains the rules which define the CISG Sphere of Application and General Provisions.

Chapter I of Part I defines the Convention's Sphere of Application. In order to define which contracts and disputes are within the scope of the CISG treaty, Articles 1–6 demarcate which sales are to be regarded as international, which kinds of transactions are to be regarded as sales of goods, which issues are governed by the treaty, etc.

A. *Main Rules of Application*

20. Article 1 contains the two main rules of Convention application. First, and (in practice) most importantly, the CISG applies to contracts for the sale of goods between parties whose places of business are in different States (a) when both these States are CISG 'Contracting States'.

1. Parties in Different Contracting States

21. Reconsider a more modern version of an example presented earlier.[21] Suppose that in the year 2020, that is, (long) after the entry into effect of the CISG in both France and the US, a French seller and an American buyer enter into a contract for the sale of wine. Suppose further that the buyer later brings an action before a French court for damages involving an alleged breach of that contract (delivery of non-conforming goods).

In this modern and quite common sale of goods situation, where the parties have their places of business in different CISG Contracting States, the French court is bound directly – by Article 1(1)(a) of the CISG treaty – to apply the CISG as the gap-filling contractual regime. That is to say, the court of such a CISG Contracting State will apply the Convention (as opposed to French or American domestic sales

21. Presented *supra*, Nos 13 et seq.

law) without recourse to (French) PIL rules.[22] Indeed, the conflict-of-laws rules have to this extent simply become superfluous since there is no longer any 'conflict' among the relevant domestic sales laws.

Moreover, if the same case was brought before a competent American court, the result as to the applicable sales law would almost surely be the same, since an American court would also be bound by treaty to apply the CISG without recourse to (American) PIL (conflict-of-laws) rules.[23]

2. Convention Applies by Virtue of PIL

22. The conclusion reached in the foregoing illustration does not mean that the advent of the CISG has completely obviated the need for PIL rules in the sales arena. Indeed, CISG Article 1(1)(b) itself presupposes the continued application of such rules in certain circumstances, in that the Convention applies to contracts of sales of goods between parties whose places of business are in different States when the rules of PIL lead to the application of the law of a (single) Contracting State. This rule – which declines in practical importance as the number of Contracting States grows – is discussed in greater detail in Chapter 3 below.

B. Contracts for the Sale of Goods

23. The Convention applies (only) to contracts for the 'sale of goods'.[24] Since the Convention does not provide a positive definition of this term, there was – at least initially – some scholarly disagreement, for example, as to whether a contract for the sale of computer software should be regarded as a sale of 'goods'.[25]

Quite apart from that (today less controversial) issue, certain transactions which undeniably relate to sales of goods (wine, cars, furniture) have quite clearly been excluded from the CISG ambit, for example: consumer sales, sales by auction and forced sales, sales of ships (etc.).[26] Nor does the Convention apply to contracts of manufacture where the buyer supplies the necessary raw materials or to mixed (sales and service) transactions where the sale of goods is but a minor element.[27] In cases where the CISG does not apply, recourse must usually be made to domestic law (via the applicable rules of PIL).

---

22. *See UNCITRAL Digest of CISG Case Law* (2016), available at www.uncitral.org/uncitral/en/case_law.html, Art. 1, para. 2. *See also infra*, No. 53.
23. *See*, e.g., Tribunale di Forli, Italy, 16 Feb. 2009 http://www.unilex.info/cisg/case/1394 (uniform law such as the CISG prevails over the applicable private international law rules). Regarding the application by an American court of the rule in UCC, §1-103 in the corresponding, *pre*-CISG situation, *see supra*, No. 14 with accompanying notes.
24. Article 1.
25. Regarding the term 'goods' under Art. 1 *see infra*, No. 58.
26. Regarding Art. 2 *see infra*, Nos 59 et seq.
27. Regarding Art. 3 *see infra*, No. 61.

C. *Validity Issues and Third-Party Rights Excluded*

24. The main substantive provisions of the CISG deal with sales contract formation (the rules in CISG Part II), and the rights and obligations of the seller and buyer arising from such a contract (Part III). Conversely, the CISG does not generally regulate issues relating to sales contract validity or the rights of third parties (property rights).[28]

D. *Product Liability*

25. The Convention does not apply to the liability of the seller for death or personal injury caused by the goods. On the other hand, the CISG rules which govern the seller's liability in damages for the foreseeable consequences of breach can and should be applied to resolve the issue of the seller's liability for damage to the buyer's property, in particular, when the buyer's loss is caused by the seller's breach (delivery of non-conforming goods).[29]

E. *The CISG and Contractual Freedom*

26. When considering the rules which regulate the Convention's applicability in a given case, it must be remembered that the Convention permits the parties to 'contract out' of the CISG or any of its individual provisions. For this reason, the courts in States which have ratified the Convention must give the parties' express agreement (the express terms of their contract) priority over the Convention gap-filling rules, at least to the extent that applicable rules of contract validity do not stand in the way.[30]

parties can still K out of CISG & express agreement will trump

II. General Provisions

A. *Interpretation*

27. Chapter II of CISG Part I contains a series of General Provisions. Among these are the important rules of interpretation set forth in Articles 7 and 8.

As regards interpretation of the CISG Convention itself, Article 7(1) requires that courts and arbitrators pay due regard to the Convention's international character and to the need to promote uniformity in its application and the observance of good faith in international trade.[31]

---

28. Unless otherwise expressly provided. Regarding Art. 4, *see* generally *infra*, Nos 62 et seq.
29. Regarding Art. 5 *see infra*, Nos 66 et seq.
30. The validity of the parties' agreement depends on the content of the applicable domestic law (Art. 4). Regarding Art. 6 *see infra*, Nos 70 et seq.
31. *See* generally *infra*, Nos 74 et seq.

Article 7(2) contains a rule for the settlement of matters which lie on or near the borderline between the Convention and domestic law: that is, matters which are governed by the Convention but not expressly settled in it.[32]

Article 8 is concerned not with the interpretation of the Convention itself, but rather with the interpretation of CISG contracts, in particular: statements made (and conduct exhibited) by parties who enter contracts governed by the Convention. Depending on the circumstances, such statements are to be interpreted pursuant to either a subjective or an objective test.[33]

B. Usages of International Trade

28. Another important CISG General Provision concerns usages of trade.

The parties to a CISG contract are, of course, bound by any usage to which they have expressly agreed,[34] but they are also bound by their prior *inter partes* contractual conduct, that is, by any practices which they have established between themselves. Beyond this, CISG merchants often agree to apply trade usages by implication, in particular such widely and regularly observed international trade usages of which CISG contracting parties ought to know.[35]

§3. Parts II and III States May Ratify One or Both

29. Taken together, CISG Parts II and III constitute the substantive core of the Convention. Each of these parts may be properly regarded as an independent unit, in that Contracting States can ratify Part II, Part III or both.[36]

§4. Formation of Contract

I. Offer and Acceptance

30. Part II of the Convention regulates the Formation of the Contract – that is, the formation of the international contract of sale. Under the Convention, as under most domestic systems, the offer and the acceptance are regarded as the two key elements in the contract formation process.

32. *See* generally *infra*, Nos 78 et seq.
33. *See* generally *infra*, Nos 81 et seq.
34. Regarding the parties' freedom to contract out of the CISG (in whole or part), *see supra*, No. 26.
35. Regarding Art. 9 *see infra*, Nos 87 et seq.
36. Regarding the Art. 92 declarations originally made (but later withdrawn) by the Scandinavian Contracting States (Denmark, Finland, Norway and Sweden), *see infra*, No. 333.

II. CISG Offer: Requirement of Definiteness

31. To constitute an offer, a proposal must meet the Convention requirement of definiteness. A proposal will meet this requirement if it indicates the goods and also (expressly or impliedly) fixes the price.[37]

III. When Offer Effective: Revocable Versus Irrevocable Offers

32. A CISG offer becomes effective upon receipt, that is, when it reaches the offeree.[38] Until that point in time, even an otherwise 'irrevocable' offer may be withdrawn. Once received, irrevocable offers (*inter alia*, some offers which fix a time for acceptance) may not be revoked during the time period concerned, although an offeree's rejection will terminate an otherwise irrevocable offer. Other (revocable) offers may be withdrawn after receipt but prior to the dispatch of an acceptance by the offeree.[39]

IV. Acceptance as Indication of Offeree's Assent

33. In order to be effective, an offeree's acceptance must be timely, and it must indicate the offeree's assent.

To be timely, the acceptance must reach the offeror within the time fixed by the offeror or within a reasonable time. In this connection, it may be noted that, unlike the rule in some domestic regimes, a CISG sales contract is *not* concluded when the offeree's acceptance is dispatched (although dispatch is the relevant point in time after which the offeror may not revoke);[40] in general, a CISG acceptance first becomes effective when it reaches the offeror.[41] In certain cases, however, the acceptance may take effect upon the performance of an act,[42] and sometimes even a late acceptance will be effective as well.[43]

V. Mirror-Image Rule and Battle of Forms

34. The CISG employs the well-known 'mirror-image' rule. To be effective as an acceptance, a reply must match the offer in all material respects; a reply containing material alterations or additions serves as a rejection and counter-offer. These rules are significant as regards the much-discussed 'battle of forms'.[44]

---

37. Regarding Art. 14 *see infra*, Nos 99 et seq.
38. As to when an indication of intention 'reaches' the addressee, *see* Art. 24 and *infra*, No. 133.
39. Regarding Arts 14–17 *see infra*, Nos 99 et seq.
40. Regarding Art. 18 *see infra*, Nos 112 et seq.
41. Regarding the 'conclusion' of the contract under Art. 23 *see infra*, No. 132.
42. Regarding the withdrawal of an acceptance under Art. 22 *see infra*, No. 131.
43. Regarding determination of the period of time for acceptances and late (yet effective) acceptances under Arts 20 and 21, *see infra*, Nos 126 et seq.
44. Regarding the 'battle of forms' and Art. 19, *see infra*, Nos 122 et seq.

§5. SALE OF GOODS: CISG PART III

35. Part III of the CISG, entitled Sale of Goods, contains the substantive rules of greatest practical significance for international sales.

I. Obligations, Rights and Remedies

36. As with any bilateral contract, a CISG contract imposes obligations on both parties.

Simply stated in terms of the parties' primary duties, the seller is obligated to deliver the goods, and the buyer is obligated to pay for them. Each party's primary CISG obligation (to deliver, to pay) confers on the other party a right to expect performance of that obligation or, in the alternative, a right to demand remedial relief for breach.

Although Part III of the CISG is broken down into five separate chapters, this basic theme pervades this part of the Convention text.

II. Part III Provisions Brief Overview of Chapters I–V

37. Chapter I of CISG Part III, entitled 'General Provisions', contains selected rules relating to fundamental breach (Article 25) and to specific performance (Article 28), both of which serve as adjuncts to the more specialized remedial rules in Convention Chapters II and III. In addition, Chapter I of Part III contains general provisions regarding delays in notification (Article 27) and contract modification (Article 29).

Chapter II of Part III lays down the supplementary rules regarding the 'Obligations of the Seller' and provides the buyer with various remedies for the seller's breach, whereas Chapter III of Part III defines the corresponding 'Obligations of the Buyer' and provides the seller with a catalogue of remedies for buyer's breach. Chapter IV of Part III regulates the question of the 'Passing of Risk' (risk of loss).

Finally, Chapter V of Part III, entitled 'Provisions Common to the Obligations of the Seller and the Buyer', supplements both the General Provisions in Chapter I and the more specialized remedial rules in Chapters II and III of Part III by dealing generally with such topics as anticipatory breach, damages for breach, liability exemptions, the effects of avoidance and the preservation of the goods.

III. Obligations of the Parties

A. Obligations of the Seller

38. The CISG summarizes the various obligations of the seller as follows: the seller must deliver the goods, hand over any documents relating to them and transfer the property in the goods, as required by the contract and this Convention.[45] The key to the seller's performance is thus to deliver the right goods at the right place and at the right time, i.e., as required by the contract and the Convention. Because the Convention respects the parties' freedom to define their own obligations, etc.,[46] the main purpose of default (supplementary) rules such as those regarding the proper place and time for seller's performance is to fill in any contractual 'gaps' which may exist.[47] Still, many CISG default rules, such as those regarding conformity (quality) of the goods, are likely to assume considerable importance in actual practice, precisely because many international sales contracts leave numerous gaps on this issue. So, except where the parties (validly) have agreed otherwise, the goods do not conform with the contract unless they are both fit for ordinary purposes (purposes for which goods of the same description would ordinarily be used) and fit for any particular purpose expressly or impliedly made known to the seller at the time of the conclusion of the contract.[48]

B. Obligations of the Buyer

39. Similar considerations apply with respect to the buyer's primary obligation to pay the right price at the right time and place, that is, as required by the contract and the Convention.[49] Once again, CISG default rules regarding the proper place and time for buyer's performance serve mainly to fill in such contractual gaps as may exist in the concrete case.[50] The Convention also contains a supplementary rule for those cases where a validly concluded contract does not expressly or implicitly fix the price which the buyer is to pay, but the relationship between the application of this gap-filling rule (in Article 55) and the rule in Article 14 has been the subject of differing interpretations.[51]

---

45. Article 30.
46. Regarding Art. 6, *see supra*, No. 26 and *infra*, Nos 70 et seq.
47. Regarding Arts 31–34, *see infra*, Nos 150 et seq. Regarding Art. 35, *see infra*, Nos 165 et seq.
48. Except (as regards fitness for particular purpose) where the circumstances show that the buyer did not rely, or that it was unreasonable for him or her to rely, on the seller's skill and judgment. *See infra*, No. 167.
49. Article 53.
50. Regarding Arts 57–59 (place and time of performance) *see infra*, Nos 243 et seq.
51. Regarding Art. 14 *see infra*, Nos 100 et seq. Regarding Art. 55 *see infra*, No. 241.

IV. Remedies

A. Supplementary Remedial Regime

40. When both parties perform their obligations as required by the contract and the Convention, there is no need for the various remedies for breach set forth in Part III of the CISG. Indeed, even assuming a breach, the Convention's supplemental remedial scheme becomes relevant only to the extent that the parties themselves have not (validly) set forth the contractual remedies available in such cases to the injured party concerned. Then again, even a carefully drafted contract which sets a clear standard for performance (and thus breach) is often analogous to 'an imperfect statute' which provides no penalties.[52] When the text of the parties' international sales contract is imperfect in this sense, one must look to the CISG default regime to fill in the gaps.

B. Enforceable Contracts and Remedies for Breach

41. For every breach of an 'enforceable' sales contract, there must be some remedy.[53] Therefore, a seller's promise to deliver goods, and/or a buyer's promise to pay for them, may be described as enforceable if – and only if – the promisee (the recipient of a given promise) is entitled to some remedy for breach: for example, to a judgment decreeing specific performance, a money judgment (damages), a proportionate reduction in price (etc.).

C. Three Basic Forms of Remedial Relief

42. All significant forms of remedial relief can be classified in terms of the three basic courses of action which modern legal systems – including the CISG – make available to a party injured by a contractual breach.[54]

First, specific relief is designed to make the promisor do what he or she promised to do; i.e., specific relief requires a breaching promisor to perform that promise (to deliver or pay) *in natura*.

Second, substitutionary relief requires the breaching promisor to pay some amount of money to compensate the loss suffered by the promisee.

The third major remedial category is the right to terminate, that is, to allow the injured party to put an end to the contractual relationship.

---

52. L. Fuller & W. Perdue, 'The Reliance Interest in Contract Damages I', *The Yale Law Journal* 46 (1937) 52, 58.
53. *See* J. Lookofsky, *Consequential Damages in Comparative Context* (1989), available at https://jura.ku.dk/jurabog, Part 2.
54. For a comparison of domestic systems generally, *see* G. Treitel, *Remedies for Breach of Contract* (1988) and Lookofsky, *ibid.* (1989), Part 4 (comparing American and Scandinavian systems). Both specific and substitutional relief serve to protect the 'expectation interest' by attempting to put the promisee in the position he or she would have been in, had the contract been performed: *accord* E.A. Farnsworth, *Contracts* 4th ed. (2004), para. 12.1.

D. Relationship among Remedies

43. Whether a given breach entitles an injured promisee (buyer or seller) to relief within one or more of these three fundamental categories depends both on the particular circumstances and on the applicable CISG rule(s). Of course, the right to demand specific performance (require that the promisor perform) is not compatible with the right to terminate (demand an end to the obligations of both parties),[55] but there is no mutual exclusivity as between the right to demand either specific performance or termination (on the one hand) and the right to demand damages (on the other).

E. Specific Performance as Primary Convention Remedy

44. Although some domestic systems regard specific performance as exceptional,[56] this remedy appears first on the CISG list, allowing, for example, the buyer to require that the seller deliver the goods (if he or she has not yet done so) or deliver substitute goods (if the goods delivered do not conform) or cure defective delivery or – in the case of buyer's breach – require that the price be paid.[57]

However, the right to require performance under the Convention is subject to a number of important restrictions. Thus, even if the CISG (Part III) rules would, as a starting point, entitle one party to require performance of any obligation by the other, a national court in a Contracting State is not bound to enter a judgment for specific performance unless that court would do so under its own (domestic) law in respect of similar contracts of sale not governed by the Convention.[58]

F. Monetary Compensation as Primary Remedy in Practice

45. Specific performance is the Convention's remedial starting point (under Article 46), but just as damages tend to dominate within the domestic remedial context, monetary compensation for breach of promise has clearly established itself as the primary remedy in international practice pursuant to the CISG.[59]

---

55. By definition, a party who 'terminates' a contract puts an end to both parties' right to demand specific relief.
56. *See* Treitel, *supra* note 54, Ch. III. American commentators have noted a trend in American courts towards a greater availability of this – for Common lawyers – 'exceptional' remedy: *see*, for example, E.A. Farnsworth, *Contracts* (2004), Ch. 12(B) and J. White & R. Summers, *Handbook of the Law under the Uniform Commercial Code* 6th ed. (2010), s. 7-6.
57. Regarding Art. 46 and seller's breach, *see* Nos 216 et seq. Regarding Art. 62 and buyer's breach, *see* Nos 257 et seq.
58. Regarding Art. 28 *see infra*, Nos 140 et seq.
59. Numerous CISG reported decisions involve buyers' claims for monetary relief: *see* generally *infra*, Nos 290 et seq. But we find relatively few reported CISG decisions dealing with buyer's right to demand that the seller provide substitute goods or cure, and even fewer CISG decisions involving the buyer's right to 'require delivery': *see infra*, Nos 214 et seq.

As regards damages for breach, there had been some initial disagreement among commentators as to whether the CISG adopts the fault-liability preference of Civilian systems or the no-fault position of the Common law.[60] More recently, the no-fault interpretation has emerged as the dominant (and clearly better) CISG view, but the Convention rules regarding liability exemptions (i.e., situations involving alleged impossibility of performance, force majeure, etc.) still deserve careful attention, not least in light of the continuing controversy regarding the role of the CISG in situations involving 'hardship'.[61]

Also, worthy of note in the monetary compensation context is the more limited form of monetary relief known to Civilians – and the CISG – as the proportionate price reduction.[62]

G. Avoidance and the Right to Terminate

46. The Convention deals with the termination remedy under the heading of 'avoidance' of the contractual relationship.[63] The primary effect of avoidance is to release both parties from their obligations under the contract, subject to any damages which may be due.[64] The Convention limits access to the avoidance remedy, not only by restricting avoidance to cases of fundamental breach[65] but also by widening the seller's right to cure.[66]

V. Passing of Risk

47. Chapter IV of Part III regulates the Passing of Risk. The general CISG rule is that loss of (or damage to) the goods after the risk has passed to the buyer does not discharge the buyer from his or her obligation to pay the price.[67] The CISG ties the passing of risk to the last significant act by which the seller completes delivery.[68]

60. *Compare*, for example, the views advanced by B. Nicholas, 'Force Majeure, and Frustration', *American Journal of Comparative Law* 27 (1979) 231 with those of J. Lookofsky, 'Fault and No-Fault in Danish, American and International Sales Law. The Reception of the 1980 United Nations Sales Convention', *Scandinavian Studies in Law* 27 (1983) 109.
61. Regarding Arts 45 and 61, *see infra*, Nos 211 and 254. Regarding Art. 79, *see infra*, Nos 302 et seq. Regarding hardship, *see infra*, No. 308.
62. Regarding Art. 50, *see infra*, Nos 232 et seq.
63. Regarding the (very different and more narrow) use of the term 'avoidance' by reason of mistake under American domestic law, *see* the *Restatement of Contracts 2nd.* §152.
64. Regarding Art. 81(1), *see infra*, No. 315. Pursuant to Art. 81(2), discussed *infra*, No. 317, a party who has performed the contract either wholly or in part may claim restitution from the other party.
65. Regarding Art. 25, *see infra*, Nos 136 et seq.
66. *See infra*, Nos 183 et seq. and 221 et seq.
67. Unless the loss or damage is due to an act or omission of the seller. Regarding Art. 66 *see infra*, Nos 268 et seq.
68. Regarding Arts 67–70, *see infra*, Nos 271 et seq.

VI. Anticipatory Breach

48. The CISG rules concerning anticipatory breach are in some respects closely related to the remedy of avoidance for fundamental breach.[69] Depending on the circumstances, one party's anticipatory breach may provide the other with grounds for suspending performance already commenced.[70]

§6. FINAL PROVISIONS: DECLARATIONS, ETC.

49. Part IV of the Convention contains a number of important Final Provisions, *inter alia*, the right of signatory States to make certain declarations (reservations) to specified articles and/or parts of the CISG. These include the right of States to declare that they wish to be bound only by the Convention's Part II (Contract Formation) or Part III (Sale of Goods) rules,[71] the right of States to declare that they will not be bound by the 'PIL' rule in subparagraph (1)(b) of Article 1[72] and the rule which permits States to recognize only sales contracts and modifications if in writing.[73]

§7. OVERVIEW OF CHAPTERS 3–6

50. The following chapters of this *Encyclopaedia* monograph contain a more detailed analysis of the 101 Articles of the Convention. The analysis is organized under the following headings: Scope and General Provisions (CISG Part I) is discussed in Chapter 3; Sales Contract Formation (CISG Part II) is discussed in Chapter 4; Obligations, Risk and Remedies (all governed by CISG Part III) are discussed in Chapter 5; and the Final Provisions of CISG Part IV are reviewed in Chapter 6.

69. *See infra*, Nos 281 et seq.
70. Regarding seller's stoppage in transit by reason of buyer's insolvency, etc., *see infra*, No. 283.
71. Regarding Art. 92 and the Scandinavian States, *see infra*, No. 333.
72. *See infra*, No. 336.
73. Regarding Art. 96, *see infra*, No. 337.

Chapter 3. Convention Scope and General Provisions

§1. Sphere of Application

51. Chapter I of CISG Part I (Articles 1–6) deals with the Convention's Sphere of Application.

In order to determine whether the CISG applies to a given transaction and/or whether it governs a given sales dispute, we must ask:

- whether the transaction meets one of the internationality tests set forth in Article 1;
- whether the transaction represents a sale of goods as required by Articles 1, 2 and 3;
- whether the particular issue or matter in dispute is governed by the CISG (Articles 4 and 5); and
- whether the parties have exercised their freedom to contract out of the Convention entirely (Article 6).

I. Internationality under Article 1

52. As a starting point, the Convention applies in cases falling within one of the two categories set forth in Article 1, paragraph 1, subparagraphs (a) and (b):

> 1. This Convention applies to contracts of sale of goods between parties whose places of business are in different States:
>   a. when the States are Contracting States; or
>   b. when the rules of PIL lead to the application of the law of a Contracting State. ↳ if choice of law leads to law of Contracting State, CISG applies

A. *Parties' Places of Business in Different Contracting States*

53. Common to subparagraphs (1)(a) and (1)(b) is the requirement that the sales contract in question be 'international', that is, the sale is between parties whose 'places of business'[74] are in *different States*. This is the (always) necessary – but in itself insufficient – condition for the application of the Convention by virtue of the main Article 1(1) rule. If a party has more than one place of business, reference should be made to Article 10 (*infra* No. 91).

If, in a given situation, the different States in which the parties reside happen to be CISG *Contracting* States (States which have acceded to the Convention), then the Convention applies by virtue of subparagraph (1)(a). For example, if a contract

74. While the CISG text does not define 'place of business', the term is generally understood to mean 'the place where commercial activities are carried out and that [is] characterized by a certain duration, stability as well as a certain autonomy': *see* F. Ferrari & M. Torsello, *International Sales Law – CISG in a Nutshell* 2nd ed. (2018), at 80–81.

for the sale of wine is entered into in January 2020 between a seller in France and a buyer in California (France and the US being different Contracting States), both French and American courts are bound by Article 1(1)(a) of the treaty to apply the CISG as the gap-filling regime. In this situation, the Convention applies *without* any recourse to rules of PIL;[75] indeed, in this situation, there is no conflict between the sales laws of the US and France.[76]

Originally, at the time of their CISG ratifications, Denmark, Finland, Norway and Sweden made declarations (reservations) under Article 92; the effect of these declarations was that – in respect to matters governed by CISG Part II (Formation of Contract) – the Scandinavian States were *not* 'Contracting States' within Article 1(1)(a).[77] Recently, however, these four Scandinavian States withdrew their Article 92 declarations.[78]

B. Convention Application by PIL

54. Subparagraph (1)(b) of Article 1 becomes relevant when the subparagraph (1)(a) criterion is not met, that is, when one or both parties to the contract do not reside in CISG Contracting States.

For example, if a contract for the sale of wine is made in January 2020 between a seller in France and a buyer in England, French courts would not be bound by Article 1(1)(a) to apply the CISG as the gap-filling regime: the contract is of course between parties residing in different States, but because the United Kingdom (as of January 2020) is still not a CISG Contracting State, the different States concerned are not different Contracting States. (Of course, English courts are not bound to apply the Convention either.) But the Convention becomes applicable nonetheless, at least in a French forum court, if the applicable rules of PIL – i.e., the choice-of-law (also known as conflict-of-laws) rules of the forum – lead to the application of the law of a (single) Contracting State.[79]

75. *See*, e.g., Tribunale di Forli, Italy, 16 Feb. 2009 http://www.unilex.info/cisg/case/1394 (uniform law such as CISG prevails over the applicable private international law rules). *Accord*: F. Ferrari & M. Torsello, *International Sales Law – CISG in a Nutshell* 2nd ed. (2018), at 36.
76. *See* para. 6 of the *Secretariat's Commentary* to Art. 1(1)(a) of the 1978 UNCITRAL Draft Convention, A/CONF. 97/5 (Art. 1(1)(a) applies 'even if the rules of private international law of the forum would normally designate the law of a third country'). *See also* P. Winship, 'Private International Law and the U.N. Sales Convention', *Cornell International Law Journal* 21 (1988) 487 also at https://scholarship.law.cornell.edu/cgi/viewcontent.cgi?article=1201&context=cilj, pp. 519–520; *see also UNCITRAL CISG Case Digest*, Art. 1, para. 2, available at www.uncitral.org/uncitral/en/case_law.html.
77. The declarations do not, however, affect the possible application of Part II by virtue of Art. 1(1)(b): *see also infra*, No. 54. For a more complete discussion of the effect of the Art. 92 declarations, *see* J. Lookofsky, 'Alive and Well in Scandinavia: CISG Part II', *Journal of Law & Commerce* 18 (1999) 289–299; *see also infra*, No. 333.
78. For details, *see infra*, No. 333.
79. Note that although Art. 1(1)(b) functions on the basis of such private international law (PIL) rules, the 1(1)(b) rule is not itself a PIL (conflict-of-laws) rule. *Compare*: Rechtbank Oost-Brabant, Netherlands, 28 Feb. 2018, available at http://www.unilex.info/cisg/case/2162 (Dutch seller and English buyer had agreed on application of the Convention, so CISG held governing law pursuant to Art. 1(1)(b); *see also infra*, No. 75 with note 171).

To continue with the same example (a contract for the sale of wine between a seller in France and a buyer in England), French courts are bound to apply the CISG Convention if the applicable French PIL rule leads to the application of French law (which, of course, is the law of 'a' Contracting State). And indeed, this would seem to be the *likely* result, since France is a party to the 1955 Hague Convention on the Law Applicable to International Sales of Goods,[80] and since the main choice-of-law default rule under this 1955 Convention is that the 'seller's law' (in this case: the law of France) applies;[81] therefore, we would expect a French court to conclude that the Convention applies by virtue of subparagraph (1)(b) of Article 1. In similar fashion, a court in Argentina (a CISG State) has held a contract between a seller in India (not a CISG State) and an Argentine buyer to be governed by the CISG pursuant to Article 1(1)(b), since Argentine PIL rules led to the application of Argentine law (the law of the place of delivery).[82]

As previously noted, the Scandinavian States (Denmark, Finland, Norway and Sweden) at the time of their CISG ratifications made Article 92 declarations with respect to CISG Part II, but these declarations, which were subsequently withdrawn, impacted only on CISG Article 1(1)(a); they never affected the obligation of courts in the Scandinavian States to apply the rule in Article 1(1)(b) in cases where one party to the contract concerned resided in a Scandinavian State.[83]

C. Article 95 Declaration – opts out of 1(1)(b) – PIL leading to CISG

55. The PIL rule in Article 1(1)(b) was not embraced by all those involved in the drafting of the CISG. This led to the declaration set forth in Article 95, whereby a Contracting State may declare that it will not be bound by subparagraph (1)(b) of Article 1 of the Convention.[84] China and the US are among the States which have availed themselves of this declaration.[85]

In cases where only one party to a given international contract resides in a Contracting State, a court in a State which has made an Article 95 declaration will apply

80. *See supra*, No. 14.
81. *See* Art. 3(1) of the 1955 Hague Convention. For an exception, *see* Art. 3(2).
82. Cámara Nacional de Apelaciones en lo Comercial de Buenos Aires, 7 Oct. 2010, available at http://unilex.info/cisg/case/1597.
83. For a more complete discussion of the effect of the Art. 92 declarations, *see* J. Lookofsky, 'Alive and Well in Scandinavia: CISG Part II', *Journal of Law & Commerce* 18 (1999) 289–299; *see also infra*, No. 333. Regarding the subsequent withdrawal of these reservations *see* J. Lookofsky, 'The Rise and Fall of CISG Article 92', in *Festschrift für Ulrich Magnus* (Mankowski & Wurmnest eds, 2014).
84. *See infra*, No. 333.
85. Other States in this category are the Czech Republic, Singapore, Slovakia and Saint Vincent and the Grenadines. For current status, *see* www.uncitral.org/uncitral/en/uncitral_texts/sale_goods/1980CISG_status.html. The US reservation was motivated by the allegedly unsettled and unpredictable status of private international law. *See* F. Gabor, 'Stepchild of the New *Lex Mercatoria*: Private International Law from the United States Perspective', *Northwestern Journal of International Law & Business* 8 (1988) 538.

(not Article 1(1)(b), but) the forum State's rules of PIL to select the applicable sales law,[86] although it is still possible that this process will lead to the application of the CISG.[87]

It should also be noted that a Contracting State which has not made an Article 95 declaration (e.g., Germany) would not be likely to apply Article 1(1)(b) in respect of any Contracting State that has made an Article 95 declaration (e.g., China).[88]

D. Parties in Different States Disregarded in Exceptional Cases

56. The so-called internationality element, common to both subparagraph (1)(a) and (1)(b) of Article 1, is that the parties to the contract have their places of business in different States.[89] However, paragraph 2 of Article 1 narrows the scope of this general criterion:

> 2. The fact that the parties have their places of business in different States is to be disregarded whenever this fact does not appear either from the contract or from any dealings between, or from information disclosed by, the parties at any time before or at the conclusion of the contract.

The underlying logic of this provision is clear. If the parties concerned neither know nor ought to know that they reside in different States, they have no reason to know that the contract which they enter is international, and so they would hardly expect the CISG to be the applicable law. In such a special situation, it is appropriate to disregard the fact that the parties actually do reside in different States. By

---

86. *See* US District Court, 22 Feb. 2011, *Princesse D'Isenbourg et CIE Ltd. v. Kinder Caviar, Inc. and Kinder Caviar, Inc. v. United Airlines, Inc.*, available at http://www.unilex.info/cisg/case/1558 (Art. 1(1)(a) CISG not satisfied since UK not Contracting State; CISG application by virtue of international private law rules also excluded due to US reservation to Art. 1(1)(b) pursuant to Art. 95; Kentucky law (UCC) applied to merits as State with most significant relationship with transaction).

87. *See* P. Winship, 'The Scope of the Vienna Convention on International Sales Contracts', in *International Sales* (Galston & Smit eds, 1984), also available at https://www.cisg.law.pace.edu/cisg/biblio/winship5.html, at 1–32. *See also Prime Start Ltd. v. Maher Forest Products Ltd. et al.*, decided 17 Jul. 2006 by a US Federal District Court (in Washington State), available at http://cisgw3.law.pace.edu/cases/060717u1.html; Flechtner & Brand, 'Opting in to the CISG … ', in *A Tribute to Joseph M. Lookofsky* (Andersen & Henschel eds, 2015), Ch. 5, discussing, *inter alia*, the U.S. District Court's decision in *FPM Financial Services, LLC v. Redline Products*, 17 Sep. 2013, available at http://cisgw3.law.pace.edu/cases/130917u1.html. *See also* generally F. Ferrari & M. Torsello, *International Sales Law – CISG in a Nutshell* 2nd ed. (2018), at 105 ff (distinguishing several lines of cases and concluding that Art. 95 reservation impacts CISG application solely in cases where forum located in Reservation State whose PIL rules lead to forum State's own law).

88. Upon ratifying the Convention Germany made a declaration to that effect. *See* www.uncitral.org/uncitral/en/uncitral_texts/sale_goods/1980CISG_status.html. *See also* Schlechtriem, 'Uniform Sales Law – The Experience with Uniform Sales Laws in the Federal Republic of Germany', *Juridisk Tidsskrift vid Stockholms Universitet* (1991–1992), also at https://cisgw3.law.pace.edu/cisg/biblio/schlech2.html, at 6 and *infra*, No. 336.

89. *See supra*, No. 53.

disregarding this fact, and thus the internationality criterion common to the application of subparagraphs (1)(a) and (1)(b), a court would reach the result that the Convention does not apply to the transaction concerned.

E. Irrelevant Factors: Nationality, Civil-Commercial

57. Paragraph 3 of Article 1 ensures that additional factors do not impact on the main (paragraph 1) rule. Paragraph 3 provides as follows:

> 3. Neither the nationality of the parties nor the civil or commercial character of the parties or of the contract is to be taken into consideration in determining the application of this Convention.

Because the Convention applies in 'international' situations, that is, when the parties (whatever their nationality) have their respective places of business in different States, the contracts in question will usually be commercial in nature, in that both parties to the contract are likely to be merchants in the usual sense. But this need not be the case for the Convention to apply, and the fact that the civil-commercial distinction is relevant in some domestic systems is of no significance as regards the applicability of the CISG. What is relevant in this connection, and as developed more fully below, is that most consumer-type transactions are excluded from the Convention sphere by virtue of Article 2(a).

II. Transaction Must Be a Sale of Goods Within Articles 1–3

A. Article 1: Sales, Goods (E.g., Computer Software), Etc.

58. Article 1 makes it clear that the Convention rules apply only to 'sales of goods' (in the French Convention text: *contrats de vente de marchandises*). Apart from the fact that Articles 2 and 3 expressly exclude some transactions which might otherwise fall within that category,[90] the CISG text does not contain any definition of the term 'sale' or of the term 'goods'.

Although Convention terms like these deserve an 'autonomous' interpretation,[91] we need not blind ourselves to a few basic notions widely accepted under most domestic regimes, for example, the fact that a contract for the *distribution* of goods is not *itself* a contract of 'sale';[92] and that means that the CISG does not apply by

90. *See infra*, Nos 59 et seq.
91. Regarding Art. 7(1), *see infra*, Nos 75 et seq.
92. Whereas an individual sales contract entered into pursuant to an exclusive distribution agreement is subject to the CISG: *see*, for example, OLG Koblenz (Germany), 17 Sep. 1993, CLOUT Case 281, available at http://cisgw3.law.pace.edu/cases/930917g1.html; Foreign Trade Court of Arbitration of the Serbian Chamber of Commerce, 28 Jan. 2009, available at http://www.unilex.info/cisg/case/1432; Federal Court of Australia, 20 Apr. 2010, available at http://www.unilex.info/cisg/case/1641; Cour d'appel de Reims (France), 30 Apr. 2013, available at http://www.unilex.info/cisg/case/1724.

default to a distribution agreement, i.e., unless the parties to that distribution agreement themselves elect to 'contract in' to the CISG.[93]

A related distinction is that a sale is not a lease.[94] That said, the highest German court held in 2014 that the *repurchase obligations* pursuant to a *leasing* contract were subject to the Convention regime.[95]

Assuming the transaction qualifies as a sale, we turn our attention to the term 'goods' (*marchandises*). Now, since goods have traditionally been equated with moveable 'things' in domestic contexts,[96] we would expect that the subject matter of an international sale must also be a 'moveable' thing,[97] that is, a thing which can be transferred (from one place to another) by a carrier or other medium, although not necessarily by a physical medium. Clearly, real property (*immeuble*) lies outside the concept of a moveable thing, just as know-how and goodwill have little or no link with the generally accepted notion of goods.[98]

Looking beyond these inherent restrictions, however, there is good reason to understand the CISG goods notion as broadly as possible, so as to cover all 'moveables' and not just 'corporeal' things.[99] For this and other reasons, most courts and commentators now agree that the Convention should *at least* apply to true sales (even if dubbed 'licenses') of *standard computer programs* (software), even though the intangible content of such a program is likely to be protected by an intangible property right.[100] Indeed, even when computer programs are sold/downloaded over

93. Arbitration Court of the International Chamber of Commerce, Arbitral award No. 11849 (2003), abstract available at www.unilex.info/cisg/case/1160 ('The Arbitrator shall apply the 1980 UN Convention on the International sale of Goods for what is not expressly or implicitly provided for under the contract.').
94. *Accord* F. Ferrari & M. Torsello, *International Sales Law – CISG in a Nutshell* 2nd ed. (2018), at 116 f.
95. *See* Bundesgerichtshof, Germany, 28 May 2014, available at http://www.unilex.info/cisg/case/1832.
96. This is, for example, true under American and Scandinavian sales law. Regarding Scandinavian law, *see* J. Lookofsky & V. Ulfbeck, *Køb: Dansk Indenlandsk Købsret* 5th ed. (2020), Ch. 2.3. *See also* Schwenzer/Hachem in Schlechtriem & Schwenzer, *Commentary* 4th ed. (2016), 33 f., emphasizing that the traditional French domestic term for 'goods' (*objets mobiliers*) employed in the French version of the ULIS text was replaced in the CISG context with *marchandises*.
97. *See* J. Lookofsky, *Understanding the CISG* 5th Worldwide ed. (2017), §2.5.
98. *See*, for example, Schwenzer/Hachem, *supra* note 96 at 35.
99. *See* generally J. Lookofsky, 'In Dubio Pro Conventione? Some Thoughts about Opt-outs, Computer Programmes and Preemption under the 1980 Vienna Sales Convention CISG', *Duke Journal of Comparative and International Law* 13 (2003), available at https://scholarship.law.duke.edu/djcil/vol13/iss3/11/. *See also* Schwenzer/Hachem, *supra* note 96 at 34 f.; F. Diedrich, 'Maintaining Uniformity in International Uniform Law Via Autonomous Interpretation: Software Contracts and the CISG', *Pace International Law Review* VIII (1996) 303, 306; Brunner, Meier, et al., 'Article 2 [Exclusions from the Convention]', in *Commentary on the UN Sales Law (CISG)* (Brunner & Gottlieb eds, 2019) at 29. *But compare* F. Ferrari, 'Specific Topics of the CISG', *Journal of Law and Commerce* 15(1) (1995) 66–67, emphasizing that (standard) programs are usually [in 1995] embodied in a corporeal medium (disks); F. Ferrari & M. Torsello, *International Sales Law – CISG in a Nutshell* 2nd ed. (2018) at 119 (opining that only sale of software made available by means of tangible support subject to CISG).
100. *See generally* J. Lookofsky, *Understanding the CISG* 5th Worldwide ed. (2017), §2.5. *See*, also, e.g., CLOUT Case 1586: Rechtbank Midden, Netherlands, 25 Mar. 2015, available at http://www.unilex.info/cisg/case/1979 (even if software not recorded on tangible medium, nevertheless regarded as 'goods' within the meaning of Art. 1 CISG). *See also* CLOUT Case 749, OGH Austria, 21 Jun. 2005 (supply of standard software programs on data storage mediums considered sale of

the Internet (i.e., even when the programs are not embodied in a tangible medium, such as a CD or DVD), the CISG default rules are well suited to regulate the parties' obligations and remedies for breach.[101] And although some have maintained that contracts for the delivery of non-standard programs should be held to lie outside the CISG scope, the arguments presented for such a distinction remain unconvincing,[102] in that the CISG expressly equates contracts for the supply of goods to be manufactured or produced with contracts for the sale of finished goods,[103] and since the relationship between the value of the physical elements embodied in the particular good (e.g., the disc which 'carries' the program) and the value of the technology or information needed to manufacture or process the good seems irrelevant. If, however, the service element in a given mixed (sales/service) transaction – for example, the supplier's post-delivery obligation to perform maintenance on the computer system sold under the same contract – is found to predominate the transaction (taken as a whole), then Article 3(2) will ensure that the (whole) contract is removed from the CISG scope.[104]

B. Sales Contracts Expressly Excluded: Article 2

1. Consumer Sales

59. Article 2 of the CISG provides that the Convention does not apply to the kinds of sales specified in Article 2, paragraphs (a)–(f).

Taking a closer look at the first excluded item, we note that the Convention does not apply to sales:

---

moveable goods). Sales of books and compact disks are clearly governed by the CISG, even though the intangible content of the book (story) or disk (music, video image) is protected by an intangible property right.

Significantly, a transaction/contract which bears the earmarks of a true 'sale' is subject to the CISG, notwithstanding the fact that the supplier of the software refers to the transaction/contract as a 'licence'. The issue of whether a given transaction qualifies as a 'sale' or a 'license' is up to the court concerned. *See*, e.g., Rechtbank Midden, Netherlands, 25 Mar. 2015 (contractual description of agreement as 'license' *not* determinative). The fact that B can only (legally) use purchased software in ways which respect intellectual property rights does not turn a transaction with the earmarks of a sale into a licence. *Accord: Softman Products Co., LLC v. Adobe Systems Inc.*, U.S.D.C. (California), 19 Oct. 2001, 2001 WL 1343955; *compare* Gillette, Walt, *The UN Convention … Theory and Practice* 2nd ed. (2016), at 53–54 (difficulty distinguishing these transaction types).

101. *See*, e.g., CLOUT Case 1586: Rechtbank Midden, Netherlands, 25 Mar. 2015, *ibid.*, and Lookofsky, *ibid.*, at 21, both sources supporting the view that the CISG should be applied to standard and specialized software sales contracts, even if the programs are transferred electronically. *Accord* Brunner, Meier, et al, *supra* note 99, at 29 (programs directly downloaded over the Internet are goods because CISG does not differentiate regarding manner in which goods reach buyer); Schwenzer/Hachem in Schlechtriem & Schwenzer *Commentary* 4th ed. (2016), at 34.

102. *Accord* Lookofsky at *id.*; Brunner/Meier, et al., at *id.* (widely held view that CISG does not apply to sales of software for development of customized software should not be followed); Diedrich, *supra* note 99. *See also* CLOUT Case No. 281, OLG Koblenz, Germany, 17 Sep. 1993, available at http://cisgw3.law.pace.edu/cases/930917g1.html (term goods to be interpreted broadly).

103. *See* Art. 3(1).

104. *See infra*, No. 61.

(a) of goods bought for personal, family or household use, unless the seller, at any time before or at the conclusion of the contract, neither knew nor ought to have known that the goods were bought for any such use. …

Many States have enacted special statutes designed to protect the rights of consumers who buy goods for personal, family or household use (etc.).[105] By virtue of the applicable PIL (choice-of-law) rules, such consumer-protection statutes are also likely to be applied to protect the interests of consumers who enter international (consumer) sales contracts, for example, when a given consumer purchases goods while travelling abroad or via the Internet (e-commerce).

CISG Article 2(a) ensures that the Convention will not displace the operation of domestic consumer-protection statutes, even if the transaction is otherwise international in the Article 1 sense. So, if a buyer who resides in CISG State A buys goods for personal, family or household use from a seller whose place of business is in CISG State B, the CISG will not apply,[106] unless such seller, at any time before or at the conclusion of the contract, neither knew nor ought to have known that the goods were bought for such use.[107]

2. Additional Exclusions

60. In addition to the subsection exclusion applicable to consumer sales, subsections (b)–(f) of Article 2 provide that the Convention does not apply to sales:

(b) by auction; (c) on execution or otherwise by authority of law; (d) of stocks, shares, investment securities, negotiable instruments or money; (e) of ships, vessels, hovercraft or aircraft; (f) of electricity.

The exclusion of sales by auction (b) and on execution (c) are attributed to the special character of such sales and to the special nature of the applicable domestic law rules.[108] The exclusion of stocks, shares, investment securities, negotiable instruments and money (d) was also intended to avoid conflict with mandatory rules of domestic law applicable to international securities and currency transactions. The exclusion of ships, vessels (etc.) (e) is attributed to special (registration) rules often

105. Various examples of such statutes are found in American legislation, at both the State and Federal levels: *see*, for example, E.A. Farnsworth, *Contracts* 4th ed. (2004), para. 4.29. Even more numerous examples are to be found within the context of the European Union: *see*, for example, J. Lookofsky, 'The State of the Union in Contract and Tort', *American Journal of Comparative Law* XLI (1993) 89.

106. That is, Art. 1(1) notwithstanding. *See*, for example, Oberster Gerichtshof, Austria, 11 Feb. 1997, CLOUT Case 190, available at http://cisgw3.law.pace.edu/cases/970211a3.html, holding that the CISG was not applicable to the sale of Lamborghini automobile purchased for buyer's personal use.

107. *See*, e.g., Oberlandesgericht Stuttgart, Germany, 31 Mar. 2008, CLOUT Case 1232 (seller reasonably believed buyer entered contract in its professional capacity; seller had not been informed about intention of buyer's employee to use car for private purposes).

108. *See*, e.g., Schweizerisches Bundesgerichts (8 Nov. 2016), CLOUT Case 1770, http://www.unilex.info/cisg/case/2126 (online auction, Austrian domestic law applied).

applicable to these kinds of goods, but there has been disagreement among courts and commentators as to where to draw the line between, for example, an excluded ship or vessel and a (smaller) boat.[109]

C. Contract of Sale Versus Contract for Services: Article 3

61. Article 3 of the CISG is designed to distinguish between *sales*, that is, where the supplier's main obligation is to supply goods, and transactions where the supplier's main obligation is to supply labour or other *services*. Article 3 provides as follows:

> 1. Contracts for the supply of goods to be manufactured or produced are to be considered sales unless the party who orders the goods undertakes to supply a substantial part of the materials necessary for such manufacture or production.
> 2. This Convention does not apply to contracts in which the preponderant part of the obligations of the party who furnishes the goods consists in the supply of labour or other services.

The first, very obvious point to be noted in this connection is that a contract for the distribution of goods is not a contract of sale.[110] The same is true of a contract to provide market research.[111]

Since contracts for the supply of goods to be manufactured or produced generally fall within the CISG scope (unless the party who orders the goods undertakes to supply a substantial part of the materials necessary for such manufacture or production), such a supply of goods transaction ought not be regarded as a contract for the sale of a service or as a mixed sales/service contract, even though the value of the labour and services rendered in connection with the production of the goods are seen as a significant – or even the dominant – element in the transaction concerned.[112]

However, paragraph (1) makes it clear that a transaction which might otherwise be considered a CISG sale of goods falls outside the Convention scope if the buyer undertakes to supply a substantial part of the materials necessary for such manufacture or production. Although the term 'substantial' (in the French language version: '*essentielle*') in paragraph (1) is hardly precise,[113] a given buyer's supply of,

---

109. *See* Rechtbank Middleburg, Netherlands, 2 Apr. 2008, available in UNILEX (CISG not applied to purchase of sailing yacht); *compare* Gerechtshof Leeuwarden, Netherlands, 31 Aug. 2005, available at http:// cisgw3.law.pace.edu/cases/050831n1.html (CISG applied to sale of six motor boats). *Compare* Honnold/Flechtner, *Uniform Law for International Sales* 4th ed. (2009), at 53–54 and Schlechtriem/Hachem in Schlechtriem & Schwenzer *Commentary* 4th ed. (2016), at 57–58.

110. *See also supra*, No. 58.

111. *See* OLG Köln (Germany), 26 Aug. 1994, CLOUT Case 122, also reported in UNILEX.

112. *See supra*, No. 58.

113. *Accord*: F. Ferrari & M. Torsello, *International Sales Law – CISG in a Nutshell* 2nd ed. (2018), at 121 (referring to the French version and rightly stressing the importance of the quality and function of given materials).

for example, 70%–80% of the total raw materials needed for production of the goods would presumably remove the transaction from the CISG scope.[114]

According to the rule in paragraph (2), where a supplier undertakes to supply a mixture of goods and services – for example, a contract whereby the supplier not only undertakes to provide the buyer with a computer system but also promises to service and/or upgrade the system at regular intervals – the CISG will apply if the sales element clearly represents the 'preponderant' part of the total transaction.[115] If a purely financial means of measurement were to be applied, this would presumably translate to more than 50% of the total value of the obligations concerned.

III. Issues Excluded from Convention Scope: Validity, Property and Delict

62. Article 4 of the Convention distinguishes between (on the one hand) rules which regulate sales contract *formation* and the parties' *rights and obligations*, both of which are governed by the CISG, and (on the other hand) questions relating to sales contract *validity* and *property* in the goods, both of which lie outside the CISG scope:

> This Convention governs only the formation of the contract of sale and the rights and obligations of the seller and buyer arising from such a contract. In particular, except as otherwise expressly provided in this Convention, it is not concerned with:
>
> a. the validity of the contract or of any of its provisions or of any usage;
> b. the effect which the contract may have on the property in the goods sold.

Those who are familiar with the content of Parts II and III of the Convention (outlined in Chapter 2 above and discussed more fully in Chapters 4–6 of this monograph) might view Article 4 as an *ex tuto* kind of provision, the main effect of which is to reaffirm that which already follows by logical implication from the content of the rules set forth in CISG Parts II and III, i.e., that the Convention 'governs only' the formation of the sales contract (Part II) and the rights and obligations of the seller and the buyer arising from such contract (Part III); conversely, it was *not* designed to govern (most) validity questions or property questions relating to the rights of third parties,[116] etc.

---

114. *Accord* Honnold/Flechtner, *supra* note 109, at 64–65. *See also* Opinion No. 4 of the CISG Advisory Council, available at http://cisgw3.law.pace.edu/cisg/CISG-AC-op4.html.
115. *See* Opinion No. 4 of the CISG Advisory Council, *ibid.*, and, for example, Handelsgericht Zürich (Switzerland), 26 Apr. 1995, CLOUT Case 196, also reported in UNILEX, holding that a contract for the sale and installation of a fitness device was a 'sales contract' governed by the CISG.
116. For a validity exception, *see infra*, No. 63. Since the Convention governs only 'the rights and obligations of the *seller and the buyer* arising from [a contract of sale]', the highest court in France has held that the CISG did not govern the rights of a French third party against an American seller who issued an end-user guarantee: *see* Cour de Cassation, 5 Jan. 1999, CLOUT Case 241, setting aside the curious decision of Cour d'appel de Grenoble, 15 May 1996, CLOUT Case 204, also reported in UNILEX.

In a few respects, however, Article 4 has proved to be a controversial rule, not least in CISG theory.[117] One point which has generated considerable academic debate is the extent to which the rules of the Convention governing contractual liability (damages for breach of obligations arising from the sales contract) serve to displace (i.e., pre-empt) domestic law rules of delictual liability,[118] *inter alia*, liability in tort for negligent misrepresentation and domestic product liability rules grounded in delict.[119] A related question is the extent to which the CISG rules which permit avoidance by reason of, e.g., non-conformity displace (i.e., pre-empt) domestic rules which permit contract avoidance by reason of mistake.[120]

A. *Contractual Validity & Domestic Law*

63. Although the CISG is, by its own terms, not 'concerned' with the validity of the contract, there are a few exceptions, and these explain why the general rule set forth in Article 4 is modified by an exception which reads: 'except as otherwise expressly provided in this Convention'. One such exception is the CISG rule of 'formal validity' laid down in Article 11;[121] a related provision is Article 29(2).[122]

These exceptions notwithstanding, the main rule remains clear: the Convention is 'not concerned' with the 'validity' of the contract or of any of its provisions, and this means that *domestic* rules of law must be used to resolve the great majority of problems which fall under the validity label, *inter alia*, questions which relate to the doctrines of mistake, fraud, duress (threat) and the reasonableness of contract terms.[123]

In other words, the validity of the parties' contract (and its individual terms) cannot be resolved on the basis of the Convention's gap-filling rules: not only because Article 4 expressly so states but also because the CISG simply does not contain the

117. *See* generally U. Schroeter, 'Contract Validity and the CISG', *Uniform Law Review* 22 (2017) 47 (concluding that most validity issues are governed by domestic law, but that some validity issues are governed by CISG, and that the line is sometimes difficult to draw).
118. *See infra*, section C.
119. *See infra*, section D.
120. *See infra*, section A.
121. *See infra*, Nos 92 et seq.
122. *See infra*, Nos 142 et seq.
123. For a comparison between Danish domestic validity rules and the validity provisions of the UNIDROIT Principles of International Commercial Contracts, *see* J. Lookofsky, 'The Limits of Commercial Contract Freedom: Under the UNIDROIT "Restatement" and Danish Law', *American Journal of Comparative Law* XLVI (1998) 485–508, also available at www.cisg.law.pace.edu/cisg/biblio/lookofsky2.html.

As regards mistake, some commentators have argued that the CISG avoidance rules displace (some) domestic rules permitting a mistaken buyer to rescind: for a comparison of the widely diverging views on this point *see* H. Hartnell, 'Rousing the Sleeping Dog', *The Yale Journal of International Law* 18 (1993) 72–78; *compare*, for example, P. Schlechtriem, 'Uniform Sales Law – The Experience with Uniform Sales Laws in the Federal Republic of Germany', *Juridisk Tidsskrift vid Stockholms Universitet* (1991/1992), also at https://cisgw3.law.pace.edu/cisg/biblio/schlech2.html, 11–12; *see also infra*, No. 226. *Compare* F. Ferrari & M. Torsello, *International Sales Law – CISG in a Nutshell* 2nd ed. (2018), at 146 ff (solution to pre-emption/coexistence dilemma complex; numerous mistake-types preclude a single solution).

tools which judges and arbitrators need to police international sales agreements against unfairness.[124] Indeed, the CISG drafters made no attempt whatsoever to prescribe the legal effect of, for example, a mutual mistake as to the existence of the subject matter of the contract, economic duress (e.g., a seller's threat of non-performance unless a price-increase is secured), an unreasonable disclaimer or limitation of liability, etc.

So if, for example, a seller in Sweden sells goods to a buyer in France, and if the express terms of their contract incorporate the seller's standard terms which purport to disclaim all liability in the event of breach, the validity (and thus enforceability) of that disclaimer is a matter which lies outside the CISG scope.[125] And since the applicable rules of PIL in such a situation would likely point to Swedish domestic law,[126] the disclaimer will only be effective (i.e., displace the CISG gap-filling remedial regime) if it is held to satisfy the 'reasonableness' requirement set forth in the Swedish Contracts Act.[127]

B. Delictual Obligations & Concurrent Remedies

64. According to Article 4, the Convention governs only the (*inter partes*) rights and obligations which arise by virtue of the parties' contract. Conversely, the Convention does not govern rights and obligations vis-à-vis third parties, nor does it govern delictual obligations (the law of tort, principles of liability for negligence, etc.).

So, in order to evaluate (e.g.) a product liability claim brought by a third-party consumer (C) against CISG merchant-seller (A) for injuries to C's person or property, national courts have no alternative but to apply domestic rules of law – this notwithstanding the fact that (A) sold the goods concerned to merchant (B) who then sold them to (C).[128] Similar considerations apply, for example, to a seller's claim for damages against his or her buyer for bad-faith termination of contractual negotiations (*culpa in contrahendo*); for if no (binding) CISG contract between these parties has been made, the situation can hardly be described as involving rights and obligations arising from the contract.[129]

---

124. As regards policing agreements against unfairness under American law, *see* generally E.A. Farnsworth, *Contracts* 4th ed. (2004), Ch. 4.
125. As regards surprising standard terms and Art. 2.20 of the UNIDROIT Principles *see* Lookofsky, *supra* note 123.
126. In this situation, both Swedish and French courts would apply the 1955 Hague Convention to determine the law applicable to the validity question: *see supra*, Nos 13 et seq. and *infra*, No. 80.
127. Under 36 of the Danish Contracts Act, a contract can be amended or held unenforceable, in whole or in part, if enforcement would be unreasonable or contrary to accepted standards of fair dealing. In making this determination, consideration is given to the circumstances at the time of contracting, the content of the contract and circumstances which have later occurred. A very similar rule applies in other Scandinavian States. As regards the validity of contractual limitations and disclaimers in relation to Art. 35, *see* generally *infra*, Nos 173 et seq.
128. *See also infra*, Nos 66 et seq.
129. *Accord* P. Schlechtriem in Schlechtriem & Schwenzer, *Commentary* 2nd English ed. (2005), at 182 with No. 36. *But compare* Schroeter in the 4th (2016) ed. of that *Commentary* at 259 f.

A related, more controversial issue is the extent to which courts and arbitrators should apply arguably competing (concurrent) domestic remedies to *supplement* the CISG remedial regime.[130] For example, domestic rules of law which justify rescission by reason of negligent misrepresentation as to the quality of goods delivered might (or might not) be allowed to 'compete' with the CISG avoidance regime,[131] just as a seller's liability for the economic consequences of such a misrepresentation might (or might not) be allowed to supplement the Convention's own damages regime, for example, allowing a buyer to advance a claim even after expiration of the two-year cut-off period in Article 39(2).[132]

Since domestic solutions to given legal problems sometimes vary from State to State, a decision to allow rule-competition between the CISG and domestic law might sometimes affect the outcome of a given CISG case. For this reason, courts and arbitrators are likely to exercise restraint before they permit domestic rules to supplement the solution provided by the Convention regime.[133] That said, there are good arguments in favour of allowing such rule-competition,[134] and this explains why *most* national courts which have faced this problem have held that the Convention does *not* pre-empt (trump) domestic rules which lie in the 'borderland' between contract and delict (tort).[135] Although this position also finds considerable

130. That is, remedies pursuant to the law applicable by virtue of applicable rules of private international law. The choice of law may be complicated, *inter alia*, by the problem of whether to 'characterize' the particular dispute as one of contract and/or tort. *See*, for example, *Arcado Sprl v. Haviland SA*, Case No. 9/87 [1989] ECC 1. *See also* J. Hill & A. Chong, *International Commercial Disputes* 4th ed. (2010), §5.6.8, n. 288 (whether concurrent claims regarded as being contractual and tortious under domestic law are allowed will depend on law of forum). Regarding jurisdiction to adjudicate contractual claims under the Brussels Regulation, *see* J. Lookofsky & K. Hertz, *Transnational Litigation & Commercial Arbitration* 4th ed. (2017), pt. 2.2.2(A).

131. Under, for example, American domestic law, avoidance might be allowed for a fraudulent misrepresentation without concern for its materiality (Farnsworth, *supra* note 124, §§4.10–4.15) whereas avoidance under CISG Art. 49(1)(a) requires a fundamental breach. *Compare Stawski Distributing Co., Inc. v. Zywiec Breweries PLC*, US District Court (N.D. Illinois), 6 Oct. 2003, 2003 WL 22290412 (provisions of Illinois Beer Industry Fair Dealing Act (IBIFDA) which limit right of foreign brewers (sellers) to terminate contracts with American wholesalers (buyers) not pre-empted (trumped) by arguably competing avoidance provisions of the CISG).

132. *See* generally J. Lookofsky, 'In Dubio Pro Conventione? Some Thoughts about Opt-outs, Computer Programmes and Preëmption under the 1980 Vienna Sales Convention CISG', *Duke Journal of Comparative and International Law* 13 (2003), also available at http://law.duke.edu/journals/djcil/articles/djcil13p0263.htm. Regarding the CISG two-year cut-off rule, *see infra*, Nos 193–194.

133. *Accord ibid. See also* the opinion of Chief Justice Rubenstein in *Pamesa v. Mendelson* (2009), para. 73, available at http://cisgw3.law.pace.edu/cases/090317i5.html: 'the trial court was essentially correct when it agreed to consider the claim that [S] was negligent in manufacturing the tiles ... I have not reached this conclusion lightly because it can be argued that the Convention [is] intended to regulate the relationship between the parties in its entirety'.

134. Regarding tort solutions in competition with Arts 5 and 35, *see* generally J. Lookofsky, 'Loose Ends and Contorts in International Sales: Problems in the Harmonization of Private Law Rules', *American Journal of Comparative Law* 39 (1991) 403 and *infra*, No. 69. Regarding the availability of concurrent remedies in product liability claims *see infra*, No. 69.

135. For an example of a US Federal Court decision supporting this view, *see Miami Valley Paper v. Lebbing Engineering & Consulting GmbH*, 2006 WEST LAW 2924779 (S.D. Ohio), also at http://cisgw3.law.pace.edu/cases/061010u1.html#cx. Following this line of cases, the Israeli Supreme

support in CISG theory,[136] some commentators, arguing that rule-competition represents a threat to uniform Convention application, have taken a different view,[137] just as some CISG precedents accord with that pre-emptive line of reasoning.[138]

In deciding whether or not to allow rule-competition between the CISG contractual regime and a given non-contractual (delictual or tort) liability regime under domestic law, many courts and commentators attach considerable significance to the 'operative facts' which a plaintiff must establish in order to activate the respective claims concerned.

Suppose, for example, that buyer (B) seeks to recover damages for breach from seller (S), alleging that S failed to supply B with goods fit for a specific purpose set forth in the parties' CISG contract of sale. To succeed on that contractual claim, B need only establish that the goods which S delivered were, in fact, unfit for that purpose. But if B also (or alternatively) seeks to hold S liable by virtue of domestic

---

Court has allowed domestic remedies for negligent misrepresentation to supplement the Convention remedial regime, *see Pamesa v. Mendelson* (2009), *supra* note 133; *see also* citations in that Israeli decision to numerous American, Canadian and Australian precedents in *accord* with this view.

136. *See* generally J. Lookofsky, *Understanding the CISG* 5th ed. (2017), §4.6; Lookofsky, 'Not Running Wild with the CISG', *Journal of Law and Commerce* 29(1) (2011); Lookofsky, 'In Dubio' (*supra* note 132); F. Ferrari & M. Torsello, *International Sales Law – CISG in a Nutshell* 2nd ed (2018), at 149–151, concurring with Lookofsky ('In Dubio ... ' at *id.*) and rejecting view that CISG pre-empts all domestic tort law (i.e., when protected interests do not overlap domestic tort law not excluded *a priori*; rather, concurrent application of domestic law depends on whether *cumul* excluded or permitted under applicable law). The ULIS Conventions of 1964, which preceded the CISG (*see supra*, No. 11), expressly excluded a buyer's recourse to domestic law in the case of non-conforming goods (ULIS Arts 34, 53), except in cases of fraud (ULIS Art. 89), but the CISG drafters – hoping it would be possible to create a separate, internationally uniform set of validity rules – refrained from including a similar provision in the CISG. The subsequent failure of the international legislator to achieve its original (uniform validity rule) goal hardly speaks in favour of a CISG interpretation which uniformly pre-empts domestic law.

137. *See*, for example, I. Schwenzer in Schlechtriem & Schwenzer, *Commentary* 4th ed. (2016), at 618, opining that the CISG leaves 'no room for domestic remedies based on the seller's innocent or negligent misrepresentation ... whether they be founded on *culpa in contrahendo* or tort'. According to Professor Schwenzer (*ibid.*), this 'especially applies to negligent misrepresentation under Anglo-American law', but Professor Schwenzer's hard-line opinion conflicts sharply with a substantial body of judicial precedent emanating from Common law jurisdictions: *see Pamesa v. Mendelson* (2009), *supra* note 133, with citations to numerous American, Canadian and Australian precedents on point. Note in this connection that permitting a CISG party to avail itself of a concurrent domestic remedy does not necessarily violate the principle of 'uniform application' prescribed by Art. 7: *see infra*, No. 77 with No. 8 and generally J. Lookofsky, 'Not Running Wild with the CISG', *Journal of Law & Commerce* 29 (2011) 141 https://jlc.law.pitt.edu/ojs/index.php/jlc/article/view/27, at 150; Lookofsky, *Understanding the CISG* 5th Worldwide ed. (2017), §4.6 at 83 (emphasizing role of negligence as *tort-based* 'operative fact'). *Compare* Gillette & Walt, *UN Convention CISG, Theory & Practice* 2nd ed., at 81–82 (arguing 'displacement' easier to apply); U. Schroeter, 'Defining the Borders of Uniform International Contract Law: The CISG and Remedies for Innocent, Negligent, or Fraudulent Misrepresentation', *Villanova Law Review* 53 (2013) 553, 564 (arguing that, from merchant-perspective, focus on facts avoids surprising application of foreign domestic rules).

138. *See* LG Aachen (Germany), 14 May 1993, RIW 1993, 760–761, also reported in UNILEX (application of CISG precluded recourse to domestic law regarding mistake as to quality of goods); OLG Thüringen (Germany), 26 May 1998, CLOUT Case 280, at http://cisgw3.law.pace.edu/cases/980526g1.html (lack of sufficient notice within scope of CISG also extends to exclude other concurrent remedies, such as claim for tortuous liability).

rules of tort, arguing that S negligently or fraudulently misrepresented that the goods were fit for B's purposes, the 'operative facts' which trigger Convention liability are *not the same* as the operative facts which trigger liability under domestic tort law, and for this reason, the CISG and domestic rule-sets should be allowed to compete.[139] After all, 'contractual and delictual remedies have coexisted in many jurisdictions for centuries, and a given State's ratification of the sales Convention does not imply its intention to merge contract with tort'.[140]

Consider, for example, the tort of negligent misrepresentation as set forth in the American *Restatement (Second) of Torts*, § 552, which has been adopted as the law in the State of Kentucky and in many other American States. According to § 552: 'One who, in the course of his business ... supplies false information for the guidance of others in their business transactions, is subject to *liability* for pecuniary loss caused to them by their justifiable reliance upon the information, *if he fails to exercise reasonable care or competence in obtaining or communicating the information.*' Since the tort of negligent representation defines an *independent duty* for which recovery in tort for economic loss available, a US District Court has held that negligent misrepresentation is *completely different from a claim for breach of a contract* and that such a tort claim is not controlled (or pre-empted) by the CISG.[141]

C. *Convention Not Concerned with Property in Goods*

65. As indicated in the first sentence of Article 4, the Convention governs (only) *inter partes* rights and obligations. Conversely, according to paragraph (b) of Article 4, the Convention is not concerned with the effect which the contract may have on the property in the goods sold.[142]

For this reason, the question of whether a sale of goods to a good-faith buyer serves to cut off the rights which creditors or other third parties might otherwise

139. *Compare* C. Gillette & S. Walt, *Sales Law. Domestic and International* 3rd ed. (2016), at 56–57, with notes 89–90 (if domestic law claim involves *fact not involved* in breach of warranty claim, domestic law continues to govern), citing US District Court, 13 Dec. 2009, *Electrocraft Arkansas, Inc. v. Electric Motors, Ltd et al.*, available at http://www.unilex.info/cisg/case/1490 (CISG preempts Electrocraft's state law claims only if such claims fall within scope of CISG: citing *Asante Technologies, Inc. v. PMC-Sierra, Inc.*, available at http://cisgw3.law.pace.edu/cases/010727u1.html, where CISG pre-empted state law contract claim; *Miami Valley Paper, LLC v. Lebbing Engineering & Consulting GmbH*, *supra*, note 135, where CISG did not prevent plaintiff from pleading negligent misrepresentation and fraudulent inducement). In *Electrocraft* itself, plaintiff *conceded* that its negligence/strict liability claim was based on *same factual allegations* as its CISG breach-of-contract claim; *see also infra* with notes 140–141.

140. *Electrocraft Arkansas, id.*, citing J. Lookofsky, 'In Dubio Pro Conventione? Some Thoughts about Opt-Outs, Computer Programs, and Preemption under the 1980 Vienna Sales Convention (CISG)', *Duke Journal of Comparative & International Law* 13 (2003) 263, 286.

141. *See* US District Court, 18 Apr. 2008, *Sky Cast, Inc. v. Global Direct Distribution, LLC*, available at http://www.unilex.info/cisg/case/1259.

142. *See*, e.g., *Coutinho & Ferrostaal GmbH v. Tracomex Ltd.*, Supreme Court of British Columbia, Canada, 13 May 2015, CLOUT Case 1579 (CISG does not address third-party rights or validity of retention-of-title clauses). *See also*, e.g., CIETAC Arbitral Award (China), 18 Apr. 2008, available at http://www.unilex.info/cisg/case/1531 (Chinese domestic law applicable as regards transfer of ownership; title reverted when goods returned to seller).

have in those goods is not a CISG concern, but rather an issue to be decided under the otherwise applicable domestic rules of law. Similarly, the right of a seller to obtain restitution of goods delivered may well be restricted by local laws protecting the rights of buyer's creditors.[143] Similarly, the Convention does not deal with the right of retention.[144]

D. Product Liability

66. Article 5 of the CISG makes it clear that the Convention rules do not apply to certain claims which fall within the 'product liability' heading. Article 5 provides as follows:

> This Convention does not apply to the liability of the seller for death or personal injury caused by the goods to any person.

1. Liability for Death or Personal Injury

67. Within domestic systems, the term 'product liability' denotes the liability of sellers (including manufacturers, producers and others) for personal injury and/or property damage caused by defective goods. In many domestic systems, such product liability claims are seen as grounded solely in delictual (tort) principles; other systems view such claims as grounded both in contract and in tort, in which case the rules of contractual and delictual liability are sometimes (depending on the system concerned) allowed to 'compete'.[145]

Clearly, a product liability claim advanced by a person who is not a party to a CISG contract cannot be governed by the CISG, simply because *all* third-party claims lie outside the CISG by virtue of Article 4.[146] But even as regards *inter partes* product liability, Article 5 expressly excludes CISG application as regards the seller's liability (to the buyer) for *death or personal injury* caused by the goods.

---

143. *See infra*, No. 317. *See*, e.g., Tribunale d'appello del Ticino, Switzerland, 20 Apr. 2016, available at http://www.unilex.info/cisg/case/1995 (restitutionary rights provided for in Art. 81 CISG contractual in nature, cannot affect property issues expressly excluded from the scope of the Convention (Art. 4); issue of whether buyer under duty to retransfer property to seller left to otherwise applicable law).

144. *See also* OLG Koblenz (Germany), 16 Jan. 1992, CLOUT Case 226, also reported in UNILEX, holding that CISG did not regulate the *validity* of a 'retention-of-title' clause; CLOUT Case 613, US District Court (N.D. Illinois), 28 Mar. 2002, available at www.cisg.law.pace.edu/cases/020328u1.html#uab (CISG not applied to retention-of-title clause; under US domestic law, third-party lender perfected security interest); OLG Stuttgart, Germany, 20 Dec. 2004, available at http://cisgw3.law.pace.edu/cases/041220g1.html. *Compare*, re. parties' *agreement* to a retention-of-title clause, cisg-online.org, case 5289.

145. *See* J. Lookofsky, 'In Dubio Pro Conventione?', *supra* note 132, text with notes 108–123. Some systems which allow competition (concurrence) between contractual and delictual claims nonetheless refuse to admit tort-based product liability claims for 'pure economic loss': *see*, for example, *East River S.S. Corp. v. Transamerica Delaval, Inc.*, 476 US 858 (1986).

146. *Supra*, Nos 62 et seq.

Therefore, a CISG seller's liability for death or personal injury can only be governed by the domestic law applicable by virtue of PIL rules.[147]

2. Damage to Buyer's Property Distinguished

68. This leaves a relatively narrow, yet commercially significant product liability question within the CISG regime, and this relates mainly to the seller's liability to the buyer for *damage to the buyer's property* caused by the seller's delivery of non-conforming goods (i.e., as opposed to damage to the goods themselves).[148] So if, for example, a given seller delivers a leaky fish tank which causes damage to the buyer's business premises or if that seller delivers virus-infected fish causing damage to the buyer's existing stock, the Convention remedial regime can be used to determine the seller's liability for the buyer's loss,[149] in that a leaky tank or virus-infected fish are goods which do 'not conform' under Article 35 of the CISG,[150] and the delivery of non-conforming goods renders a CISG seller liable for all loss suffered by the other party as a consequence of the breach.[151]

Finally, to take a different kind of example, suppose a buyer (B), by virtue of domestic law rules, is held liable for the death or personal injury of a third person (TP), and that TP's death or injury was caused by non-conforming goods which were supplied to B by seller (S) under a CISG contract. In this situation, some commentators argue that the Convention regime should govern B's claim against S for *indemnification*, since B's claim relates, arguably, to 'pecuniary loss' (as opposed to a claim for 'liability of the seller for death or personal injury caused by the goods to any person' under Article 5),[152] but most other commentators rightly reject that 'expansionistic' view of Article 5.[153]

---

147. *See* Art. 7(2), discussed *infra* in Nos 78 et seq.
148. Claims by the buyer for damage to the goods themselves are *not* 'product liability' claims (accord: EU Product Liability Directive, Art. 9(b)), but rather claims of *non-conformity* which, of course, are 'governed' by the CISG. *Compare* CISG AC Opinion No. 12, at http://www.cisg.law.pace.edu/cisg/CISG-AC-op12.html, note 33 (characterizing – for some unknown reason – the views of the present author (previously expressed in 13 *Duke Journal of Comparative & International Law* 263, 2003) as '*contra*' the obvious position taken here).
149. *See* Handelsgericht Zürich (Switzerland), 26 Apr. 1995, available at www.cisg.law.pace.edu/cases/950426s1.html; OLG Thüringen, Germany, 26 May 1998, CLOUT Case 280, available at http://cisgw3.law.pace.edu/cases/980526g1.html.
150. Regarding Art. 35 *see* generally *infra*, Nos 162 et seq.
151. Regarding Art. 74 *see infra*, Nos 291 et seq. Regarding the possibility of a liability 'exemption' for unknowable defects under Art. 79, *see infra*, Nos 302 et seq.
152. *See*, e.g., CISG AC Opinion No. 12, available at http://www.cisg.law.pace.edu/cisg/CISG-AC-op12.html (conceding that this interpretation may seem, on its face, to ignore the language 'to any person' in Art. 5.); Schwenzer/Hachem in Schlechtriem & Schwenzer *Commentary* 4th ed. (2016), at 97–98 (arguing that such recourse is not excluded).
153. *See* F. Ferrari & M. Torsello, *International Sales Law – CISG in a Nutshell* 2nd ed. (2018), at 137–138 (buyer's claims for pecuniary loss resulting from claim against buyer by its own customer for personal injury caused by goods excluded from CISG scope); C. Brunner, F. Meier, et al., 'Article 5 [Exclusion of Liability for Death or Personal Injury]', in *Commentary on the UN Sales Law (CISG)* (Brunner & Gottlieb eds, 2019), at 74 (CISG does not govern regress claims for personal injuries arising from defective goods).

3. Competition Between Convention and Domestic Delictual Rules

69. Because claims for buyer's property damage are often regulated, not only by contractual regimes but also by domestic rules of delict (tort, negligence, strict product liability, etc.), a question arises as to whether these domestic delictual rules: (a) should be displaced (pre-empted) in the international sales context by the CISG regime,[154] or (b) whether the two rule-sets should be allowed to compete.[155] Good reasons can be advanced for allowing some degree of rule-competition (concurrent claims) in this context,[156] especially in situations where the facts which trigger Convention liability are *not the same* as the facts which trigger liability under domestic law;[157] but the contrary view (rejecting competition between rule-sets) also finds support in other academic opinion and at least one CISG precedent.[158]

IV. Freedom of Contract: Convention as Supplementary Regime

70. Article 6 of the CISG reaffirms the well-known principle of contractual freedom as well as the nature of the Convention as a supplementary (default rule-set) regime. Article 6 provides as follows:

> The parties may exclude the application of this Convention or, subject to article 12, derogate from or vary the effect of any of its provisions.

154. As already indicated, due to the operation of Arts 4 and 5, the liability for death or personal injury to any person as well as property damage suffered by third parties will continue to be regulated by domestic rules of delict.
155. Such competition would, of course, not provide plaintiffs with a double recovery but might, for example, mean a more favourable position vis-à-vis notice requirements, statutes of limitation, etc.
156. *See* J. Lookofsky, 'In Dubio Pro Conventione? Some Thoughts about Opt-outs, Computer Programs and Preëmption under the 1980 Vienna Sales Convention CISG', *Duke Journal of Comparative and International Law* 13 (2003) 263, 286–288, also available at https://scholarship.law.duke.edu/djcil/vol13/iss3/11/; F. Ferrari & M. Torsello, *International Sales Law-CISG in a Nutshell* 2nd ed. (2018), at 138 (rejecting view that CISG exclusively applicable in property damage situations; tort action for property damage caused by non-conforming goods should not be barred by failure to notify within reasonable time under Art. 39); *accord* P. Schlechtriem in Schlechtriem & Schwenzer, *Commentary* 2nd English ed. (2005), at 80; *but compare* Schwenzer/Hachem in the 4th (2016) ed. of the same work, p. 97 f.
157. *Accord*: F. Ferrari & M. Torsello, *International Sales Law – CISG in a Nutshell* 2nd ed. (2018), at 149–151, citing J. Lookofsky, 'In Dubio Pro Conventione?', *supra* note 132. *See also supra*, No. 64.
158. *See* Honnold/Flechtner, *Uniform Law for International Sales* 4th ed. (2009), at 95–102 (nonetheless describing contrary view previously advanced by Professor Schlechtriem as 'intriguing and meriting the most careful consideration'); *see also* OLG Thüringen (Germany), 26 May 1998, CLOUT Case 280, at http://www.unilex.info/cisg/case/509 (lack of sufficient notice within scope of CISG also extends to exclude other concurrent remedies, such as claim for tortuous product liability).

A. Contracting Out

71. As is generally the case with respect to domestic sales laws, the CISG is designed primarily to serve as a supplementary regime which fills contractual 'gaps' in international sales contexts.[159] For this reason, Article 6 expressly gives parties to an international sales contract the right to 'contract out' of the CISG – in whole or in part.

If, for example, a seller in France and a buyer in Russia expressly agree that their sales contract shall be 'governed by the Swedish Sale of Goods Act (*Köplagen*)', then that domestic sales law regime will *displace* the CISG, even though French and Russian courts and arbitrators otherwise (absent the just-stated clause) would apply the Convention to the contract between the parties concerned, simply because they reside in different CISG Contracting States.[160]

In order to determine whether or not a well-positioned party should, at the time of contracting, seek to exclude CISG application to the contract in question, that party – and his or her legal counsel – should, of course, consider the advantages and disadvantages of Convention application. That said, the many 'pros' of CISG application will most often likely outweigh the 'cons'.[161]

For those who nonetheless would seek to contract out of the CISG, careful contract drafting is advised: a clause in a contract (or general standard conditions) which states that, for example, 'French law' or 'Polish law' or 'Ukrainian law' applies, will *not* be interpreted as displacing the CISG, simply because the CISG has become an *integral part* of French and Polish and Ukrainian law.[162]

Note that CISG Article 8 governs the interpretation of the clauses in the foregoing examples,[163] just as Article 14 the Convention might govern the issue of whether

159. *See* generally *supra*, Ch. 1.

160. *Accord*: F. Ferrari & M. Torsello, *International Sales Law – CISG in a Nutshell* 2nd ed. (2018), at 45–46 (when domestic/internal law of Contracting State chosen as the law applicable, CISG will not apply). Regarding Art. 1(1)(a) *see supra*, No. 53.

161. *See* C. Brunner, 'Introduction', in *Commentary on the UN Sales Law (CISG)* (Brunner & Gottlieb eds, 2019), at 9–10 (among the pros: widely adopted, easily accessible multilingual text, allowing multinational corporations to submit sales contracts to single regime with level playing field, but for some legal counsel, a key con can be relative lack of experience with CISG).

162. The great majority of reported CISG decisions support this view. *See*, for example, LG Düsseldorf (Germany), 11 Oct. 1995 www.unilex.info/cisg/case/234 (applying CISG on the basis of Art. 1(1)(a), even though seller's standard terms expressly provided for application of 'German law'; Court noted choice of law of Contracting State as governing law could not in itself amount to implied exclusion of CISG, because the *CISG is part of law of that State*). *See also* OLG Koblenz (Germany), 17 Sep. 1993 (No. 2 U 1230/91), RIW 1993, 934–938 (parties' choice of 'French law', coupled with 1(1)(b) rule, led to application of CISG). *Accord* ICC award No. 7565/1994, reported in UNILEX; Supreme Court of Poland, 17 Nov. 2008 http://www.unilex.info/cisg/case/1723 (express choice of law of Contracting State not exclusion of CISG); Gdansk Court of Appeal, Poland, 22 Jan. 2014, http://www.unilex.info/cisg/case/1983 (general conditions of sale which governed commercial relationship between parties determined Polish law as applicable law; Convention applied as part of Polish law); Int'l Commercial Arbitration Court at the Ukrainian Chamber of Commerce and Industry, Ukraine, 23 Jan. 2012 http://www.unilex.info/cisg/case/1876; U.S. District Court, 31 Jul. 2013, *It's Intoxicating, Inc., v. Maritim Hotelgesellschaft mbH and D. Zimmer*, http://www.unilex.info/cisg/case/1815 (reference to 'Georgia law' not effective opt-out).

163. In situations like these, where the starting point is that the CISG applies automatically (by default) pursuant to Art. 1(1), the issue of how to interpret statements like 'German law', 'French law' and

a purported opt-out clause contained in one party's standard terms has been incorporated as part of the overall CISG contract concerned.[164]

72. Even when the parties to an international sales contract do not elect to displace the CISG regime in its entirety, they will often contract out to a more limited extent, for example, where the contract expressly incorporates the Incoterms.[165]

Another common example of partial contracting out is provided in situations where certain terms are set forth in a standard form agreement containing, for example, a clause obligating the seller to repair or replace non-conforming goods, perhaps supplemented by an express disclaimer or limitation of liability in damages,[166] etc. In such situations, the parties' rights and obligations will be governed by a combination of: (a) the express contractual provisions, (b) the applicable domestic rules of validity (which may limit the effect of the express provisions),[167] and (c) the supplementary Convention rules.[168]

B. Contracting In

73. In some common international sales situations, the CISG does *not* automatically apply, for example, because the parties do not reside in Contracting States,[169] and/or because the Convention would not apply for other reasons, for example, because the contract concerns the sale of a ship.[170] In cases like these, the contract in question will, as a starting point, be governed by the domestic sales (and sales contract formation) rules determined by the choice-of-law rules of PIL. If, however,

---

'the laws of Switzerland' is governed by CISG Art. 8 (discussed *infra*, Nos 81 et seq.); that is, a court in a CISG Contracting State is bound to apply Art. 8 to determine whether the parties concerned have (or have not) exercised their freedom to contract out of the Convention rule-set, without resort to conflict-of-laws rules (*see supra*, No. 53). In other words, you are 'in' (the Convention) until you (according to *its* rules) 'opt out'. *Accord:* Honnold/Flechtner, *Uniform Law for International Sales* 4th ed. (2009), at 110 with note 23. For a more complex and (it is submitted) less convincing view, *see* Schwenzer/Hachem in Schlechtriem & Schwenzer, *Commentary* 4th ed. (2016), 103–104. The fact that the party who *drafted* a standard form *intended*, for example, 'French law' to mean French domestic law should not lead to the application of that law, unless that is also how the other party – or a reasonable person in the position of the other party – would interpret such a clause. As regards unclear clauses, the *contra proferentem* maxim can supplement (or be deemed part of) Art. 8; *see* Schmidt-Kessel in *Commentary*, *ibid.*, at 178.

164. Regarding Art. 14, *see infra*, Nos 100 ff. Applying logic similar to that set forth in the preceding note, the contract formation rules in CISG Part II should be used to determine whether parties who reside in different Contracting States have actually concluded (formed) an agreement to contract out. *Accord*: J. Bailey, 'Facing the Truth', *Cornell International Law Journal* 32 (1999) 273, 303.
165. *See infra*, No. 152.
166. *See* generally J. Lookofsky, *Understanding the CISG* 5th Worldwide ed. (2017), §7.1. Regarding liability arising from the operation of Arts 35, 45 and 74, *see infra*, Nos 162, 211 and 290 et seq.
167. Indeed, in the example just described, domestic mandatory rules (regarding the validity of the purported disclaimer) may limit the effectiveness of an express disclaimer: *see supra*, No. 63.
168. *Compare* Court of Cassation, Belgium, 7 Mar. 2014, CLOUT Case 1713 (when placing order buyers stated their general and special terms and conditions would apply; CISG held not applicable).
169. *See supra*, Nos 52–57.
170. *See supra*, No. 60 with accompanying note.

the parties concerned regard the Convention regime as preferable to the more provincial solution dictated by choice-of-law rules, they can contract in to the Convention, that is, even though it would not apply by default.[171]

Note in this connection and depending on the circumstances, that a court might interpret a general reference to 'New York law' as evidencing an intent to contract in to the Convention, that is, even in a case where the Convention would not otherwise (in the absence of an opt-in clause) apply.[172]

§2. General Provisions

74. Chapter II of Part I of the CISG is headed General Provisions. Among these are important rules regarding interpretation – both as regards interpretation of the Convention itself and as regards interpretation of those sales contracts to which the Convention applies.

I. Convention Interpretation: Uniformity and Good Faith

75. Article 7 contains two rules regarding the interpretation of the Convention itself (as opposed to interpretation of contracts subject to the Convention).[173] The first of these rules, Article 7(1), provides as follows:

> 1. In the interpretation of this Convention, regard is to be had to its international character and to the need to promote uniformity in its application and the observance of good faith in international trade.

76. For purposes of the present analysis, it will be convenient to divide the discussion of the rule of interpretation set forth in Article 7(1) into two parts, and to begin here (in No. 76) with the part which serves as a command (to Contracting

171. If, during the negotiations, both parties seek to contract out of the Convention but cannot agree on a domestic rule-set to replace it, the CISG remains applicable under the default rule in Art. 1(1)(a): *see* US District Court, 18 Jan. 2011, *Hanwha Corporation v. Cedar Petrochemicals, Inc.*, available at http://www.unilex.info/cisg/case/1583 (applying CISG Art. 8(2) to resolve merits, court found parties had not reached binding agreement).

172. *Accord* P. Winship, 'The Scope of the Vienna Convention on International Sales Contracts', in *International Sales* (Galston & Smit eds, 1984), also available at https://www.cisg.law.pace.edu/cisg/biblio/winship5.html, at 1–32; regarding the American Art. 95 declaration *see supra*, No. 55. Courts have reached similar results applying the rule in CISG Art. 1(1)(b): *see supra*, No. 71 and, for example, OLG Düsseldorf (Germany), 8 Jan. 1993, CLOUT Case No. 48, available at www.cisg.law.pace.edu/cases/930108g1.html (parties' express choice of 'German law' made CISG applicable by virtue of Art. 1(1)(b), notwithstanding fact that Turkish seller did not reside in CISG State).

173. Regarding Art. 8 and the interpretation of contracts subject to the Convention, *see infra*, Nos 81–86.

States and their courts) to interpret the Convention by having 'regard … to its international character and to the need to promote uniformity in its application'.[174]

To better understand the nature of this command to have 'regard', we do well to bear in mind the various primary and secondary sources of CISG law, and in this connection, we recall that the Convention is a supranational 'statute', that is, a piece of international legislation which binds those States which have agreed to abide by it. For this reason, the courts of all CISG Contracting States are clearly bound to give effect to the individual provisions set forth in the treaty text itself. So, when a question arises as to how a given rule or term in the Convention should be understood, the most simple and natural starting point for the interpretation of that provision is likely to be the 'plain meaning' of the treaty's 'black-letter' text.[175] This is, after all, the *primary source* of CISG law.

Note in this connection that Norway originally incorporated the CISG into Norwegian law through the Norwegian Sale of Goods Act which, at that time, governed both domestic and international contracts of sale. Regrettably, this sometimes led Norwegian courts to resolve CISG cases without reference to CISG 'black letter' rules![176] Fortunately, in November 2014, the CISG was incorporated into Norwegian law by direct reference to the CISG text,[177] thus putting Norway on the same footing as all other Contracting States.

In many cases, however, the meaning and/or proper application of (the six, equally authentic versions of) a given Convention provision will not be plainly clear, and this can give rise to more than one possible interpretation of that rule and/or its proper application in a given concrete case. In these situations, Convention interpreters can and should seek guidance in (reliable) *secondary sources* of the meaning to be attributed to CISG rules of law.[178]

Since the Convention is a legislative enactment (an international treaty), some CISG interpreters see reason to search for evidence of the international legislator's 'intent'. But unlike the readily understandable and well-organized legislative history (*travaux préparatoires*) which often accompanies domestic legislation, the CISG legislative history consists mainly of the countless discussions and debates among numerous national representatives which accompanied the drafters' formulation of individual treaty terms. For this reason, the CISG legislative history, while

174. As regards the second part of the Art. 7(1) rule (concerning 'the observance of good faith in international trade'), *see infra*, No. 77.
175. *See* Art. 31 of the 1969 Vienna Convention on the Law of Treaties. Regarding the six equally authentic, but not always completely consistent versions of the treaty, *see* Art. 101 and *infra*, No. 340. Regarding, for example, the US Supreme Court's 'literal' interpretation of the Hague Evidence Convention, *see Société Nationale Industrielle Aerospatiale v. U.S. Dist. Court for Southern Dist. of Iowa*, 482 US 522 (1987). *See also* J. Hellner, 'The UN Convention on International Sales of Goods – An Outsider's View', *Ius Inter Nationes: Festschrift für Stefan Riesenfeld* (1983).
176. *See*, e.g., Agder Appeals Court, Norway, 7 Jun. 2013, CLOUT Case 1635.
177. *Ibid.*, note 5.
178. *See* Art. 32 of the 1969 Vienna Convention on the Law of Treaties. Regarding the six equally authentic versions of the treaty text, *see infra*, No. 340.

voluminous,[179] rarely provides solid evidence of the CISG drafters' (common) intent with respect to any given treaty rule.[180]

A related observation applies to CISG interpretations based on ULIS. For although certain CISG provisions resemble ULIS rules, that does not necessarily mean that the legislators who drafted ULIS possessed the same legislative intent as those who drafted the CISG.[181] Nor should the unofficial Secretariat Commentary to the 1978 Draft Convention be regarded as an authoritative CISG guide.[182]

This leads to the question of the relationship between the CISG and the UNIDROIT Principles of International Commercial Law (4th ed. 2016) – *inter alia*, the extent to which courts and arbitrators can – as posited in the Principles' own Preamble – apply individual UNIDROIT Principles to help *interpret* individual CISG Convention provisions.[183] Although good arguments can be made on both sides of this issue, the fact is that many decision makers have already resorted to the application of the Principles in this way,[184] and it seems unlikely that scholarly criticism of this technique will put an end to the practice anytime soon.

(A related sub-issue – to be considered later – concerns the extent to which individual UNIDROIT Principles can rightly be applied to *supplement* (as opposed to interpret) individual CISG rules,[185] e.g., whether the CISG 'exemptions' rule in Article 79 can be supplemented by the UNIDROIT 'hardship' regime.)[186]

For various reasons, and in some cases perhaps even unwittingly, national courts have sometimes interpreted the CISG in accordance with well-entrenched domestic

---

179. For a comprehensive collection of CISG conference documents, *see* J. Honnold, *Documentary History of the 1980 Uniform Law for International Sales* (1989). *See also* the online history of individual CISG rules available at http://cisgw3.law.pace.edu/cisg/text/cisg-toc.html.

180. For an exception (regarding intuitive evidence that the CISG drafters obviously did *not* intend that 'damages' under Art. 74 include attorneys' fees) *see infra*, No. 292. As regards the use of CISG documentary history as an interpretative aid (in general), Professors Honnold and Flechtner, *Uniform Law* 4th ed. (2009), at 599 urge restraint: 'Interpretation based on discussions by a large legislative body is more meaningful for decisions of broad issues of policy than for detailed applications'.

181. Many European commentators place great emphasis on decisions interpreting the provisions of the ULIS, notwithstanding the fact that numerous CISG States (including the US) were clearly opposed to – and therefore never ratified – the ULIS: *see supra*, No. 11.

182. An American proposal to draft an official Commentary to the 1980 Convention was *rejected*: *see* P. Winship, 'The Scope of the Vienna Convention on International Sales Contracts', in *International Sales* (1984), also available at https://www.cisg.law.pace.edu/cisg/biblio/winship5.html, at 1–27. The UN Secretariat's *Commentary* to the 1978 Draft Convention (A/CONF. 97/5), while providing some useful insights, will never attain worldwide recognition as an official and authoritative source of Convention interpretation. For this reason alone, one should reject the proposal by Bailey, 'Facing the Truth', *Cornell International Law Journal* 32 (1999) 273 at 300, to adopt the Commentary as the 'official' (American) commentary to the CISG.

183. As set forth in the Preamble of the UNIDROIT Principles (http://www.unilex.info/principles/text): 'The[se Principles] may be used to *interpret* or supplement international uniform law instruments' (emphasis added). *See also* Ferrari & Torsello, *supra* note 160, at 66–67.

184. *See*, e.g., Cámara Nacional de Apelaciones en lo Comercial, Argentina, http://www.unilex.info/cisg/case/2037, 16 Oct. 2013 (applying Art. 7.4.1–7.4.6 of the UNIDROIT Principles on damages to interpret CISG Arts 74–76 and thus to determine the 'current price' of egg products sold by an Argentinian seller to a Danish buyer).

185. That is as posited in the UNIDROIT Principles Preamble (*supra* note 183). *See infra*, No. 79, text with notes 228 et seq.

186. *See infra*, No. 308.

views, *inter alia*, in cases where Convention terminology seems reminiscent of (older) local law.[187] The main problem here, of course, is that a given interpretation based on a given domestic viewpoint might lead to what CISG interpreters in other jurisdictions would regard as a clearly wrong CISG result.[188]

In an attempt to guard against such inappropriate solutions, Article 7(1) *commands* Contracting States (and their) courts to 'have regard' to the *international* character of the Convention and the need to promote *uniformity* in its application.[189] To this end, CISG arbiters should undertake an independent (autonomous) interpretation of the treaty, with a view towards achieving results acceptable to other CISG Contracting States.[190] To be sure, the flexible command set forth in paragraph (1) of Article 7 – i.e., to have some unspecified measure of 'regard' to the stated desiderata – hardly compels courts and arbitrators to pursue the uniformity goal at all costs,[191] but it does at least represent an important factor to be taken into consideration when interpreting a given CISG rule.

As regards *case law* (precedent), it is significant that no supranational court is competent to interpret the CISG.[192] And yet, since Article 7(1) requires courts to display (due) regard to the international character of the Convention and to the need to promote uniformity in its application, national courts are bound to 'have regard' to CISG foreign precedents[193] – a task made easier in recent years by CLOUT (Case

187. The striking similarity between CISG Art. 74 and the Common law *Hadley v. Baxendale* rule prompted some provincial observations in the *Delchi* case, CLOUT Case 138, available at http://cisgw3.law.pace.edu/cisg/wais/db/cases2/951206u1.html. *See also* US Court of Appeals, 14 Feb. 2011, *Dingxi Longhai Dairy, Ltd. v. Becwood Technology Group L.L.C.*, available at http://www.unilex.info/cisg/case/1564 ('case law interpreting analogous provisions of [UCC] Article 2 … may also inform a court where the language of the relevant CISG provisions tracks that of the UCC').

A somewhat related and similarly disruptive phenomenon, which Professor Ferrari has dubbed the 'outward trend', concerns the projection of foreign law onto the provisions of an international instrument where these provisions refer to legal concepts unknown in the system in which the interpreter is trained. *See generally* F. Ferrari, 'Autonomous Interpretation Versus Homeward Trend Versus Outward Trend in CISG Case Law', *Uniform Law Review* 22 (2017) 244.

188. For example, some German courts in earlier CISG-related decisions seem to have read the inspection and notice rules in CISG Arts 38 and 39 as if they were restatements of the (very strict) requirements laid down in German domestic law: *see infra*, Nos 187 et seq.
189. In this context, the verb 'shall' is to be understood as a (polite but obligatory) command.
190. Professor Flechtner, emphasizing the flexible nature of the (regard is to be had) command in Art. 7(1), has made an interesting case for a 'regional' CISG interpretation: *see* H. Flechtner, 'Another CISG Case in the US Courts: Pitfalls for the Practitioner and the Potential for Regionalized Interpretations', *Journal of Law & Commerce* 15 (1995) 127, 132 et seq.
191. *Compare* L. Mistelis, 'More About the CISG Advisory Council', www.cisgac.com/default.php?sid=149: 'The Council is guided by the mandate of Art. 7 of the Convention as far as its interpretation and application are concerned: the *paramount* regard to international character of the Convention and the need to promote uniformity' (emphasis added).
192. This contrasts, for example, with the competency of the European Court of Justice to interpret the Brussels Regulation on Jurisdiction and Judgments.
193. *See* J. Lookofsky, 'CISG Foreign Case Law: How Much Regard Should We Have?', in *The Draft UNCITRAL Digest and Beyond: Cases, Analysis and Unresolved Issues in the U.N. Sales Convention* (Ferrari, Flechtner & Brand eds, 2004), 216, 217; *see also* Lookofsky, 'Digesting CISG Case Law: How Much Regard Should We Have?', *Vindobona Journal of International Commercial Law*

Law on UNCITRAL Texts), with the essence of individual CLOUT decisions conveniently collected and organized in the *Digest of CISG Case Law*,[194] not to mention the Pace Law Albert H. Kritzer CISG Database (CISGW3) and UNILEX systems, both of which comprise large numbers of CISG decisions rendered by courts and arbitral tribunals around the world.[195]

Of course, since decisions rendered by even the highest courts of other jurisdictions can at best achieve status as *persuasive* (as opposed to binding) CISG precedent, a truly international interpretation of the Convention remains a most difficult task.[196] And yet, it is both significant and encouraging that an increasing number of national courts refer to foreign CISG case law and often find these precedents persuasive.[197] Unpersuasive foreign precedents, on the other hand, need not be followed.[198]

Next on the scale of secondary CISG authority (i.e., after CISG case law) comes CISG *scholarly opinion*, i.e., the views of academics and Convention commentators worldwide, as expressed in their books, articles and other publications.

Although it is difficult to assess the impact of such CISG scholarship in an international context, especially given the propensity of national courts to rely mainly on home-grown scholarly opinion,[199] CISG scholars have in any case generated an enormous quantity of CISG-related literature. Usually, this scholarship reflects the opinion of only one author (or two),[200] but the collective opinions issued in the name of the CISG Advisory Council (CISG AC) constitute a noteworthy exception.

---

and Arbitration 8 (2004) 181. *Accord*: H. Flechtner, 'The Several Texts of the CISG in a Decentralized System: Observations on Translations, Reservations and Other Challenges to the Uniformity Principle in Article 7(1)', *Journal of Law & Commerce* 17 (1998) 187. *See also* Court of Appeal, The Hague (Netherlands), 22 Apr. 2014, English abstract available at http://www.unilex.info/cisg/case/1900 (absent supranational Court to ensure uniform CISG interpretation and application, national judges and arbiters *required*, in accordance with Art. 7, to *take into consideration* foreign case law, which though not binding, has persuasive authority).

194. For online access to these UNCITRAL sources, *see* https://uncitral.un.org/en/case_law.

195. The Pace Law School Institute of International Commercial Law's 'Albert Kritzer CISG Database' (www.iicl.law.pace.edu/cisg/cisg) includes Professor Kritzer's original and comprehensive 'CISGW3' database (now 'archived' but still worthwhile and usable at www.cisg.law.pace.edu). The UNILEX database of CISG cases and materials is available online at http://www.unilex.info/instrument/cisg.

196. *Accord*: Flechtner, *supra* note 193, at 210.

197. *See*, e.g., Foreign Trade Court of Arbitration of the Serbian Chamber of Commerce, 28 Jan. 2009, available at http://www.unilex.info/cisg/case/1432 (arbitration referred to relevant foreign case law as means to achieve uniform interpretation and application of Convention according to Art. 7(1)); High Court of New Zealand, 30 Jul. 2010, at http://www.unilex.info/cisg/case/1595 (relying on Art. 7(1), court cited foreign case law (and scholarly writings) addressing question of non-conformity as result of non-compliance with public permission requirements).

198. *See* Lookofsky, *supra*, note 193, at 186: because there is no established system or scale to evaluate the weight of CISG foreign precedent, the persuasive – or unpersuasive – nature of any given foreign decision will depend on various factors, including (but not limited to) the *force of the reasoning* in the (foreign) opinion and the apparent *soundness of the result*; it may also depend on the *prominence of the (foreign) court* and whether the decision has *support in other jurisdictions*.

199. *See* (e.g.) Bundesgerichtshof, Germany, 28 May 2014, available at http://www.unilex.info/cisg/case/1832 (citing, in addition to a long list of *German* academic views, CISG Advisory Council Opinion No. 13).

200. *See*, e.g., the wealth of material cited and/or directly available at http://www.cisg.law.pace.edu/cisg/biblio/biblio.html.

Although collectively authored opinions are not necessarily more cogent or persuasive than individually authored opinions,[201] CISG AC opinions have in recent years been cited with increasing frequency,[202] and a Netherlands Court of Appeal has gone so far as to declare (in dictum) that it regards them as highly persuasive.[203]

A significant number CISG academics – including those who belong to the CISG AC collective – often adopt 'expansionist' CISG positions, i.e., positions which favour (e.g.) the application of the Convention in arguably borderline situations, whereas most national courts seem to have adopted a more cautious, less expansionist approach.[204] That said, we should recognize that the interpretation and application of developing CISG case law and scholarly opinion cannot be regarded as a 'mathematical' science,[205] especially since both these secondary sources can *at most* provide persuasive (as opposed to binding) authority as regards the proper (best) interpretation and application of the CISG rule concerned.[206] For this reason, it seems appropriate and useful to view the most difficult aspects of CISG interpretation as part of an ongoing international 'work in progress' and to expect some degree of CISG 'legal pluralism' as inevitable, a 'reality that will never (and perhaps should never) disappear completely'.[207]

77. When interpreting the CISG treaty, courts and arbitrators also must be mindful of the *second* part of Article 7(1): 'regard is [also] to be had' to the observance of *good faith* in international trade.

Hardly by accident, this second part of the Article 7(1) rule, which commands national courts to *interpret* the Convention in *good faith*, falls short of domestic analogues which expressly require contracting *parties* to *act* (perform their duties) in

201. *See* Flechtner & Lookofsky, 'Zapata Retold: Attorneys' Fees Are (Still) Not Governed by the CISG', *Journal of Law and Commerce* 26 (2007) 1, 7; U. of Pittsburgh Legal Studies Research Paper. Available at SSRN http://ssrn.com/abstract=1334299: 'The Advisory Council is, quite obviously, not an "international legislature" … the Council is comprised merely of self-appointed representatives of the CISG scholarly community. It is certainly a distinguished group of scholars, but organizing themselves into a (private) body gives their opinions no more inherent authority concerning the meaning of the CISG than the opinions of other scholars: Advisory Council opinions have authority only insofar as they present a *convincing* analysis.'
202. *See*, e.g., US District Court, S.D.N.Y., 28 Sep. 2011, *Cedar Petrochemicals Inc. v. Dongbu Hannong Chemical Ltd*, available at http://www.unilex.info/cisg/case/1643; Bundesgerichtshof, Germany, 28 May 2014, available at http://www.unilex.info/cisg/case/1832 (citing, in addition to *German* academic views, CISG AC Opinion No. 13).
203. *See* (e.g.) Court of Appeal, The Hague (Netherlands), 22 Apr. 2014, available at http://www.unilex.info/cisg/case/1900 (noting that the CISG AC, established by private initiative and consisting of leading experts in the field, aims at uniform interpretation and provides highly authoritative (*gezaghebbende*) opinions on uniform CISG application and interpretation).
204. *See* generally J. Lookofsky, 'Not Running Wild with the CISG', *Journal of Law & Commerce* 29 (2011), also available at http://papers.ssrn.com/sol3/papers.cfm?abstract_id=2376353.
205. *Accord* J. Lookofsky, 'Loose Ends and Contorts in International Sales', *American Journal of Comparative Law* 39 (1991), also at http://cisgw3.law.pace.edu/cisg/biblio/lookofsky6.html.
206. Regarding the Art. 7 issue of 'how much regard' courts in a given CISG jurisdiction should have to foreign CISG precedent, *see* text *supra* with notes 189 ff. and generally Lookofsky, 'Digesting CISG Case Law: How Much Regard Should We Have?', available at https://www.cisg.law.pace.edu/cisg/biblio/lookofsky9.html.
207. *See* P. Berman, 'The Inevitable Legal Pluralism Within Universal Harmonization Regimes: The Case of the CISG', *Uniform Law Review* 21(1) (2016).

accordance with good faith; indeed, the absence of a good-faith-performance rule in the CISG reflects the fact that *some* Convention drafters had feared the uncertain consequences of legislating at the international level with respect to just that kind of obligation.[208]

But now, after some thirty years of Convention interpretation and application by national courts, the distinction between good-faith interpretation and good-faith performance has become somewhat blurred, not least because Article 7(2) provides for the settlement of certain CISG matters on the basis of the 'general principles' on which the Convention is based.[209] And since good faith has been identified as one such general principle, a number of courts and commentators –located primarily in Civilian (as opposed to Common Law) domestic jurisdictions – have cited Article 7 as authority for the proposition that the parties to a CISG contract are indeed obligated to *act* in good faith;[210] a French appellate court, for example, has required a party to pay damages because that party's *conduct* was contrary to the principle of good faith in international trade laid down in Article 7.[211]

II. Convention Interpretation: Matters Governed but Not Settled

78. Whereas paragraph 1 of Article 7 provides general rules for the interpretation of the sales treaty, paragraph 2 of Article 7 contains a special rule designed for the settlement of matters 'governed' by but not expressly 'settled' in the Convention. This provision provides as follows:

> 2. Questions concerning matters governed by this Convention which are not expressly settled in it are to be settled in conformity with the general principles on which it is based or, in the absence of such principles, in conformity with the law applicable by virtue of the rules of private international law.

79. Article 7(2) provides a potentially powerful tool which courts and arbitrators can use to plug so-called internal gaps in the express Convention text. By locating a relevant CISG general principle for the resolution of a given governed-but-not-settled matter, courts and arbitrators can remain within the four corners of the treaty in situations where they otherwise would need to revert to other (usually domestic) rules of law.[212]

---

208. *See* J. Honnold/Flechtner, *Uniform Law for International Sales* 4th ed. (2009), at 134 with note 23 (describing the good-faith rule in Art. 7(1) as a compromise between two divergent views).
209. *See infra*, Nos 78–80.
210. *See* generally C. Andersen, 'Good Faith? Good Grief!', *International Trade and Business Law Review* 17 (2014) 310, also available at http://ssrn.com/abstract=2675008; M. Bridge, 'Good Faith, the Common Law, and the CISG', *Uniform Law Review* 22 (2017) 98, also available at https://doi.org/10.1093/ulr/unw059.
211. *See* Cour d'appel de Grenoble, France, 22 Feb. 1995, CLOUT Case 154, abstract available at www.unilex.info/cisg/case/83.
212. Article 7(2) addresses so-called *internal* gaps, i.e., issues that fall within (are 'governed by') the CISG's material sphere of application pursuant to Art. 4 and not excluded in Arts 2–6. By contrast, so-called *external* gaps concern issues excluded from the CISG's sphere of application pursuant to Art. 4, making them subject to the domestic law designated by applicable conflict of law rules. *See*

Courts and commentators have identified a considerable number of CISG general principles for use within the Article 7(2) context, including some hardly controversial CISG principles, such as 'reasonableness',[213] estoppel (*venire contra factum proprium*)[214] and 'full compensation'.[215]

Note, however, that these and other identifiable CISG general principles can only help settle (otherwise unsettled) 'matters' which can rightly be described as *governed* by the Convention (*les matières régies par la présente Convention*). Conversely, certain other matters – such as those relating to the validity of the sales contract, third-party rights, limitation periods,[216] etc. – are 'external gaps' clearly *not governed* by the Convention which can only be settled by resort to rules which lie completely outside the Convention ambit, that is (usually) domestic rules of law.[217]

Note also in this connection that some matters which are CISG-governed – and therefore also capable of being settled by means of Article 7(2) – might alternatively (and perhaps even preferentially) be resolved/settled by means of *analogy*.[218] Suppose, for example, that a decision maker must determine whether an e-mail qualifies as a 'writing' under Article 13. Now, since Article 13 clearly 'governs' the 'matter' of how to define a 'writing',[219] we might regard the e-mail issue as a matter (within a larger matter) which is governed but not settled by the CISG and then settle that matter with the general principle, arguably reflected in Article 13, that the Convention is 'receptive' to other forms of writing which are functional equivalents of telegram and telex.[220] But we might also resolve that same matter without resorting to the Article 7(2) mechanism at all, simply by making an analogy between e-mail and the kinds of 'writing' listed expressly in the Convention text.[221] Either way, CISG case law now confirms that e-mail and telefax communications are valid written CISG contract forms.[222]

C. Brunner & P. Wagner, 'Article 7 [Interpretation of the Convention and Gap-Filling]', in *Commentary on the UN Sales Law (CISG)* (Brunner & Gottlieb eds, 2019), at 86.

213. *See* P. Schlechtriem and other sources cited at www.cisg.law.pace.edu/cisg/text/reason.html#schl.

214. Regarding this general principle, *see* U. Schroeter in Schlechtriem & Schwenzer, *Commentary* 4th ed. (2016), Art. 27, para. 16; *accord* Müller-Chen, also in the 4th ed. of the *Commentary*, Art. 45, para. 16(bb).

215. Regarding Art. 74 *see* Nos 291 et seq.

216. *See*, for example, Cour de Justice Genève (Switzerland), 10 Oct. 1997, CLOUT Case 249, abstract at www.unilex.info/cisg/case/309 (matter of limitation period not governed by CISG; matter governed by Swiss domestic law, applicable to contract by virtue of Swiss private international law rules).

217. *See* note 212 *supra*. *See also supra*, Nos 62 et seq.; Lookofsky, 'Loose Ends and Contorts', *American Journal of Comparative Law* 39 (1991) 407; H. Hartnell, 'Rousing the Sleeping Dog', *The Yale Journal of International Law* 18 (1993). *See also infra*, No. 80.

218. *Accord*: F. Ferrari & M. Torsello, *International Sales Law – CISG in a Nutshell* 2nd ed. (2018), at 24 (Art. 7(2) also covers other methods of legal reasoning, such as analogical application; indeed, recourse to analogical application prevails over recourse to general CISG principles).

219. *See infra*, Nos 97 et seq.

220. *See* (using this technique, albeit more cautiously as regards electronic communications) Schmidt-Kessel, in *Commentary* 4th ed. (2016), 221 f.

221. *See* Lookofsky, *Understanding the CISG* 5th Worldwide ed. (2017), §2.11.

222. *See* Supreme Court of the Czech Republic, 17 Dec. 2013, CLOUT Case 1450, available at https://www.uncitral.org/clout/clout/data/cze/clout_case_1450_leg-3214.html.

That said, courts and scholars sometimes differ as to which matters can (or cannot) rightly be classified as 'CISG-governed'. Consider, for example, the issue of set-off: i.e., the right of a given debtor (A) to counter (balance) creditor (B)'s claim against him (A) with a claim which (A) has against (B). Although the term 'set-off' is nowhere to be found in the Convention text, a significant minority of scholars and courts have taken the view that set-off (at least in certain CISG contexts) is rightly regarded not only as a matter 'governed' by the CISG but also as a matter capable of being 'settled' by the application of general CISG principles.[223]

An arbitral award rendered in Vienna concerning the calculation of interest illustrates the potential inherent in Article 7(2) for even more expansionistic rule-making.[224] Although Article 78 expressly provides for the payment of interest (on the price and other sums in arrears),[225] this black-letter provision does not set (or provide any means to set) the interest rate, simply because those who drafted the Convention could not agree on this point.[226] For this reason, most courts and arbitrators have filled this 'gap' in the treaty by resorting to domestic law, but in this Vienna arbitration, the sole arbitrator decided nonetheless that the rate of interest was a matter governed but not settled by the CISG and then proceeded to settle the matter (the rate) by reference to the general CISG principle of 'full compensation', that is, the principle that a CISG promisee should be compensated for all (foreseeable) losses caused by the other party's breach. In doing so, the arbitrator thus found the means to 'settle' a matter which (in 1980) could not be settled by the Vienna treaty drafters themselves.[227]

A related, equally controversial question concerns the relationship between the CISG and the UNIDROIT Principles of International Commercial Law (4th ed. 2016) – in particular, the extent to which courts and arbitrators – as posited in the Principles' own Preamble – can apply individual UNIDROIT Principles to *supplement* (as opposed to interpret) individual CISG Convention provisions.[228] Although good arguments can be made on both sides of this issue, not least on the 'no' side,[229] the fact is that some decision makers have already resorted to the application of the Principles in this way,[230] and it seems unlikely that scholarly criticism of this technique will put an end to this practice.

223. *See* U. Magnus, 'CISG and Set-Off', Ch. 12 in *A Tribute to Joseph M. Lookofsky* (Andersen & Henschel eds, 2015); Schwenzer/Hachem, *Commentary* 4th ed. (2016), at 85 (preferring minority view that set-off encompassed where both claims based on CISG). *But see* F. Ferrari & M. Torsello, *International Sales Law – CISG in a Nutshell* 2nd ed. (2018), at 139 f. (set-off outside the CISG's scope of application).

224. *See* Internationales Schiedsgericht der Bundeskammer der gewerblichen Wirtschaft – Wien, awards No. SCH-4366, 15 Jun. 1994, CLOUT Case 93, available at www.uncitral.org/uncitral/en/case_law/abstracts.html.

225. *See infra*, Nos 300 et seq.

226. *See* generally Honnold/Flechtner, *Uniform Law* 4th ed. (2009), 602–606.

227. *Accord* LG Aachen (Germany) of 20 Jul. 1995, abstract in UNILEX at www.unilex.info/cisg/case/125, which *expressly rejected* an Art. 7(2) solution to the interest-rate problem, noting that the Vienna Convention drafters *tried but failed* to solve the interest-rate problem.

228. As set forth in the Preamble of the UNIDROIT Principles (http://www.unilex.info/principles/text): 'The[se Principles] may be used to interpret or *supplement* international uniform law instruments' (emphasis added).

229. *See*, e.g., F. Ferrari & M. Torsello, *International Sales Law – CISG in a Nutshell* 2nd ed. (2018), at 66–67 (critical of this aspect of the UNIDROIT Preamble, since the gap-filling rule in CISG Art.

A particularly controversial example of 'expansionist' CISG decision-making by means of Article 7(2) gap-filling will be considered later under the heading of 'hardship'.[231]

80. In instances when a decision maker cannot discern any general CISG principle with which to settle the governed-but-not-settled issue at hand, the last part of Article 7(2) requires that the matter be settled in conformity with the [substantive] law applicable by virtue of the (applicable) rules of PIL. Usually, the PIL (choice-of-law) rules at the decision maker's disposal will point to a *domestic* substantive law rule.[232] In some commercial situations, however, the applicable substantive rule might be an international rule of substance located within the larger body of *lex mercatoria.*[233]

III. Interpretation of Statements by Parties

81. Unlike Article 7 (which concerns the interpretation of the text of the CISG treaty), the subject matter of Article 8 is CISG *contract* interpretation, that is, the interpretation of 'statements' made by (and other conduct of) a party to a CISG international contract of sale. Article 8 provides as follows:

(1) For the purposes of this Convention, statements made by and other conduct of a party are to be interpreted according to his intent where the other party knew or could not have been unaware what that intent was.
(2) If the preceding paragraph is not applicable, statements made by and other conduct of a party are to be interpreted according to the understanding that a reasonable person of the same kind as the other party would have had in the same circumstances.
(3) In determining the intent of a party or the understanding a reasonable person would have had, due consideration is to be given to all relevant circumstances

---

7(2) requires resort to general principles upon which *CISG* is based, not external rules such as UNIDROIT Principles). *But compare* C. Brunner & P. Wagner, 'Article 7 [Interpretation of the Convention and Gap-Filling]', in *Commentary on the UN Sales Law (CISG)* (Brunner & Gottlieb eds, 2019), at 88 (UNIDROIT Principles which are 'compliant with CISG general principles' may be relied upon to help fill CISG internal gap).

230. *See* Brunner & Wagner, preceding note, and, e.g., Cour de Cassation (Supreme Court of France), 17 Feb. 2015.

231. Regarding the 2009 decision of the highest Belgian court, expanding the reach of Art. 79 to cover hardship, *see infra* under No. 308.

232. *See supra*, No. 79. *See also* (e.g.) Cour d'appel de Colmar (France), 6 Nov. 2013, CLOUT Case 1507 (issue of whether buyer's action was time-barred *not governed* by the CISG, so French court applied 1955 Hague Convention on Law Applicable to International Sales, which led to Art. 477 of German Civil Code).

233. Within an arbitral context, *see* Lowenfeld, '*Lex Mercatoria*: an Arbitrator's View', *Arbitration International* 6 (1990) 133. *See also* Hertz & Lookofsky, *Transnational Litigation & Commercial Arbitration* 4th ed. (2017), Ch. 6.2.3. *See also* G. Born, *International Commercial Arbitration* (2009), 2232–2237.

of the case including the negotiations, any practices which the parties have established between themselves, usages and any subsequent conduct of the parties.

A. *Subject Matter of Article 8: Statements and Conduct*

82. Article 8 deals with the interpretation of 'statements' made by the parties to a CISG contract, including the statements made by the offeror and the offeree during the contract formation process (as regulated by CISG Part II).

Indeed, Article 8 was originally drafted precisely with CISG sales contract formation in mind.[234] Ultimately, however, Article 8 came to be placed in Part I of the Convention, and for this reason, Article 8 is rightly regarded as a CISG General Provision, that is, a provision which is relevant not only as regards statements made by the parties in connection with CISG contract formation (Part II of the Convention) but also (as more fully explained in the following) as regards other, arguably even more important aspects of CISG contract interpretation.

83. Since Article 8 expressly covers statements made by a [single] party, courts in Germany and elsewhere rightly use this provision to interpret sales agreements which contain statements drafted (and thus 'made') by one party and then signed (accepted) by the other.[235]

And although it might seem harder to apply Article 8 to interpret the 'intent' underlying the terms of a document prepared with the full participation of both parties, it is now generally accepted that Article 8 also applies to the interpretation of such (very common) 'joint statements'.[236] Indeed, it is now clear that Article 8 even

234. *See* Honnold/Flechtner, *Uniform Law for International Sales* 4th ed. (2009), at 153 with note 1.

235. *Compare*, for example, LG Oldenburg (Germany), 28 Feb. 1996, available at http://cisgw3.law.pace.edu/cases/960228g1.html (Dutch buyer ordered three 'truck-loads' eggs from German seller; reasonable seller should have understood buyer's statement/order to mean three *full* truck-loads). *See also* Bundesgerichtshof (Germany), 31 Oct. 2001, CLOUT Case 445, available at http://cisgw3.law.pace.edu/cases/011031g1.html (issue of whether seller's standard terms incorporated in contract resolved by CISG rules on contract formation and contract interpretation, including Art. 8).

236. *See*, e.g., Supreme Court of Switzerland, 22 Dec. 2000, available at http://www.unilex.info/cisg/case/729 (relevant contract language interpreted according to Art. 8(2), i.e., according to understanding of reasonable person); Schmidt-Kessel in Schlechtriem & Schwenzer, *Commentary* 4th ed. (2016), 145. To justify this result, one might well argue that the interpretation of such 'joint statements' is a matter governed but not expressly settled by the Convention, and the matter is easily 'settled' in conformity with the general interpretation principles laid down in Art. 8. Regarding Art. 7(2) *see supra*, Nos 78 et seq. Taking a more restrictive view, and without resorting to Art. 7(2), Professors Honnold and Flechtner, *supra* note 234, at 154 with note 3, have argued that para. (2) of Art. 8 applies when a jointly executed instrument contains 'statements' prepared (and thus 'made') by one party and signed ('accepted') by the other, but when both parties 'participate fully' in preparing the instrument, he argues that only para. (3) would apply.

applies to the interpretation of CISG contract terms dealing with matters not otherwise governed by the Convention at all, for example, the interpretation of an arbitration clause contained in that contract.[237]

B. Subjective and Objective Tests

84. Depending on the circumstances, the statements of the parties are to be interpreted pursuant to either a subjective or an objective test. One party's statements and conduct are to be interpreted subjectively, according to his (or her) intent under paragraph (1), where the other party knew or could not have been unaware what that intent was.[238] Where, however, such other party neither knew nor could have been so aware, the first party's statements are to be interpreted objectively under paragraph (2), according to the understanding that a reasonable person in the same circumstances would have had.[239]

Although Article 8 clearly 'governs' the 'matter' of CISG contract interpretation,[240] we could hardly expect these few lines of text to serve as an effective replacement for the mountain of transnational jurisprudence accumulated elsewhere on this important subject. For this reason, courts and arbitrators sometimes supplement the black-letter law in Article 8(2) with other widely accepted contract interpretation principles such as *contra proferentem*. To provide justification (authority) for applying that principle within the Convention context, these arbiters can either read 'between the lines' of Article 8(2) to divine its underlying meaning[241] and/or divine a corresponding CISG 'general principle';[242] alternatively, they might look outside the Convention, to *lex mercatoria* and the like.[243]

237. *See* Lookofsky, *Understanding the CISG* 5th Worldwide ed. (2017), §2.12. *See*, e.g., the award of 21 Jun. 1996 by Schiedsgericht der Handelskammer – Hamburg, Germany, CLOUT Case 166, abstract available at www.unilex.info/cisg/case/196 (interpreting arbitration agreement according to understanding of reasonable person and taking relevant circumstances into account (Art. 8 CISG), the tribunal held that assistance of specialized lawyer was to be expected). *See also*, e.g., Danish Eastern High Court of Appeal (Østre Landsret), 27 Jun. 2018, CLOUT Case 1828 (pursuant to Art. 8(1) arbitration clause in CISG-governed contract interpreted, to the extent possible, in accordance with parties' mutual intent).

238. *See*, e.g., Danish Eastern High Court at *id.* (parties intended to reach compromise on issue of jurisdiction under which arbitral proceeding should be instituted in domicile of respondent; English version of arbitration clause underlined by seller during negotiations held to reflect this compromise). *See also* Supreme Court of Poland, 28 Nov. 2013, available at http://www.unilex.info/cisg/case/1993 (buyer aware of seller's intent re. prepayment).

239. *See*, for example, interpreting buyer's conduct, Bundesgerichtshof (Germany) 25 Nov. 1998, CLOUT Case 270, available at http://cisgw3.law.pace.edu/cases/981125g1.html.

240. Regarding Art. 7(2) *see supra*, No. 79.

241. *Accord* Honnold/Flechtner, *Uniform Law* 4th ed. (2009), para. 107.1 (Art. 8(2) – which has 'roots' in classic *contra proferentem* rule – places *burden* on one who drafts a contract *to communicate clearly* to a reasonable person in same position as other party); *see also* CISG AC Opinion No. 13 (citing Honnold/Flechtner at *id*).

242. Regarding Art. 7(2) *see supra*, No. 79. *See* Lookofsky in *The Draft UNCITRAL Digest and Beyond: Cases, Analysis and Unresolved Issues* (Ferrari/Flechtner/Brand eds, 2004), at 232 (Art. 8 is at least consistent with letter and spirit of *contra proferentem*).

243. *See* UNIDROIT Principles, Art. 4.6 at http://www.unidroit.org/instruments/commercial-contracts/unidroit-principles-2010/398-chapter-4-interpretation/936-article-4-6-contra-proferentem-rule and

C. Due Consideration to All Relevant Circumstances

85. Paragraph (3) is a qualification of the objective interpretation test set forth in paragraph (2). In determining the intent of a party or the understanding a reasonable person would have had, due consideration is to be given to *all relevant circumstances* of the case, including the negotiations, etc.

D. Common Law Parol Evidence Rule and Article 8

86. According to Article 11 of the Convention (discussed more fully below), a CISG contract need not be in writing. But the parties to a typical CISG contract will usually memorialize their understanding (their joint statements) in a written document, thus raising the question: is a court in a CISG State asked to interpret such a document free to consider evidence to the effect that one party, during the negotiations, made an arguably contradictory oral statement (which might be interpreted as evidence of that party's true contractual intent)?[244]

According to the Convention, the answer to that hypothetical question is clearly yes: just as most national courts regularly consider such oral evidence under their own domestic (procedural) law, CISG Article 8 expressly requires that 'due consideration' be given to all (potentially) relevant circumstances in CISG cases, including the negotiations. For that reason, virtually all Convention commentators have argued, quite rightly, that the so-called parol evidence rule,[245] still in effect pursuant to the domestic contract law of some (but not all) Common law jurisdictions,[246] is not compatible with the CISG.[247] Following this view, virtually all courts, including

---

(e.g.) China, 7 Jan. 2000, CIETAC Arbitration proceeding, English translation at http://cisgw3.law.pace.edu/cases/000107c1.html ('Tribunal *cannot locate a guide from the CISG* [but a]ccording to the *basic principle* of contract interpretation – *contra proferentem* – if contract terms supplied by one party are unclear, an interpretation against that party shall be adopted.'). *See also* Lookofsky, *Understanding the CISG* 5th Worldwide ed. (2017), §2.12 at 44. Regarding (e.g.) the applicability of the *contra proferentem* maxim to standard form disclaimers and limitations of liability *see* Lookofsky, *ibid.*, §7.3 at 176 f.

244. For example, within the Art. 35 context, whether a given oral statement made by the seller should be interpreted as a supplement and/or modification of the seller's subsequent written description of the goods. For a concrete illustration of this particular problem, *see* Lookofsky, 'Loose Ends and Contorts', *American Journal of Comparative Law* 39 (1991), 407–410.

245. Despite its 'procedural' appearance, the parol evidence is a rule of substantive contract law. According to Arthur Corbin's classic, yet still viable definition (*Contracts*, para. 573), the general part of the exception-riddled parol evidence 'rule' can be stated as follows: when two parties have made a contract and have expressed it in a writing to which they have both assented as the complete and accurate integration of that contract, evidence, whether parol [oral] or otherwise, of antecedent understandings and negotiations will not be admitted for the purpose of varying or contradicting the writing.

246. Outside the CISG context, the parol rule is regarded as a formalistic anachronism by Civilian jurists, and it remains a source of embarrassment to at least some commentators within the Common law realm: *see* Honnold/Flechtner, *supra* note 241, at 164–166. Years ago, the English Law Commission concluded that the so-called rule does not (under English law) exclude evidence which, in the interests of justice, ought to be admitted: *see* Halsburry's Monthly Review, March 1986 at 12–13.

247. *See* Lookofsky, *ibid.*, at 55.

nearly all American courts which have addressed the issue, have held that Article 8 precludes application of the parol evidence rule in cases otherwise governed by the CISG.[248]

The CISG thus frees (even American) courts from formalistic (parol evidence) constraints, but the rule laid down in Article 8(3) provides no simple solution to the harder problem of whether a given oral statement – assuming it was 'made' by a party to a written CISG contract – should actually be treated as 'part' of the contract as a whole.[249] Some contract drafters, seeking to pre-empt the occurrence of this particular interpretation problem, include an express 'merger clause' in their standard form contracts, but depending on subsequent circumstances, the effectiveness of such a clause might nonetheless itself be brought into question.[250]

IV. Commercial Custom and Usage

87. By virtue of CISG Article 9, commercial custom and usage can become an integral part of an international contract of sale. Article 9 provides as follows:

1. The parties are bound by any usage to which they have agreed and by any practices which they have established between themselves.
2. The parties are considered, unless otherwise agreed, to have impliedly made applicable to their contract or its formation a usage of which the parties knew or ought to have known and which in international trade is widely known to, and regularly observed by, parties to contracts of the type involved in the particular trade concerned.

A. Express Agreement and Inter Partes Course of Dealing

88. The single sentence in paragraph (1) of Article 9 addresses two situations. The first relates to the uncommon situation where the parties to a given international sales contract have actually agreed in advance to be bound by a given trade usage.

248. *See* CLOUT Case 222: *MCC-Marble Ceramic Center Inc. v. Ceramica Nuova D'Agostino S.p.A.*, 144 F.3d 1384 (11th Cir. 1998), citing, *inter alia*, the views of Bernstein & Lookofsky, *Understanding the CISG in Europe* (1997), 29. *See also Mitchell Aircraft Spares Inc. v. European Aircraft Service AB*, 23 F.Supp. 2nd 915 (N.D.Ill.1998). *Accord:* Opinion, No. 3 of the CISG Advisory Council, available at http://cisgw3.law.pace.edu/cisg/CISG-AC-op3.html. *But see Beijing Metals & Minerals Import/Export Corp. v. American Business Ctr., Inc.*, 993 F. 2nd 1178 (5th Cir. 1993).

249. In English law, the corresponding problem is usually phrased in terms of 'intent' and 'reliance' on (mis)representation/warranty. *See*, for example, *Dick Bentley Productions Ltd. v. Harold Smith (Motors) Ltd.* [1965] 2 All E.R. 65 (Lord Denning: representation is warranty if intended to be acted on and in fact acted on).

250. So-called merger (or integration) clauses seek to nullify the effect of all prior agreements and understandings not expressed in the writing: *see MCC-Marble Ceramic Center Inc. v. Ceramica Nuova D'Agostino S.p.A.*, *supra*, but such clauses remain problematical: *see* Lookofsky, *Understanding the CISG* 5th Worldwide ed. (2017), §§4.5 and 7.3; *compare* Honnold/Flechtner, *supra* note 241, at 165 (unhesitatingly giving full effect to these clauses under Art. 6). *See also infra*, No. 146 with note 373.

Beyond this, paragraph 1 also addresses far more common cases where the parties to a given sales transaction have impliedly established a usage by virtue of their own prior dealings.[251] Within this latter context, courts have had occasion to consider what it takes to establish such a practice.[252]

B. Implied Incorporation of Commercial Usage

89. Paragraph (2) of Article 9 lays down the requirements for the implied incorporation of a given usage in the particular international trade. To be applicable in a given situation, the usage must be one which the parties knew or ought to have known and which in international trade is widely known to, and regularly observed by, parties to contracts of the type involved in the particular trade concerned.[253]

90. An international custom which fulfils the stated Article 9 criteria takes precedence over the Convention's supplementary rules, that is, both the contract formation rules of CISG Part II and the gap-filling rights and obligations as defined in Part III. For example, the ability of a CISG buyer to pursue his or her claim in respect of a given non-conformity may depend on the existence of an established practice (between the parties concerned) or a wider trade usage regarding the buyer's inspection of goods (within the particular trade concerned).[254] To take another example: trade usage can affect an international seller's right to claim interest for late payment at the rate specified in its standard business terms, i.e., even if those standard terms – absent the usage – might not pass the 'incorporation' test.[255]

251. This part of CISG Art. 8 corresponds to what the American Uniform Commercial Code, §2-205(1) calls a 'course of dealing'.

252. *See*, e.g., *Calzaturificio Claudia s.n.c. v. Olivieri Footwear Ltd.*, WESTLAW 16482 (S.D.N.Y. 1998), CLOUT Case 413, available at www.cisg.law.pace.edu/cases/980406u1.html#ta (buyer disputed seller's allegation that previous transactions between same parties rendered delivery 'ex works' a contractual term).

253. *See*, for example, Gerechtshof Hertogenbosch (The Netherlands), 24 Apr. 1996, abstract available at www.unilex.info/cisg/case/224, holding that the buyer, an experienced businessman in the trade concerned, could not have been unaware of the widespread use of standard terms referred to by seller in its confirmation of buyer's order, nor of specific provisions on interest, which were not of such a character that buyer could not have expected them, especially since these parties had done business together in the past. *See also* Audiencia Provincial, Barcelona, Spain, 13 May 2014, available at http://www.unilex.info/cisg/case/1901 (English is *lingua franca* in international trade, also demonstrated by fact that buyer communicated with seller in English, inferring buyer was in position to understand invoices issued by seller).

254. Regarding Art. 35 *see infra*, Nos 162 et seq.

255. *See*, for example, Gerechtshof Hertogenbosch (The Netherlands), 24 Apr. 1996, *supra* note 253. Regarding the incorporation of standard terms within the CISG context, *see* generally *infra*, No. 174.

V. Place of Business: Rules for Exceptional Cases

91. A number of Convention rules refer to a party's place of business.[256] Article 10(a) is a general CISG provision which provides that if a party has more than one place of business, then the relevant place of business is the one with the closest relationship to the contract and its performance.[257] Applying this rule in a case where an Austrian buyer purchased goods from the Swiss branch of a company with headquarters in Liechtenstein (notably, a *non*-contracting State), a Swiss court held the contract was governed by the CISG, since it was the Swiss branch which had the closest relationship to the contract and its performance.[258]

Under the rule in Article 10, paragraph (b), if a party does not have a(ny) place of business, reference is to be made to that party's habitual residence.

VI. No Writing Requirement for CISG Contract

92. CISG Article 11 provides as follows:

> A contract of sale need not be concluded in or evidenced by writing and is not subject to any other requirement as to form. It may be proved by any means, including witnesses.

So this is the Convention's starting point: a CISG sales contract need not be in writing.[259]

A. Relation to Formal Requirements under Domestic Law

93. But since some domestic legal systems attach great importance to their formal writing requirements, the CISG drafters decided to create a derogation option, so as to ensure that the Convention would be acceptable for those States as well.

B. Article 12: (Article 96) Declarations in Derogation of Article 11

94. For this reason, Article 12 of the CISG provides as follows:

256. *See* Arts 1 (*supra*, No. 52), 12 (*infra*, No. 94), 20(2) (*infra*, No. 127), 31(c) (*infra*, No. 155), 42(1)(b) (*infra*, No. 203), 57(1)(a) (*infra*, No. 243), 69(2) (*infra*, No. 275) and 96 (*infra*, No. 337).
257. This having regard to the circumstances known to or contemplated by the parties at any time before or at the conclusion of the contract: *see* Art. 10(a).
258. *See* Bezirksgericht der Saane (Switzerland), 20 Feb. 1997, CLOUT Case 261, abstract available at www.unilex.info/cisg/case/403.
259. It should, however, be noted that the rule in Art. 11 does not bar the parties from agreeing to impose formal requirements (Art. 6), nor does it necessarily negate certain regulations (and sanctions) in States which require a writing for purposes of administrative control or for enforcement of exchange control laws. *See* A/CONF./97/5, *Secretariat's Commentary* to Art. 10 of the 1978 draft, para. 2.

> Any provision of Articles 11, 29 or Part II of this Convention that allows a contract of sale or its modification or termination by agreement or any offer, acceptance or other indication of intention to be made in any form other than in writing does not apply where any party has his place of business in a Contracting State which has made a declaration under Article 96 of this Convention. The parties may not derogate from or vary the effect of this article.

95. Article 96 provides as follows:

> A Contracting State whose legislation requires contracts of sale to be concluded in or evidenced by writing may at any time make a declaration in accordance with article 12 that any provision of article 11, article 29, or Part II of this Convention, that allows a contract of sale or its modification or termination by agreement or any offer, acceptance, or other indication of intention to be made in any form other than in writing, does not apply where any party has his place of business in that State.[260]

96. Since less than ten Contracting States have made Article 96 declarations,[261] the declaration is likely to be at issue in cases where only one of the parties to a CISG contract resides in such a declaring State.

And in such cases, according to the view taken here (which also represents the majority view), the effect of that Article 96 declaration is limited:[262] a forum court asked to apply the formal domestic law requirements of the declaring State (as opposed to Article 11) should do so only when that court's rules of PIL lead to the application of the declaring State's law.[263]

VII. Definition of Writing

97. Article 21(2), concerning late acceptance, and Article 29(2), concerning contract modification, are Convention rules which make use of the term 'writing'.[264] Article 13 defines this term as follows:

> For the purposes of this Convention 'writing' includes telegram and telex.

260. Regarding Arts 12 and 96 *see also infra*, No. 337.
261. As of July 2021, Argentina, Armenia, Belarus, Chile, Democratic People's Republic of Korea, Paraguay, the Russian Federation, Ukraine and Vietnam have made such (currently effective) declarations.
262. *See* Schmidt-Kessel in Schlechtriem & Schwenzer, *Commentary* 4th ed. (2016), at 215 with note 8, citing, *inter alia*, Bernstein & Lookofsky, *Understanding the CISG in Europe*, §2-14 and Lookofsky, *United Nations Convention*, No. 96 in the 2004 ed. of the present *Encyclopaedia* monograph. *Compare*: Honnold/Flechtner, *supra* note 241, at 187–191 (generally in favour of the position taken here, but reverting to the view originally taken by Honnold, that is, for employment of domestic form requirements of a non-reserving State when Art. 12 is triggered and PIL principles point to the law of a non-reserving State).
263. For further details and citations *see infra*, No. 337.
264. *See infra*, Nos 128 and 146.

98. According to Article 13, the term 'writing' *includes* telegram and telex. However, Article 13 does not expressly exclude other, more modern means of electronic communication, such as telefax transmissions and (now, more importantly) e-mail, and it seems both logical and reasonable to conclude that also these means of communication should be treated as writings under Article 13.[265] This matter – though not expressly settled in the Convention – is arguably governed by it, and an expansive reading of the term 'writing' to include more modern, yet clearly analogous, means of communication is hardly precluded by the letter of Article 13, just as such a flexible interpretation would seem to conform with the general principles on which the Convention (at least Article 13) is based.[266] In any case, CISG case law now confirms that e-mail communications are indeed 'writings' for purposes of Article 13.[267]

265. *See*, for example, Lookofsky, *Understanding the CISG* 5th Worldwide ed. (2017), §2.11; Honnold/Flechtner, *supra* note 241, at 192. The same opinion has been expressed by the CISG Advisory Council: *see* http://cisgw3.law.pace.edu/cisg/CISG-AC-op1.html. *Compare* (more cautiously) Schmidt Kassel in Schlechtriem & Schwenzer, *Commentary* 4th ed. (2016) at 221 f.

266. Regarding Art. 7(2) and decision-making by analogy, *see supra*, No. 79.

267. *See* Supreme Court of the Czech Republic, 17 Dec. 2013, CLOUT Case 1450. Recall in this connection that the Convention does not generally require that agreements be in writing (Art. 11); note also in this connection that Arts 21(2) and 29(2) do not require that a 'writing' (when otherwise required, for example, by virtue of Art. 12) be signed.

Chapter 4. Sales Contract Formation

99. Assuming that the sales contract in question falls within the CISG sphere,[268] questions relating to the formation of that contract will be governed by CISG Part II (Articles 14–24).

Previously, a limitation as to the applicability of CISG Part II derived from Article 92, by which a CISG Contracting State may declare that it will 'not be bound' by CISG Part II. And indeed, the Scandinavian States (Denmark, Finland, Norway and Sweden) had at the time of their CISG ratifications all made Article 92 declarations/reservations. But since these States subsequently withdrew these declarations, and since no other CISG States have made them, the practical significance of this limitation is now near nil.[269]

§1. The Offer

I. Minimum Requirements

100. The offer is the starting point – and often also the focal point – in the contract formation process. In order to qualify as a CISG 'offer' – that is, a communication capable of being accepted by an offeree (addressee) – a given proposal must meet certain minimum requirements. Paragraph 1 of Article 14 provides as follows:

> 1. A proposal for concluding a contract addressed to one or more specific persons constitutes an offer if it is sufficiently definite and indicates the intention of the offeror to be bound in case of acceptance. A proposal is sufficiently definite if it indicates the goods and expressly or implicitly fixes or makes provision for determining the quantity and the price.

A. Definiteness & Intention to Be Bound. Offer Addressed to Specific Persons

101. Article 14(1) indicates that the key elements of a CISG offer are definiteness and the intention of the offeror (obligor) to be bound.

As regards intention to be bound, the offeror is properly regarded as the master of his or her offer; that is, an offer is to be *interpreted* in accordance with Article 8, i.e., according to the offeror's own intent, at least in cases where the offeree knew or could not have been unaware what that intent was.[270] Absent clear evidence of

268. *See supra*, Nos 51 et seq.
269. The only remaining practical concern in this connection relates to the possibility that litigation could arise in relation to a CISG contract which was formed (between a Scandinavian and a non-Scandinavian party) at a point in time when the Scandinavian Art. 92 declarations applied. For a more complete discussion of the (rapidly diminishing) effect of the Art. 92 declarations, *see infra*, No. 333.
270. Regarding Art. 8(1), *see supra*, Nos 81 et seq.

such subjective intent, the focus shifts to the understanding of a reasonable offeree in that position.[271] For example, in the determination of whether standard contract terms are to be considered as part of a given offer and (ultimately) part of the contract concerned, special regard must be given to Article 8(2).[272]

As regards the requirement of definiteness, the second sentence of Article 14(1) provides that a proposal is sufficiently definite if it: (a) indicates the goods and (b) expressly or implicitly fixes or makes provision for determining the quantity and price. For example, a purchase order which identifies the goods as type 'XYZ' software as well as the compensation to be paid (e.g., per unit) would surely satisfy these minimum requirements,[273] just as an order for chinchilla pelts of 'middle or better quality' at a price 'between 35 and 65 German marks' has been held sufficiently definite under Article 14.[274]

Note in this connection that the Convention recognizes that the contract can make provision for subsequent specification of the quantity and/or quality of the goods. In this connection, the Convention provides a mechanism whereby the seller can fill the gap left by a buyer who fails to make specifications as otherwise required by the contract.[275]

A proposal which fails to satisfy the requirement of definiteness cannot qualify as a CISG offer, nor can it qualify as a counter-offer under Article 19(1).[276] But if a given CISG offer seems incomplete at first blush, custom and usage may serve to fill it out. In a Hungarian case, a seemingly nebulous oral offer by a German seller was held sufficiently definite under Article 14(1), in that the quality, quantity and price of the goods were impliedly fixed by the parties' prior course of dealing in accordance with Article 9(1), since the seller repeatedly had delivered goods previously ordered by the buyer, who had regularly and without objection paid the price after delivery.[277]

---

271. Article 8(2). *See*, for example, Oberster Gerichtshof (Austria), 20 Mar. 1997, CLOUT Case 189, abstract available at www.unilex.info/cisg/case/254 (determination of whether offer sufficiently definite based on understanding of reasonable person in same circumstances).
272. *See* F. Ferrari & M. Torsello, *International Sales Law-CISG in a Nutshell* 2nd ed. (2018), at 175.
273. *See* LG München, 8 Feb. 1995, CLOUT Case 131, available at www.cisg.law.pace.edu/cases/950208g4.html (computer program called *Graphiplus*, order contained name of program and price).
274. *See* Austrian Supreme Court (Oberster Gerichtshof) of 10 Nov. 1994, CLOUT Case 106, available at http://cisgw3.law.pace.edu/cases/941110a3.html#ua (agreement as to price range did not preclude conclusion of valid contract since under Art. 55 (*infra*, No. 241) if price is not explicit or implicit in contract parties considered to have agreed on usual market price).
275. Regarding Art. 65 *see infra*, No. 266.
276. *See infra*, Nos 118 et seq. and OLG Frankfurt am Main (Germany), 4 Mar. 1994, CLOUT Case 121, available at http://cisgw3.law.pace.edu/cases/940304g1.html (Supreme Court confirmed order sufficiently definite to constitute offer under Art. 14 CISG, since could be perceived as such by reasonable person in same circumstances as seller, Art. 8(2)–(3), and considering behaviour of buyer who accepted goods and sold them further without questioning price; price sufficiently definite to make application of Art. 55 unnecessary).
277. *See* Court of Budapest of 24 Mar. 1992, CLOUT Case 52, abstract available at www.unilex.info/cisg/case/19. *See also* commentary by Vida in IPRax 1993 at 263. Regarding Art. 9 *see supra*, Nos 87 et seq. *Compare* US District Court (S. D., New York) 21 Aug. 2002, CLOUT Case 579, available at www.cisg.law.pace.edu/cases/020821u1.html#uab (plaintiff alleged facts, including industry usage that buyers could rely on implied supply commitments, that would support finding that plaintiff's initial proposal was sufficiently definite under Art. 14).

If a particular proposal addressed to one or more specific persons is sufficiently definite, it will qualify as a CISG offer; proposals not so addressed must be evaluated in accordance with Article 14, paragraph 2.[278]

B. Problem of Price-Gap

102. The most controversial aspect of Article 14 concerns the requirement of definiteness in relation to price. A proposal is 'sufficiently definite' if it (indicates the goods and) fixes or makes provision for determining the price, but does that mean (*e contrario*) that a proposal which leaves the price term 'open' is not sufficiently definite, thus precluding the formation of a (binding/valid) contract?

Although the proper interpretation of the price-definiteness requirement has been tied to related factors in Article 55,[279] most courts and commentators agree that a price-gap is not necessarily fatal to an offer under Article 14,[280] especially given the importance which Article 14 attaches to the parties' intention,[281] and considering that Article 6 permits the parties to derogate from nearly any CISG provision, including (courts and commentators agree) Article 14(1).[282] However, the highest French court has held that a contract between an Argentinean seller and a French buyer for the sale of Williams pears was not validly concluded, since the parties had not agreed on a minimum price (or quantity).[283]

Courts and arbitrators faced with a price-gap issue in a CISG contract are encouraged to discern the intention of the parties in the concrete case, so as to determine whether or not they intended their agreement to bind. In making this determination, arbiters should apply the flexible principles set forth in Article 8;[284] if on this basis, it appears that the parties (expressly or impliedly) intended to be bound by their agreement, including its open price term, that intention should prevail.[285]

If there is price-gap issue, arbiters must look to intention of parties to have price left open or understood by implication

278. *See infra*, No. 103.

279. This provision provides a gap-filling reference to the price generally charged in cases where a contract has been 'validly concluded but does not expressly or implicitly fix or make provision for determining the price'. *See infra*, No. 241.

280. Clearly, the second sentence of Art. 14(1) does *not* say or imply that a proposal is invalid (for indefiniteness) if it *fails* to fix the price. Rather, this sentence is best understood as a 'safe harbour' rule: *see* Honnold/Flechtner, *Uniform Law for International Sales* 4th ed. (2009), at 210.

281. *Supra*, Nos 100 et seq.

282. *See* Landgericht Neubrandenburg, Germany, 3 Aug. 2005, available at http://cisgw3.law.pace.edu/cases/050803g1.html (according to Art. 6 CISG parties entitled to exclude the requirements of Art. 14(1) sentence two). *Accord*: Honnold/Flechtner, *supra* note 280, at 211; Lookofsky, *Understanding the CISG* 5th Worldwide ed. (2017), §3.2.

283. *See* Cour de Cassation, 7 Feb. 2012, available at http://www.unilex.info/cisg/case/1673 (agreement as to 'base' price for French company to start marketing product did not mean minimum contractual price had been fixed).

284. *Supra*, Nos 81 et seq.

285. Although some CISG commentators would condition that conclusion upon a subsequent validity determination under domestic law pursuant to Art. 55. *See infra*, No. 241.

C. Invitation to Make Offers Distinguished

103. The CISG distinguishes between an offer, which binds the offeror, and an invitation that others make offers, which does not. Paragraph (2) of Article 14 provides:

> 2. A proposal other than one addressed to one or more specific persons is to be considered merely as an invitation to make offers, unless the contrary is clearly indicated by the person making the proposal.

This provision reaffirms the starting point in paragraph (1): a proposal not addressed to one or more specific persons is to be interpreted – presumptively – as an invitation to make offers.[286] However, a proposal clearly evidencing an intention to be bound should be treated as a true offer (which is subject to the various rules which apply to offers and their acceptance in CISG Part II).

There are few, if any, reported decisions applying paragraph (2).[287]

II. Time Offer Takes Effect; Right to Withdraw

104. Assuming a proposal meets the requirements for an offer set forth in CISG Article 14, the next step may be to determine when that offer takes effect. This point in time is significant as regards the offeror's right to 'withdraw' an offer prior to the time of its receipt by the offeree. Article 15 provides as follows:

> 1. An offer becomes effective when it reaches the offeree.
> 2. An offer, even if it is irrevocable, may be withdrawn if the withdrawal reaches the offeree before or at the same time as the offer.

According to Article 15, paragraph (1), an offer becomes effective when it 'reaches' the offeree. Whereas an offer made orally may be said to reach the recipient immediately (as soon as it is made), a written communication first reaches the offeree when it is actually delivered to the offeree or to his or her place of business.[288] According to paragraph (2) of Article 15, an offer may be withdrawn if the withdrawal reaches the offeree before or at the same time as the offer. Indeed, since an offer does not take effect prior to its receipt by the offeree (the recipient), it is even possible for the offeror to 'withdraw' an offer which, by its own terms, is irrevocable.

Although few, if any, Article 15 decisions have been reported,[289] it should be noted that an offeror's ability to 'withdraw' in accordance with this provision relates

286. The converse proposition – that is, that a proposal addressed to one or more specific persons *is* considered to be an offer – does not necessarily follow from para. (2).
287. *See UNCITRAL CISG Case Digest* of Art. 14, available at https://uncitral.un.org/en/case_law/digests.
288. The term 'reach' is defined in Art. 24: *see infra*, No. 133.
289. *See UNCITRAL CISG Case Digest* of Art. 15 (2016 ed.), available at https://uncitral.un.org/en/case_law/digests.

only to an offer which has not (yet) reached the offeree; only such an offer, which has not become effective, can be withdrawn. This is to be distinguished from the right to 'revoke' under CISG Article 16 (discussed below), that is, the right of an offeror to call back an offer which has reached the offeree and therefore already taken effect.

III. Offeror's Right to Revoke

105. Once an offer, not effectively withdrawn, has reached the offeree, the issue is the offeror's right to revoke (call back) his or her offer.

In some legal systems, the default rule is that every offer received is deemed to be irrevocable (binding), at least for a reasonable time;[290] in other (e.g., Common law) systems, the starting point is that offers do not generally bind the offeror until such time as the offeree actually accepts the offer.[291]

Article 16 of the CISG, which represents a compromise between these domestic extremes, provides as follows:

1. Until a contract is concluded, an offer may be revoked if the revocation reaches the offeree before he has dispatched an acceptance.
2. However, an offer cannot be revoked:
   a. if it indicates, whether by stating a fixed time for acceptance or otherwise, that it is irrevocable; or
   b. if it was reasonable for the offeree to rely on the offer as being irrevocable and the offeree has acted in reliance on the offer.

A. Revocability Is General Rule

106. The starting point in Article 16, paragraph (1), is that CISG offers are revocable, in that, an offer which, having reached the offeree, has become effective may be revoked if the revocation reaches the offeree before he or she has dispatched an acceptance.[292]

Although paragraph (1) seems to accord with the view traditionally taken in some Common law systems, two comparative points may be noted. The first point is this: the fact that an offer may be revoked before an acceptance is dispatched does not imply that a CISG contract is concluded when the acceptance is dispatched.[293]

290. This is the view taken in Scandinavia: *see* para. 1 of the essentially uniform Scandinavian Contracts Acts.

291. This is the traditional Common law view and the view still held in England. Regarding the American view, *see infra*, No. 106.

292. *See* Higher Court in Ljubljana, Slovenia, 9 Apr. 2008, translation available at http://cisgw3.law.pace.edu/cases/080409sv.html (attempted revocation received by offeree after acceptance dispatched (and also after offeree had shipped goods) ineffective under Art. 16(1)).

293. Note that under the Common law view, an acceptance made by a non-instantaneous means of communication is effective upon dispatch, thus concluding the contract, whereas the rule in CISG Art. 23 is closer to the Civilian view: *see infra*, No. 132.

The second, particularly important point is that paragraph (1) of Article 16 must be read in conjunction with the two significant modifications contained in paragraph (2); interestingly, from a comparative point of view, both these modifications (exceptions to the revocability rule) find analogues in the corresponding American law of contracts and sales.[294]

B. Modification: Offer Indicating Irrevocability

107. The first exception to the Article 16(1) rule derives from the familiar principle that the offeror is the 'master' of the offer. According to subparagraph 2(a): an offer to enter an international contract of sale which itself indicates that it is irrevocable cannot be revoked. The offeror may make the requisite indication of irrevocability either by stating a fixed time for acceptance or by some other means.

The main message of subparagraph 2(a) is that the CISG offeror is bound by his or her word. If, for example, the offeror makes his or her offer on 1 February and states that the offer 'will be held open' until a specific date (e.g., '15 February'), this represents a clear indication of irrevocability – in effect, a binding promise that the offer will, in fact, be held open until then; for this reason, such an offer cannot validly be revoked during the time stated, even if the offeror should later change his or her mind.

C. Offer Fixing Time for Acceptance

108. Although Article 16 has caused little difficulty in practice,[295] one aspect of subparagraph (2)(a) has provoked doctrinal debate.[296] The issue here is whether an offer which merely 'fixes a time for acceptance' should – for that reason alone – be interpreted as irrevocable.

Suppose, for example, that the offeror states that the offeree's acceptance 'must be received before 1 March'. Some might read this phrase as relating only to the time frame for acceptance; others might say the offeror – by providing the time frame for acceptance – has also (impliedly) indicated that the offer is irrevocable during the stated period.

Some distinguished commentators, drawing upon the less-than-clear legislative history of this provision, have adopted a middle-of-the-road position, maintaining that an offer like this gives rise to a 'rebuttable presumption' of irrevocability.[297] It is submitted, however, that each such case must be decided on its own facts; i.e., each individual offer should be interpreted on its own terms. Depending on the circumstances and the larger contractual context, the fact that a given offer contains a

---

294. *See* §2-205 of the Uniform Commercial Code and §87 of the *Restatement (2d) of Contracts*.

295. *See UNCITRAL CISG Case Digest* of Art. 16 (2016 ed.), available at https://uncitral.un.org/en/case_law/digests.

296. Regarding the controversy, *see* (e.g.) E.A. Farnsworth, 'Formation of Contract', in *International Sales* (Galston & Smit eds, 1984), 3–11; Honnold/Flechtner, *Uniform Law* 4th ed. (2009), at 217–218; Schroeter in Schlechtriem & Schwenzer, *Commentary* 4th ed. (2016), at 322–323.

297. *See* Schroeter, *ibid.*, at 323 with note 47.

statement relating to the time for acceptance (e.g., the statement in the example above) may – or may not – be interpreted as (also) implying a promise not to revoke.[298]

D. *Modification: Action in Reliance*

109. Subparagraph (2)(b) of Article 16 provides a further modification of the starting point set forth in paragraph (1). An offer may not be revoked if it was reasonable for the offeree to act in reliance on the offer, and the offeree has in fact acted in reliance on it.

For example, this rule might be applied in a situation where B relies on an (otherwise revocable) offer made by S, in that B, before accepting S' offer, offers to resell the same goods to C. If S revokes his or her offer to B after C effectively accepts the offer made by B, but before B effectively accepts the offer by S, the key issue is whether it was reasonable for the offeree (B) to have acted in reliance on the offer by S; if the reliance was not reasonable, the revocation by S must be held rightful under Article 16(1), and that means that B's (late) acceptance is without legal effect.

Although few, if any, reported decisions have involved Article 16(2)(b),[299] American courts applying American domestic law have often had occasion to apply an analogous reliance-based rule, whereby an offeree's reliance can preclude the revocation of an otherwise revocable offer, but only if that reliance was 'reasonably foreseeable' by the offeror.[300] Although Article 16(2)(b) demands an autonomous (Article 7) interpretation, and though the word foreseeability is not mentioned in 16(2)(b), the foreseeability of the offeree's reliance could rightly be regarded as a relevant factor when assessing the reasonableness of an offeree's act of reliance under the CISG. It would, for example, hardly seem reasonable for a CISG offeree to conduct an extensive – and expensive – investigation concerning the advisability of acceptance, unless such an investigation was reasonably foreseeable by the offeror.[301]

IV. Effect of Rejection

110. In most domestic systems, a rejection by the offeree serves to 'kill' (extinguish) the offer made by the offeror. Article 17 of the CISG provides a rule which accords with this basic idea: 'An offer, even if it is irrevocable, is terminated when a rejection reaches the offeror.'

---

298. *See* Art. 8, *supra*, No. 81.
299. *See UNCITRAL CISG Case Digest* of Art. 16 (2016 ed.), available at https://uncitral.un.org/en/case_law/digests.
300. Unlike subpara. (2)(b) of Art. 16, which asks whether the offeree has reasonably relied, the key issue under §87(2) of the *Restatement (2d) of Contracts*, is whether the offeror should reasonably expect his offer to induce reliance.
301. *Compare* the assessment of this example in the *Secretariat Commentary*, A/CONF./97/5, Comment 8 to Art. 14 of the 1978 Draft.

Article 17 was designed for a simple, limited purpose: the protection of the reasonable expectations of the offeror. Having received a rejection (or non-conforming acceptance) from the offeree,[302] the offeror should be free to take his or her business elsewhere. Indeed, even if the offeror was originally bound by an irrevocable offer, that offer dies when the rejection is received.

§2. Acceptance under Articles 18–22

111. Articles 18–22 of CISG Part II deal with the subject of acceptance.

I. Acceptance: Indication of Assent

112. Paragraph (1) of Article 18 tells us which kinds of statements or conduct by the offeree constitute a true (legally effective) acceptance:

> 1. A statement made by or other conduct of the offeree indicating assent to an offer is an acceptance. Silence or inactivity does not in itself amount to acceptance.

113. According to the rule in paragraph (1), an acceptance may consist of a statement or of 'other conduct', for example, the seller's conduct in shipping the goods which the buyer has offered to buy, or the buyer's conduct in opening a letter of credit.[303] Quite apart from the form which the offeree's communication may take, the statement or conduct in question must, of course, provide an indication of the offeree's assent.

Since the CISG does not impose upon the offeree a general duty to reply, silence or inactivity does not – in itself – amount to acceptance. Therefore, the offeror cannot bind the offeree in advance merely by stating that silence will be treated (interpreted) as an indication of the offeree's assent. However, if the offeree initiates a given transaction by soliciting an offer, then he or she – the offeree – may bind himself or herself in advance by indicating that an offer, if subsequently received, will be deemed accepted absent contrary indication by the offeree within a specified period.[304]

302. As regards a purported acceptance which varies from the content of the original offer, *see* Art. 19 and *infra*, Nos 118 et seq.

303. *Magellan International Corporation v. Salzgitter Handel GmbH*, US Dist. Ct. (ND Ill.), 7 Dec. 1999, CLOUT Case 417, available at www.cisg.law.pace.edu/cases/991207u1.html#unc (contract concluded with buyer's acceptance reasonably inferred from issuing of letter of credit).

304. *See* Cour de cassation (France), 27 Jan. 1998, CLOUT Case 224, available at http://cisgw3.law.pace.edu/cases/980127f1.html (applying *principle* in Art. 18(1) in case where buyer, who requested that goods purchased be modified, accepted them without reservation). *See also* Østre Landsret (Eastern Appellate Court, Denmark), 23 Apr. 1998, CLOUT Case 309, available at http://cisgw3.law.pace.edu/cases/980423d1.html (offeree's silence did not constitute acceptance).

II. Time Acceptance Takes Effect

A. *When Assent Reaches Offeror*

114. Paragraph (2) of Article 18, which determines the point in time at which an acceptance (under the first paragraph) becomes effective, provides as follows:

> 2. An acceptance of an offer becomes effective at the moment the indication of assent reaches the offeror. An acceptance is not effective if the indication of assent does not reach the offeror within the time he has fixed or, if no time is fixed, within a reasonable time, due account being taken of the circumstances of the transaction, including the rapidity of the means of communication employed by the offeror. An oral offer must be accepted immediately unless the circumstances indicate otherwise.
>
> By virtue of paragraph (2), an acceptance becomes effective upon the timely arrival of the offeree's indication of assent.[305] So, to be effective, the acceptance must arrive, and it must arrive in time.

B. *Receipt Theory*

115. An important consequence of the so-called receipt theory of acceptance, as adopted by the CISG in Article 18(2), is that the sender of the acceptance (the offeree) bears the risk of transmission, that is, the risk that his or her acceptance, although sent (dispatched), may never actually arrive, for example, if an acceptance sent by regular mail goes astray, or if an acceptance sent by e-mail never reaches its destination (the offeree's inbox). So, absent contrary prior agreement, the offeree's acceptance must in some manner actually 'reach' the offeror; if not, the legal consequences generally associated with the acceptance of a CISG offer will not take effect.

C. *Acceptance Within Time Fixed or Reasonable Time*

116. In accordance with the principle that the offeror is the master of the offer, the acceptance must not only reach the offeror but also do so within the time frame which the offeror has fixed.[306] If no time has been fixed, the CISG default rule is that the acceptance must reach its destination within a reasonable time, taking due account of all the circumstances. Thus, an offer sent by e-mail will require a more prompt reply than an offer sent by traditional post (snail mail).[307] Absent contrary indication, an oral offer requires an immediate acceptance.

---

305. As to when such a communication 'reaches' the offeror, *see* Art. 24, discussed *infra*, No. 133. Once the acceptance becomes effective, a contract is formed pursuant to Art. 23: *see infra*, No. 132.
306. Regarding the time at which such a period begins to run, *see* Art. 20 and *infra*, No. 126.
307. *See* generally CISG AC Opinion No. 1, Electronic Communications under CISG, 15 Aug. 2003, available at http://cisgw3.law.pace.edu/cisg/CISG-AC-op1.html#art18-2.

D. Assent by Performance of Act

117. As regards the time at which acceptance takes effect, paragraph (3) of Article 18 provides for cases where the offeree assents by performing an act:

> (3) However, if, by virtue of the offer or as a result of practices which the parties have established between themselves or of usage, the offeree may indicate assent by performing an act, such as one relating to the dispatch of the goods or payment of the price, without notice to the offeror, the acceptance is effective at the moment the act is performed, provided that the act is performed within the period of time laid down in the preceding paragraph.

In many cases, the offeror will call upon the offeree to indicate assent by a statement of intention, that is, a notification which serves as a promise by the offeree to act at some future point in time.

Sometimes, however, the offeror will request – or at least impliedly condone – that the offeree accepts without actually making such a statement. For example, the offeror may request or condone that the offeree accepts by performing an act, for example, shipping the goods ordered by the offeror. A similar understanding may follow from a 'course of dealing' established between the particular parties concerned or from a broader usage among merchants within the particular trade.[308]

In all such cases, assuming the act is performed within the time fixed by the offeror or within a reasonable time, the offeree's acceptance becomes effective at the moment the act is actually performed,[309] and this is true irrespective of whether the offeror is notified of the act's performance or not.[310] Once the act which constitutes acceptance has been performed, the offeror cannot effectively revoke; indeed, even an offer which might have been revocable initially (when made by the offeror) cannot be revoked after the offeree's acceptance.[311]

III. Mirror-Image and Battle of Forms

A. Introduction

118. The offeror (the party who makes a CISG offer) is the master of that offer. Article 19 of the CISG serves to link this golden rule both to the 'mirror-image' concept of acceptance and to the much-discussed commercial phenomenon known as the 'battle of forms'. Article 19(1) provides as follows:

308. Regarding these concepts under Art. 9, *see supra*, Nos 87 et seq.
309. *See*, for example, OLG Frankfurt am Main (Germany), 23 May 1995, CLOUT Case 291, available at www.cisg.law.pace.edu/cases/950523g1.html (seller's delivery can constitute acceptance by performance).
310. *See* Schroeter in Schlechtriem & Schwenzer, *Commentary* 4th ed. (2016), at 348 (bluntly rejecting Honnold's contrary view).
311. This conforms with the corresponding principle laid down in Art. 16(1): *see supra*, Nos 105 et seq.

> A reply to an offer which purports to be an acceptance but contains additions, limitations or other modifications is a rejection of the offer and constitutes a counter-offer.

B. Non-matching Reply Is Rejection and Counter-Offer

119. Article 19(1) conforms with the traditional theory set forth in domestic contractual regimes: because CISG sales obligations (like other contractual obligations) are initiated by expressions of mutual agreement, an acceptance must match the offer. So the CISG starting point is that a reply by the offeree which purports to be an acceptance of the offer, but which does not actually reflect the terms of the offer, constitutes – not an acceptance, but rather – a rejection of that offer (and thus, at most, a counter-offer).[312]

C. Independent Communication Not Rejection

120. Then again, not every non-conforming reply will purport to be an acceptance of the offer in question. Sometimes, for example, a reply which makes enquiries or suggests the possibility of additional terms is intended to explore the willingness of the offeror to bargain (accept terms more favourable to the offeree) while leaving open the possibility that the offeree may later accept the offeror's original terms.[313] If such an independent communication is a reasonable interpretation of the offeree's intent,[314] it will not constitute a rejection (coupled with a counter-offer).

D. Limited Exception to Mirror-Image Rule

121. Although paragraph (1) of Article 19 provides that a reply purporting to be an acceptance which does not reflect the terms of the offer constitutes a rejection and counter-offer, Article 19, paragraph (2) carves out an exception to the general mirror-image rule:

---

312. *See*, for example, OLG Hamm (Germany), 22 Sep. 1992, CLOUT Case 227, available at http://cisgw3.law.pace.edu/cases/920922g1.html#ua (buyer requested wrapped bacon; seller's reply to deliver unwrapped bacon was rejection and counter-offer). *See also* OLG Frankfurt am Main (Germany), 23 May 1995, CLOUT Case 291, available at www.cisg.law.pace.edu/cases/950523g1.html (delivery by seller of quantity less than that ordered by buyer constituted rejection and counter-offer). *See also* US Court of Appeal (9th Cir. 5 May 2003) *Chateau des Charmes Wines Ltd. v. Sabate U.S.A Inc., Sabate S.A.*, CLOUT Case 576, available at http://cisgw3.law.pace.edu/cases/030505u1.html#ca (additional or different terms in acceptance relating to settlement of disputes considered to alter terms of offer materially).

313. *See Secretariat's Commentary*, A/CONF./97/5, Comment 4 to Art. 17(1) of the 1978 Draft.

314. Regarding contract interpretation pursuant to Art. 8 *see supra*, Nos 81 et seq.

> However, a reply to an offer which purports to be an acceptance but contains additional or different terms which do not materially alter the terms of the offer constitutes an acceptance, unless the offeror, without undue delay, objects orally to the discrepancy or dispatches a notice to that effect. If he does not so object, the terms of the contract are the terms of the offer with the modifications contained in the acceptance.

Application of the exception created by paragraph (2) of Article 19 is likely to arise within the context of a so-called battle of forms.

E. *The Battle of Forms*

1. Introduction

122. An international contract of sale is not always the product of a formal negotiation. In many cases, the parties exchange brief communications (e.g., by e-mail), and these are often coupled with (or followed by) the supply and/or exchange of standard forms of agreement. In these and similar instances, the offeree's reply will very likely signal a purported acceptance, even though the standard terms contained in the acceptance are not at all likely to match the offer or the (different) standard terms to which it may refer.[315] Should the non-conforming reply be treated as an acceptance?

Irrespective of whether a given case involves competing sets of (buyer's and seller's) standard terms or (more simply) one party seeking to impose its standard terms on the other, courts often face the threshold issue of whether the standard terms in question can be characterized as 'contained' (*incorporated*) in the communication concerned. In this connection, the rule of CISG contract interpretation in Article 8 informs us that the mere reference in a given offer (or acceptance) to the offeror's (or offeree's) standard terms, the content of which is not expressly set forth in that communication, is not likely to be held sufficient for this purpose;[316] if, however,

---

315. *See* (e.g.) US District Court, *CSS Antenna, Inc. v. Amphenol-Tuchel Electronics, GMBH*, 8 Feb. 2011, available at http://www.unilex.info/cisg/case/1593 (well-established practice between parties that buyer sent purchase order form to seller and seller sent back purchase confirmation form, which contained reference to its standard terms).

316. *See*, e.g., US District Court, preceding note (forum selection clause in seller's standard terms had not become part of contract; referring to Art. 8, court noted that purchase confirmation form failed to mention the forum clause and that language used in standard terms was ambiguous and did not clearly show seller's intent to have those terms govern contract, nor did evidence show that buyer had actual knowledge of the seller's standard terms: purchase confirmation forms sent directly to buyer's billing department where no one had authority to enter contracts; nor were general conditions ever discussed during negotiations). *Accord*: US District Court, 10 Sep. 2013, *Roser Technologies v. Carl Schreiber GmbH*, available at http://www.unilex.info/cisg/case/1877 (reference to standard terms on seller's website not sufficient). *See also*, e.g., Rechtbank Utrecht, Netherlands, 21 Jan. 2009, available at http://www.unilex.info/cisg/case/1594 (simple reference to standard terms insufficient; irrelevant that German suppliers usually so refer in their contracts with sellers at domestic level, since seller did not prove use of general conditions customary in international trade); Rechtbank Rotterdam, Netherlands, 25 Feb. 2009, available at http://www.unilex.info/cisg

the party who intends to incorporate its terms makes its intention (that its terms will apply) clear to the other party, the result under Article 8 is likely to be different.[317]

2. Materiality Test

123. In order to help resolve cases where the content (terms) of a given offer and a purported acceptance – perhaps accompanied by the offeree's standard terms – do not match, CISG Article 19 sets forth a limited exception to the traditional mirror-image rule, an exception which is regulated by a materiality test. The effect of this exception – intended by the CISG drafters to reflect the will of most contracting parties – is that immaterial inconsistencies between the communications and or standard forms of the parties do not pose a barrier to the transaction concerned. A purported acceptance which contains additional or different terms which do not materially alter the terms of the offer constitutes a true acceptance, and the terms of the contract become the terms of the offer with the modifications contained in the acceptance. Only if the offeror, without undue delay, objects to the (immaterial) discrepancy will the reply by the offeree qualify as a rejection.

/case/1573 (not sufficient that seller referred to standard terms in numerous invoices, since text of terms not made available before contracting); Oberlandesgericht Celle (Germany), 24 Jul. 2009, available at http://www.unilex.info/cisg/case/1472 (seller confirmed order in message stating its standard terms – as set out on its website and displayed in its business facilities – would apply to contract; issue whether terms incorporated into parties' contract resolved in accordance with Arts 14 and 18, together with Art. 8, in that recipient of such proposal must have reasonable possibility to become aware of terms; would be violation of good-faith principle (Art. 7) and – as held by Bundesgerichtshof, 9 Jan. 2002 (UNILEX) – of the parties' general duty of cooperation and information if recipient were obliged to enquire about content and bear risk of unknown terms). *Accord*: Oberlandesgericht Naumburg, 13 Feb. 2013, available at http://www.unilex.info/cisg/case/1697 (under German domestic law and according to *some* non-German court interpreting the CISG on this issue, mere reference to standards terms can be sufficient for incorporation, but better Convention view is that party relying on such terms must submit or make them sufficiently available to the other party); Court of Appeal, the Hague (Netherlands), 22 Apr. 2014, available at http://www.unilex.info/cisg/case/1900 (as clarified by CISG AC Opinion No. 13, standard terms regarded as being included in contract not only when parties expressly or impliedly agreed to their inclusion and other party had reasonable opportunity to read them; in this case, no such reasonable opportunity since terms only retrievable on seller's website; nor did Court accept argument that seller referred to its conditions in parties' prior contracts, as no evidence that buyer had reasonable opportunity to note terms on those prior occasions). *See also* Austria, Oberster Gerichtshof, 29 Jun. 2017 at http://www.unilex.info/cisg/case/2129; Rechtbank Midden, Netherlands, 16 Nov. 2016 at http://www.unilex.info/cisg/case/2127.

317. *See* Oberlandesgericht Munchen, 14 Jan. 2009 http://www.unilex.info/cisg/case/1496 (during negotiations, buyer was informed of seller's intention to have its general terms and conditions govern contract; moreover, extracts of such terms had been reproduced in confirmation orders, some of which buyer had countersigned without objection; fact that general terms were written in English, a foreign language, irrelevant). *See also* US District Court, 21 Jan. 2010, *Golden Valley Grape Juice and Wine, LLC v. Centriys Corporation/Centriys Corporation v. Separator Technology Solutions Pty Ltd.*, available at http://www.unilex.info/cisg/case/1510 (court found manufacturer's e-mail offer to seller with sales quote adequate under Art. 14, since manufacturer's general conditions attached to quote; seller's incorporation of quote in its proposal to buyer was acceptance by conduct).

Note in this connection that the 'materiality' issue in Article 19 would seem to arise only in situations where the standard terms proffered by the acceptor are rightly regarded as having been incorporated,[318] e.g., in a case where the seller replies to (purports to accept) the buyer's purchase order by both referring in its acceptance to its (seller's) standard terms and also by actually attaching them to that acceptance, with the likely result that the arbiter will regard those terms as part of the *content* of the acceptance concerned. Then, and only then, need the arbiter decide whether that acceptance, including the standard terms incorporated in it, contains a material alteration.

3. Materiality Defined

124. CISG Article 19 is not the first sales statute which attempts to provide a solution to the familiar problem of the non-conforming acceptance (and the battle of forms).[319] But, the CISG solution in Article 19(3) has not met with widespread approval, nor do the numerous, often conflicting decisions interpreting the rule help to set things straight.[320]

Judged solely by its wording, and when compared to some bolder domestic formulations, Article 19 seems to represent a limited and conservative exception to the general mirror-image rule. This is because paragraph (3) of Article 19 defines material alteration in the broadest of terms:

> Additional or different terms relating, among other things, to the price, payment, quality and quantity of the goods, place and time of delivery, extent of one party's liability to the other or the settlement of disputes are considered to alter the terms of the offer materially.

Indeed, since paragraph (3) sets forth such a wide-ranging and non-exhaustive (among other things) list of provisions deemed material in the Article 19 sense, one prominent commentator found it difficult to even imagine variations that would not be material,[321] and CISG case law on point certainly confirms that many alternations are classified as material.[322]

Then again, first impressions can prove deceptive upon closer analysis. For example, a German court has held that a clause requiring notice by the buyer of defects within thirty days after the date of the seller's invoice may be regarded as

318. *See* generally *supra*, No. 122.

319. For an analysis of the complex and controversial rule in §2-207 of the American Uniform Commercial Code *see* White & Summers, *Handbook of the Law under the Uniform Commercial Code* 6th ed. (2010), §2-3. Regarding a 2001 proposal to amend this rule *see ibid.*, §2-4.

320. *See* generally Schroeter in Schlechtriem & Schwenzer, *Commentary* 4th ed. (2016), at 351 et seq.

321. E.A. Farnsworth, 'Formation of Contract', in *International Sales* (Galston & Smit eds, 1984), at 3–16.

322. *See*, for example, decision of OLG München (Germany), 8 Feb. 1995, CLOUT Case 167, available at www.cisg.law.pace.edu/cases/950208g2.html (significant reduction of time for delivery was material modification of seller's offer). *See also* Cour de cassation, 16 Jul. 1998, CLOUT Case 242, available at www.cisg.law.pace.edu/cases/980716f1.html (clause conferring jurisdiction on French court was material alteration).

non-material under Article 19(2), notwithstanding the fact that the buyer's failure to notify within the stated time period effectively insulates the seller from all liability claims based on non-conforming goods.[323] A Chinese arbitral award provides another example of a non-material term.[324]

It is also significant that some scholars treat Article 19(3) as merely establishing a rebuttable presumption of materiality.[325] Following this approach, the highest court in France, in a case where a seller's reply stated a higher quantity of paving stones than that set forth in the buyer's purchase order (offer), held that the presumption that the seller's reply constituted a material alteration was rebutted – this because the buyer, who had failed to object to the discrepancy, had also willingly paid part of the price.[326]

A related important point is that it is not possible to understand Article 19 in isolation from other Convention provisions. For example, a reply containing an additional term (as opposed to a modification) which conforms to international trade usage will not constitute a material addition even if it deals with a topic listed in paragraph (3).[327]

4. Cases Not Resolved by Article 19

125. Finally, it should be emphasized that Article 19 does not provide machinery capable of solving all problems likely to arise within the context of a battle of forms.

One typical sales situation which has frequently challenged national courts concerns cases where the forms exchanged do not entirely match (e.g., the seller's form limits liability for breach, while the buyer's form provides for the opposite result), but where the parties nonetheless proceed to perform their main obligations (to

323. *See* Landgericht Baden-Baden of 14 Aug. 1991, CLOUT Case 50, abstract available at www.unilex.info/cisg/case/13 (time limit for notice of defects as fixed in the general conditions of the seller had become part of the contract since a term contained in the acceptance indicating that notice of defects must be given within thirty days after the date of invoice could not be considered a material modification of the terms of the offer); *see also Journal of Law & Commerce* 12 (1993) 227.

324. *See* China International Economic and Trade Arbitration Commission, People's Republic of China, 17 Sep. 2003, available at http://cisgw3.law.pace.edu/cases/030917c1.html (change from three deliveries with 500 tonnes, 700 tonnes, and 800 tonnes in each to four deliveries with 500 tonnes in each considered immaterial because there was no change in total quantity).

325. *See*, e.g., F. Ferrari & M. Torsello, *International Sales Law-CISG in a Nutshell* 2nd ed. (2018), at 198; Schroeter, *supra* note 320, at 356 (provision merely contains rebuttable presumption). Some scholars in this group emphasize that terms relating to the subjects listed in Art. 19(3) *are* considered (*sont considérés*) material; the provision does not say that they *must* be so considered: *see* Magnus in Staudinger, *Kommentar*, Art. 19, Rd. Nr. 16 and authors cited there.

326. The court also noted that the buyer did not object to the seller's method of calculation of the paving stones to be delivered, thereby accepting it. *See* Cour de cassation (France), 27 May 2014, available at http://www.unilex.info/cisg/case/1879.

327. *Accord*: Honnold/Flechtner, *supra* note 296, at 247. *Compare* Oberlandesgericht Graz (Austria), 7 Mar. 2002, CLOUT Case 537, available at http://cisgw3.law.pace.edu/cases/020307a3.html (declaration of acceptance conditional on credit insurance acceptance diverged from original proposal, thus constituting a counter-offer; buyer knew seller would have entered contract only on condition of credit insurance acceptance). Regarding trade usage under Art. 9, *see supra*, Nos 87 et seq.

deliver and pay) without regard to the contractual discrepancy and its potential consequences. In such cases, some sort of CISG 'contract by conduct' must be said to exist,[328] but the terms of that contract may later become the subject of some dispute. One possible solution (arguably closest to the black-letter solution set forth in Article 19) would be to give preference to the standard terms of the party who got in the battle's 'last shot';[329] in other cases, a more fair solution would be to let the conflicting terms cancel each other out (the so-called knockout approach)[330] and then look to the substantive solution supplied by the CISG gap-filling rule.[331] Arguably, the 'astonishingly amount of academic attention' directed at Article 19 far exceeds the provision's importance in practice.[332]

Note that once a contract has been validly concluded on the basis of the Contract Formation rules in CISG Part II, a subsequent unilateral communication (from one contracting party to the other) does not become part of (or modify) the agreement originally reached. This point was made clear in a case decided in 2003 by a US Court of Appeals. A Canadian winery (B) agreed by telephone to buy 1.2 million corks from (S), the US subsidiary of a French manufacturer. Together with each of the eleven shipments which ensued, S sent an invoice stating (in French) that 'Any dispute arising under the present contract is under the sole jurisdiction of the Court of Commerce of [... France].' B took delivery and paid for each shipment, but made no objection (or comment) in relation to the clause. Later, claiming that wine bottled with the S-corks was tainted by cork flavours, B filed suit in a US Federal Court against S (and its French parent). Reversing the District Court's decision, the Court of Appeals held that the forum clauses proffered by S had not (by virtue of CISG Article 19 or otherwise) become part of the prior oral agreement between the parties.[333]

---

328. *See*, e.g., Landgericht Kehl, Germany, 6 Oct. 1995, abstract at www.unilex.info/cisg/case/163 (parties' performance established derogation from Art. 19 or waiver of enforcement of conflicting standard terms); Oberlandesgericht München (Germany), 11 Mar. 1998, CLOUT Case 232, available at http://cisgw3.law.pace.edu/cases/980311g1.html (by performing the contract buyer accepted standard terms that differed from offer). Regarding an acceptance by conduct under Art. 18, *see supra*, No. 117.
329. *See*, e.g., Oberlandesgericht Köln, 24 May 2006, CLOUT Case 824, available at http://cisgw3.law.pace.edu/cases/060524g1.html (seller and buyer exchanged general terms and conditions; court held interpretation of contracts with conflicting terms leads to application of at least those provisions which do not differ; beyond this, so-called last shot doctrine applies). *Compare* F. Ferrari & M. Torsello, *International Sales Law-CISG in a Nutshell* 2nd ed. (2018), at 201 f. (knockout view cannot be shared, since it has no basis in CISG's formation rules).
330. *See*, e.g., Bundesgerichtshof, Germany, 9 Jan. 2002, available at http://cisgw3.law.pace.edu/cases/020109g1.html (application of 'knock-out' doctrine); *See also* Schroeter in Schlechtriem & Schwenzer, *Commentary* 4th ed. (2016), at 367; *accord* Brunner & Murmann, et al., 'Article 4 [Issues Covered and Excluded; Validity and the Effect on Property Interest in the Goods Sold]', in *Commentary on the UN Sales Law (CISG)* (Brunner & Gottlieb eds, 2019), at 66.
331. If, for example, one form disclaims liability for breach and the other does not, the CISG gap-filling rule is to allow the injured party full (expectation) damages for breach. Regarding Art. 74 *see infra*, Nos 291 et seq.
332. Schroeter in Schlechtriem & Schwenzer, *Commentary* 4th ed. (2016), at 365.
333. *See Chateau des Charmes*, CLOUT Case 576, available at http://cisgw3.law.pace.edu/cases/030505u1.html#ca (oral agreements between S and B as to kind of cork, quantity and price sufficient to create complete & binding contracts; terms of agreements did not include forum selection clause; under Art. 29, contract may be modified or terminated by parties' mere agreement, but additional

IV. Time Period for Acceptance: Default Rules

126. As noted previously, a CISG acceptance must reach the offeror within the time which the offeror has fixed.[334] If the offeror has fixed the time period for acceptance (e.g., 'you have four days to accept'), it is important to identify the point in time when that period begins to run by default (i.e., absent contrary indication by the offeror). Paragraph (1) of Article 20 provides as follows:

> A period of time for acceptance fixed by the offeror in a telegram or a letter begins to run from the moment the telegram is handed in for dispatch or from the date shown on the letter or, if no such date is shown, from the date shown on the envelope. A period of time for acceptance fixed by the offeror by telephone, telex or other means of instantaneous communication, begins to run from the moment that the offer reaches the offeree.

As regards periods fixed by instantaneous means of communication (e.g., telephone), the time begins to run from the moment the offer reaches the offeree. As regards non-instantaneous communications (e.g., letters sent by post),[335] however, the CISG default rule is that the period begins to run from the moment the communication is handed in for dispatch or from the date shown on the letter;[336] to this extent, Article 20(1) stands in contrast to the rule that the acceptance first becomes effective when it reaches the offeree.[337]

V. Official Holidays, Etc.

127. A hardly controversial rule regarding the effect of official holidays or non-business days on the period of acceptance is set forth in Article 20(2).[338]

---

or different terms relating to settlement of disputes alter the terms of the offer materially; no indication that B evidenced affirmative assent to forum selection clauses in invoices; B merely performed its obligations under oral contract; nothing in Convention suggests failure to object to unilateral attempt to alter material terms of valid agreement is 'agreement' under Art. 29).

334. Regarding Art. 18(2), *see supra*, No. 114.

335. The CISG Advisory Council has expressed the opinion that e-mail communications are non-instantaneous communications and should be treated as such: *see* Opinion No. 3, Comment 20.3, available at http://cisgw3.law.pace.edu/cisg/CISG-AC-op1.html.

336. As always, the offeror – who remains the master – can set forth another solution in the offer itself.

337. Regarding Art. 15(1), *see supra*, No. 104.

338. 'Official holidays or non-business days occurring during the period for acceptance are included in calculating the period. However, if a notice of acceptance cannot be delivered at the address of the offeror on the last day of the period because that day falls on an official holiday or a non-business day at the place of business of the offeror, the period is extended until the first business day which follows.'

VI. Exceptions to Timely Acceptance Rule

A. *The Rule and the Exceptions*

128. As noted previously with respect to the general Article 18(2) rule, an acceptance is not effective if the indication of assent does not reach the offeror within the time he or she has fixed within a reasonable time. Article 21 of the CISG provides the following two exceptions to the rule:

(1) A late acceptance is nevertheless effective as an acceptance if without delay the offeror orally so informs the offeree or dispatches a notice to that effect.
(2) If a letter or other writing containing a late acceptance shows that it has been sent in such circumstances that if its transmission had been normal it would have reached the offeror in due time, the late acceptance is effective as an acceptance unless, without delay, the offeror orally informs the offeree that he considers his offer as having lapsed or dispatches a notice to that effect.

B. *Notification by Offeror Accepting Late Acceptance*

129. According to Article 18(2), a late acceptance is of no effect, and so the offer to which such an acceptance seeks to reply will usually lapse. However, under the exception set forth in Article 21(1), a late acceptance is nevertheless effective as such if the offeror promptly notifies the offeree to that effect. In such event, the acceptance becomes effective upon its receipt (and before the subsequent notice by the offeror).[339]

C. *Acceptance Timely in Normal Circumstances*

130. Article 21(2) deals with a somewhat more complex situation: the late acceptance shows that it has been sent in such circumstances that if its transmission had been normal, it would have reached the offeror in due time. In this case, the CISG drafters chose to follow the 'Scandinavian' (domestic) rule:[340] the late acceptance is effective as such unless the offeror promptly informs the offeree that he or she considers his or her offer as having lapsed.

VII. Withdrawal of Acceptance

131. The CISG rule regarding withdrawal of an offer has been previously discussed.[341] As regards withdrawal of an acceptance, Article 22 provides as follows:

339. This differs from the result which obtains in systems which treat a late acceptance as a counter-offer: *see Secretariat's Commentary*, A/CONF./97/5, Comment 3 to Art. 19(1) of the 1978 Draft.
340. *See* Art. 4(2) of the (essentially uniform) Scandinavian Contracts Acts.
341. Regarding Art. 15 *see supra*, No. 104.

> An acceptance may be withdrawn if the withdrawal reaches the offeror before or at the same time as the acceptance would have become effective.

It follows from Article 22 that an acceptance may not be withdrawn after it has become effective: once the acceptance is in effect, the contract is in effect in its entirety;[342] so any attempt to withdraw the acceptance after this point will constitute a breach by the offeree.

§3. Acceptance Effective; Contract Concluded

132. According to Article 23 of the CISG:

> A contract is concluded at the moment when an acceptance of an offer becomes effective in accordance with the provisions of this Convention.

This rule, which establishes the point in time when a CISG contract is concluded, works in tandem with the rule in Article 18(2) which provides that an acceptance becomes effective at the moment the indication of assent reaches the offeror.[343]

§4. Declaration of Intention: Definition of Reach

133. Part II of the Convention concludes with Article 24 which defines the point in time at which a declaration of intention (offer, acceptance, etc.) is considered to reach the addressee:

> For the purposes of this part of the Convention, an offer, declaration of acceptance or any other indication of intention reaches the addressee when it is made orally to him or delivered by any other means to him personally, to his place of business or mailing address or, if he does not have a place of business or mailing address, to his habitual residence.[344]

342. Regarding Art. 23, *see infra* (text directly below).
343. Assuming that, as in the usual case, the acceptance reaches the offeror within the time fixed, etc. Regarding Art. 18, *see supra*, Nos 112 et seq.
344. The definition of the term 'reach' has significance in relation to Arts 15, 16, 17, 18, 20, 21 and 22. As regards electronic communications, *see* Opinion No. 1 of the CISG Advisory Council, available at http://cisgw3.law.pace.edu/cisg/CISG-AC-op1.html: 'The term "reaches" corresponds to the point in time when an electronic communication has entered the addressee's server, provided that the addressee expressly or impliedly has consented to receiving electronic communications of that type, in that format, and to that address.'

Chapter 5. Obligations, Risk and Remedies

§1. Sale of Goods: Five Chapters in CISG Part III

134. Part III of the CISG, entitled Sale of Goods, contains the substantive rules of greatest practical significance for international sales. Part III is subdivided into five separate chapters.

§2. General Provisions

I. Introduction

135. Chapter I of CISG Part III, consisting of Articles 25–29, is entitled General Provisions.

Some of these general provisions, in particular those which relate to the remedies of avoidance and specific performance,[345] serve as adjuncts to the more specialized remedial rules in Chapters II and III of Part III regarding seller's and buyer's breach. Chapter I of Part III also contains other general provisions, applicable to both parties, regarding delays in notification and contract modification.[346]

II. Avoidance and Fundamental Breach

A. *Fundamental Breach Defined*

136. The first – and arguably the most important – general provision in Chapter 1 of Part III relates to the rules which permit an injured party to put an end to ('avoid') the contract, that is, in CISG parlance, the remedy of avoidance.

In most cases, the relevant CISG rules (set forth in Chapters II and III of Part III) require that a breach be 'fundamental' before an injured party will be permitted to avoid.[347] Article 25 supplements these rules by providing the necessary definition of the term fundamental breach:

> A breach of contract committed by one of the parties is fundamental if it results in such detriment to the other party as substantially to deprive him of what he is entitled to expect under the contract, unless the party in breach did not foresee and a reasonable person of the same kind in the same circumstances would not have foreseen such a result.[348]

345. *See infra*, Nos 136 et seq. and Nos 140 et seq.
346. *See infra*, Nos 139 and 146.
347. Regarding Art. 49 (avoidance for seller's breach) *see infra*, Nos 225 et seq.; regarding Art. 64 (avoidance for buyer's breach) *see infra*, Nos 261 et seq.
348. In the view of most courts and commentators, the time of the conclusion of the contract is the relevant moment for the determination of foreseeability. *See* F. Ferrari & M. Torsello, *International Sales Law – CISG in a Nutshell* 2nd ed. (2018), at 419.

B. Substantial Detriment

137. Article 25 defines fundamental breach in terms of (foreseeable) substantial detriment. This means that, for example, as regards the buyer's right to avoid upon seller's late delivery,[349] the buyer (the injured party) must allege and prove that the delay has caused him or her to suffer a detriment which substantially (perhaps even more than 'materially') deprives him or her of what he or she is entitled to expect under the contract.[350] In addition, the detriment suffered by the injured party must be one which the breaching party (in this example: the seller) reasonably ought to have foreseen.

Avoidance is generally regarded as an exceptional CISG remedy, to be exercised restrictively. Still, the question of whether the injured party suffers a substantial detriment as a result of a given breach and whether such detriment is foreseeable by the other party requires a concrete evaluation of the nature of the obligation breached (i.e., whether the breach relates to non-delivery or non-payment, non-conforming delivery, etc.), as well as the other circumstances of the particular case. In some situations, even the breach of a secondary obligation can amount to a fundamental breach.[351]

Since a party to a CISG contract who fails to live up to his or her obligations in full is not necessarily guilty of a 'fundamental' breach,[352] a draftsman seeking greater protection for a given client (e.g., a buyer) might seek to incorporate an express contractual provision which states, for example, that the seller's delivery of the goods on a stated date is 'of the essence', perhaps adding (for the sake of additional clarity) that the buyer's duty to pay the price is 'conditioned' on seller's delivery on the date stated.[353]

A closer examination of the right to avoid will be undertaken below in connection with the individual, more specific rules regarding seller's and buyer's

349. Article 49: *see infra*, Nos 225 et seq.

350. CISG Art. 25 reflects the corresponding rules in most domestic systems: 'The most important principle is that the default [breach] attains a certain minimum degree of seriousness.' *See* Schroeter in Schlechtriem & Schwenzer, *Commentary* 4th ed. (2016), at 417, quoting Treitel, *Remedies for Breach*, No. 161. It has been suggested that a 'substantial' deprivation under the CISG may be more than what Common lawyers would consider as 'material' under their corresponding domestic law. *See* H. Flechtner, 'Remedies under the New International Sales Convention: The Perspective from Article 2 of the U.C.C.', *Journal of Law and Commerce* 8 (1998) 53, 75. The application of similar terminology in the Convention provisions dealing with anticipatory breach tends to support this argument: *see* Flechtner at *ibid.* and *infra*, Nos 282 et seq.

351. *See* generally CISG Advisory Council Opinion No. 5, available at http://www.cisgac.com/cisgac-opinion-no-5/. *See also*, for example, OLG Germany, CLOUT Case 2, available at www.cisg.law.pace.edu/cases/910917g1.html (fundamental breach of duty to preserve exclusivity).

352. In a CISG case decided by a German court (Amtsgericht Oldenburg on 24 Apr. 1990, available at http://cisgw3.law.pace.edu/cases/900424g1.html), an Italian seller contracted to deliver fall fashions to a German buyer in four instalments (specified as follows: 'July, August, September, +'). When the first lot arrived at the end of September, the buyer refused acceptance and returned the goods; the seller sued for damages. In a questionable decision, the court found for the seller, holding that the breach was within the period specified in the contract and not fundamental under Art. 49(1)(a); the court also cited the absence of a 'Nachfrist' (Art. 47) notice under Art. 49(1)(b).

353. Regarding the parties' freedom to contract out of the CISG default rule regime (in whole or, as suggested here, in part), *see supra*, No. 72.

breach.[354] For the present, it may be noted that the uncertainty which may sometimes surround the elastic fundamental breach standard has been counterbalanced to some degree by the establishment of a supplementary *Nachfrist*-type avoidance rule, in that the issuance of a (reasonable) *Nachfrist* warning may obviate the injured party's need to demonstrate a fundamental breach.[355] As further elaborated below, the buyer's right to avoid by reason of the delivery of non-conforming goods may be restricted by the seller's right to cure.[356]

C. When Avoidance Declaration Effective

138. Like Article 25, Article 26 is a general provision relating to the right of either injured CISG party (seller or buyer) to avoid.

Because avoidance can have serious consequences for the party in breach (requiring, for example, that a breaching seller retake possession of the goods on foreign soil), Article 26 provides that a declaration of avoidance of the contract is effective only if made by notice to the other party.[357]

Assuming the injured party is entitled to avoid, for example, by reason of a fundamental breach or by reason of the breaching party's failure to duly comply with a reasonable *Nachfrist* notice, a single Article 26 notice will suffice: unlike some domestic systems, the Convention does not first require a warning–notice which declares in advance the injured party's intention to avoid.[358]

III. Delay or Error in Transmission

139. Article 27 of the Convention deals with delays or errors in transmission:

> Unless otherwise expressly provided in this Part [III] of the Convention, if any notice, request or other communication is given or made by a party in accordance with this Part and by means appropriate in the circumstances, a delay or error in the transmission of the communication or its failure to arrive does not deprive that party of the right to rely on the communication.

---

354. Regarding avoidance for seller's fundamental breach under Art. 49, *see infra*, No. 225. Regarding Art. 64 (avoidance for buyer's breach) *see infra*, Nos 261 et seq.
355. The CISG *Nachfrist* rule owes its nickname to a similar, yet substantively different rule in German domestic law. Regarding seller's non-delivery and Arts 47(1) and 49(1)(b), *see infra*, Nos 220 and 226. Regarding buyer's non-payment and Arts 63(1) and 64(1)(b), *see infra*, Nos 260 and 261.
356. Regarding Art. 48, *see infra*, Nos 221 et seq.
357. The contract is avoided as of the point in time when the notice takes effect, that is, upon its dispatch. *See infra*, No. 139. Depending on the circumstances, a declaration of avoidance may be revoked even after it takes effect. *See ibid.*
358. *See* A/CONF./97/5, *Secretariat's Commentary* to Art. 24 of the 1978 draft. As already indicated, the Convention permits the issuance of a *Nachfrist* warning which may serve to obviate the need to establish a fundamental breach. Regarding seller's non-delivery and Arts 47(1) and 49(1)(b), *see infra*, Nos 220 and 226. Regarding buyer's non-payment and Arts 63(1) and 64(1)(b), *see infra*, Nos 260 and 261.

Assuming that a given communication is made in accordance with Part III of the Convention and by means appropriate in the circumstances, such a communication is generally effective upon dispatch.[359] Thus, as a general Part III rule, and in contrast with the rules applicable to certain communications in Part II,[360] Article 27 places the risk of delay or error in transmission upon the addressee. If, for example, the buyer sends a notice advising the seller that the goods delivered are defective, but that notice is lost during transmission, the buyer retains his or her rights to remedial relief.[361] There are, however, a number of exceptions to this general Part III rule.[362]

IV. Specific Performance

A. *Specific Performance and Forum Law*

140. As noted previously, and as more fully developed later in connection with the discussion of remedies for breach, the Convention accepts – as a starting point – the logic of Civil law systems with respect to specific performance: if a promisor fails to perform his or her promise, the most natural means of promise enforcement is to simply require that the promisor perform the promised act: for example, require that the seller deliver that which has not yet been delivered (Article 46(1)), or remedy a defective delivery by (re)delivery of goods which conform to the contractual description (Article 46(2)), or (in the case of buyer's breach) require that the price agreed be paid (Article 62).[363] But as regards all these rules, Article 28 sets forth an important general proviso:

> If, in accordance with the provisions of this Convention, one party is entitled to require performance of any obligation by the other party, a court is not bound to enter a judgment for specific performance unless the court would do so under its own law in respect of similar contracts of sale not governed by this Convention.

In contrast with Civil law systems, Common law systems have traditionally placed the remedy of specific performance in a low position on the remedial scale, and Article 28 – which was primarily designed to accommodate the Common law view – is evidence of the compromise which the Convention's remedial system represents.

---

359. Regarding possible revocation of an avoidance declaration *see infra*, No. 227 with note 680.

360. Regarding Art. 18(2), *see supra*, No. 114.

361. *See* Art. 39 (*infra*, Nos 190 et seq.) and, for example, Honnold/Flechtner, *Uniform Law for International Sales* 4th ed. (2009), at 286–287.

362. Regarding Art. 47(2), *see infra*, No. 220 with accompanying note; regarding Art. 48(4), *see infra*, No. 224 with accompanying note; regarding Art. 63(2), *see infra*, No. 260 with accompanying note; regarding Art. 65(1)–(2), *see infra*, No. 266 with accompanying note; regarding Art. 79(4), *see infra*, No. 311.

363. *See* generally *supra*, No. 44. Regarding Art. 46 (seller's breach) *see infra*, Nos 214 et seq. Regarding Art. 62 (buyer's breach) *see infra*, Nos 257 et seq.

B. Award of Specific Performance: Two-Step Process

141. Article 28 requires that a court (or arbitral tribunal) asked to require performance under the Convention engage in a two-step process: first, the court must determine whether the remedial rules in Chapters II or III of Part III themselves would make specific performance available to the injured party in the particular case.[364] Then, if the answer to the first question is yes, the court must proceed to apply the safety-valve test in Article 28.

So, even when a court holds that the applicable (Chapter II or III) Convention rule would require a non-performing party to perform, that court must also consider whether such specific relief would be available pursuant to the domestic sales law of the forum State. And if specific relief would not be so available under the domestic rules, the forum court is not bound to require performance under the Convention.[365]

On the one hand, it may be said that Article 28 tends to maintain domestic conceptions of the proper role for specific performance, even though the Convention, in general, must be interpreted with the need for international uniformity in mind.[366] On the other hand, it should be remembered that the role of Article 28 in practice will be severely limited: although this provision might sometimes be invoked to hamper the effort of a seller still in possession to recover the price, monetary damages will always remain a viable alternative;[367] and an injured buyer will only rarely seek to enforce the seller's performance by judicial means, in that the remedy of (avoidance and) damages will nearly always be preferred.[368]

V. Modification and Termination

A. No Formal Requirements

142. As previously emphasized, a CISG contract of sale need not be concluded in or evidenced in writing, just as CISG contracts are not generally subject to any other requirement as to form.[369]

Following up on this theme, Article 29 eliminates such formal requirements as regards CISG contract modification and contract termination. The general rule is set forth in paragraph (1):

---

364. Regarding Art. 46 (seller's breach) *see infra*, Nos 214 et seq. Regarding Art. 62 (buyer's breach) *see infra*, Nos 257 et seq.

365. Regarding the application of Art. 28, *see* generally Lookofsky, *Understanding the CISG* 5th Worldwide ed. (2017), §6.4. *See also* generally, Kastely, 'The Right to Require Performance in International Sales', *Washington Law Review* (1988) 63, 607, and Müller-Chen in Schlechtriem & Schwenzer, *Commentary* 4th ed. (2016), at 482 et seq. Regarding specific performance in Civil and Common law systems, *see* G. Treitel, *Remedies for Breach of Contract* (1988), Ch. 3.

366. Regarding Art. 7(1), *see supra*, Nos 75 et seq.

367. Regarding the seller's right to secure specific performance *see infra*, Nos 257 et seq. Regarding the seller's right to damages *see infra*, Nos 254 and 289 et seq.

368. Regarding buyer's right to damages under Art. 45 *see infra*, Nos 211 and 289 et seq.

369. Regarding Art. 11, *see supra*, Nos 92 et seq.

A contract may be modified or terminated by the mere agreement of the parties.

143. Article 29(1) serves to extend the Article 11 rule: unless the parties otherwise agree, a contract to modify or terminate a CISG agreement need *not* be in writing.[370]

B. Relationship to Consideration under Common Law

144. Beyond this, Article 29(1) helps exclude the application of other domestic conceptions. Thus, under rules traditionally applicable in Common law jurisdictions, a one-sided modification of a sales contract was not binding by virtue of the mere agreement of the parties. If, for example, a buyer promised to pay the seller more than the price originally agreed, but got nothing in return, that buyer's promise was not binding under the traditional Common law rule: the seller could not demand something for nothing, since some kind of 'consideration' was required to make the buyer's promise bind. Indeed, in England and certain other Common law jurisdictions, this is still the case.

Now, however, as regards international contracts subject to the CISG, lack of consideration is not a defence available to the promisor who would allege that his or her unilateral CISG promise (to pay more) should not bind.

145. Then again, dispensing with the consideration requirement has not dispensed with the real problem which sometimes lurks in the one-sided modification kind of case. Article 29 states only that a CISG sales contract, once entered, may be modified by the mere agreement between the parties, but the 'validity' question of whether a promise to modify is valid and binding in the concrete case – or whether the modification has been extorted by economic duress – lies outside the Convention scope. Therefore, it is still necessary to distinguish between modifications arrived at by threats and extortion (economic duress) on the one hand, and honest, acceptable business standards on the other hand.[371] And it is submitted that this side of the Article 29 problem must be left to the applicable domestic law.[372]

370. Regarding the modification in para. (2), *see* discussion *infra*, No. 146.

371. *See* generally J. Lookofsky, *Consequential Damages in Comparative Context* (1989), https://jura.ku.dk/jurabog, at 34–39.

372. *Accord*: US Court of Appeals for the Third Circuit, US, 19 Jul. 2007 (*Valero Marketing & Supply Company v. Greeni Trading Oy*), CLOUT Case 846, available at http://cisgw3.law.pace.edu/cases/070719u2.html ('Although [seller] asserted at trial that it agreed to the September 14 Agreement because it felt that it was a "take it or leave it" proposition, the record is clear that [seller] did assent to that agreement. [Seller] does not argue that it was under duress.'). *See also* Schlechtriem in Schlechtriem & Schwenzer, *Commentary* 2nd English ed. (2005), 330 with notes 13–14, and Schroeter, 4th ed. of the same work at 495 with notes 9–10 (both citing Lookofsky, 'Loose Ends and Contorts in International Sales', *American Journal of Comparative Law* 39 (1991) 403 at 412) as well as the views expressed by Lookofsky in a prior edition of this *Encyclopaedia* monograph). Regarding questions of validity and CISG Art. 4 *see also supra*, Nos 62 et seq.

Under American domestic (validity) law, a seller's outright refusal to deliver without additional compensation has been held to constitute a threat made in violation of the duty to deal in

C. Contract Requiring Written Modification or Termination

146. Paragraph (2) of Article 29 addresses the situation where the contract between the parties contains a clause which requires any contract modification or termination to be in writing:

> (2) A contract in writing which contains a provision requiring any modification or termination by agreement to be in writing may not be otherwise modified or terminated by agreement. However, a party may be precluded by his conduct from asserting such a provision to the extent that the other party has relied on that conduct.

The first sentence of Article 29(2), which conforms with the general freedom-of-contract rule in Article 6, clearly applies to clauses which seek to deny contractual effect to subsequent oral agreements and modifications.[373] The starting point here is that such no-oral-modification clauses are to be given effect, at least with the proviso that such clauses, if abusive or unreasonable, may be prohibited by domestic validity rules.[374]

A more difficult question is to determine what constitutes reliance-inducing conduct under the 'estoppel' safety valve established by the second sentence of Article 29(2), just as the proper construction (interpretation) of a given no-oral-modification clause may give rise to a difficult question regarding the relationship between that sentence and the general rule in Article 6.[375]

§3. Obligations of the Seller and Buyer's Remedies for Breach

I. Introduction

147. Chapter II of CISG Part III (Articles 30–52) sets forth the supplementary (gap-filling) Convention regime regarding the obligations of the seller; this chapter

---

good faith. *See* White & Summers, *Uniform Commercial Code* 6th ed. (2010), §2-7 discussing *Roth Steel Products v. Sharon Steel Corp.*, 705 F. 2nd 134 (6th Cir. 1983) – a case which shows that the issues of duress, good faith and unconscionability go hand in hand. English precedents include the *Atlantic Baron* case [1979] Q.B. 705, *Atlas Express Ltd. v. Kafco Ltd.* [1989] 3 W.L.R. 389, and *Williams v. Roffey Bros. Ltd.* [1990] 2 W.L.R. 1153, C.A. Regarding the corresponding German domestic law, *see* Schroeter, *ibid.*, at 495.

373. *Compare* so-called merger clauses which are designed to deprive prior or contemporaneous oral agreements of contractual effect. Regarding merger clauses and 'parol evidence' *see supra*, No. 86, text with note 250.

374. *Accord* Schroeter, *supra* note 372, at 506 with note 105; Schlechtriem in the 2nd ed. of the same work at 330 with note 13 (citing Lookofsky (1991) 39 *American Journal of Comparative Law* 412). Schroeter (at *id.* with note 104) would also apply this rule by analogy to 'merger clauses' (*see* preceding note).

375. *See* Honnold/Flechtner, *Uniform Law* 4th ed. (2009), at 302 et seq. *See also*, Schlechtriem, *ibid.*, at 335 (need to apply flexible approach means that courts will enjoy considerable discretion). *See* generally R. Hillman, 'Article 29(2) of the United Nations C.I.S.G.: A New Effort at Clarifying the Legal Effect of "No Oral Modification" Clauses', *Cornell International Law Journal* 21 (1989) 449. Regarding estoppel as a general CISG principle, *see supra*, No. 79.

also provides the buyer with various remedies in the event of the seller's breach. Many of these provisions must be read in conjunction with other CISG rules: not only the Part I and Part III General Provisions previously discussed[376] but also the other general (common) provisions set forth in Chapter V of Part II (Provisions Common to the Obligations of the Seller and of the Buyer).[377]

II. Summary of Seller's Obligations

148. The various obligations of the CISG seller are summarized in Article 30:

> The seller must deliver the goods, hand over any documents relating to them and transfer the property in the goods, as required by the contract and this Convention.

149. As explained in the following, the message summarized in Article 30 (and more fully detailed in the provisions which follow) that rule is that the CISG seller must deliver the 'right' goods at the 'right' place and at the 'right' time, that is, as required by the contract and this Convention. Because the Convention respects the parties' freedom to define their own obligations, etc.,[378] it must always be remembered that the primary purpose of default CISG rules such as those regarding the proper place and time for seller's performance is to fill in such contractual gaps as may exist in the agreement actually reached between the parties in the concrete case.

III. Delivery of the Goods and Handing Over of Documents

A. *Introduction*

150. Section I of Chapter II (Articles 31–34) concerns delivery of the goods and handing over of documents. The first rule in this section deals with the place of delivery, which is particularly important not only as regards the seller's delivery obligation as such but also as regards the operation of the Convention rules regarding the Passing of Risk.[379]

376. Regarding Arts 6–9 and 25–29, *see supra*, Nos 70 et seq. and 135 et seq.
377. Regarding Arts 71–88, *see infra*, Nos 280 et seq.
378. Regarding Art. 6, *see supra*, Nos 70 et seq.
379. Regarding Ch. IV of Part III (Arts 66–70), *see infra*, Nos 267 et seq.

B. *Place of Delivery*

1. Gap-Filling Rules

151. Article 31 sets forth the default rules which define the place of delivery in a contract governed by the CISG, that is, the gap-filling rules which apply absent an express contractual provision or international usage to the contrary.[380]

2. Incoterms

152. In as much as the precise demarcation of the place of delivery is a key function of the Incoterms regime, the CISG default rules in section I of Chapter II should also be read in light of such Incoterms as may apply by virtue of the parties' agreement or by virtue of custom. In many cases, the Incoterms will be made applicable by virtue of an express contractual provision, for example, a term which incorporates by reference an Incoterm place-of-delivery term.[381] Another possibility is that the Incoterms may become operational by virtue of the parties' practices between themselves or by virtue of a wider international trade usage.[382]

3. Contracts of Carriage: Delivery to First Carrier

153. The general CISG default rule as regards the place of delivery is set forth in Article 31, paragraph (a):

> If the seller is not bound to deliver the goods at any other particular place, his obligation to deliver consists:
>
> a) if the contract of sale involves carriage of the goods – in handing the goods over to the first carrier for transmission to the buyer.

154. In virtually all cases where the CISG applies, the buyer and seller will have their places of business in different States.[383] And in the great majority of these cases, the parties' contract will expressly or impliedly contemplate the 'carriage of the goods' (from one State to another) via a carrier, that is, an independent third

380. Regarding Art. 6, *see supra*, Nos 70 et seq.; regarding Art. 9, *see supra*, Nos 87 et seq.
381. For example, a contract term expressly providing that the seller is to deliver the goods: 'C.I.F. (Incoterms)'. The Incoterms were last updated and revised in 2020. Regarding the ICC Incoterms 2000, *see* the Report of the United Nations Secretary-General: A/CN. 9/479 of 10 Apr. 2000. *See also infra*, No. 269.
382. Re the parties' practices, *see supra*, No. 88. Regarding the rather strict requirements of CISG Art. 9(2), *see supra*, Nos 89 et seq. *Accord*: F. Ferrari & M. Torsello, *International Sales Law-CISG in a Nutshell* 2nd ed. (2018), at 65 (Incoterms *can* be binding upon parties pursuant to Art. 9(2), *provided* prerequisites listed in that provision are met).
383. Regarding Art. 1, *see supra*, Nos 52 et seq.

party not under seller's or buyer's direct control.[384] In these numerous and typical cases, Article 31(a) provides that the seller fulfils his or her delivery obligation by handing over the goods to the first such carrier for transmission to the buyer.

4. Cases Not Involving Carriage

155. Paragraphs (b) and (c) of Article 31 are designed to provide default rules for those less common cases where an international sales contract does *not* contemplate carriage by an independent carrier. In these cases, the obligation to delivery consists:

> (b) if, in cases not within the preceding subparagraph, the contract relates to specific goods, or unidentified goods to be drawn from a specific stock or to be manufactured or produced, and at the time of the conclusion of the contract the parties knew that the goods were at, or were to be manufactured or produced at a particular place – in placing the goods at the buyer's disposal at that place;
>
> (c) in other cases – in placing the goods at the buyer's disposal at the place where the seller had his place of business at the time of the conclusion of the contract.

156. Where paragraph (a) does not apply, and the goods are specific goods in a specific place, such as a particular painting currently on exhibit in a given art gallery, the default rule in paragraph (b) requires the seller to place the goods at the buyer's disposal at that specific place. The same delivery rule expressly applies to 'unidentified goods to be drawn from a specific stock or to be manufactured or produced'.

In the other cases to which subparagraph (c) refers, that is, those contemplating neither carriage nor specific goods in a specific place, etc., the seller's obligation is to place the goods at the buyer's disposal at the seller's place of business.

5. Notice of Consignment

157. In cases which actually involve carriage of the goods, Article 32 provides three default rules which supplement the seller's primary delivery obligation.[385]

The first of these supplementary obligations concerns goods not clearly identified to the contract, in that the seller must give the buyer notice of the consignment specifying the goods.[386] The second and third supplementary obligations are

---

384. Indeed, even if the contract does not expressly refer to the use of a carrier, the distance which separates the parties and/or their practices may carry the necessary implication. *Accord* Honnold/ Flechtner, *Uniform Law* 4th ed. (2009), at 311.

385. As set forth in Art. 31(a): *see supra*, No. 153.

386. Article 32(1) provides:

designed to help ensure that the necessary carriage contracts will be concluded, and that the appropriate insurance in respect of the carriage will be obtained.[387]

6. Place of Delivery and Jurisdiction

158. In some legal systems, a connection exists between substantive contract law rules regarding the place of performance (to deliver or pay) and rules of procedure which determine juridical jurisdiction. This is, for example, true to a certain extent under American law,[388] as well as under Canadian law,[389] and the same was also true in Europe during the period when the Brussels *Convention* on Jurisdiction & Judgments applied.[390]

Now, however, the jurisdiction of courts in European Union (EU) Member States to adjudicate a CISG case involving an action against an EU domiciliary is determined 'autonomously' under Article 7(1)(b) of the Brussels I *Regulation*.[391] This provision defines 'the place of performance of the obligation in question' in a sale of goods case as the 'place ... where, under the contract, the goods were delivered or should have been delivered'.

Previously, commentators had disagreed as to whether the place of delivery under CISG Article 31 might be relevant as regards the application of the Brussels place-of-performance rule, but in the *Car Trim* case (2010), the EU Court of Justice held

---

1. If the seller, in accordance with the contract or this Convention, hands the goods over to a carrier and if the goods are not clearly identified to the contract by markings on the goods, by shipping documents or otherwise, the seller must give the buyer notice of the consignment specifying the goods.

387. Article 32(2)–(3) provides:

1. If the seller is bound to arrange for carriage of the goods, he must make such contracts as are necessary for carriage to the place fixed by means of transportation appropriate in the circumstances and according to the usual terms for such transportation.
2. If the seller is not bound to effect insurance in respect of the carriage of goods, he must, at the buyer's request, provide him with all available information necessary to enable him to effect such insurance.

388. American State and Federal courts have assumed jurisdiction against out-of-State defendants in cases where, by virtue of a 'long-arm' statute, the forum is the 'place of performance' (place of payment). Regarding the application of the Florida long-arm statute, in conjunction with Due Process requirements, in *Burger King Corp. v. Rudzewicz*, 471 US 462 (1985), *see* J. Lookofsky & K. Hertz, *Transnational Litigation & Commercial Arbitration* 4th ed. (2017), Ch. 2.5.2(A).

389. *See* (e.g.) Cour d'appel de Quebec, 12 Apr. 2011, available at http://unilex.info/cisg/case/1646 (court applied CISG to determine the place performance of American buyer's obligation to pay price; established practice between parties that Quebec was place of performance; no place of payment established in accordance with Art. 57 CISG except buyer's practice, known to the seller, of paying price in Gaspesie, thus conferring jurisdiction on Canadian court).

390. During this period CISG Arts 31 and 57 had in some cases been relevant in the application of Art. 5(1) of the 1968 Brussels Convention.

391. Regarding jurisdiction under the Brussels I Regulation (Recast 2012), *see* generally J. Lookofsky & K. Hertz, *EU-PIL: European Union Private International Law in Contract and Tort* 3rd ed. (2017), Ch. 2.2.2(A).

EU member in CISG case will give jx to place of delivery when no place of performance is chosen

that, in the absence of a choice-of-forum clause, the place of performance under Article 7(1)(b) is to be determined without recourse to gap-filling substantive rules of law such as those in CISG Article 31.[392]

To be sure, if a given CISG contract expressly designates the *place of delivery*, and that place is within an EU Member State (X), then X-State courts will have jurisdiction to decide an action brought, for example, by a buyer against a seller domiciled in (X), e.g., in respect of delayed or non-conforming delivery. In the absence of such an express provision (or an express choice-of-forum clause), however, jurisdiction will lie with the courts at the place where the goods were physically transferred or should have been physically transferred to the buyer at their *final destination*.[393] Interestingly (though perhaps also confusingly), this place will *not* normally be the default place of delivery under CISG Article 31(a), that is, the place where the goods are handed over to the first carrier.

The Brussels place-of-performance rule has similar implications as regards the jurisdiction of EU courts in actions relating to a CISG buyer's obligation to pay the price.[394]

C. *Time of Delivery*

159. Article 33 concerns the time of delivery:

> The seller must deliver the goods: (a) if a date is fixed by or determinable from the contract, on that date; (b) if a period of time is fixed by or determinable from the contract, at any time within that period unless circumstances indicate that the buyer is to choose a date; or (c) in any other case, within a reasonable time after the conclusion of the contract.

Within the CISG context, an express contractual provision will nearly always take precedence over the supplementary Convention rule.[395] Absent an express provision regarding the date or time period fixed by or determinable from the contract, the CISG default solution as regards the time of delivery is keyed to the familiar, yet elastic reasonableness test, whereby the reasonable interests and expectations of both parties must be taken into account.

---

392. *Car Trim v. KeySafety Systems*, Case C-381/08, decided 25 Feb. 2010 (autonomy of linking factors in Art. 7(1)(b) precludes application of rules of private international law of Member State where action is brought and substantive law which would be applicable thereunder). *See* Lookofsky & Hertz, *ibid.*, pp. 89–105.
393. That is the place where the physical transfer of the goods took place, as a result of which the purchaser obtained, or should have obtained, actual power of disposal over those goods at the final destination. Regarding *Car Trim* and *Electrosteel Europe SA v. Edil Centro SpA*, Case C-381-08 (9 Jun. 2011), *see* Lookofsky & Hertz, *ibid.*
394. That is, CISG Art. 57 is no longer relevant as regards the jurisdiction of EU Member State courts in these cases either. *See infra*, No. 244.
395. Regarding Art. 6, *see supra*, Nos 70 et seq.

Taken together, the seller's obligation to deliver and the buyer's obligation to pay are rightly regarded as 'constructive conditions concurrent'.[396] So if the buyer fails to perform its obligation, the seller will, absent contrary agreement (e.g., to extend credit), be entitled to withhold its performance (delivery) – this even though the Convention does not expressly so state.[397]

D. *Contracts of Carriage: Documents*

160. If the contract involves carriage, the seller will often dispatch the goods on terms whereby documents controlling their disposition (e.g., a negotiable bill of lading) will not be handed over to the buyer except against payment of the price.[398] Article 34 sets forth certain supplementary provisions which relate to this situation.[399] These seemingly superfluous rules were made necessary by reason of the CISG drafting technique.[400]

IV. Conformity of the Goods and Third-Party Claims

161. CISG Part III, Chapter II, section II (Articles 35–44) covers a topic of great practical importance: conformity of the goods and third-party claims.

A. *Conformity of the Goods*

162. A substantial portion of all sales litigation relates to claims by buyers that the goods are in some sense defective, that is, in that they do not conform to that which has been agreed. As regards international sales subject to the CISG, Article 35 lays down the supplementary rules.

396. *See also infra*, No. 246.
397. *See* Arrondissementsrechtbank Arnhem, 31 Jan. 2008, available at http://www.unilex.info/cisg/case/1340 (CISG contains no provision giving either party right to withhold performance, but case law and doctrine agree such a right can be inferred from Art. 58).
398. Regarding Art. 58, *see infra*, Nos 245 et seq.
399. Article 34 provides as follows:

> If the seller is bound to hand over documents relating to the goods, he must hand them over at the time and place and in the form required by the contract. If the seller has handed over documents before that time, he may, up to that time, cure any lack of conformity in the documents, if the exercise of this right does not cause the buyer unreasonable inconvenience or unreasonable expense. However, the buyer retains any right to claim damages as provided for in this Convention.

400. The first sentence of Art. 34 confirms the rule in Art. 6: *see supra*, Nos 70 et seq. Regarding the second sentence and the cure rule applicable to the goods themselves, *see infra*, Nos 183 et seq. Regarding the drafting technique, *see* Honnold/Flechtner, *Uniform Law* 4th ed. (2009), at 325.

B. Distinction Between Contractual and Delictual Claims

163. Before proceeding to examine the all-important conformity rules in Article 35, it should be remembered that the Convention governs only contractual rights.[401] Depending on the circumstances in the particular case, a given forum court might therefore find that certain domestic law rules relating to non-contractual duties can supplement – and complicate – the international regime.[402]

For example, even in a case where a seller cannot be said to have assumed (or breached) any contractual (promissory) commitment in the Article 35 sense, the applicable domestic law of tort (delict) might still provide the buyer with damages for losses suffered by reason of reliance on negligent misrepresentation,[403] just as the buyer's claim for rescission arising by reason of a fraudulent misrepresentation regarding the quality of the goods could serve to supplement the CISG avoidance rules.[404] Similarly, courts might allow a product liability claim grounded in domestic rules of tort (negligence) to compete with a CISG claim for damages grounded in the seller's no-fault liability for damage to the buyer's property when the seller has delivered non-conforming goods.[405]

C. Conformity with Express Contractual Requirements (Description, Guarantee, Etc.)

164. Putting such tort-related considerations aside, we turn our focus to the all-important contract-based rules in CISG Article 35. The first of these provides as follows:

> (1) The seller must deliver goods which are of the quantity, quality and description required by the contract and which are contained or packaged in the manner required by the contract.

---

401. Regarding Art. 4 *see* generally *supra*, Nos 62 et seq.

402. *Supra,* No. 65.

403. Regarding the relationship between contractual (CISG) and domestic delictual claims under Israeli law, *see* the *Pamesa v. Mendelson* (2009), available at http://cisgw3.law.pace.edu/cases/090317i5.html (trial court essentially correct in considering claim that seller negligent in manufacturing goods). In American tort law, the tendency is clearly to treat a misrepresentation action as a separate matter from the contract; *see*, for example, *Miami Valley Paper* (*supra*, No. 64, note 138) citing J. Lookofsky, 'In Dubio Pro Conventione? Some Thoughts about Opt-outs, Computer Programs and Preëmption under the 1980 Vienna Sales Convention CISG', *Duke Journal of Comparative and International Law* 13 (2003), also available at https://scholarship.law.duke.edu/djcil/vol13/iss3/11/. *See* generally J. Lookofsky, 'Not Running Wild with the CISG', *Journal of Law and Commerce* 29(1) (2011), also at https://papers.ssrn.com/sol3/papers.cfm?abstract_id=2376353.

404. *See supra*, Nos 63–64. *But compare* F. Ferrari & M. Torsello, *International Sales Law – CISG in a Nutshell* 2nd ed. (2018), at 217 (whenever misleading information relates to goods, situation must be deemed to fall within the scope of Art. 35, so application of concurrent domestic rules precluded).

405. *See* generally *supra*, No. 69.

Paragraph (1) of Article 35 serves to express the familiar contractual principle whereby the obligations of the parties are, in the first instance, defined by their own agreement.[406]

In one simple yet illustrative CISG case,[407] a Turkish company had promised to deliver 1,000 tonnes of fresh cucumbers to a buyer doing business in Germany, but the seller allegedly delivered less than that amount. Since the CISG applied, the seller was obligated to deliver goods of the quantity required by the contract, and so delivery of less than 1,000 tonnes constituted a contractual breach.[408]

Another straightforward illustration of the Article 35(1) principle involved a German seller's obligation to deliver steel bars in lots to a Syrian buyer.[409] The contract expressly permitted a weight variation of 5%, but since some of the bars delivered fell outside this range, the seller was held to have breached its obligation to deliver steel bars which, as of the passing of risk, conformed to the quality and description required by the contract.[410]

Depending on the circumstances, the fact that the contract expressly describes the goods as possessing a particular quality (X) might be understood to impliedly exclude a different quality (Y). In a Finnish case, the contract expressly provided for the delivery of 40,000 kilos of 'steam treated' powdered paprika which the buyer used in seasoning mixes produced in accordance with its customers' recipes. In addition to being steam treated, however, the powdered paprika delivered by the seller had also been radiated – this in contradiction of an impending EU Directive. On this basis, the Finnish court held that the goods failed to conform to the contract under Article 35(1).[411]

Since Article 35(1) requires that the seller deliver goods of the quality and description 'required by the contract', the seller must, *inter alia*, deliver goods which conform with an express contractual guarantee – for example, if the seller warrants or guarantees that a machine will run for a 'minimum of 10,000 working hours'. Indeed, for purposes of Article 35(1), there may be little difference between such a performance guarantee and the seller's mere description of the performance-characteristics of the goods.[412]

---

406. Regarding Art. 6, *see supra*, Nos 70 et seq. *See also* J. Lookofsky, 'Tooling up for Warranties with the CISG Case Digest', *CILE Studies, The CISG and the Business Lawyer: The UNCITRAL Digest as a Contract Drafting Tool* 4 (2008).
407. *See*, for example, Oberlandesgericht Düsseldorf (Germany), 8 Jan. 1993, CLOUT Case 48, also available at www.cisg.law.pace.edu/cases/930108g1.html.
408. However, since timely notice of non-conformity was not given pursuant to Arts 38(1) and 39(1), the buyer lost the right to rely on the alleged breach. Regarding this aspect of the case, *see infra*, Nos 187 et seq.
409. ICC Case No. 6653/1993, CLOUT Case 103, abstract available at www.unilex.info/cisg/case/36.
410. The conformity determination is usually made as of the passing of risk, even though the lack of conformity first becomes apparent at a later point in time: regarding Art. 36, *see infra*, Nos 180 et seq.
411. *See* Court of Appeal, Turku, Finland, 24 May 2005, English translation available at http://cisgw3.law.pace.edu/cases/050524f5.html.
412. For this reason, it is difficult to see the need for the 'special' guarantee rule set forth in para. (2) of Art. 36: *see infra*, No. 182. On the other hand, an express guarantee with respect to durability, etc., may be significant if interpreted as a contractual deviation from the usual two-year period in para. (2) of Art. 39: *see infra*, No. 195.

That said, an agreement as to quality within the purview of Article 35(1) need not take the form of express words. If, prior to the conclusion of a contract for the sale of marble, the buyer provides the seller with a sample or model marble slab, thus indicating the buyer's expectations, and the seller does not indicate his or her unwillingness or inability to deliver goods of that kind, then the characteristics of the slab will impliedly become part and parcel of parties' contract under Article 35(1), that is, their (implied) agreement with respect to the quality of the goods.[413]

CISG case law also confirms that the parties' agreement as to packaging need not be expressed in words. An Italian seller sold parmesan cheese knowing that it would be resold in France (the buyer's country), but the cheese was subsequently delivered in packaging that did not comply with French food-labelling regulations. Holding that the goods did not conform to the contract within the meaning of Article 35, the French court took pains to interpret the parmesan seller's intent under Article 8, finding it indisputable, by virtue of the relations pursued by the parties for at least several months, that the seller knew the parmesan sachets ordered by the buyer would be marketed in France, and that this knowledge imposed a duty on the seller to interpret the order as pertaining to goods which complied with the marketing regulations of the French market.[414] Along similar lines, goods not accompanied by instructions written in a language which (the seller ought to know) was not understandable to the buyer do not conform to the contract.[415]

D. Supplementary Convention Obligations

1. Introduction: Implied Obligations, Express Disclaimer, Etc.

165. Paragraph (2) of Article 35 sets forth a series of implied obligations as to the quality of the goods which the Convention, as a starting point, imposes on every CISG seller. For this reason, today's international buyer is legally entitled to expect the goods to possess certain basic qualities, even if the contract does not expressly so state.[416]

Before proceeding to discuss the significant impact of the individual implied obligations set forth in Article 35(2), however, it should be noted that these duties are not to be implied in cases where the parties have (validly) agreed otherwise.

---

413. *See*, for example, OLG Graz (Austria), 9 Nov. 1995, available at http://www.unilex.info/cisg/case/370, as reported in UNILEX. As noted in the decision, the same result can be reached by analogy with Art. 35(2)(c), a rule directly applicable where the seller provides the sample or model: *see infra*, No. 170.

414. Cour d'appel, Grenoble, 13 Sep. 1995, CLOUT Case 202, available at www.unilex.info/cisg/case/151 and at http://cisgw3.law.pace.edu/cisg/wais/db/cases2/950913f1.html#cx. *See also* R. Henschel, *The Conformity of Goods in International Sales* (2005), at 185–187. *See also infra*, No. 170 with note 439.

415. *See* F. Ferrari & M. Torsello, *International Sales Law – CISG in a Nutshell* 2nd ed. (2018), at 265, citing LG Darmstadt (Germany), 9 May 2000, available at http://www.unilex.info/cisg/case/501 (missing product-information in French and Italian; buyer lost right to rely on alleged non-conformity due to failure to provide timely notice).

416. *See Secretariat Commentary*, Comment 13 at 94 (regarding Art. 33 of the 1978 Draft).

In other words, an express (*caveat emptor*) provision in the contract – for example, whereby the seller 'undertakes no obligations whatsoever in respect of the goods fitness for ordinary and/or particular purposes' – will serve to displace (negate) the obligations otherwise implied by subparagraphs (a) and (b) of Article 35(2), provided that the express provision (disclaimer, etc.) is valid under the applicable domestic rules of law.[417]

2. Fitness for Ordinary Purposes

166. Article 35(2) is comprised of four subparts: (a)–(d). All apply to all CISG contracts, unless the parties have agreed otherwise. The standards stated in these subparts are cumulative; that is, the goods do not conform to the contract unless they meet the standards of all applicable subparts.

Subparagraphs (a) and (b) of Article 35(2) contain the gap-filling implied obligations which are of greatest practical importance:[418]

> (2) Except where the parties have agreed otherwise, the goods do not conform with the contract unless they:
> a. are fit for the purposes for which goods of the same description would ordinarily be used;
> b. are fit for any particular purpose expressly or impliedly made known to the seller at the time of the conclusion of the contract, except where the circumstances show that the buyer did not rely, or that it was unreasonable for him to rely, on the seller's skill and judgment. …

As regards the first test of non-conformity – set forth in subparagraph (a) – it is significant that goods often are ordered simply by denoting their general description, that is, without any indication to the seller as to the buyer's particular purpose (intended special use).[419] In such cases, subparagraph (a) will be especially relevant, since, absent agreement to the contrary, the seller automatically undertakes an implied obligation that the goods sold will – at the minimum – be fit for the purposes for which goods of the same description would ordinarily be used. For this reason, the highest French court has held that ceramic ovenware which was not resistant to high oven temperatures was not fit for ordinary (baking) purposes,[420]

---

417. *See supra*, Nos 63 and 72 and *infra*, Nos 173 et seq. Although the Convention does not obligate the buyer to undertake a *pre*-contractual inspection of the goods, a limited *caveat emptor*-type exception applies under Art. 35(3): *see infra*, No. 172.
418. *See UNCITRAL Digest of CISG Case Law*, Art. 35 (2016 ed.), available at https://uncitral.un.org/en/case_law/digests.
419. *See* A/CONF./97/5, *Secretariat's Commentary* to Art. 33 of the 1978 Draft Convention.
420. *See* Cour de cassation, France, 17 Dec. 1996, CLOUT Case 206, available at http://cisgw3.law.pace.edu/cases/961217f1.html.

and a Spanish court has held that a machine forming part of a production line was unfit for its purpose (production in that line) when it failed to produce a single part.[421]

Within the context of international trade, resale must be considered an ordinary use;[422] and so a CISG buyer who purchases for resale is entitled to expect goods which are resalable in the ordinary course of business. What is resalable will then depend upon the reasonable expectations of the ultimate purchasers. If, for example, a furniture merchant purchases sofas for resale to consumers, the goods are not fit for ordinary purposes if the cushions slide forward when the consumers sit down.[423]

When it comes to perishable food products, consumption by ordinary consumers must of course be considered an ordinary purpose (use). Ordinary does not mean perfect, however, and the German Supreme Court (BGH) has held that New Zealand mussels sold by a Swiss seller to a German buyer were fit for ordinary purposes, notwithstanding the fact that the mussels delivered contained cadmium at a level higher than that recommended by the German Federal Department of Health:[424] more generally, the court held that the quality requirements imposed by public law in the buyer's country are only relevant in the context of Article 35(2) if the seller had good reason to know of their existence.[425] In another German case, emphasizing the parties' prior commercial dealing, the delivery of paprika not complying with the minimum standards of German public law was held to constitute a breach of the seller's implied promise under Article 35(1).[426]

---

421. *See* Fuenlabrada Court of First Instance, 11 May 2012, at CLOUT Case 1343, also at http://www.unilex.info/cisg/case/1824.

422. *See* A/CONF./97/5, *Secretariat's Commentary* to Art. 33 of the 1978 Draft Convention.

423. *See* Pretura della giurisdizione di Locarno-Campagna, Switzerland, 27 Apr. 1992, CLOUT Case 56, available at www.cisg.law.pace.edu/cases/920427s1.html. In this case, however, the buyer lost the right to rely on the non-conformity because of failure to provide timely notification under Art. 39: *see infra*, Nos 187 et seq.

424. *See* BGH, 8 Mar. 1995, CLOUT Case 123 available at www.cisg.law.pace.edu/cases/950308g3.html. Significantly, the cadmium in the mussels delivered would pose a risk only to persons who consumed great quantities. Moreover, the maximum level fixed by the Department was the subject of a recommendation, as opposed to a binding directive. The BGH did not address the question of whether under Art. 35 the goods must be of 'average' quality or merely 'merchantable', since the buyer in the case concerned had not established (in the court below) that the mussels delivered contained more cadmium than New Zealand mussels in general. For a commentary, *see* Schlechtriem in IPRax 1996 at 12. *See also* J. Lookofsky, 'Tooling Up for Warranties with the CISG Case Digest', *CILE Studies, The CISG and the Business Lawyer: The UNCITRAL Digest as a Contract Drafting Tool*, vol. 4 (2008), ¶¶ 7 et seq.

425. *See* BGH, *ibid. Accord Medical Marketing International, Inc. v. Internazionale Medico Scientifica S.r.l.*, 1999 WL 311945 (E.D. La.), 1999 US Dist. LEXIS 7380, also reported in UNILEX: the medical equipment supplied by the Italian seller did not comply with American public law; citing (and distinguishing) the 1995 BGH decision (*see* preceding note), the arbitrators found that, due to special circumstances, the seller knew or should have known of the regulations at issue. *See also* Lookofsky, 'Tooling Up', *ibid.*

426. L.G. Ellwangen, 21 Aug. 1995 http://unilex.info/cisg/case/164. *See also* Bundesgerichtshof (Germany), 26 Sep. 2012, available at http://www.unilex.info/cisg/case/1684 (buyer of clay for potato grading could reasonably expect separated potatoes to be fit for animal feeding without washing them thoroughly after grading, especially since such cleansing was not mandatory under the relevant legal framework).

Subsequently, the High Court of New Zealand summarized the (German) 'New Zealand Mussels Case' rule and its exceptions as follows:

> As a general rule, the seller is not responsible for compliance with the regulatory provisions or standards of the importing country, even if he or she knows the destination of the goods, unless:
>
> a. The same regulations exist in the seller's country.
> b. The buyer drew the seller's attention to the regulatory provisions and relied on the seller's expertise.
> c. The seller knew or should have known of the requirements because of special circumstances, including the fact that:
>   – the seller has maintained a branch in the importing country,
>   – a long-standing connection between the parties,
>   – seller has often exported into the buyer's country,
>   – the seller has promoted its products in the buyer's country.[427]

The kind of goods which are sometimes described as 'durable' goods (washing machines, industrial machinery, automobiles, etc.) are not fit for their ordinary purposes unless they remain durable (usable) for an ordinary period of time. A new refrigerator with a lifespan of only a few weeks or months of use would clearly not be fit for the ordinary purposes to which refrigerators are usually put (long-term use).[428] The precise period is, of course, a determination which will vary depending on the nature of the particular goods, and the CISG can hardly be expected to provide detailed guidance on this point.[429]

The CISG standard which requires that goods be fit for 'ordinary' purposes has been compared to such domestic standards as 'merchantable' quality or 'average' quality.[430] Citing a third academic theory,[431] as well as the general CISG principle of 'reasonableness', a Dutch arbitral tribunal has held a CISG seller bound to deliver condensate (crude oil mix) of *reasonable* quality.[432]

---

427. *See* High Court of New Zealand, 30 Jul. 2010, *RJ & AM Smallmon v. Transport Sales Limited and Grant Alan Miller*, available at http://www.unilex.info/cisg/case/1595 (fact that seller had previously advertised and exported trucks in Australia insufficient to prove it knew or should have known of applicable Australian regulations); affd. by Court of Appeal of New Zealand, 22 Jul. 2011, CLOUT Case 1256, also at http://www.unilex.info/cisg/case/1617.
428. *Accord* (as regards fitness for *particular* purpose) Landgericht München, Germany, 27 Feb. 2002, English translation available at http://cisgw3.law.pace.edu/cases/020227g1.html (clear to seller that buyer sought to acquire goods as *permanent* furniture for its offices; although no specific contract provision dealing with lifespan, implied that parties agreed to long-term operational life; court assumed impliedly operational lifetime of three years).
429. *See also infra*, Nos 181–182.
430. *See* BGH, 8 Mar. 1995, *supra*. *See also* Landgericht Coburg, Germany, 12 Dec. 2006, available in translation at http://cisgw3.law.pace.edu/cases/061212g1.html (goods that meet expectations of average user).
431. Originally advanced by Bernstein & Lookofsky, *Understanding the CISG in Europe* (1997), §4.7 (CISG buyers' reasonable expectation of reasonable use value for money).
432. *See* the award of Netherlands Arbitration Institute in the *Rijn Blend* case, 15 Oct. 2002, Nos 71 and 117. Applying this standard, the tribunal held that the Rijn Blend delivered in 1998 did not meet the reasonable quality requirement for at least two reasons (price and the long-term nature of the

3. Fitness for Particular Purposes

167. Prior to the conclusion of the contract, the seller may have been made aware of the particular purpose to which the goods will be put. If so, the seller assumes an implied obligation under Article 35(2)(b) that the goods are fit for such purpose, in that the buyer may reasonably rely on the seller's skill and judgment in this respect.

In one relevant example, a French seller and a Portuguese buyer had concluded a contract for the sale and dismantlement of a second-hand aircraft hangar. The French court held that the seller had breached the contract by delivering certain elements which were not fit for the particular purpose which the buyer had made known to the seller (reassembling the hangar in the original way). In this situation, once the buyer's particular purpose was made known to the seller, the buyer was entitled to expect goods fit for that purpose.[433]

In other cases, however – where the buyer either does not make his or her particular purpose known, or does not rely on the seller's skill and judgment, or if it is unreasonable for the buyer to so rely – no obligation as to fitness for the buyer's particular purpose will be implied.

168. In some cases, the implied obligations set forth in subparagraphs (2)(a) and (2)(b) of Article 35 will overlap, in that a given buyer's particular purpose may well correspond to the purpose to which such goods are generally put. For example, a Swiss arbitral tribunal has held that 'pocket ash-trays' with dangerously sharp edges were unfit for ordinary use,[434] but the same goods might also be described as unfit for their particular purpose.[435] In such overlapping instances, any failure to comply with the reasonable reliance test in subparagraph (2)(b) will be inconsequential as regards the establishment of a contractual breach in relation to subparagraph (2)(a).

4. Conditions and Warranties under Domestic Law Distinguished

169. The implied obligations set forth in subparagraphs (2)(a) and (2)(b) of Article 35 resemble the obligation to supply what Common lawyers call (a) merchantable goods and (b) goods fit for the purpose. But, in contrast with traditional

---

sales contracts). The award, available at http://cisgw3.law.pace.edu/cases/021015n1.html, has been cited with approval by Schwenzer in Schlechtriem & Schwenzer, *Commentary* 4th ed. (2016), at 602 with note 108, in that 'reasonable quality' focuses on the buyer's justified expectations, as does Art. 35(2)(b). Regarding CISG general principles *see supra*, Nos 78 et seq.

433. *See* Cour d'appel de Grenoble, Chambre Commerciale, 26 Apr. 1995, abstract available at www.unilex.info/cisg/case/109.

434. *See* Bundesgericht, Switzerland, 10 Oct. 2005, abstract at www.unilex.info/cisg/case/1094.

435. *See*, e.g., Landgericht München, Germany, 27 Feb. 2002, English translation available at http://cisgw3.law.pace.edu/cases/020227g1.html (clear to seller that buyer sought to acquire goods as permanent furniture for its offices; although no specific contract provision dealing with lifespan, implied that parties agreed to long-term operational life, at least three years).

English and American terminology, the CISG subsumes the delivery of unfit-for-purpose goods under the heading of goods which do 'not conform' with the contract. And since the CISG seller cannot be said to have breached a 'condition' or 'warranty' (in the Common law sense),[436] no remedial consequences can be deduced solely on the basis of the quality implications of Article 35.[437]

5. Sample or Model; Packaging

product = must match sample

170. Article 35, subparagraph (2)(c) imposes a further obligation upon the seller regarding conformity to the qualities of goods which the seller has held out to the buyer as a sample or model. By virtue of this CISG provision, if a seller of Swiss cheese or of computer software provides his or her buyer with a sample of same, the seller is (impliedly) obligated to deliver goods which conform to the sample.[438] Subparagraph (2)(d) of Article 35 requires that the goods be contained or packaged in the manner usual for such goods or, where there is no such manner, in a manner adequate to preserve and protect the goods. For example, as regards the first of these criteria, a CISG seller who is – or should be – aware of the buyer's intention to purchase foodstuffs which can be resold in France, in conformity with French law, must deliver goods which are wrapped in the manner required by French law.[439]

As previously noted, neither of these Article 35(2) duties is to be implied in cases where the parties to the CISG contract have (validly) agreed otherwise.[440]

---

436. Such Common law terminology is foreign to the Convention. Regarding implied conditions under the English Sale of Goods Act UK (1979), *see* G. Treitel, *The Law of Contract* 12th ed. (2007), paras 18-053 et seq., and *compare* the corresponding 'implied warranties' in §§ 2-313, 2-314, and 2-315 of the American Uniform Commercial Code.

437. Regarding the CISG buyer's right to recover damages for seller's non-conforming delivery, *see infra*, Nos 209 et seq.; Regarding the right to avoid in the event of such breach, *see infra*, Nos 226 et seq. As already indicated (*supra*, No. 64), the Convention addresses only *inter partes* problems: thus, CISG Art. 35 regarding conformity of the goods displaces, for example, an American seller's warranties vis-à-vis his buyer, but the Convention contains no counterpart to UCC §2-318.

438. *See*, for example, LG München (Germany), 8 Feb. 1995, CLOUT Case 123, available at http://cisgw3.law.pace.edu/cases/950208g1.html. Some might reach the same result by the application of Art. 35(1), in that the sample provided will usually serve to indicate the quality 'required by the contract', that is, without the need to resort to a gap-filling rule; Regarding the 'express warranty' created by sample or model under American domestic law, *see* White & Summers, *Uniform Commercial Code* 6th ed. (2010), §9-6. Regarding CISG samples, *see also* J. Lookofsky, 'Tooling Up for Warranties with the CISG Case Digest', *CILE Studies, the CISG and the Business Lawyer: The UNCITRAL Digest as a Contract Drafting Tool*, vol. 4 (2008), ¶ 11. Regarding the special situation where a CISG *buyer* provides the sample or model, *see supra*, No. 164.

439. *See* Cour d'appel de Grenoble (France), Chambre Commerciale, 13 Sep. 1995, CLOUT Case 202, cited *supra*, No. 164 with note 415 as regards Art. 35(1); the Court's opinion refers only/generally to 'Article 35'. *See also* COMPRIMEX award of 29 Apr. 1996, available at http://cisgw3.law.pace.edu/cases/960429m1.html.

440. *See supra*, No. 165.

E. *Seller's Knowledge of Defect Irrelevant*

171. The seller's implied obligations are not generally dependent upon the seller's state of mind. In other words, the seller is obligated to deliver goods which meet the requirements set forth in Article 35(2)(a)–(d) whether or not he or she 'knew or could have been aware' of a given non-conformity at the time of contracting.[441]

And as highlighted later, the seller's state of mind is also essentially irrelevant when it comes to the Convention's supplementary remedial rules: the CISG seller is liable in damages on a no-fault basis, *inter alia*, for breach of the implied obligation to deliver conforming goods.[442]

F. *Caveat Emptor and Pre-contractual Inspection of Goods*

172. As already indicated, the CISG seller automatically (by default) undertakes the Convention catalogue of implied obligations with respect to fitness for purpose, etc., set forth in Article 35(2) – at least in the absence of an express contractual provision to the contrary (a warranty-limitation, disclaimer of liability, or the like).[443]

Moving in a slightly seller-friendly direction, however, Article 35(3) of the Convention represents a limited remnant of the classical *caveat emptor* (buyer-beware) rule. According to this provision, the seller is not liable under subparagraphs (2)(a)–(d) for any lack of conformity of the goods if, at the time of the conclusion of the contract, the buyer 'knew or could not have been unaware' of such lack of conformity.[444]

So, although the CISG does not impose upon the buyer any pre-contractual duty to inspect,[445] a buyer who in fact undertakes such an inspection and actually becomes 'aware', for example, that the goods offered for sale are not fit for a particular intended purpose, is assumed to purchase such goods as he or she finds them; the same is true of a buyer who for some other reason 'could not have been unaware' of such lack of conformity – a test which is arguably more buyer-friendly

441. *Compare* the corresponding qualification as regards third-party claims based on industrial or intellectual property in Art. 42, discussed *infra*, Nos 201 et seq. Regarding the seller's knowledge of buyer's 'particular purpose', *see supra*, No. 167.

442. *See infra*, No. 211. Regarding the effect of an Art. 79 'exemption', *see infra*, Nos 302 et seq.

443. As regards disclaimers and liability limitations, etc., *see infra*, Nos 173 et seq.

444. According to the French version of the treaty text:

> Le vendeur n'est pas responsable, au regard des alinéas a) à d) du paragraphe précédent, d'un défaut de conformité que l'acheteur connaissait ou ne pouvait ignorer au moment de la conclusion du contrat.

So in the French version, the alternative to 'knew' (*connaissait*) is 'could not ignore (*ne pouvait ignorer*). *See* generally J. Lookofsky, "Cator Can't Compete: Caveat Emptor under CISG Article 35(3)?"', Chapter 10 in *The CISG Convention and Domestic Contract Law. Harmony, Cross-Inspiration or Discord?* (J. Lookofsky & M. Andersen eds, 2014), also available at http://ssrn.com/abstract=2573770.

445. Regarding Art. 38, *see infra*, Nos 190 et seq.

than the familiar 'ought to know' standard.[446] In such clear-cut situations, i.e., where the buyer knew or could not have been unaware of the non-conformity in question, it seems fair to maintain a *caveat emptor*-type rule (what you see is what you get), that is, the otherwise implied obligations in subparagraphs (2)(a)–(2)(d) notwithstanding, assuming at least that the seller concerned was not herself guilty of fraudulent conduct.[447]

G. Disclaimer and Limitation of Liability

1. Introduction

173. A subject of great practical significance is the seller's ability to disclaim or limit his or her implied obligations as regards quality and/or the extent of his or her liability for breach of those obligations.

As already emphasized, the implied obligations set forth in Article 35(2) apply by default, i.e., '[e]xcept where the parties have agreed otherwise'. This proviso is in accord with the general Article 6 freedom-of-contract rule, in that the parties may derogate from or vary the effect of any [Convention] provisions. 'Repair-or-replace' clauses, for example, are among the common tools by which the seller's seek to adjust the remedies otherwise available to buyers in cases where the goods delivered do not conform.[448]

Beyond this, an express contract term might provide that the seller 'accepts no responsibility whatsoever that the goods are fit for any particular purpose, whether or not such purpose has been made known to him', thus purporting to displace the implied obligation set forth in Article 35(2)(b). But that implied obligation will only

446. *See*, for example, Tribunal Cantonal Valais (Switzerland), 28 Oct. 1997, CLOUT Case 219, available at http://cisgw3.law.pace.edu/cases/971028s1.html (buyer who actually tested tractor before purchase must have been aware of obvious defects); Federal Court of Australia, *Castel Electronics Pty. Ltd. v. Toshiba Singapore Pte. Ltd.*, 20 Apr. 2011, available at http://www.unilex.info/cisg/case/1641 (Art. 35(3) excludes liability only where specific circumstances giving rise to defect concerned were known or could not have been unknown by buyer when contract made); District Court Horsens (Denmark), 7 Dec. 2012, CLOUT Case 1364. *See* generally Lookofsky, 'Cator Can't Compete', *supra* note 444, at 136.

447. *See* OLG Köln (Germany), 21 May 1996, CLOUT Case 168, available at http://cisgw3.law.pace.edu/cases/960521g1.html (documents incorrectly indicated car first registered in 1992 and that mileage was low; even if buyer (car dealer) 'could not have been unaware' of non-conformity, the fraudulent seller could not rely on Art. 35(3)). In this situation the German court rightly opined that a seller guilty of fraudulent conduct cannot avail itself of the safety valve in Art. 35(3), *even if* the buyer's conduct could be described as 'grossly negligent'. *Accord* F. Ferrari & M. Torsello, *International Sales Law – CISG in a Nutshell* 2nd ed. (2018), at 274 (when more blame falls upon seller than negligent buyer, e.g., when seller hides defects, Art. 35(3) does not apply; solution justified by general CISG principle that negligent buyer deserves more protection than fraudulent seller). *See also* Lookofsky, 'Cator Can't Compete', *supra* preceding note, at 139 f.

Although para. (3) does not expressly apply to an Art. 35(1) express promise of quality, the same principle might well be applied by analogy. *Compare* Schwenzer in Schlechtriem & Schwenzer, *Commentary* 4th ed. (2016), at 614 with note 229, citing sources that indicate disagreement on the relationship between Art. 35(1) and 35(3).

448. *See supra*, No. 72.

be displaced if the (seemingly burdensome) clause in question is held *incorporated* into the overall contract, if it is *interpreted* in accordance with the draftsman's (liability-disclaiming) intent, and if domestic rules of *validity* do not get in the way. These conditions are discussed separately under heads 2–4 below.

2. Incorporation of Disclaimer

174. As already indicated, a given disclaimer or limitation of liability will not always achieve the (draftsman's) intended effect. For one thing, a given clause will only be effective if the clause can be described as incorporated into the contract, that is, as having become an integral part of the overall contract of sale. A disclaimer clause is likely to be hidden amidst the 'boilerplate' language in a seller's standard form, and courts will not always read surprising and/or unreasonably burdensome fine-print clauses as part of the deal. The Supreme Court of Germany, for example, has refused to allow a CISG seller to seek refuge in standard terms of agreement in a situation where the buyer had no reasonable access to their content.[449] CISG Article 19, which can be applied in a 'battle-of-forms' scenario, can also be relevant with respect to the incorporation of a disclaimer or liability limitation in one party's standard form.[450]

3. Interpretation of Disclaimer

175. Even a disclaimer clause which is deemed to be incorporated in the contract concerned will only achieve its intended effect if it is interpreted as 'covering' the situation concerned. In this connection, the Convention's reasonable-man standard (in Article 8) is likely to be applied, in that limitations and (especially) disclaimers of warranty and/or liability will continue to be construed narrowly (*contra proferentem*) by national courts, that is, against the draftsman,[451] unless the draftsman can prove, that it was the intent of both parties (e.g.) that the seller should not be liable in the event of (negligent) non-performance of his or her contractual duties, express or implied.[452]

A significant precedent in this connection is the finding by an arbitral tribunal in Stockholm that an express warranty concerning the quality of new machinery did not derogate from Article 35(2), since it contained 'only positive terms concerning the qualities that the goods would possess, and not negative terms relieving the

449. BGH, 31 Oct. 2001, CLOUT Case 445, available at http://cisgw3.law.pace.edu/cases/011031g1.html (standard conditions could only become part of offer if attached to it or otherwise placed at disposal of offeree.).
450. *See supra*, No. 123.
451. Regarding Art. 8, *see supra*, Nos 81 et seq. Regarding the applicability of the *contra proferentem* maxim in the CISG context *see* (e.g.) Bundesgerichtshof, Germany, 28 May 2014, available at http://www.unilex.info/cisg/case/1832 (citing, in addition to the views of *German* academics, CISG Advisory Council Opinion No. 13).
452. *See supra*, No. 79.

seller of responsibilities'.[453] In effect, the tribunal interpreted the seller's express guarantee – that the machine concerned was 'made of the best materials with first class workmanship, brand new and unused' – as a supplement to (as opposed to a disclaimer of) the seller's implied CISG quality obligations.[454]

4. Validity of Disclaimer

176. Even where a given clause passes the incorporation and interpretation hurdles just described, the validity issue remains. As previously noted, the validity of the contract, hereunder the validity of a limitation or disclaimer of the implied obligations set forth in Article 35(2), is an issue which lies outside the CISG; and since the Convention is simply 'not concerned with' the validity of the contract or of any of its provisions, the validity of a clause purporting to disclaim or severely limit the application of CISG default liability rules must be settled in accordance with the applicable domestic law.[455]

5. Examples of the Application of Domestic Validity Rules

177. For example, under Swedish (and other Scandinavian) domestic law, a purported warranty or liability disclaimer will only be effective – even as between CISG merchants – if it passes a reasonableness test.[456] When the reasonableness of a disclaimer in a CISG contract is tested under American domestic law, the relevant question is whether the disclaimer is 'unconscionable' (UCC §2-302).[457] German courts have tested the validity of CISG liability disclaimers along similar lines.[458]

---

453. *See UNCITRAL Digest of CISG Case Law* (2016 ed.), Art. 35, note 25 and accompanying text, citing the award rendered by the Arbitration Institute of the Stockholm Chamber of Commerce, 5 Jun. 1998, CLOUT Case No. 237, full text available at http://cisgw3.law.pace.edu/cisg/wais/db/cases2/980605s5.html#ta. 'In the Tribunal's opinion, it cannot be sufficient to include in the contract warranties dealing in positive terms with general aspects of quality, as is the case in the present Contract. In fact, Clause 13 of the Contract would seem to contain exactly the sort of undertaking to which Art. 35(1) refers and which shall be supplemented, unless the parties agree otherwise, with the subsequent general "guarantees" of the article. Hence, the Tribunal cannot find that the parties have derogated in the Contract from the CISG provisions on fitness for purpose.'

454. *See* J. Lookofsky, 'Tooling Up for Warranties with the CISG Case Digest', *CILE Studies, the CISG and the Business Lawyer: The UNCITRAL Digest as a Contract Drafting Tool*, vol. 4 (2008), ¶ 5.

455. Regarding Art. 4(a) *see supra*, Nos 62 et seq.

456. Regarding the 'general clause' (§36) of the Uniform Scandinavian Contracts Acts, *see* generally, J. Lookofsky, 'The Limits of Commercial Contract Freedom: Under the UNIDROIT "Restatement" and Danish Law', *American Journal of Comparative Law* XLVI (1998) 485–508.

457. That is, assuming that the relevant rules of private international law point to American law. *See* generally, J. Lookofsky, 'Loose Ends and Contorts in International Sales', *American Journal of Comparative Law* 33 (1991) 403, 410 et seq.

458. *See* OLG Köln (Germany), 21 May 1996, CLOUT Case 168, available at http://cisgw3.law.pace.edu/cases/960521g1.html (contract documents incorrectly indicated car first registered in 1992 and that mileage was low; Italian seller, acting fraudulently, had breached Art. 35(1) duty to deliver confirming goods and could not rely on clause excluding liability for lack of conformity, since clause was invalid under German domestic law).

Quite apart from such instances of express censorship of unreasonable terms, national courts can also reach similar results by employing more covert judicial means, in that courts sometimes seem willing to 'interpret' their way 'around' an unfair – albeit incorporated and technically valid – disclaimer clause.[459]

6. Validity Versus Substance

178. In some contexts, courts may have to confront the fact that the line between (domestic) validity and (CISG) substance is not always clear.

To take one relevant example of the relationship between these conceptions, an unusual clause does not become 'part of the contract' under German law if the other party did not have reason to expect it under the circumstances, especially as regards the 'appearance' of the contract.[460] The German statute which lays down this rule, while formally tied to rules of contract formation, functions as a rule of validity and should (when otherwise applicable) therefore supplement – and not be displaced (pre-empted) by – the rules which regulate CISG contract formation or the seller's obligations under the CISG regime.[461]

According to §2-316(2) of the American Uniform Commercial Code (UCC), a warranty disclaimer is without effect unless it is 'conspicuous' and mentions the word 'merchantability'. While it might well be argued that this too is a validity rule (in some respects similar to the German provision just noted), the merchantability requirement is so closely tied to American substantive law (UCC §2-313) that it presumably renders the rule in §2-316(2) inappropriate – and arguably also ineffective – in the CISG context.[462] That interpretation of the inapplicability of §2-316(2) in the CISG context notwithstanding, an American court could still hold a given disclaimer (which passes the incorporation and interpretation tests) 'unconscionable' under UCC §2-302.[463]

459. *See supra*, No. 175.

460. BGB §305c(1), available in English translation at www.gesetze-im-internet.de/englisch_bgb/englisch_bgb.html#BGBengl_000P305c.

461. *See* J. Lookofsky, *Understanding the CISG* 5th Worldwide ed. (2017), at 182–183. *Compare* Art. 2.1.20(1) of the *UNIDROIT Principles of International Commercial Contracts* (International Institute for the Unification of Private Law 4th ed. (2016)), 'No term contained in standard terms which is of such a character that the other party could not reasonably have expected it, is effective unless it has been expressly accepted by that other party.' As with similar domestic law constructs, this UNIDROIT 'Formation' provision is best characterized as a validity (reasonableness) rule: *see* J. Lookofsky, 'The Limits of Commercial Contract Freedom', *American Journal of Comparative Law* 46 (1998) 485, 495–508.

462. *Accord* Honnold/Flechtner, *Uniform Law* 4th ed. (2009), at 340. Regarding 'merchantability' under American and English substantive law, *see supra*, No. 169.

463. *See supra*, Nos 174–177. It should nonetheless again be emphasized that, as between merchants, UCC §2-302 is applied very sparingly by American courts.

7. Convention as Validity Yardstick

179. Although the CISG is (generally) 'not concerned with' validity (Article 4), it has been argued that the Convention serves not just as a gap-filler but also as a 'yardstick':[464] Since the CISG remedial system aims at justice between the parties,[465] it may be seen as providing a fair (substantive) default regime in the average case, and this makes it relevant as regards the proper application of validity rules which strive to maintain a reasonable balance between contractual obligations and remedial relief.

Of course, the CISG does not represent the only fair remedial regime, but a remedial alternative set forth in the parties' contract should, at the minimum, provide each party with the potential for *minimum adequate remedial relief.* So if, for example, the contract in question is based on standard terms which place an unreasonable limit on the buyer's right to claim damages or to avoid in the event fundamental breach, in that these terms fail to provide the buyer with alternative remedial relief, the reasonableness-tests of domestic law, perhaps acting in tandem with the CISG general principle of good faith, can serve to (re)activate the supplementary CISG remedial rule.[466] Indeed, if an oppressive standard term contradicts CISG fundamental principles (*Grundwertungen*), a court might deny the term effect for that reason alone, that is, even if the term in question would be valid under the otherwise applicable domestic law.[467]

464. *See* P. Schlechtriem, 'The Sellers Obligations under the United Nations Convention on Contracts for the International Sale of Goods', in *International Sales* (Galston & Smit eds, 1984), at 6-6 (regarding clauses imposed through the use of standard terms, etc.).

465. J. Hellner, 'The Vienna Convention and Standard Form Contracts', in *International Sale of Goods: Dubrovnik Lectures* (Volken Sarcevic eds, 1986), 351.

466. The (arguably) 'general' CISG good-faith principle (*supra,* Nos 77 et seq.) *accords* the award rendered by the Arbitration Institute of the Stockholm Chamber of Commerce on 5 Jun. 1998, CLOUT Case 237, extensive extract available at http://www.unilex.info/cisg/case/338. In this case, an American seller and Chinese buyer had concluded a contract for the sale of a press for the production of frame rails for light trucks. The seller, who first had received buyer's notice of defects some three years after delivery, was held liable in damages, notwithstanding the fact that the contract expressly provided the buyer with an eighteen-month warranty period. The contract also contained a clause excluding consequential or incidental damages, but the text of the award in UNILEX does not reveal the nature or extent of the damages awarded. *Compare* Cour d'appel Bourges, France, 7 Jan. 2016, cited *infra,* note 533.

467. *Accord* Oberster Gerichtshof (Austria), 7 Sep. 2000, CLOUT Case 428, abstract available at www.unilex.info/cisg/case/473 (German seller's terms provided S could cure defects, replace goods (gravestones) or refund the price, whereas B could not withhold payment; term restricting B's right to withhold payment (valid under German domestic law) did not contravene CISG fundamental principles, since term would be narrowly interpreted so as not to deprive B of its fundamental CISG right to avoid or claim compensation if the goods remained useless despite S' attempts to cure).

H. Time of Conformity Determination

1. Introduction

180. As discussed in the foregoing (Nos 164 et seq.) Article 35 sets forth the conditions which must be satisfied in order for the goods to conform to the contract and the CISG. Article 36 provides a rule which defines the point in time at which the conformity of the goods is to be judged.

2. The General Rule

181. The general rule is set forth in Article 36, paragraph (1):

> The seller is liable in accordance with the contract and this Convention for any lack of conformity which exists at the time when the risk passes to the buyer, even though the lack of conformity becomes apparent only after that time.

This rule is tied to the rules regarding the passing of risk set forth in Articles 66 et seq., as sometimes supplemented or replaced by analogous Incoterms provisions.[468] And it is logical that the CISG conformity determination takes place as of the passing of risk, in that, according to Articles 66 et seq., the risk passes at the point in time when the seller delivers the goods, that is, performs his or her primary obligation under the CISG contract of sale.

Although the risk of accidental loss or destruction usually passes to the buyer when the seller hands the goods over to a carrier (for transmission to the buyer),[469] Article 36(1) makes it clear that the seller remains liable for any non-conformity existing at that particular point in time, that is, even if the non-conformity in question first becomes discoverable by the buyer at a later point in time.[470]

In this connection, it is important to note that goods will generally not be considered fit for ordinary and/or special purposes unless they are of such quality that they *remain fit* for such purposes for a reasonable period of time after delivery.[471] If, however, the goods are fit (conforming) when delivered, but are later damaged

468. *See infra*, Nos 267 et seq. *See also* US District Court, S.D.N.Y., 28 Sep. 2011, *Cedar Petrochemicals Inc. v. Dongbu Hannong Chemical Ltd.* available at http://www.unilex.info/cisg/case/1643 (allocation of risk between seller and buyer for non-conformity under F.O.B. clause not in contradiction with Art. 36 CISG. F.O.B. terms imply seller liable if goods damaged before risk has passed to buyer; if damage occurs afterwards, buyer liable).

469. *Ibid.*

470. *See*, for example, the COMPRIMEX award of 29 Apr. 1996 reported in UNILEX, available at http://www.unilex.info/cisg/case/258 (seller liable for non-conformity – inadequate packaging – which existed when risk passed, even though non-conformity first became apparent later). Regarding time limitations which may preclude the buyer from asserting non-conformity discovered after delivery, *see* Arts 38–44, discussed *infra*, Nos 190 et seq.

471. *Compare infra*, No. 182 regarding lack of conformity which 'occurs' after delivery.

by the carrier's or some other TP's negligent act, the seller will have performed his or her obligations, and the buyer's only recourse will be against the carrier or such other person.

3. Subsequent Non-conformity

182. Paragraph (2) of Article 36 purports to provide a supplement to the general rule:

> The seller is also liable in accordance with the contract and this Convention for any lack of conformity which occurs after the time indicated in the preceding paragraph and which is due to a breach of any of his obligations, including a breach of any guarantee that for a period of time the goods will remain fit for their ordinary purpose or for some particular purpose or will retain specified qualities or characteristics.

As already emphasized in connection with the discussion of Article 35 above, CISG goods are not considered fit for ordinary or particular purposes unless they are fit and remain fit (for such purposes) for a reasonable time, that is, the period during which such goods normally/usually remain fit, assuming normal use. Article 36(1) shows that the relevant time for the entire non-conformity determination is the time at which the goods are delivered; conversely, the relevant point in time is not the time at which the non-conformity 'appears' (becomes apparent). For example, if the seller delivers washing machines which – due to a latent defect – are not capable of running more than a few weeks, such machines should be described as non-conforming as of the date of their delivery (even though this non-conformity might first be discovered later, when the machines break down).[472]

Article 36(2) expressly covers situations where, due to seller's breach, a given non-conformity occurs after delivery. This would seem to be a rule of extremely limited application which might render the seller liable in certain unusual situations not covered by the rule in paragraph (1). It would, for example, cover the situation where the seller – during the course of an attempt to cure a given non-conformity in goods previously delivered – bungles the job, thus giving rise to a (second) non-conformity (which did not exist at the time of delivery).

Apart from such cases, the main thrust of the rule in Article 36(2) seems difficult to understand.[473] Article 36(2) seems mainly directed at a breach of a guarantee that the goods will remain fit or will retain specified qualities or characteristics. But in cases where the seller breaches an express or implied 'guarantee' of this kind, the breach 'occurs' at the time of delivery; so a seller who delivers washing machines

472. *Accord* (as regards fitness for particular purpose) Landgericht München, Germany, 27 Feb. 2002, English translation available at http://cisgw3.law.pace.edu/cases/020227g1.html (clear to seller that buyer sought to acquire goods as permanent furniture for its offices; although no specific contract provision dealing with lifespan, implied that parties agreed to long-term operational life; court assumed impliedly operational lifetime of three years).

473. *Accord*: Schwenzer in Schlechtriem & Schwenzer, *Commentary* 4th ed. (2016), at 626.

which (e.g.) are guaranteed to last three years commits a breach at the moment he or she delivers goods not capable of lasting three years.[474] And since such guaranty-breaches would appear to fall within the general rule in Article 36(1), there was hardly any real need for the purportedly 'clarifying' guaranty-provision in the paragraph (2) rule.[475] Fortunately, the provision seems not to have caused more trouble than it was designed to avoid.[476]

I. Seller's Right to Cure Defects

1. Cure in Context

183. A CISG seller who delivers non-conforming (e.g., defective) goods will ordinarily become liable for breach in accordance with the Convention's remedial scheme (as defined in section III of Chapter II).[477] However, by providing a seller who delivers before the agreed delivery date with a certain right to 'cure' (remedy) deficiencies and/or non-conformities in the goods so delivered,[478] Article 37 gives the seller in this situation an opportunity to limit the range of remedial relief which might otherwise be available to the injured buyer. According to this provision:

> If the seller has delivered goods before the date for delivery, he may, up to that date, deliver any missing part or make up any deficiency in the quantity of the goods delivered, or deliver goods in replacement of any non-conforming goods delivered or remedy any lack of conformity in the goods delivered, provided that the exercise of this right does not cause the buyer unreasonable inconvenience or unreasonable expense. However, the buyer retains any right to claim damages as provided for in this Convention.

474. *See supra*, No. 166. *See also* Honnold/Flechtner, *supra* note 462, at 346, noting that the legislative intent may have been to include the seller's implied obligations under Art. 35 within the scope of an Art. 36 'guarantee'. *See also*, for example, the COMPRIMEX award of 29 Apr. 1996 reported in UNILEX (seller liable for non-conformity – inadequate packaging – which existed when the risk passed, even though the non-conformity first became apparent later on).

475. *See* A/CONF./97/5, *Secretariat's Commentary* to Art. 34(2) of the 1978 Draft Convention, indicating that the drafters found it necessary to 'clarify' the rule in Art. 36(1).

476. *See* cases cited in UNCITRAL CISG Case Law Digest (2016 ed.), Art. 36, available at https://uncitral.un.org/en/case_law/digests.

477. *See infra*, Nos 209 et seq. *See also* the more general remedial rules set forth in Ch. I (*supra*, Nos 136 et seq.) and Ch. V (*infra*, Nos 280 et seq.).

478. Distinguish the *buyer's* right to *demand* that the seller repair (cure) under Art. 46(3), discussed *infra*, No. 219.

2. Article 37, Fundamental Breach and Avoidance

184. As indicated previously in connection with Article 25,[479] and as developed more fully below in the discussion of buyer's remedies for seller's breach,[480] a buyer is entitled to avoid a CISG contract if the seller's failure to perform amounts to a fundamental breach.

In cases where the seller delivers earlier than the date required by the contract and the Convention, and it becomes apparent that the goods do not conform (with respect to quality or quantity), Article 37 provides a seller with the means to limit the injured buyer's right to avoid. Given these special circumstances, unless it becomes 'clear' that the seller will not cure (or cannot cure without causing the buyer unreasonable inconvenience or expense), the buyer cannot avoid until the actual delivery date has passed.[481] The same is true if the non-conformity is effectively cured before the delivery date, for the buyer cannot then be said to suffer a detriment which substantially deprives him or her of what he or she was entitled to expect.[482]

185. Article 37 should also be considered in conjunction with Article 48, which provides the seller with the right to cure even after the date of delivery.[483]

J. Notice of Non-conformity Required

186. When a CISG buyer claims that the goods delivered do not conform to the contract, it is important – and fair – that the seller be made aware of the precise nature of that buyer's claim, *inter alia*, to provide the seller with an opportunity to investigate and possibly remedy (cure) the non-conformity.[484] Even a seller who would challenge the buyer's non-conformity claim should be allowed to document his or her own position.[485]

For these reasons, Article 39 of the Convention conditions the buyer's right to remedial relief upon the giving of timely and sufficient notice to the seller as regards the particular non-conformity concerned.[486] As more fully explained below, this is an extremely important provision which works in tandem with the (equally important) requirements for timely examination set forth in Article 38.

---

479. *Supra*, Nos 136 et seq.
480. Regarding avoidance under Art. 49, *see infra*, Nos 225 et seq.
481. In the case of anticipatory breach, Art. 37 can restrict avoidance under Art. 72 (this provision is discussed *infra*, Nos 285 et seq.).
482. *See* discussion *infra*, No. 226.
483. *See* discussion *infra*, Nos 221 et seq.
484. As regards cure, *see* Arts 37 (*supra*, Nos 183 et seq.) and 48 (*infra*, Nos 221 et seq.).
485. *Infra*, Nos 209 et seq.
486. As regards Art. 39 *see infra*, Nos 190 et seq.

K. Examination of Goods

1. Timely Examination

187. Article 38 lays down the rules which define the concept of timely examination. Paragraph (1) of Article 38 sets forth the general rule:

> The buyer must examine the goods, or cause them to be examined, within as short a period as is practicable in the circumstances.

The 'short-as-practicable' examination period set forth in Article 38 must be considered in connection with the buyer's duty to notify under Article 39 within a 'reasonable' time. Obviously, a CISG buyer cannot provide his or her seller with the requisite notice of a given non-conformity under Article 39 before that buyer becomes aware that the non-conformity in question actually exists. In most situations, the buyer will acquire the requisite awareness when he or she undertakes a post-delivery examination of the goods.

The default rule in CISG Article 38(1) requires the buyer to undertake (or arrange for) such an examination, at the place of 'delivery',[487] within as short a period as is practicable in the circumstances. For this reason, most courts have required CISG buyers to move quickly, but if the contract involves carriage of the goods, the examination may at least be deferred until after the goods have arrived at their destination, because inspection is presumed to first become practicable at that time.[488]

The timeliness of both the examination and the subsequent notice pursuant to the CISG rules will depend, *inter alia*, on the nature of the goods in question as well as the customs prevailing in the particular trade. In the case of perishable goods, for example, courts are likely to require near-immediate examination,[489] and although the time periods laid down in Articles 38(1) and 39(1) are distinct and different, a court which determines that near-immediate examination is practicable in the circumstances under Article 38 might also find it reasonable to require near-immediate

487. *See*, e.g., Rechtbank Breda, Netherlands, 16 Jan. 2009, available at http://www.unilex.info/cisg/case/1387 (contract provided for carriage of watermelons for buyer's account and risk; under Art. 38 buyer obliged to examine before transportation to Netherlands; seller liable only for defects at the time of shipment when risk passed under Arts 35(1) & 36(1)).

488. *See* Art. 38(2), discussed *infra*, No. 189 and International Court of Commercial Arbitration, Chamber of Commerce & Industry of the Russian Federation, decision of 24 Jan. 2000, in CISGW3. *See also* Art. 38(3) which deals with cases where the goods are redirected in transit or redispatched.

489. *See*, for example, OLG Saarbrücken, 3 Jun. 1998, CLOUT Case 290 (in international flower trade reasonable for buyer to inspect on same day goods were received). Quite apart from the dictates of Art. 38, when the goods deteriorate quickly, a prompt examination is required if the buyer is to establish non-conformity as of the passing of risk under Art. 36 (*see supra*, No. 181); Gerechtshof-Arnhem, Netherlands, 9 Mar. 2010, available at http://www.unilex.info/cisg/case/1919 (buyer of pasta should have examined immediately after delivery).

notice of the examination results under Article 39.[490] In other circumstances, notice given several weeks or months – or (in unusual circumstances) even years – after delivery may suffice.[491]

As a starting point, the parties have the power to derogate from the rules in Articles 38–39, so as to require (e.g.) notice 'within five working days after delivery',[492] just as a seller can waive his or her right to object to the propriety of a buyer's examination of the goods.[493]

2. Nature of Examination

188. Article 38(1) describes only the time for buyer's examination, not the intensity thereof. It must be assumed, however, that this intensity question is a matter which is 'governed' by the Convention (and not domestic law),[494] and that the examination required is one which is reasonable in the circumstances, not one which would reveal every possible defect.[495]

More generally, the nature (intensity) of the examination required will depend, *inter alia*, on international usages in the trade concerned.[496] Arguably, a buyer not having the requisite technical expertise and special equipment could not be expected to effect an examination for hidden defects discoverable only by such technical means.[497] It has, for example, been held that a buyer had no duty to examine video screen machinery to determine whether it lacked basic electrical safety features;[498] similarly, a middleman who purchases goods in sealed containers would not normally be expected to undertake (or secure) a laboratory analysis of the contents prior to resale.[499]

490. Since the time frames for inspection and the subsequent giving of notice are based on independent criteria, same-day notice should only be required where also 'practicable' under Art. 39(1), discussed *infra*, No. 192. *See*, e.g., Cour d Cassation (France), 4 Nov. 2014, available at http:www.unilex.info/cisg/case/1917 (French buyer of Christmas trees received complaints from its customers in mid-December; buyer could have discovered defects no later than Christmas; buyer's notification to Dutch seller in February not timely). *Compare* Vestre Landsret (Danish Western High Court of Appeal), 10 Nov. 1999, available at www.cisg.law.pace.edu/cases/991110d1.html (Christmas trees sold in December; notice of defects two days after delivery was timely, but avoidance declaration seven days later was too late).

491. *See infra*, Nos 190 et seq. *See also* cases cited in *UNCITRAL CISG Case Law Digest* (2016 ed.), available at https://uncitral.un.org/en/case_law/digests, Art. 38, paras 11–19 (indicating the numerous factors to be considered and the wide range of permissible time periods).

492. *See* Rechtbank Arnhem, Netherlands, 11 Feb. 2009, available at http://www.unilex.info/cisg/case/1439 ('5 Arbeitstagen ab Lieferungsdatum'; derogation (Art. 6) reasonable, considering perishable nature of goods (trees) and buyer's agreement to seller's standard terms).

493. *See* cases cited in *UNCITRAL CISG Case Law Digest* (2016 ed.), *supra* 451, Art. 38, paras 6–7.

494. Regarding this aspect of Art. 7(2), *see supra*, Nos 78 et seq.

495. Regarding the 'general principle' requiring *reasonable* conduct, *see supra*, Nos 79–80.

496. *See* A/CONF./97/5, *Secretariat's Commentary*, No. 3 to Art. 36 of the 1978 Draft Convention. *See also infra*, Nos 191–192.

497. *See* A/CONF./97/5, *Secretariat's Commentary*, No. 3 to Art. 36 of the 1978 Draft Convention.

498. Landgericht München, Germany, 27 Feb. 2002, available at http://cisgw3.law.pace.edu/cases/020227g1.html.

499. *See*, for example, LG Paderborn (Germany), 25 Jun. 1996, abstract in UNILEX at www.unilex.info/cisg/case/191, where seller delivered PVC containing a lower percentage of a certain substance

CISG case law indicates a certain measure of disagreement on this important question, however, and some courts have taken a highly demanding (i.e., seller-friendly) stance as regards the nature of the examination required. In one case, the German buyer of forty-eight pairs of shoes was held to have lost all remedial rights by failing to undertake a *thorough* examination at the time of delivery.[500] In another instance, a buyer who first gave notice of defects twenty-four days after delivery of adhesive foil covers lost all remedial rights, since the buyer had not processed a sample immediately upon delivery (processing which, in the court's view, was practicable).[501]

The sufficiency of a given sampling for examination will depend on the concrete circumstances.[502] In one case brought before a German court, the buyer lost its right to rely on an alleged non-conformity when it failed to undertake a random sampling as well as stress tests in a situation not involving much effort or excessive costs.[503] If the buyer faces the risk of large consequential losses, he or she may need to examine the goods more thoroughly.[504]

---

than the percentage agreed in the contract: in this situation, the buyer had not lost the right to rely on the lack of conformity by failing to examine the PVC before receiving customers' complaints, since the defective composition could only be discovered by special chemical analysis which buyer was not bound to have made. *Accord*: BGH (Supreme Court of Germany), 25 Jun. 1997, CLOUT Case 235, available at www.cisg.law.pace.edu/cases/970625g2.html (exact nature of defect first discoverable after processing).

500. *See* LG Stuttgart of 31 Aug. 1989, CLOUT Case 4, available at www.cisg.law.pace.edu/cases/890831g1.html. Since improper sewing, measurement and poor colour quality could not be considered latent defects, the buyer's duty to examine and discover (discoverable) defects upon delivery was not discharged by a superficial examination of a few (conforming) pairs; consequently, the court held that notice of non-conformity given to the seller sixteen days after delivery, when the buyer's customers began to complain of non-conformities not revealed by the prior inspection, was too late. The apparent severity of this particular decision is ameliorated by the fact that the seller had been 'forewarned' by customer complaints concerning a first lot of shoes delivered previously, so he had special reason to promptly and carefully examine all shoes delivered in the second lot.

501. *See* OLG Karlsruhe (Germany), 25 Jun. 1997, CLOUT Case 230, available at www.cisg.law.pace.edu/cases/970625g1.html. While acknowledging that Arts 38 and 39 are less severe than the corresponding provisions in German domestic law, the court found that this CISG buyer could (and should) have given notice within ten to eleven days.

502. *See*, for example, Landgericht Aschaffenburg, Germany, 20 Apr. 2006, available at http://cisgw3.law.pace.edu/cases/060420g1.html (sampling sufficient for deliveries of large quantities of goods); *compare* Kantonsgericht Schaffhausen, Switzerland, 27 Jan. 2004, CLOUT Case 892, available at www.cisg.law.pace.edu/cases/040127s1.html (random sampling for mass production items, but not sufficient for 'small series').

503. Oberlandesgericht Dresden, Germany, 8 Nov. 2007, English translation available at http://cisgw3.law.pace.edu/cases/071108g1.html. *Compare* Oberlandesgericht Köln, Germany, 12 Jan. 2007, available at http://cisgw3.law.pace.edu/cases/070112g1.html (examination required only if cost and effort in reasonable proportion to expected benefits).

504. If a superficial examination or sampling reveals deviations in such circumstances, the goods should then be processed in a test run. *See* Landgericht Aschaffenburg, Germany, 20 Apr. 2006, available at http://cisgw3.law.pace.edu/cases/060420g1.html#ch.

3. Contract of Carriage: Examination May Be Deferred

189. For the many international sales cases involving carriage of the goods, the rule in Article 38, paragraph (1), is supplemented by paragraphs (2) and (3).

Paragraph (2) of Article 38 provides:

> If the contract involves carriage of the goods, examination may be deferred until after the goods have arrived at their destination.

The main (general) rule in paragraph 1 of Article 38 (discussed in the foregoing sections) applies, *inter alia*, if the contract involves carriage. In these, as in other cases, the examination is to be effected within as short a period as is practicable in the circumstances.

In cases involving carriage, however, the circumstances will often dictate the application of the special rule in paragraph 2, for in these (carriage) cases, 'examination may be deferred until after the goods have arrived at their destination'.[505] In such cases, inspection is presumed to first become practicable at that point in time.

Article 38(2) is supplemented by a rule which provides for a further extension in certain cases where the goods have been redirected in transit or redispatched.

Paragraph (3) of Article 38 provides:

> If the goods are redirected in transit or redispatched by the buyer without a reasonable opportunity for examination by him and at the time of the conclusion of the contract the seller knew or ought to have known of the possibility of such redirection or redispatch, examination may be deferred until after the goods have arrived at the new destination.

According to German CISG case law, a buyer who would invoke Article 38(3) bears the burden of proving that the seller was aware of the possibility that the goods would be redirected in transit, and that the buyer did not have a reasonable opportunity to examine the goods before they were redispatched.[506]

505. *See* Art. 38(2) of *UNCITRAL Digest of CISG Case Law* (2016 ed.): in such cases, it will often not be convenient or even possible for the buyer to examine the goods at the point of delivery, and thus in fairness the period for examination should not begin running at that point.

506. In a German decision involving a large quantity of used shoes, the fact that the Ugandan buyer would have had to fly to Kenya in order to examine the goods at the place of delivery before transshipment to Uganda (and that such an examination might have triggered Kenyan custom duties) did *not* relieve the buyer of the duty to examine the goods in Kenya. *See* Landgericht Frankfurt, Germany, 11 Apr. 2005, CLOUT Case No. 775, available at http://cisgw3.law.pace.edu/cases/050411g1.html. For a commentary rightly critical of this decision, *see* H. Flechtner, 'Funky Mussels, a Stolen Car, and Decrepit Used Shoes: Non-conforming Goods and Notice Thereof under the United Nations Sales Convention', *Boston University International Law Journal* 26(1) (2008), available at http://papers.ssrn.com/sol3/papers.cfm?abstract_id=1144182.

L. Notice of Discoverable Defects & Consequences of Failure to Notify

1. The General Rule

190. Against the background of Article 38, which provides a general (short-as-practicable) time frame for the inspection of delivered goods, Article 39 sets forth the general rule regarding the consequences of the buyer's failure to give notice of a discoverable defect. Paragraph (1) of Article 39 provides the general rule:

> The buyer loses the right to rely on a lack of conformity of the goods if he does not give notice to the seller specifying the nature of the lack of conformity within a reasonable time after he has discovered it or ought to have discovered it.

2. Notice of Discoverable Defects & Consequences of Failure to Notify

191. Under Article 38, and as previously discussed, the buyer must undertake a reasonable examination of the goods as soon as practicable after delivery. Then, if such reasonable and timely examination reveals that the goods do not conform in some specific respect, Article 39(1) requires that the buyer provide the seller with specific notice of such non-conformity within a reasonable time.

Just as some courts have taken an unusually demanding (i.e., seller-friendly) stance with respect to the intensity and timeliness of the *examination* required by Article 38(1),[507] the same is true as regards the specificity and timeliness of the *notice* with respect to any non-conformity which that examination reveals.[508]

As regards the requirement in Article 39(1) that the buyer *specify* (identify) the non-conformity, a German CISG decision rendered in 1989 held that a buyer of certain wearing apparel lost all her remedial rights, since the notifications (allegedly) sent to the seller/manufacturer re. 'poor workmanship and improper fitting' did not specify the nature of the alleged non-conformities with sufficient precision.[509] Ten years later, however, the German *Bundesgerichtshof* issued a ruling which seemed to relax the specificity requirements in cases like this.[510] Some subsequent German cases have nonetheless maintained a strict stance,[511] whereas other decisions (in

507. *See supra*, No. 188.
508. If the notice requirements posed by some German courts (to German and foreign buyers alike) with respect to Art. 39(1) sometimes seem overly harsh, it may be because these courts have not taken sufficient note of the difference between the CISG 'reasonable time' standard in Art. 39(1) and the corresponding ULIS rule which required that notice be given *promptly*.
509. *See* Landgericht München, 3 Jul. 1989, CLOUT Case 3, available at www.cisg.law.pace.edu/cases/890703g1.html.
510. BGH (Germany), 3 Nov. 1999, CLOUT Case 319, available at www.cisg.law.pace.edu/cases/991103g1.html (sufficient that buyer passed on end-users' complaints indicating general nature of non-conformity in question).
511. Oberlandesgericht Karlsruhe, Germany, 8 Feb. 2006, CLOUT Case 721, available at http://cisgw3.law.pace.edu/cases/060208g1.html (identify the lack of conformity exactly); Oberlandesgericht Celle, Germany, 10 Mar. 2004, CLOUT Case 597, available at http://cisgw3.law.pace.edu/cases/0

Germany and elsewhere) have adopted a more flexible position.[512] So in this respect, CISG Article 39 case law remains non-uniform.

In cases where the buyer gives timely notice of a serious non-conformity, but does not, in the first instance, specify that defect with sufficient precision, it would seem fair – and in accord with both the spirit and black letters of the Convention[513] – to require the seller to demand that the buyer provides a (prompt) supplementary specification,[514] that is, instead of allowing the seller (perhaps guilty of a fundamental breach) to escape all liability on the basis of a technicality. Following a similar approach when evaluating the propriety of a buyer's written notice of a pony's lack of conformity, a Danish court took into account the fact that the buyer, before the final diagnosis of the pony's condition was made, had continuously advised the seller of the pony's worsening condition.[515]

As regards the requirement that the requisite notice be given within a reasonable time, it should first be emphasized that what is reasonable often will depend on the nature of the goods in question and/or the custom regarding notice in that particular trading context. So, just as it will usually be reasonable to require that the buyer of perishable goods examine them immediately, it may also be reasonable to require immediate notice of the examination results concerned.[516] Allowing buyers somewhat more flexibility in these situations, the highest court in France has defined a two-month maximum notification period under Article 39(1) in the case of non-conforming goods which are perishable (or intended to be sold within a very short period of time).[517]

40310g1.html (buyer must describe non-conformity as precisely as possible). *But compare* Bundesgericht (Supreme Court), Switzerland, 13 Nov. 2003, CLOUT Case 885, available at http://cisgw3.law.pace.edu/cases/031113s1.html (suggesting that the German translation of Art. 39 used by German-speaking courts requires greater precision than the official CISG text).

512. *See*, for example, the Swiss decision cited in the previous note. *See also* Hof van Beroep Gent, Belgium, 28 Jan. 2004, translation available at http://cisgw3.law.pace.edu/cases/ 040128b1.html (notice should be specific enough to make it possible to conclude that goods purchased not in conformity with contract, thus enabling seller to make judgment about buyer's complaint, decide on measures regarding furnishing of proof, etc.); Landgericht Stuttgart, Germany, 15 Oct. 2009, available at http://cisgw3.law.pace.edu/cases/091015g1.html (specific enough to allow seller to comprehend claim and take appropriate steps in response, for example, examine the goods, secure necessary evidence for potential disputes, arrange for a substitute delivery or otherwise remedy the lack of conformity, or have recourse against a supplier).

513. Regarding the good-faith principle expressed in Art. 7, *see supra*, Nos 75 et seq.

514. *Accord*: Landgericht Bamberg, Germany, 23 Oct. 2006, English translation available at http://cisgw3.law.pace.edu/cases/061023g1.html (in 'age of technology' seller expected to ask questions if he desires more precise information). Regarding the 'duty to reply' imposed upon the offeree in CISG Art. 21(2), *see supra*, No. 128; Regarding the duty to act in good faith as a CISG 'general principle', *see supra*, No. 78.

515. *See* the decision of the City Court of Copenhagen, Denmark, 19 Oct. 2007, CLOUT Case 992, available at http://cisgw3.law.pace.edu/cases/071019d1.html (after pre-existing injury to pony discovered, buyer had continuously advised seller as to pony's worsening condition; later, upon final diagnosis, buyer promptly notified seller and declared contract avoided).

516. *See*, for example, OLG Saarbrücken, 3 Jun. 1998, CLOUT Case 290, available at http://cisgw3.law.pace.edu/cases/980603g1.html (in international flower trade reasonable for buyer to inspect and give notice of lack of conformity on same day goods received).

517. *See* Cour de Cassation, France, 4 Nov. 2014, available at http://www.unilex.info/cisg/case/1917 (buyer could have discovered Christmas tree defects immediately after delivery and, in any case,

As regards non-perishables, however, some buyers may enjoy even greater flexibility. Referring to prior CISG foreign case law, a Spanish court in 2012 held that in the case of non-perishable goods, where a delay in notification did not adversely affect the seller's activities vis-à-vis third parties, the time period referred to in Article 39(1) first begins to run when the buyer becomes certain, rather than merely suspecting, that the goods are defective.[518]

Since the timeliness of a given inspection and subsequent notice of alleged defects ought to depend on the concrete circumstances, at least in the case of non-perishables,[519] the Supreme Court of France has rightly decided to leave this (highly discretionary) determination in the hands of the individual French judges.[520] Other (e.g., American and Italian) courts have taken similarly flexible positions, with one US District Court holding that the determination of what period of time is 'practicable' or 'reasonable' is a factual one, dependent on the circumstances of the particular case.[521]

Other courts have taken a more rigid view in defining what constitutes a reasonable time under Article 39(1). In one of the earlier (very strict) German cases on point, it was found that the buyer could have processed a sample of the non-perishable goods immediately upon their delivery and (therefore) could have discovered and given notice of defects within ten to eleven days after delivery. For this

---

no later than Christmas; notwithstanding fact that the buyer had received complaints from its clients in mid-December, it waited until February to inform seller).

518. *See* Fuenlabrada Court of First Instance, 11 May 2012, CLOUT Case 1343, also at http://www.unilex.info/cisg/case/1824 (buyer had complied with Art. 39, since not possible to find hidden defect until machine in operation).

519. *Compare*, as regards perishables, text *supra* with note 517.

520. *See*, for example, Cour de Cassation (France), 26 May 1999, CLOUT Case 315, available at www.cisg.law.pace.edu/cases/990526f1.html (buyer of rolled metal sheets gave notice five weeks after deliveries commenced; timely under Arts 38(1) and 39(1)). *See also* Cour d'appel de Versailles, 29 Jan. 1998, CLOUT Case 225, at www.cisg.law.pace.edu/cases/980129f1.html (buyer sent notice of non-conformity two weeks after provisional test of two high-tech machines at seller's premises; one month after second test, buyer sent notice refusing to take delivery until certain modifications made; further letters specifying defects sent six months after delivery of first machine and eleven months after delivery of second. Held: *all* these notices satisfied requirements of Art. 39). *See also* Cour d'appel de Colmar, 24 Oct. 2000, CLOUT Case 400, available at www.cisg.law.pace.edu/cases/001024f1.html (notice of defects in glue given two months after discovery held timely).

521. *See* US District Court for the Northern District of Illinois, 29 May 2003 (*Chicago Prime Packers, Inc. v. Northam Food Trading Co.*, et al.), available at http://cisgw3.law.pace.edu/cisg/wais/db/cases2/030529u1.html#cs (equipment designed to produce plastic gardening pots, not practicable to require notification within a few weeks); *see also* US District Court, S.D., Michigan (*Shuttle Packaging Systems, L.L.C. v. Jacob Tsonakis*, INA S.A., et al.), 17 Dec. 2001, CLOUT Case 578, available at www.cisg.law.pace.edu/cases/011217u1.html. *See also*, e.g., Tribunale di Bolzano, Italy, 27 Jan. 2009, available at http://www.unilex.info/cisg/case/1671 (in assessing reasonable time under Art. 39(1), consider all relevant circumstances, in particular nature of goods, since goods in present case non-perishable (industrial equipment), notice four months after delivery held reasonable); but *compare* Tribunale di Reggio Emilia, 12 Apr. 2011, http://www.unilex.info/cisg/case/1644 (notice more than two months after delivery of ceramics not reasonable); Tribunale di Forli, Italy, 16 Feb. 2009, http://www.unilex.info/cisg/case/1394 (notice thirteen months after delivery of cisterns not reasonable).

reason, notice given twenty-four days after delivery was deemed too late, thus depriving the buyer of all remedial rights.[522]

Still, other courts have sought to find a compromise solution to the Article 39(1) conundrum, one which takes account of the wide range of corresponding timely notice conceptions under domestic law. Thus, a Swiss court held in 1997 that notice of non-conformity was timely if given within one month after delivery, describing this period as a good compromise between the German and the (far more lenient) American views.[523] Taking a similar approach in 1998, the German Supreme Court (*Bundesgerichtshof*) established one month as a general – that is, standard or generally acceptable – notification period.[524] This seems at least to be a step in the right direction, although one should seriously question whether the Convention provides national courts with authority to reduce the flexible Article 39(1) standard to a mathematical formula, even if such a formula might be said to advance the goal of uniform CISG application.[525] So if a given CISG seller of non-perishable goods has not been prejudiced (e.g.) by a two-month defect-notification 'delay', the buyer ought not to be deprived of its legitimate rights.[526] In any event, the pronouncement of a Swiss appellate court in 2016 that notice under Article 39(1) must be given 'immediately' represents a regrettable step backward.[527]

According to Article 39(1), and as already indicated, if the buyer does not provide the seller with the requisite notice within the allowable time, he or she loses the 'right to rely' on the lack of conformity. In other words, the starting point of the Convention is that the buyer loses the right to assert any and all of the various remedies otherwise provided under the Convention for seller's breach (the right to require performance, the right to avoid, to the right to claim damages or a proportionate reduction).[528]

522. Notwithstanding the fact that the parties had a long-standing business relationship: *see* OLG Karlsruhe (Germany), 25 Jun. 1997, CLOUT Case 230, available at www.cisg.law.pace.edu/cases/970625g1.html. *Compare* OLG München (Germany), 11 Mar. 1998, CLOUT Case 232, available at www.cisg.law.pace.edu/cases/980311g1.html (notice given four months after delivery of textiles held untimely/unreasonable under Art. 39 and also in violation of express contract clause requiring written notice of defects within fourteen days of delivery).

523. *See* Obergericht Kanton Luzern (Switzerland), 8 Jan. 1997, CLOUT Case 192, available at www.cisg.law.pace.edu/cases/970108s1.html.

524. BGH, 3 Nov. 1999, CLOUT Case 319, available at www.cisg.law.pace.edu/cases/991103g1.html. *See also* OLG Oldenburg, 5 Dec. 2000, UNILEX.

525. *Accord* F. Ferrari & M. Torsello, *International Sales Law – CISG in a Nutshell* 2nd ed. (2018), at 279 (recourse to presumptive periods do not reflect flexibility of 'reasonable time' standard); Opinion No. 3 of the CISG Advisory Council, available at http://cisgw3.law.pace.edu/cisg/CISG-AC-op2.html: 'No fixed period, whether fourteen days, one month or otherwise, should be considered as reasonable in the abstract without taking into account the circumstances of the case.'

526. *See*, e.g., Audiencia Provincial de Madrid, Spain, 14 Jul. 2009, available at http://www.unilex.info/cisg/case/1621 (flags intended for world cup promotion defective; considering nature of goods and final destination to second buyer, first buyer's notice *two months* after discovery of defects reasonable).

527. Cour d'appel civile du Tribunal Contonal de Vaud (Switzerland), 29 Feb. 2016, CLOUT Case 1772 (with National Correspondent Professor Schroeter noting that the Court, alleging this to be the 'majority view', ignored the majority of CISG case law and commentary).

528. Regarding the various remedies generally available to buyer for seller's breach, *see infra*, Nos 209 et seq. (regarding s. III of Ch. II) and *infra*, Nos 280 et seq. (regarding Ch. V).

This severe starting point is, however, modified by two other CISG rules. The first of these safety valves is set forth in Article 40 which provides that a seller who is (or should be) aware of given non-conformity (which the buyer has been unable to detect) cannot enjoy the protection which Articles 38 and 39 provide.[529]

Second, pursuant to Article 44, a buyer may seek to provide the court or arbitral tribunal with a reasonable excuse for his or her failure to notify, thereby seeking (partial) refuge from the severity of the Article 39(1) rule.[530]

It should also be noted that Article 39 is subject to the parties' power to derogate from or vary the effect of any provision of the Convention under Article 6. Provided such agreements (often included in one party's standard terms) meet the ordinary requirements regarding incorporation and interpretation,[531] they have generally been enforced, at least to the extent they are judged reasonable by the standards of Article 39.[532] It is, on the other hand, also important to note that a seller's express guarantee as to durability, e.g., that cement plates are 'guaranteed to last for 10 years', does not automatically extend the buyer's duty to notify of defects within a reasonable time after their discovery.[533]

3. Latent Defects under Article 39(1)

192. A buyer who fails to discover (and give timely notice regarding) a *discoverable* defect loses the right to rely thereon. In other words, a buyer who ought to have discovered a defect (i.e., could have done so during the course of a reasonable examination), but did not, is treated the same as a buyer who actually discovers a defect, but fails to notify the seller of that defect (on time).[534]

There is, however, no Article 39 obligation upon the buyer to provide prompt notice of 'latent' defects, defined for present purposes as defects which are so well hidden that they are not discoverable by ordinary means (i.e., by the reasonable

529. Regarding seller's 'bad faith' and CISG case law under Art. 40, *see infra*, No. 197.
530. Regarding excuses under Art. 44 *see infra*, Nos 207 et seq.
531. As to these requirements, *see* generally *supra*, Nos 174 et seq.
532. *See* Rechtbank van Koophandel, Mechelen, Belgium, 18 Jan. 2002, abstract available at www.unilex.info/cisg/case/941 (seller's barely legible fine-print standard terms (in German) requiring notice by Dutch buyer within twenty-four hours held not incorporated in parties' contract); *compare* Rechtbank Arnhem, Netherlands, 11 Feb. 2009, at http://cisgw3.law.pace.edu/cases/090211n1.html (seller's standard terms providing for notice of lack of conformity within five working days after delivery held reasonable, taking into account perishable nature of goods); *compare* also Oberlandesgericht München, Germany, 11 Mar. 1998, abstract available at www.unilex.info/cisg/case/299 (fourteen days' notice of non-conformity held validly agreed, since reasonable under Art. 39 CISG).
533. Such an express durability guarantee was given by the seller in the case decided by Cour d'appel Bourges, France, 7 Jan. 2016, available in UNILEX (http://www.unilex.info/cisg/case/1965), but since the buyer first notified the seller of (hidden) defects some three years after their discovery, the buyer lost all its rights. *Compare* Arbitration Institute of the Stockholm Chamber of Commerce, 5 Jun. 1998, CLOUT Case 237, at http://cisgw3.law.pace.edu/cases/980605s5.html, discussed *supra* note 466.
534. *Compare* Landgericht Stuttgart, 31 Aug. 1989 (CLOUT Case No. 4), available at www.cisg.law.pace.edu/cases/890831g1.html (buyer aware of defects in previous shipment, so careful examination of subsequent shipment required).

inspection required by Article 38). Therefore, if a buyer conducts a reasonable inspection, but first discovers a latent defect at some later point in time – perhaps even several months after delivery – he or she is then required to provide the seller with the necessary Article 39 notice within a reasonable time after that, that is, after the latent non-conformity is (or should reasonably have been) discovered.[535]

M. Absolute (Two-Year) Cut-Off Rule

193. Paragraph (2) of Article 39 supplements the general (reasonable time) rule in paragraph (1) by providing an 'absolute' cut-off rule, that is, a maximum time period after which the buyer – 'in any event' – loses the right to rely on a given non-conformity. Paragraph (2) provides:

> In any event, the buyer loses the right to rely on a lack of conformity of the goods if he does not give the seller notice thereof at the latest within a period of two years from the date on which the goods were actually handed over to the buyer, unless this time-limit is inconsistent with a contractual period of guarantee.

Note by way of introduction that the two-year period set forth in Article 39(2) provides a time limit as regards a buyer's notice of non-conformity; unlike the UN Limitation Convention,[536] the CISG rule does *not* provide a time limit within which an action against the seller must be brought.[537]

535. *See* A/CONF./97/5, *Secretariat's Commentary*, Comment No. 3 to Art. 37 of the 1978 Draft Convention. *See also* Court of Appeal, Turku, Finland, 24 May 2005, English translation available at http://cisgw3.law.pace.edu/cases/050524f5.html (examination that did not reveal radiation in foodstuffs sufficient under Art. 38, as not customary for such parties to conduct that kind of examination; for this reason buyer not denied right to rely on non-conformity under Art. 39(1)). *Compare* Hoge Raad (Netherlands), 20 Feb. 1998, CLOUT Case 833, available at http://cisgw3.law.pace.edu/cases/980220n1.html (Dutch buyer of Italian floor tiles resold to customers. Seven months after buyer's delivery to seller, buyer received complaints from customer regarding quality (allegedly worn surface dull and dark); Supreme Court held buyer should have inspected immediately after receiving complaints, and given notice to seller shortly afterwards). *Compare* also LG Düsseldorf (Germany), 23 Jun. 1994, abstract available at www.unilex.info/cisg/case/115 (buyer of aircraft engines not expected to discover possible defects before installed and put into operation, but examination four months after delivery not 'as short as is practicable in the circumstances' nor did buyer give notice within reasonable time after discovering defects).

536. The United Nations Convention on the Limitation Period in the International Sale of Goods (LPISG) determines the period during which one party can assert an international sales-related claim against the other. The LPISG provides a uniform four-year statute of limitations for international sales. *See infra*, No. 196 and J. Lookofsky, *Understanding the CISG* 5th Worldwide ed. (2017), Ch. 9.

537. *See* (e.g.) Cour de Cassation (France), 3 Feb. 2009, available at http://www.unilex.info/cisg/case/1455. *See* generally U. Schroeter, 'A Time-Limit Running Wild? Article 39(2) CISG and Domestic Limitation Periods', in *A Tribute to Joseph M. Lookofsky* (Andersen & Henschel eds. 2015), also at https://papers.ssrn.com/sol3/papers.cfm?abstract_id=2725027 (concluding that no conflict exists between the CISG's two-year cut-off rule and shorter domestic limitation periods).

N. Application of Two-Year Rule to Latent Defects

194. Because Articles 38 and 39(1) require timely inspection and notification as regards discoverable defects, Article 39(2) has particular significance for latent defects, that is, defects not reasonably discoverable upon delivery pursuant to Article 38. Although a CISG buyer, as a starting point, retains the right to rely on latent defects which first become evident after the passage of some time, Article 39(2) helps protect the seller against stale claims which may be of doubtful validity.[538]

The CISG two-year period begins to run as soon as the goods are actually handed over to the buyer, and a buyer who fails to give notice of a non-conformity before the expiration of this period loses the right to rely thereon. Therefore, a buyer who first discovers and gives notice of a latent defect after the expiration of this period (and who has not secured a guarantee which effectively extends the period) can claim no remedy, however undiscoverable the non-conformity in question might have been.[539]

The two-year period adopted by the Convention drafters might seem seller-friendly to some, but it actually represents an international compromise when seen against the background of some domestic solutions.[540] In some jurisdictions, a CISG buyer might be permitted to advance a tort-based domestic law claim for negligent misrepresentation even after the two-year period in Article 39(2) has expired.[541]

As indicated in the following, the severity of the rule in Article 39(2) may be tempered if the seller has guaranteed the goods for a period longer than two years,[542] just as a disappointed buyer may, in exceptional cases, be able to seek refuge in the safety-valve provision set forth in Article 40.[543]

O. Express Contractual Cut-Offs and Periods of Guarantee

195. Here, as in other Convention contexts, express contractual provisions, agreed to by the parties, take precedence over the CISG (supplementary, gap-filling) rules.[544] Therefore, the two-year time limit ordinarily applicable by virtue of the default rule in Article 39(2) will not apply if the parties' contract provides for a

538. *See* A/CONF./97/5, *Secretariat's Commentary*, No. 6 to Art. 37 of the 1978 Draft Convention.

539. *See* Federal Court of Australia, Australia, 13 Aug. 2010 (*Cortem SpA v. Controlmatic Pty. Ltd.*), available at www.austlii.edu.au/cgi-bin/sinodisp/au/cases/cth/FCA/2010/852.html; Cour de cassation, France, 8 Apr. 2009, CLOUT Case 1026, available at http://cisgw3.law.pace.edu/cases/090408f1.html.

540. *Compare*, for example, the one-year cut-off rule in the pre-2002 version of Art. 54 of the Danish Sales Act (*Købeloven*) and §2-607(3) of the American Uniform Commercial Code (no specific cut-off apart from 'reasonable time').

541. *See Pamesa v. Mendelson* (2009), available at http://cisgw3.law.pace.edu/cases/090317i5.html. *See also supra*, No. 64.

542. *See infra*, No. 195.

543. *See infra*, No. 196.

544. Regarding Art. 6, *see supra*, Nos 70 et seq.

different notice rule/period in their contract, for example, one which requires the buyer to give notice within a shorter period of time (assuming that period is not unreasonably short).[545]

The special proviso in the last part of Article 39(2) relates to contractual periods of guarantee, for example, a clause whereby the seller guarantees conformity of the goods for a one-year period or three-year period.[546] The problem of whether a given guarantee clause is 'inconsistent with' – and thus overrides – the gap-filling two-year period in Article 39(2) is a question of contract interpretation to be decided by the court or arbitral tribunal concerned in accordance with Article 8.[547] In one such decision, an international arbitral tribunal determined that the parties concerned did not impliedly derogate from Article 39 by virtue of an eighteen-month contractual warranty.[548]

P. Relation to Prescription Convention and Other Statutes of Limitation

196. A buyer who gives notice within the time period defined in Article 39(2) may also be required to take additional steps to preserve his or her rights. Under Articles 8 and 10 of the United Nations Limitations Convention (LPISG), the buyer must commence judicial proceedings against the seller within four years of the date when the goods were actually handed over.[549] Nations not (yet) bound by the LPISG are likely to apply the relevant domestic limitation period (statute of limitations) period identified by the applicable rules of PIL.[550]

Q. Seller Aware of Defect

197. By virtue of Articles 38 and 39, a buyer who fails to notify the seller of a given non-conformity will, in the great majority of cases, lose the right to rely thereon.

---

545. An unreasonably short cut-off period would be subject to a validity-attack: regarding unreasonable liability disclaimers and limitations, etc., *see supra*, Nos 173 et seq.
546. Such a guarantee will often be coupled to a clause setting forth the seller's right or duty to repair or replace defective goods.
547. *See* A/CONF./97/5, *Secretariat's Commentary*, No. 7 to Art. 37 of the 1978 Draft Convention (with examples indicating that a shorter, one-year guarantee would be unlikely to affect the two-year CISG limit) and *compare* Honnold/Flechtner, *Uniform Law* 4th ed. (2009), at 374 (exception at end of para. (2) relevant only when contract guarantees performance for period longer than two years).
548. *See* the award rendered by the Arbitration Institute of the Stockholm Chamber of Commerce, 5 Jun. 1998, CLOUT Case 237, available at www.cisg.law.pace.edu/cases/980605s5.html.
549. *See* the Convention on the Limitation Period in the International Sale of Goods, concluded on 14 Jun. 1974 and amended by the Protocol of 11 Apr. 1980. *See* generally J. Lookofsky, *Understanding the CISG* 5th Worldwide ed. (2017), Ch. 9. As of May 2019, the LPISG Convention (as amended by the Protocol) had entered into force in thirty States: *see* www.uncitral.org/uncitral/en/uncitral_texts/sale_goods/1974Convention_status.html.
550. *Compare* Cour de Justice Genève (Switzerland), 10 Oct. 1997, CLOUT Case 249, abstract at www.unilex.info/cisg/case/309. *See also* U. Schroeter, 'A Time-Limit Running Wild? Article 39(2) CISG and Domestic Limitation Periods', in *A Tribute to Joseph M. Lookofsky* (Andersen & Henschel eds. 2015), also at https://papers.ssrn.com/sol3/papers.cfm?abstract_id=2725027, at 348.

However, a seller who has knowledge of the defect concerned ought not be permitted to enjoy the protection which these inspection and notice provisions provide. For this reason, Article 40 provides:

> The seller is not entitled to rely on the provisions of articles 38 and 39 if the lack of conformity relates to facts of which he knew or could not have been unaware and which he did not disclose to the buyer.

Although the rule in Article 40 is generally regarded as a 'safety valve' designed to function in exceptional circumstances, it may also be regarded as an expression of the general principle which requires both CISG parties to act in good faith.[551]

A prime example of the application of Article 40 has been provided by the decision of an arbitral tribunal rendered in Sweden in 1998.[552] In this case, the tribunal held that the buyer could rely on a non-conformity first discovered some three years after delivery of the machinery in question, upon the rationale that the seller in question 'could not have been unaware' that improper installation of a certain substitute machine part could lead to a serious malfunction: the seller, who had done nothing to eliminate the risk, 'consciously disregarded' facts related to the cause of the malfunction. The tribunal further held that, by failing to provide adequate installation instructions or supervise the installation of the machine, the seller had breached its duty to disclose the non-conformity in question, and that – by virtue of the safety valve in Article 40 – the buyer was not time-barred from presenting its claim for damages.

A more recent decision by a French appellate court concerned an Italian manufacturer who supplied a French middleman buyer with tile coverings which, due to insufficient enamel coating, later proved unfit for normal use. Convinced that the seller *prior to delivery* had conducted unfavourable tests and trials but not disclosed these results to the buyer, the court held that the requirements of Article 40 had been met. So even if the buyer first gave notice of the defects more than two years after delivery, that buyer had not lost its CISG remedial rights.[553] Courts in Italy and Finland have also rendered buyer-friendly decisions in similar scenarios.[554] These decisions notwithstanding, it should be emphasized that other prominent courts have

551. Regarding the proper interpretation of the Convention having due regard, *inter alia*, to 'good faith' *see* Art. 7(1) and Nos 75 et seq. Regarding 'good faith' as a general principle pursuant to Art. 7(2) *see supra*, No. 79.
552. *See* the award rendered by the Arbitration Institute of the Stockholm Chamber of Commerce, 5 Jun. 1998, CLOUT Case 237, available at www.cisg.law.pace.edu/cases/980605s5.html.
553. *See* Cour d'appel Bordeaux, 12 Sep. 2013, available at http://www.unilex.info/cisg/case/1945.
554. *See* Tribunale di Modena, Italy, 19 Feb. 2014, at http://www.unilex.info/cisg/case/1956 (seller's criminal fraud); Turku Court of Appeal, Finland, 18 Dec. 2013, CLOUT Case 1765 (contract for painted steel girders; seller 'could not have been unaware' of fact that it delivered unpainted girders).

been reluctant to apply the Article 40 rule in the absence of clear evidence that the seller 'knew or could not have been unaware' of a given non-conformity.[555]

R. Obligation to Deliver Goods Free of Third-Party Claims

1. Introduction; Article 41

198. According to Article 30, the CISG seller must transfer the property in the goods. Elaborating this theme, the first sentence of Article 41 provides: 'The seller must deliver goods which are free from any right or claim of a third party, unless the buyer agreed to take the goods subject to that right or claim.'

199. A seller who sells goods which he or she does not own (and is not authorized to sell) commits a clear breach of the obligation laid down in Article 41;[556] the same is true where the goods delivered are encumbered by a non-disclosed security interest held by a third party. In either case, the seller's knowledge regarding the third-party interest at the time of contracting is irrelevant.[557] Beyond this, the Convention protects the buyer even against third-party claims,[558] in that the mere assertion by a third party of such a claim constitutes a breach by the seller and entitles the buyer to exercise the remedies which the Convention provides.[559] If the claim is frivolous, and/or if the seller quickly and effectively disposes of an asserted claim, the buyer who suffers no substantial detriment will not be entitled to avoid the contract by virtue of a fundamental breach.[560] However, depending on the forum jurisdiction concerned, the buyer may be able to require that the seller actually perform his or her Convention obligation to supply unencumbered goods by taking appropriate legal action (instituting or defending a lawsuit).[561] Damages for breach will be available in either event.[562]

555. *See*, for example, Oberlandesgericht Stuttgart, Germany, 31 Mar. 2008, English translation available at http://cisgw3.law.pace.edu/cases/080331g1.html#ch (car had been repainted despite contrary contractual description; no evidence that seller aware of repainting at the time of conclusion of contract; court need not decide whether seller's gross negligence sufficient in relation to Art. 40 since no evidence of gross negligence).
556. For example, when the goods delivered prove to be stolen. *See* Germany, 11 Jan. 2006, Supreme Court (*Bundesgerichtshof*), translation available at http://cisgw3.law.pace.edu/cases/060111g1.html.
557. Regarding the somewhat different rule in Art. 42, *see infra*, No. 201.
558. For example, where an insurance company claims it has become the rightful owner of a stolen car. *See* Germany, 11 Jan. 2006, Supreme Court (*Bundesgerichtshof*), translation available at http://cisgw3.law.pace.edu/cases/060111g1.html.
559. Regarding Arts 45–52, *see infra*, Nos 209 et seq.
560. *See* Honnold, *Uniform Law*, ed. Flechtner, 4th ed. (2009), Art. 41, 386–387. Regarding Art. 49, *see infra*, Nos 225 et seq.
561. Regarding specific performance, *see* Art. 46(1) (*infra*, Nos 214 et seq.) and 28 (*supra*, Nos 140 et seq.).
562. Assuming a loss suffered in consequence. Regarding Arts 74 et seq., *see infra*, Nos 291 et seq.

In one application of the Article 41 rule, an Austrian court held that a seller does not comply with the obligation to deliver goods free from any right or claim of third parties if, after formation of the contract, delivery of the goods is made subject to an export restriction.[563]

2. Third-Party Rights Distinguished

200. The Convention governs only the rights and obligations of the seller and buyer; it is 'not concerned' with the effect which the contract may have on the property in the goods sold.[564] In accordance with this principle, Article 41 makes the seller potentially liable (only) to the buyer for claims which third parties may assert against the buyer, whereas the question of whether a third party's rights are cut off by virtue of a buyer's good faith purchase from a seller under a contract otherwise regulated by the CISG lies outside the Convention scope.

3. Article 42: Claims Based on Industrial or Intellectual Property

201. Under the general rule set forth in Article 41, the seller must deliver goods which are free from any third-party right or claim. However, if such right or claim is based on industrial property or other intellectual property, the seller's obligation is governed by Article 42.[565] As regards such rights and claims (based on patents, copyrights or trademarks), paragraph (1) of Article 42 provides:

> The seller must deliver goods which are free from any right or claim of a third party based on industrial property or other intellectual property, of which at the time of the conclusion of the contract the seller knew or could not have been unaware, provided that the right or claim is based on industrial property or other intellectual property:
>
> a. under the law of the State where the goods will be resold or otherwise used, if it was contemplated by the parties at the time of the conclusion of the contract that the goods would be resold or otherwise used in that State; or
> b. in any other case, under the law of the State where the buyer has his place of business.

202. Clearly, a seller who sells goods (which he or she knows are) encumbered by third-party patent, copyright or trademark rights commits a breach of the implied Convention obligation set forth in Article 42.

563. *See* Oberster Gerichtshof, 6 Feb. 1996, CLOUT Case 176, available at http://www.unilex.info/cisg/case/202 and at www.cisg.law.pace.edu/cases/960206a3.html (in these circumstances, buyer held entitled to damages).
564. Regarding Art. 4, *see supra*, Nos 62 et seq.
565. *See* Art. 41, second sentence.

Beyond this, Article 42 protects the buyer against third-party claims, in that the mere assertion of such a claim constitutes a breach by the seller and entitles the buyer to exercise the remedies which the Convention provides.[566] If the claim is frivolous, and/or if seller quickly and effectively disposes of an asserted claim, the buyer who suffers no substantial detriment will be unable to avoid the contract by virtue of a fundamental breach.[567] However, depending on the forum jurisdiction concerned, the buyer may be able to require that the seller actually remedy his or her failure to supply claim-free goods by taking appropriate legal action (instituting or defending a lawsuit).[568] Damages for breach will be available in either event.[569]

4. Seller's Knowledge of Third-Party Right or Claim

203. Unlike the corresponding rule in Article 41, the seller's knowledge regarding a third-party right or claim at the time of contracting may be relevant when industrial or intellectual property rights are involved. In the international context, where an (alleged) infringement will usually take place outside the seller's territory, the Convention limits the implied obligation of the seller to deliver unencumbered goods.

The seller's Article 42 obligation is limited to cases where the seller, at the time of contracting, 'knew or could not have been unaware' of the right or claim concerned. In this connection, the highest court in France confirmed the lower court's finding that a professional buyer could not have been unaware that shoelaces on the footwear which the seller delivered violated a third party's trademark.[570]

Note in this connection that the seller's obligation under Article 42 is also limited by the specification of which State's industrial or intellectual property laws are relevant in this regard: (a) the State of resale or use, if contemplated by the parties at the conclusion of the contract; in other cases (b) the buyer's State of business.[571]

5. Buyer's Risk

204. Paragraph (2) of Article 42 places a further limit on the seller's obligation in two situations where the buyer clearly ought to bear the risk of a conflicting right

566. Regarding the similar rule in Art. 41, *see supra*, No. 199. Regarding the remedies set forth in Arts 45–52, *see infra*, Nos 209 et seq.
567. Regarding the similar rule in Art. 41, *see supra*, No. 199. Regarding Art. 49, *see infra*, Nos 225 et seq.
568. Regarding specific performance, *see* Art. 46 (*infra*, Nos 214 et seq.) and 28 (*supra*, Nos 140 et seq.).
569. Assuming a loss suffered in consequence. Regarding Arts 74 et seq. *see infra*, Nos 291 et seq.
570. Cour de cassation, France, 19 Mar. 2002, CLOUT Case 479, available at www.cisg.law.pace.edu/cases/020319f1.html (Court of Cassation cited sovereign discretion of trial court which found professional buyer could not have been unaware of counterfeit).
571. *See* A/CONF./97/5, *Secretariat's Commentary*, No. 6 to Art. 40 of the 1978 Draft Convention. *See also* Schwenzer in Schlechtriem & Schwenzer, *Commentary* 4th ed. (2016), at 698–700.

or claim: (a) where the buyer contracts with knowledge of the risk, and (b) where the buyer provides the specifications, etc., which created the conflict with the third-party right or claim concerned.[572]

6. Consequences of Failure to Notify

205. As in cases where an alleged breach relates to non-conforming goods (Article 35), a buyer alleging breach of an obligation under Articles 41–42 must give the seller timely and specific notice thereof. Article 43(1) provides:

> The buyer loses the right to rely on the provisions of Article 41 or Article 42 if he does not give notice to the seller specifying the nature of the right or claim of the third party within a reasonable time after he has become aware or ought to have become aware of the right or claim.

The question of timely notice after the buyer has become (or ought to have become) aware of the third-party right or claim has been addressed, *inter alia*, by the German Supreme Court in a case involving a stolen automobile. Noting that the question of what is a 'reasonable' time depends on the circumstances of each case, including the nature of the right and claim involved, the Court held that notice given more than two months after the car's seizure by the police was not timely, since the buyer, by virtue of the seizure (as a layman, that is, even before receiving lawyer's advice) ought to have become aware of a possible subsequent right or claim.[573] It is not clear from the decision whether the seller was actually prejudiced by the buyer's delay or whether that factor entered into the decision of the court.[574]

As a starting point, at least, the buyer who fails to duly notify in accordance with Article 43(1) loses the right to assert all the various remedies otherwise provided under the Convention for seller's breach (the right to require performance, to avoid, to claim damages or a proportionate reduction, etc.).[575] This starting point is modified in exceptional cases where the buyer can establish a reasonable excuse.[576] Note

572. According to Art. 42(2), the obligation of the seller under the Art. 42(1) does not extend to cases where: (a) at the time of the conclusion of the contract, the buyer knew or could not have been unaware of the right or claim; or (b) the right or claim results from the seller's compliance with technical drawings, designs, formulae or other such specifications furnished by the buyer. As noted by F. Ferrari & M. Torsello, *International Sales Law – CISG in a Nutshell* 2nd ed. (2018), at 289, the rule in Art. 42(2)(b) reflects the general principle that an obligee cannot rely on an obligor's breach to the extent that the breach was caused by the obligee's own act or omission.

573. *See* Germany, 11 Jan. 2006, Supreme Court (*Bundesgerichtshof*), CLOUT Case 822, available at http://cisgw3.law.pace.edu/cases/060111g1.html (court also found buyer failed to give seller proper notice that owner's insurer demanded that buyer turn over goods). *See also* Oberlandesgericht Dresden, Germany, 21 Mar. 2007, available at http://cisgw3.law.pace.edu/cases/070321g1.html.

574. Regarding this consideration in relation to the corresponding notice rules in Arts 38 and 39(1), *see supra*, No. 191.

575. Regarding the various remedies generally available to buyer for seller's breach, *see infra*, Nos 209 et seq. (regarding s. III of Ch. II) and *infra*, Nos 280 et seq. (regarding Ch. V).

576. Regarding excuses under Art. 44, *see infra*, Nos 207 et seq.

also that, in contrast with rule applicable in non-conformity situations governed by Article 39(2), Article 43 does not set forth a two-year cut-off period.[577]

7. Seller Aware of Third-Party Right or Claim

206. As we have seen, a buyer who fails to notify the seller of a given third-party right or claim may lose the right to rely thereon. Conversely, a seller who is aware of the right or claim concerned ought not be permitted to enjoy the protection which Article 43(1) would otherwise provide. For this reason, Article 43(2) provides that the seller is not entitled to rely on the provisions of the preceding paragraph (1) if he knew of the right or claim of the third party and the nature of it.

In contrast with the slightly more buyer-friendly rule in Article 40,[578] Article 43(2) precludes the seller from relying on the buyer's failure to notify only in cases where the seller actually knew of the right or claim of the third party; a showing that the seller could not have been unaware will not suffice.

S. Excuse for Failure to Notify of Breach

1. Nature of the Exception

207. Under Articles 39(1) and 43(1), buyers who fail to notify of an alleged breach in respect of the various obligations of the seller set forth in CISG Part III (Articles 35, 41, 42) generally lose the right to rely on such breach. And as a starting point at least, Articles 39(1) and 43(1) relate to the full range of Convention remedies otherwise available.[579] But Article 44 provides a narrow exception:

> Notwithstanding the provisions of paragraph (1) of Article 39 and paragraph (1) of Article 43, the buyer may reduce the price in accordance with Article 50 or claim damages, except for loss of profit, if he has a reasonable excuse for his failure to give the required notice.

A buyer who is found to have such a 'reasonable excuse' for his or her failure to notify does not lose all elements of the right to rely: such a buyer, while losing the right to require performance and the right to avoid, retains the right to a proportionate reduction in price, as well as a limited right to claim damages (i.e., except for profit lost by virtue of the failure to notify).[580]

---

577. The rule governing the limitation period applicable to a claim for defects in title must be drawn from the domestic law applicable by virtue of the conflict-of-laws rules of the forum. *See* F. Ferrari & M. Torsello, *International Sales Law – CISG in a Nutshell* 2nd ed. (2018), at 291 f.
578. *Supra*, No. 197.
579. *See supra*, Nos 191 and 205.
580. *See*, e.g., Tribunale di Modena, Italy, 19 Feb. 2014 http://www.unilex.info/cisg/case/1956 (buyer who lost right to terminate/avoid could nonetheless demand price reduction (Art. 83); citing Art. 84 court also awarded interest on reduction). As regards Art. 50, *see infra*, No. 232. As regards damages, hereunder for lost profits, *see infra*, Nos 289 et seq.

Although Article 44 does not refer to the buyer's obligation to examine the goods under Article 38, Article 44 has nonetheless been applied in a situation where the buyer failed to comply with the notice requirements of Article 39(1) because it did not examine the goods in a timely fashion – a delay for which that buyer had a reasonable excuse.[581]

It should be emphasized that the absolute two-year cut-off rule in Article 39(2) remains unaffected by Article 44. In this sense, Article 44 differs from Article 40 – a provision which has been applied to extend the buyer's protection beyond that two-year period.[582]

2. Reasonable Excuse

208. The difficult Article 44 question is what constitutes a reasonable excuse. The legislative history of the Convention suggests that Article 44 was drafted to meet what representatives from developing countries saw as the drastic consequences of a failure to notify under Article 39(1), and it has therefore been suggested that buyers in less developed regions may be among those likely to enjoy the benefits of a reasonable excuse.[583] That said, Article 44, by its own terms, applies to all CISG buyers, even experienced merchants, and so far most courts have interpreted the rule narrowly, providing safety-valve relief only in exceptional circumstances.[584] In the 'stolen automobile case' cited previously,[585] the German Supreme Court held that the buyer (an automobile dealer) did not have a reasonable excuse for failure to provide the seller with timely notice. In a far more controversial decision (the 'used shoe' case), a German regional court denied a merchant-buyer in a developing country (Uganda) an Article 44 excuse.[586]

These decisions notwithstanding, the developing CISG case law also shows that safety-valve rules like those in Articles 40 and 44 are applied, from time to time, so as to avoid otherwise unjust results.[587]

581. Arbitration Court of the International Chamber of Commerce, June 1999, CLOUT Case 474, abstract available at www.unilex.info/cisg/case/466 (buyer excused under Art. 44; not responsible for incorrect examination by independent inspection body).

582. *See supra*, No. 197 (citing case where buyer was allowed to rely on non-conformity discovered three years after delivery).

583. *See* Honnold/Flechtner, *Uniform Law* 4th ed. (2009), at 378–379.

584. Gerechtshof's Hertogenbosch (The Netherlands), 15 Dec. 1997, reported in UNILEX, is in *accord*: the buyer could have appointed an expert to take and examine a sample of the goods (furs) at the time of delivery; so the buyer's failure to discover the non-conformity before processing by a third party was not deemed to constitute a 'reasonable excuse'.

585. *See supra*, No. 205 Regarding Supreme Court (*Bundesgerichtshof*), 11 Jan. 2006, translation available at http://cisgw3.law.pace.edu/cases/060111g1.html.

586. Landgericht Frankfurt, Germany, 11 Apr. 2005, CLOUT Case 775, available at http://cisgw3.law.pace.edu/cases/050411g1.html. For a severely critical assessment of this decision, *see* H. Flechtner, 'Funky Mussels, a Stolen Car, and Decrepit Used Shoes: Non-conforming Goods and Notice Thereof under the United Nations Sales Convention', *Boston University International Law Journal* 26(1) (2008), available at http://papers.ssrn.com/sol3/papers.cfm?abstract_id=1144182.

587. *See*, for example, Arbitration Court of the International Chamber of Commerce, June 1999, CLOUT Case 474, abstract at www.unilex.info/cisg/case/466 (buyer excused under Art. 44; not responsible for incorrect examination by independent inspection body). Regarding the application

V. Remedies for Breach of Contract by the Seller

A. Introduction

209. Section III of Chapter II (Articles 45–52) is entitled Remedies for Breach of Contract by the Seller. These remedial rules form the core of the Convention regime.

For every breach by the seller of an enforceable CISG sales contract, there must be some remedy,[588] and Article 45(1) summarizes the remedies which the Convention makes available to the buyer for seller's breach:

> If the seller fails to perform any of his obligations under the contract or this Convention, the buyer may:
>
> a. exercise the rights provided in Articles 46 to 52;
> b. claim damages as provided in Articles 74 to 77.

B. Performance, Avoidance and Damages for Breach

210. The remedial rights referred to in subparagraph (a) of Article 45(1) and more extensively detailed in Articles 46–52 concern the buyer's right to require specific performance and the right to avoid.

Subparagraph (b) of Article 45(1) refers to the rules in Articles 74–77 which concern a CISG party's right to claim damages, in particular the extent and measurement of damages for breach.

Whether a given breach entitles a buyer to relief within one or more of these three fundamental remedial categories will always depend both on the particular circumstances and on the applicable CISG rule(s).

C. No-Fault Liability Based on Breach

211. It should at the outset be emphasized that Article 45 does more than catalogue the buyer's various CISG remedies for the seller's breach. In fact, Article 45(1)(b) constitutes the very *source* of the CISG buyer's right to claim damages for breach.[589] According to this subparagraph, the seller's failure to perform (breach) entitles the buyer to claim damages (as provided in Articles 74–77).

Since the CISG buyer may thus claim damages for any breach (failure to perform) by the seller, and since (as will be seen) Articles 74–77 deal only with the extent and measurement of damages, Article 45(1) clearly represents a *no-fault*

of the 'safety valve' in Art. 40 *see supra*, No. 197 (citing case where Chinese merchant allowed to rely on non-conformity first discovered three years after delivery).

588. *See* the Overview, *supra*, Nos 40 et seq.

589. *See* A/CONF./97/5, para. 1 of the *Secretariat's Commentary* to Art. 41 of the 1978 Draft Convention.

liability rule: that is, assuming that the injured buyer has suffered some causally related loss; the 'basis' of Convention liability in damages is the breach itself.[590]

D. Relationship among Remedies

212. As indicated previously,[591] the right to demand specific performance (i.e., to require that the seller perform) is not compatible with the right to avoid (demand an end to the obligations of both parties).[592] On the other hand, there is no mutual exclusivity as between the buyer's right to demand either specific performance or termination (on the one hand) and the right to demand damages (on the other), and Article 45(2) confirms this point: 'The buyer is not deprived of any rights he may have to claim damages by exercising his right to other remedies.'

Art 45(2): rights to specific perform/termination & damages are not mutually exclusive.

E. No Grace Period in CISG Context

213. Under some domestic legal systems, a significant delay in delivery does not necessarily give the buyer the right to avoid the contract, in that the seller may apply to a court for a 'delay of grace' (*délai de grâce*) which – if granted – effectively establishes a new delivery date.[593] Under the Convention, however, the buyer's right to avoid for fundamental breach cannot be defeated by such a *délai de grâce*.[594] Indeed, Article 45(3) expressly provides that no period of grace may be granted to the seller by a court or arbitral tribunal when the buyer resorts to any remedy for breach of contract.

Art 45(3): court/tribunal cannot give seller grace period. Only buyer can.

F. Specific Performance

1. Right to Require (Specific) Performance

214. Specific performance is the remedial starting point of the Convention, and although experienced practitioners will realize that avoidance and damages are the

---

590. The limited exemptions available to the seller under Art. 79 do not water Art. 45(1)(b) down to a rule of liability based on *culpa* or fault. *See* J. Lookofsky, 'Fault and No-Fault in Danish, American and International Sales Law. The Reception of the 1980 United Nations Sales Convention', *Scandinavian Studies in Law* 27 (1983) 109 (predicting that the fears expressed by B. Nicholas, 'Force Majeure, and Frustration', *American Journal of Comparative Law* 27 (1979) 231 would prove unfounded). Regarding subsequent case law under Art. 79, which provides clear support for the no-fault nature of CISG liability, *see infra*, Nos 302 et seq.
591. *Supra*, No. 43.
592. By definition, a party who 'terminates' a contract puts an end to both parties' right to demand specific relief.
593. Regarding, for example, the French domestic rules, *see* G. Treitel, *Remedies for Breach of Contract* (1988), 323.
594. Regarding Art. 49(1)(a), *see infra*, Nos 226 et seq. Regarding the *Nachfrist*-type warning system under Art. 49(1)(b), *see* Nos 229 et seq.

main remedies in international practice,[595] there are at least some instances where an injured CISG buyer will have occasion to demand that the breaching seller do what he or she promised to do, i.e., deliver the goods – this of course assuming of that the parties' contract does not validly deny the injured party access to that remedy (Article 6).[596]

So if a seller fails to perform his or her promise, the gap-filling Convention regime permits the buyer to require that the seller perform as promised: (1) deliver, (2) deliver substitute goods, or (3) cure defective delivery.

As regards the first of these three options, Article 46(1) provides:

> The buyer may require performance by the seller of his obligations unless the buyer has resorted to a remedy which is inconsistent with this requirement.

Paragraph (1) of Article 46 is designed to deal with the situation where the seller's breach consists of a total failure to perform. In such a situation, the buyer may demand performance unless he or she has resorted to an inconsistent remedy, that is, avoidance.[597]

buyer can't ask for avoidance and performance

2. Specific Performance and the Duty to Mitigate Damages

215. In addition to the express limitation set forth in paragraph (1) of Article 46, i.e., as regards resort to an inconsistent remedy, it has been suggested that the right to require performance should be interpreted in conjunction with an injured party's Convention obligation to mitigate damages,[598] in part because the right to compel specific performance after a market change might permit the buyer to speculate at the seller's expense.[599] However, because the Convention version of the mitigation rule applies expressly as a limitation on the right to recover damages, and because of the legislative history rejecting an amendment to that (Article 77) rule,[600] many

---

595. *See supra*, No. 45. As indicated *infra*, very few significant Art. 46 decisions have been reported. Regarding the buyer's right to avoid, *see infra*, Nos 226 et seq.; regarding damages *see* Nos 289 et seq.

596. *See*, for example, the award rendered by Arbitration Court of the International Chamber of Commerce, 2004, available at http://cisgw3.law.pace.edu/cases/041273i1.html (contract provided buyer could demand liquidated damages 'in lieu of any other remedy in respect of loss incurred by Buyer').

597. *See supra*, No. 212.

598. Regarding Art. 77, *see infra*, Nos 297 et seq.

599. *See* Lookofsky, *Understanding the CISG* 5th Worldwide ed. (2017), §6.4. *See also* Honnold/Flechtner, *Uniform Law* 4th ed. (2009), at 415.

600. *See* S. Walt, 'For Specific Performance under the United Nations Sales Convention', *Texas International Law Journal* 26 (1991) at 214.

scholars deny the application of mitigation as a limitation of the right to claim performance.[601] The very limited CISG case law on point suggests the issue is of little practical significance.[602]

3. Specific Performance Limited by Forum Law

216. Article 46(1) must be read in light of Article 28.[603] According to this latter CISG rule, a court or arbitral tribunal asked to require that a seller perform need not necessarily order such performance, even in a situation where the requirements for granting performance under Article 46(1) are satisfied.[604]

By virtue of Article 28, a forum court or arbitral tribunal which finds that the requirements of Article 46(1) are satisfied must also (i.e., as a second step) consider whether specific relief would be available to the buyer pursuant to the domestic sales law of the forum State.[605] And if that court or tribunal finds that specific relief would not be available under the corresponding domestic law, that court or tribunal is 'not bound' to require performance.

The discretionary rule in Article 28 was originally designed to meet the needs of Common law jurisdictions, in that such jurisdictions traditionally grant specific relief only in exceptional circumstances. And the rule in Article 28 has in fact been applied by a US Federal District Court in a situation where a German seller promised (but failed) to deliver hard-to-replace steel to an American buyer. In that situation, the Court rightly declared itself not bound to require delivery unless it would do under its own (domestic) law.[606]

---

601. *See* Schwenzer in Schlechtriem & Schwenzer, *Commentary* 4th ed. (2016), at 1105 f.; Walt, *ibid.*, at 214–216. Regarding mitigation and the seller's right to demand payment of the price under Art. 62, *see* A/CONF./97/5, para. 3 of the *Secretariat's Commentary* to Art. 73 of the 1978 Draft Convention and *infra,* No. 257.

602. Specific performance is a little-used remedy in the sales international context, and as of this writing, only one significant Art. 46(1) case (noted *infra,* No. 216) had been reported in UNILEX. *See also UNCITRAL Digest of CISG Case Law* (2016 ed.), available at https://uncitral.un.org/en/case_law/digests, Art. 46, para. 4 (right to require performance not often invoked; in practice aggrieved parties preferred to pursue other remedies).

603. *Supra,* Nos 140 et seq.

604. For example, where buyer (the party who is demanding performance) 'has not resorted to an inconsistent remedy'. *See supra,* No. 214.

605. Regarding specific performance in Civil and Common law systems, *see* Treitel, *Remedies* (1988), Ch. 3.

606. *See Magellan International Corporation v. Salzgitter Handel GmbH,* 1999, US District Court, CLOUT Case 417, available at www.cisg.law.pace.edu/cases/991207u1.html. In dismissing the seller's request for summary judgment, the court cited Art. 28 and stated that 'replaceability' was a central issue under the relevant American domestic sales law rule: UCC §2-716(1). The immediate effect of the ruling was to require a trial to determine whether the steel in question was, in fact, 'replaceable' (as the seller claimed); if the court found it to be replaceable, the buyer could not require delivery under the UCC, in which case the court would not be bound to require delivery under the CISG. *See also Styles v. Movie Star Muscle Cars, Inc. et al.*, 17th Judicial Circuit, State of Florida, 2017 Fla. Cir. LEXIS 9983, full text also available at CISG-online: cisg-online.org, case number 4684 (granting specific performance under Art. 28 for delivery of vintage car, as that remedy would also be granted, by way of exception, under Florida State law).

Then again, the letter of Article 28 does not limit its application to Common law systems, and the rule might also serve as a useful safety valve in other – for example, Civilian and Scandinavian – jurisdictions.[607]

The two-step process just described, involving both an analysis of the Convention and an analysis under forum law, clearly applies to cases falling under Article 46, paragraph (1), that is, where the seller does not deliver at all. Arguably, it should also apply to those forms of specific performance described in paragraphs (2) and (3).[608]

4. Require Delivery of Substitute Goods

217. Unlike Article 46(1), paragraph (2) of Article 46 deals with the situation where the goods have in fact been delivered. The problem (breach) in this situation is that the goods which have been delivered do not conform with the contract:

> If the goods do not conform with the contract, the buyer may require delivery of substitute goods only if the lack of conformity constitutes a fundamental breach of contract and a request for substitute goods is made either in conjunction with notice given under Article 39 or within a reasonable time thereafter.

Typically, the lack of conformity referred to in Article 46(2) will relate to a breach of the seller's obligation to deliver conforming goods under Article 35, but the buyer's right to require specific performance in the form of redelivery also extends to breaches which relate to the seller's obligation to deliver unencumbered goods under Article 41.[609]

In any case, to require delivery of substitute goods may entail a severe and potentially disproportionate financial burden for the seller.[610] For this reason, Article 46(2) conditions a buyer's right to require redelivery in much the same way as it conditions a buyer's right to avoid the contract entirely: like avoidance, redelivery requires a showing of fundamental breach.[611] Therefore, the buyer must suffer a detriment which substantially deprives him or her of what he or she is entitled to expect under the contract, and the detriment must also be one which this seller (or a reasonable seller) ought to have foreseen.[612]

The requirement that the breach be fundamental under Article 46(2) was of central importance in a 2007 arbitral proceeding involving a Danish seller's sale of an

---

607. Regarding, for example, limits on the right to demand performance which would otherwise be 'unduly burdensome' or 'impossible' under Scandinavian law *see* Lookofsky, *Consequential Damages*, available at https://jura.ku.dk/jurabog, 118–119.

608. *See* discussion of these provisions below.

609. *See* S. Walt, *supra* No. 215, note 600 at 217–218 (reviewing the inconclusive legislative history). Regarding Art. 41, *see supra*, Nos 198 et seq.

610. *See* A.CONF./97/5, para. 12 of *Secretariat's Commentary* to Art. 42 of the 1978 Draft Convention (costs to the seller of shipping substitute goods and of disposing of goods already delivered may exceed buyer's loss due to given non-conformity).

611. Regarding Art. 49(1) *compare infra*, Nos 226 et seq.

612. Regarding Art. 25, *see supra*, Nos 136 et seq.

American label-printing machine to a buyer in China. Given the fact that the seller, despite numerous attempts, failed to cure (repair) defects relating to 'core characteristics such as the overprint precision and the speed', the tribunal held the seller obligated to (re)deliver a quality-conforming machine within sixty days. Should the seller fail to redeliver, the buyer was held entitled to avoid the contract and, upon its return of the non-conforming machine, demand repayment of the (USD 1 million) price, thus reaffirming the fundamental nature of the Danish seller's breach.[613]

The rationale underlying this 2007 arbitral award conforms with the holdings of other courts: if the defects in question are easily repaired, the lack of conformity is not a fundamental breach. So, where the seller, in line with Article 48,[614] offers speedy repair without inconvenience to the buyer, the buyer cannot demand delivery of substitute goods under Article 46(2).[615]

In addition to the requirement that the breach be fundamental, the request for redelivery must be made in conjunction with (or shortly after) a notice which specifies the nature of the lack of non-conformity.[616] Until such time as the seller complies with its obligation to redeliver, the buyer is entitled to withhold the price.[617]

In order to be entitled to require redelivery, the buyer must be prepared to return the goods already received. In most cases, the buyer loses the right to require that the seller deliver substitute goods if it is impossible for him or her to make restitution of the goods substantially in the condition in which he or she received them.[618]

Since a proportional reduction in price entails the buyer's retention of the non-conforming goods, a buyer's resort to Article 50 would be 'inconsistent' with a demand for redelivery under Article 46(2).[619]

---

613. China International Economic and Trade Arbitration Commission, People's Republic of China, 24 Jul. 2007, English translation available at http://cisgw3.law.pace.edu/cases/070724c1.html (basing buyer's right to avoid on Art. 46(2), as confirmed by express contractual provision). Had the non -conformity in this case been cured/repaired within a reasonable time, the seller's breach would hardly have been deemed fundamental. *Compare* Oberlandesgericht Koblenz, Germany, 31 Jan. 1997, CLOUT Case 282, available at www.cisg.law.pace.edu/cases/970131g1.html (even serious non-conformity not fundamental breach as seller had offered to furnish substitute blankets). Regarding the buyer's right to avoid for fundamental breach under Art. 49, *see infra,* Nos 225 et seq.

614. As to Art. 48 and its relation to the concept of fundamental breach *see infra,* Nos 221 ff.

615. *See UNCITRAL Digest of CISG Case Law* (2016 ed.), available at https://uncitral.un.org/en/case_law/digests, Art. 46, para. 14.

616. *See* Art. 39, *supra,* No. 190.

617. *See* Supreme Court, Poland, 11 May 2007, available at http://cisgw3.law.pace.edu/cases/070511p1.html (suggesting this conclusion either by analogy with Art. 71 (*infra,* No. 282) or by virtue of a corresponding CISG general principle).

618. Regarding this Art. 82(1) rule and the exceptions set forth in Art. 82(2), *see infra*, Nos 318 et seq.

619. Article 50 is discussed *infra*, No. 232.

5. Right to Demand Redelivery Limited by Forum Law

218. To require a seller to redeliver is to require him or her to perform as promised.[620] Therefore, it is submitted – though, as yet, hardly settled – that Article 28 may work to limit Article 46(2).[621] So, even assuming that the various Convention redelivery requirements (fundamental breach, etc.) are met, a forum court ought not to be bound to require such performance under the Convention if this form of specific relief would not be available pursuant to the corresponding domestic law of the forum State.[622]

6. Buyer's Right to Require That Seller Remedy Non-conformity (Cure)

219. Under the Convention, and depending on the circumstances, a seller's non-conforming delivery may ultimately be remedied ('cured') for one of two reasons: either because the buyer demands (and is granted) this remedy or because the seller exercises his or her own right to repair.[623] It should therefore be emphasized that paragraph (3) of Article 46 deals (solely) with the *buyer's* right to require that seller remedy a defective delivery by repair:

> If the goods do not conform with the contract, the buyer may require the seller to remedy the lack of conformity by repair, unless this is unreasonable having regard to all the circumstances. A request for repair must be made either in conjunction with notice given under Article 39 or within a reasonable time thereafter.

In many situations, it will be more convenient and less expensive for the seller to repair the non-conforming goods delivered (than to provide for their return to the country of origin and then reship conforming goods from there). This helps explain why the Convention does not condition the buyer's right to demand that seller repair upon a showing of a fundamental breach. In fact, the starting point in Article 46(3) is that any breach of the seller's obligation to deliver conforming goods entitles the buyer to demand this particular kind of specific performance.[624]

However, a concrete evaluation of the situation is always required, in that the seller need not repair whenever this would be unreasonable having regard to all the

620. *Accord*: S. Walt, *supra*, 218 (order of specific performance may, under Art. 46(2), require seller to deliver substitute goods).
621. For a contrary view, *see* Honnold, *Uniform Law*, ed. Flechtner, 4th ed. (2009), Art. 46, at 415–416 (arguing that Art. 46(2) and (3) should be regarded as *lex specialis* qualifying the general provisions of Art. 28).
622. *See supra*, Nos 140 et seq.
623. Regarding seller's right to cure, *see supra*, No. 183 (regarding Art. 37) and *infra*, Nos 221 et seq. (regarding Art. 48).
624. *See*, for example, Cour d'appel de Versailles (France), 29 Jan. 1998, CLOUT Case 225, available at www.cisg.law.pace.edu/cases/980129f1.html#ca (two weeks after provisional test of machinery at seller's premises buyer informed seller's agent of non-conformities and specified improvements to be made before new test; court held buyer, in conjunction with Art. 39 notices of non-conformity, had required seller to remedy defects in compliance with Art. 46(3)).

circumstances. It would, for example, seem unreasonable to require a distant seller to utilize his or her own facilities or to travel a great distance to repair a minor defect, not only in light of the buyer's general duty to take appropriate measures to minimize loss suffered as a consequence of seller's breach[625] but also in light of the other Convention remedies at the buyer's disposal.[626]

Note in this connection that a proportional reduction in price due to non-conformity entails the buyer's retention of the non-conforming goods. For this reason, resort to a price reduction under Article 50 remedy would be 'inconsistent' with a demand that the seller cures under Article 46(3).[627]

Since the right to demand repair is rightly (albeit controversially) regarded a species of the more general right to demand performance as promised,[628] it is submitted that Article 28 should also work to limit the operation of Article 46(3).[629]

G. Nachfrist Warning: Fixing an Additional Performance Period

220. Under the main Convention rule which governs the buyer's right to avoid, the buyer is entitled to avoid only by reason of the seller's fundamental breach.[630] This rule covers both cases of non-delivery and non-conformity. In cases of non-delivery, however, the buyer may also avoid if the seller does not deliver the goods within an additional period of time fixed by the buyer.[631] CISG Article 47(1) describes the kind of additional period which may be fixed:

> The buyer may fix an additional period of time of reasonable length for performance by the seller of his obligations.

Those who drafted the main CISG avoidance rule, which gives the buyer the right to terminate in the event of a fundamental breach, envisioned situations where the buyer might have reason to doubt whether the seller would perform before a given delay in delivery becomes truly serious (i.e., a substantial detriment which would entitle the buyer to avoid). Moreover, the buyer might have reason to doubt how the

625. *Accord*: Honnold/Flechtner, *supra* note 621 at 415. Regarding Art. 77, *see infra*, Nos 297 et seq.
626. If buyer engages a third party to repair, the cost will be chargeable to the seller as damages for breach. Regarding Art. 74, *see infra*, Nos 291 et seq.
627. Article 50 is discussed *infra*, No. 232.
628. *Accord*: S. Walt, *supra*, at 217 ('form that specific performance takes depends on the circumstances').
629. *Accord*: F. Ferrari & M. Torsello, *International Sales Law – CISG in a Nutshell* 2nd ed. (2018), at 363 and 431. Regarding Art. 46(2), *see supra*, No. 218. *But see* Honnold/Flechtner, *supra* note 621 at 415–416 (arguing that Art. 46 (2) and (3) should be regarded as *lex specialis* qualifying the general provisions of Art. 28).
630. Article 49(1)(a), *infra*, No. 226.
631. Article 49(1)(b), *infra*, No. 229.

Convention requirement of fundamental breach would be applied to the circumstances of a given case;[632] and since reasonable minds can differ as to when we actually reach the 'critical mass' where a given delay (breach) becomes fundamental, a CISG buyer might find himself or herself in a precarious position, afraid to run the risk of (prematurely) taking a stand.[633]

For these reasons – and having been inspired by the similar (but not fully corresponding) *Nachfrist* provisions in German law – the CISG drafters gave the buyer the right to fix an additional period of time, a warning period (*Nachfrist*), after which the buyer may avoid without having to determine whether the delay concerned has reached (what a court might subsequently regard as) 'fundamental' proportions.[634]

However, it must be acknowledged that the flexible CISG requirement that the length of the *Nachfrist* period fixed be 'reasonable' itself introduces an element of uncertainty, in that a variety of factors enter into the calculation of whether the period fixed is to be judged reasonable or not.[635] In one decision illustrating the application of this rule, an additional time period of two weeks for the delivery of three printing machines from Germany to Egypt was arguably too short, whereas a period of seven weeks was regarded as reasonable.[636] In another case, involving a Danish-German car sale, a period of three to four weeks was found to be reasonable.[637]

The *Nachfrist* notice is designed to give the seller in breach a second delivery chance; once the seller is notified, the buyer must await the seller's reaction. During the period fixed, the buyer may not resort to any remedy he or she might otherwise have by virtue of the breach.[638]

As already emphasized, the seller's non-compliance with a given *Nachfrist* notice is sanctioned only in the case of non-delivery: only in this kind of *Nachfrist* situation will the buyer be entitled to avoid.[639] Thus, although the broad wording of

---

632. Regarding Art. 25, *see* generally *supra*, Nos 136 et seq.

633. *See* Lookofsky, *Understanding the CISG* 5th Worldwide ed. (2017), §6.10.

634. Regarding Art. 49(1)(b), *see infra*, No. 229.

635. *See* the factors noted by Huber in Schlechtriem, *Commentary* 1st English ed. (1998), at 396 (length of contractual period of delivery, buyer's recognizable interest in rapid delivery, nature of seller's obligation, nature of 'impediment' to timely delivery); similarly, Müller-Chen in the 4th (2016) ed. of the same work at 751.

636. CLOUT Case 136, Oberlandesgericht, Celle, Germany, 24 May 1995, available at http://cisgw3.law.pace.edu/cases/950524g1.html. *Compare* Tribunal of Int'l Commercial Arbitration at the Russian Federation Chamber of Commerce, 3 Dec. 2014, available at http://www.unilex.info/cisg/case/2034 (additional period of ten days fixed by buyer to deliver goods not of reasonable length in light of eight-month production time of goods sold).

637. CLOUT Case 362, Oberlandesgericht, Naumburg, Germany, 27 Apr. 1999, available at http://cisgw3.law.pace.edu/cases/990427g1.html.

638. Article 47(2) provides: unless the buyer has received notice from the seller that he will not perform within the period so fixed, the buyer may not, during that period, resort to any remedy for breach of contract. However, the buyer is not deprived thereby of any right he may have to claim damages for delay in performance.

639. Regarding Art. 49(1)(b), *see also infra*, No. 229.

Article 47(1) would seem to comprise any breach, the practical application of the provision is limited to cases involving non-delivery.[640]

H. Seller's Right to Cure after the Delivery Date

1. Introduction

221. By providing a seller who delivers early (i.e., before the contractually specified date) with a right to cure non-conformities (defects) in the goods so delivered, Article 37 gives the seller a chance to limit the damage caused by the breach and also to limit the scope of remedial relief otherwise available to the injured buyer.[641] Article 48(1) supplements this early-delivery rule with a more limited right for the seller to cure defects *after* the delivery date:

> Subject to article 49, the seller may, even after the date for delivery, remedy at his own expense any failure to perform his obligations, if he can do so without unreasonable delay and without causing the buyer unreasonable inconvenience or uncertainty of reimbursement by the seller of expenses advanced by the buyer. However, the buyer retains any right to claim damages as provided for in this Convention.

222. In most situations, an effective remedy by the seller of his or her initial failure to perform in full may be preferable to the buyer's avoidance of the contract: this will surely be the case for the seller, and it may also even be true for the buyer. To exercise his or her right under Article 48(1), however, the seller must produce a cure which is quick, convenient and certain as seen from the buyer's point of view.

2. Relation Between Cure and Avoidance under Article 49

223. Article 48(1) starts with the proviso: 'subject to Article 49' – a reference which is not completely clear on its face, and neither the rule's legislative history nor (as yet) CISG case law has definitively clarified the relationship between these important provisions.

There is, on the one hand, considerable support for the view that the seller should be allowed to cure (remedy) even serious defects in accordance with Article 48(1), that is, even in cases where a given non-conforming delivery might otherwise seem to fall within the scope of the fundamental breach rule in Article 49,[642] provided the seller, taking account of the buyer's plans for the goods, can reasonably be expected

640. *Accord*: Honnold/Flechtner, *Uniform Law* 4th ed. (2009), 418–419. If a seller fails to comply with an Art. 47(1) notice issued in respect of non-conformity, the notice can only affect the point in time at which the buyer can avoid on the basis of seller's fundamental breach: *accord* Honnold/Flechtner, *id.*, at 440 with note 13.

641. *See supra*, No. 183.

642. Article 49 is discussed in detail *infra*, Nos 225 et seq.

to repair or replace the goods within a reasonable time.[643] So, except in cases where a given breach remains incurable (by reasonable means, etc.), many commentators (and at least some courts) agree that a seller's good-faith offer to cure ought not to be defeated by the buyer's right to avoid for a fundamental breach.[644] Put another way: Article 49 might, as a starting point, 'take precedence' over Article 48(1),[645] but a breach of contract is unlikely to be regarded as fundamental in cases where timely and effective cure remains a reasonable possibility.[646]

The main ratio underlying this 'pro-cure' position is the existence of a 'dynamic' relationship among Articles 25, 48(1) and 49, the idea being that when a given non-conformity can be cured without great inconvenience to the buyer, then that non-conformity should not be regarded as a fundamental breach which triggers, for the buyer who would use it, the drastic avoidance remedy.

As emphasized in the UNCITRAL Digest of CISG Case law, however, many courts and commentators have adopted a different position: 'Avoidance of the contract ... excludes the seller's right to cure.'[647] Under this view, 'it is for the buyer to decide whether or not the contract should be avoided', and if a right to avoidance (by reason of fundamental breach) is established, 'the buyer may exercise it without restriction from the seller's right to cure'.[648] Given these (to some extent conflicting) views, contracting parties are well advised to include an express term which specifies the relationship between cure and avoidance. Indeed, many of the standard terms of parties doing business at the international level give the seller a well-defined right to cure defects within a reasonable time after delivery: according to

643. *Accord* Schroeter in Schlechtriem & Schwenzer, *Commentary* 4th ed. (2016), at 445–447. *See also*, for example, OLG Koblenz, Germany, 31 Jan. 1997, CLOUT Case 282, available at http://cisgw3.law.pace.edu/cases/970131g1.html (since seller had made offer to deliver new goods, which was refused by buyer, lack of quality did not amount to fundamental breach).

644. *See* generally Honnold/Flechtner, *supra* note 640, at 426–428. *See also,* for example, Pretura di Locarno-Campagna (Switzerland), 27 Apr. 1992, available at www.cisg.law.pace.edu/cases/920427s1.html (Swiss buyer resold living-room furniture to customer who complained goods defective; buyer who had refused seller's offer to cure held not entitled to avoid). *See also* the decision of Cour d'appel de Grenoble (France), 26 Apr. 1995, available at http://cisgw3.law.pace.edu/cases/950426f2.html (seller of used aircraft hangar partly cured non-conformity).

645. *See* generally Brunner, Akikol, et al., 'Article 48 [Cure after Date for Delivery; Requests for Clarification]', in *Commentary on the UN Sales Law (CISG)* (Brunner & Gottlieb eds, 2019), at 366–367.

646. Conversely, a breach will be regarded as fundamental and 'incurable' under Art. 48(1) where the breach in question cannot reasonably be remedied completely within an appropriate time; where the seller refuses to cure; in cases where cure is irrelevant (because *timely* conforming delivery is 'of the essence'); and where the buyer has justifiably lost confidence in the seller. *See* Brunner, Akikol, et al., at *id.*

647. *See UNCITRAL Digest of CISG Case Law* (2016 ed.), available at https://uncitral.un.org/en/case_law/digests, Art. 48, para. 2. *See also* F. Ferrari & M. Torsello, *International Sales Law – CISG in a Nutshell* 2nd ed. (2018), at 433 ('cannot be disputed' that in event of fundamental breach aggrieved party may declare contract avoided without need to grant to party in breach prior opportunity to cure).

648. UNCITRAL Digest at *id.*, text with notes 1 and 3. A few sentences later, however, the Digest (somewhat paradoxically) adds: 'a breach is rarely fundamental when the failure of performance could easily be remedied'. *See id.*, text with note 6, immediately after which the Digest (text with note 7) adds: 'This rule, however, should not be misunderstood to mean that in each case the seller must be offered an opportunity to cure before the buyer can avoid the contract.'

these terms, only in the event the breach concerned is of 'fundamental' proportions *and* the seller fails to cure that breach is the buyer entitled to avoid.[649]

3. Proposals and Notice by Seller Regarding Cure

224. The remainder of Article 48, paragraphs (2)–(4), contains a series of logical rules regarding proposals and notice by the seller regarding cure.[650]

I. Buyer's Right to Avoid for Seller's Breach

225. Article 49 embodies the main CISG rule, which provides an injured buyer with the right to avoid and thus terminate the contract, that is, put an end to the performance obligations of both parties.[651]

1. Avoidance for Fundamental Breach

226. Under some domestic statutes of sale, a 'perfect tender' rule prevails, whereby any breach (however insignificant) entitles the injured party to avoid (terminate) the contract.[652]

In international sales, however, particularly far-reaching consequences and extensive waste may follow in the wake of contract avoidance (termination), and so the general Convention rule is that avoidance requires a showing of a serious breach. According to Article 49(1)(a), the buyer may declare the contract avoided 'if the failure by the seller to perform any of his obligations under the contract or this Convention amounts to a fundamental breach of contract'. For a given breach (e.g., a delay in delivery) to qualify as a fundamental breach, the buyer must show: (a) that

649. *See* J. Lookofsky, *Understanding the CISG* (5th Worldwide ed. 2017) §7.1.
650. The text of Art. 48(2–4) is as follows:

- If the seller requests the buyer to make known whether he will accept performance and the buyer does not comply with the request within a reasonable time, the seller may perform within the time indicated in his request. The buyer may not, during that period of time, resort to any remedy which is inconsistent with performance by the seller.
- A notice by the seller that he will perform within a specified period of time is assumed to include a request, under the preceding paragraph, that the buyer make known his decision.
- A request or notice by the seller under paragraph (2) or (3) of this article is not effective unless received by the buyer.

651. *See* Art. 81, *infra*, No. 315.
652. Regarding, for example, English and American law, *see* J. Lookofsky, *Consequential Damages in Comparative Context* (1989), Part 4.3.1, available online at https://jura.ku.dk/jurabog.

timely delivery was of particular significance to him or her, and (b) that the seller knew of this significance or had good reason to know.[653]

Whether a seller's breach is fundamental will depend on the concrete circumstances.[654] To take a concrete example involving the CISG seller's obligation to deliver on time,[655] suppose the contract provides for the delivery of certain highly specialized goods (not easily obtainable elsewhere) to a given buyer (B) on a clearly specified date, for example, 31 January. If the seller delivers on 15 February, and if (B) is thereby prevented from performing an existing obligation to (re)deliver the same goods to a designated third party as agreed (say on 3 February), (B) has almost surely suffered a substantial deprivation under Article 25, but (B) will only be entitled to avoid if the original seller (or a reasonable seller in that position) had reason to know that such a breach would have such a substantial effect.[656]

As a rule, late performance does not in and of itself constitute a fundamental breach of contract. Only when the time for performance is of essential importance – either because that is so *stipulated* between the parties or because timely performance is *critical in the circumstances* (e.g., seasonal goods) – will delay amount to a fundamental breach.[657] As regards the first category, the CISG cases reported so far do not seem to involve a binding contractual provision which expressly provides that time is 'of the essence'.[658] There are, on the other hand, several cases where punctual performance was in fact critical for the buyer and where this fact was foreseeable by the seller at the time of contracting.[659]

The most challenging issues in determining whether a seller's breach is fundamental arise with respect to the delivery of defective (non-conforming) goods.[660] To be sure, a seller who delivers goods totally unfit for ordinary purposes will – at least in the case of an incurable defect – be held to have committed a fundamental breach.[661] Some courts have also held a breach to be fundamental when the goods

653. *See*, for example, the award of the ICC Court of Arbitration (Paris), No. 8128/1995, available at www.cisg.law.pace.edu/cases/958128i1.html (CISG seller knew buyer was obligated to deliver goods to third party and that, in case of late delivery, buyer had to pay a contractual penalty).

654. Regarding Art. 25, *see supra*, Nos 136 et seq.

655. Article 33: *see supra*, Nos 159 et seq.

656. Regarding this Art. 25 requirement, *see supra*, Nos 136 et seq. *See*, for example, the award of the ICC Court of Arbitration (Paris), No. 8128/1995, cited *supra* note 653, also at www.unilex.info/cisg/case/207.

657. *UNCITRAL Digest of CISG Case Law* (2016 ed.), available at https://uncitral.un.org/en/case_law/digests, Art. 49, para. 14.

658. With respect, the case cited in the *UNCITRAL Digest*, *ibid.*, with note 36, does not involve a situation where (as opined in the Digest) the parties themselves had 'stipulated' that the time for performance was of 'essential importance', and the reason that Oberlandesgericht Hamburg, Germany, 28 Feb. 1997, CLOUT Case No. 277, does not illustrate the Digest proposition is this: a delay in a contract with a CIF delivery term does not necessarily entail a fundamental breach. *Accord* Schroeter in Schlechtriem & Schwenzer, *Commentary* 4th ed. (2016), at 440–441 (also emphasizing possible custom in the trade concerned).

659. *See*, for example, Corte di Appello di Milano, Italy, 20 Mar. 1998, cited in the *UNCITRAL Digest*, *supra* with note 37 (buyer ordered seasonal knitted goods and pointed out the essential importance of delivery at the contract date, although it did so only after conclusion of the contract).

660. *UNCITRAL Digest of CISG Case Law* (2016 ed.), Art. 49, para. 16.

661. *See*, for example, Cour d'appel de Versailles (France), 29 Jan. 1998, CLOUT Case 225, available at www.cisg.law.pace.edu/cases/980129f1.html (buyer who could not use defective machines as expected entitled to avoid). *See also* LG Ellwangen, 21 Aug. 1995, available at

had substantial defects, and the buyer (or the buyer's buyer) needed the goods for manufacture.[662] The same conclusion has been reached where the non-conformity related to illegal additives.[663]

It must, however, be emphasized that avoidance in an international sales context is regarded as a particularly severe – and therefore exceptional – remedy, and many courts have therefore shown great reluctance to allow a buyer injured by a breach to avoid by reason of non-conforming delivery and thus put an end to the whole CISG contractual relationship, not least in cases where possible alternative uses or resale were available.[664]

If a given buyer requires more certainty than that provided by the flexible, gap-filling rule in Article 49(1), then that buyer might opt for a contractual term which expressly departs from the 'substantial deprivation' standard. Such a clause might, for example, expressly 'condition' the buyer's duty to pay upon the seller's punctual and fully conforming delivery.[665] Similar protection might be achieved by a clause which expressly provides that 'any non-conformity in the goods delivered by the seller shall be regarded as a fundamental breach'.[666]

Few, if any, reported Article 49 cases involve the interpretation or effect of buyer-friendly clauses which (as just illustrated) expressly 'upgrade' contractual quality

---

www.cisg.law.pace.edu/cases/950821g2.html (paprika not meeting minimum standards of German food law). Regarding Art. 35(2)(a)–(b), *see supra*, Nos 165 et seq. Regarding the relationship between Art. 49(1)(a) and 'curable' defects under Art. 48 *see supra*, No. 223 and, for example, Pretura di Locarno-Campagna (Switzerland), 27 Apr. 1992, CLOUT Case 56, at www.cisg.law.pace.edu/cases/920427s1.html, where a Swiss buyer resold living-room furniture to a local customer who then complained that the goods were defective (sitting on sofas caused cushions to slide forward); the Swiss buyer was held not entitled to avoid, *inter alia*, because he had refused to accept an offer by his Italian seller to cure the non-conformity by replacing the upholstery.

662. *See UNCITRAL CISG Case Digest* (2016 ed.) of Art. 25, *citing Cour de cassation*, France, 26 May 1999, available at http://cisgw3.law.pace.edu/cases/990526f1.html (metal sheets absolutely unfit for the foreseen kind of manufacture by the buyer's sub-buyer). *See also* Bundesgericht, Switzerland, 18 May 2009, available at http://www.unilex.info/cisg/case/1460 (actual performance of machine delivered *well below* performance required under contract, so buyer substantially deprived of justified expectation (Art. 25) and entitled to declare contract terminated pursuant to Art. 49(1)(a)).
663. *See Cour de Cassation*, France 23 Jan. 1996, CLOUT Case No. 150, available at http://cisgw3.law.pace.edu/cases/960123f1.html (artificially sugared wine forbidden under EU and national laws).
664. *See*, for example, German Supreme Court (Bundesgerichtshof), 3 Apr. 1996, CLOUT Case 171, available at www.cisg.law.pace.edu/cases/960403g1.html (avoidance is remedy of 'last resort'; breach not fundamental since buyer failed to show resale of non-conforming cobalt sulphate would be unreasonably difficult). *See also*, for example, Swiss Supreme Court (Schweizerisches Bundesgericht), 28 Oct. 1998, CLOUT Case 248, available at http://cisgw3.law.pace.edu/cases/981028s1.html (German sellers delivered frozen meat containing excessive fat and worth 25% less than conforming goods to Swiss buyer/wholesaler; considering buyer's ability to process or resell goods at lower price, court held non-conformity not significant enough to entitle buyer to avoid).
665. For example: 'The buyer's duty to pay for the goods under this contract is expressly conditioned upon delivery by the seller of goods which conform to their contractual description and specifications in each and every respect. Should the goods fail to so conform, the buyer shall have the right to declare the contract avoided and to return the goods to the seller at the seller's expense.'
666. Regarding the parties' freedom to contract out (in whole or, as suggested here) in part, *see supra*, No. 72.

stipulations to the level of express conditions.[667] The question of whether a given stipulation is 'of the essence' is of course a matter of interpretation under Article 8 CISG,[668] but the fact that some courts have held or indicated that breach of a certain quality-related obligation would be regarded as fundamental,[669] such as an obligation to supply unsweetened apple juice concentrate,[670] or soy protein not genetically modified,[671] does not (as elsewhere opined) imply that the parties themselves had agreed in advance that breach of such terms would be regarded as fundamental.[672] In fact, the German court in the apple juice case concerned held that the delivery of sweetened apple juice was not fundamental,[673] and the holding of the Swiss court that delivery of genetically modified beans was a fundamental breach was based on that court's own interpretation of a quality 'certification' (as opposed to an express agreement between the parties).[674]

Finally, it may be noted that a buyer not otherwise entitled to avoid the sales contract due to non-conformity pursuant to CISG Article 49(1)(a) might, at least in exceptional circumstances and in some jurisdictions, be held entitled to rescind the contract pursuant to the applicable domestic law regarding the effects of misrepresentation, fraud, duress and the like.[675]

---

667. *But see* Schroeter in Schlechtriem & Schwenzer, *Commentary* 4th ed. (2016), at 442–444 (citing specific quality descriptions which, according to Schroeter, constitute party definitions of the fundamental importance of certain quality features).
668. *Accord* (to this extent): CISG Advisory Council Opinion No. 5, 'The buyer's right to avoid the contract in case of non-conforming goods or documents', available at http://www.cisgac.com/cisgac-opinion-no-5/.
669. *Ibid.*
670. OLG Stuttgart, Germany, 12 Mar. 2001, translation available at www.cisg.law.pace.edu/cases/010312g1.html (buyer not entitled to avoid because no fundamental breach under Art. 49(1)(a); even though goods delivered had been mixed with glucose syrup and could therefore no longer be referred to as 'apple juice concentrate', breach did not substantially deprive buyer of justifiable expectation under contract).
671. Appellationsgericht Basel-Stadt, Switzerland, 22 Aug. 2003, CLOUT Case 887, available at www.cisg.law.pace.edu/cases/030822s1.html.
672. *Compare* CISG Advisory Council Opinion *supra* note 668, No. 5.
673. Thus lowering the court's observations on the issue discussed here to mere *dictum*. *Accord* Schroeter *supra* note 667, at 444 with note 231.
674. *But see* CISG Advisory Council Opinion *supra* note 668, No. 5.
675. Regarding the potential for overlap between the Convention and domestic validity rules, *see* generally *supra*, Nos 63–64; *but see*, for example, LG Aachen (Germany), 14 May 1993, CLOUT Case 47, available at http://cisgw3.law.pace.edu/cases/930514g1.html (application of CISG precluded recourse to domestic law regarding mistake as to the quality). Under American domestic law, avoidance might be allowed for a fraudulent misrepresentation without concern for its materiality (*see* Farnsworth, *Contracts* 4th ed. (2004), §4.12), whereas under CISG Art. 49(1)(a), a fundamental breach is the *sine qua non* for avoidance (Huber in Schlechtriem, *Commentary* 1st English ed. (1998), No. 5 at 416).

   The Hague Sales Conventions of 1964, which preceded the CISG, and which were ratified by very few States, expressly excluded the buyer's right of recourse to domestic law in the case of non-conforming goods (ULIS Arts 34 and 53), except in cases of fraud (ULIS Art. 89); the CISG Convention, however, contains no similar provisions, apparently because some Vienna drafters hoped it would be possible to create a separate treaty on 'validity' (which also would have dealt with the concurrent remedy issue): *see* Huber *ibid.*, at 370 with note 86.

2. Declaration of Avoidance

227. Article 49(1)(a) entitles the buyer to 'declare' the contract avoided. Such a declaration of avoidance is effective only if made by notice to the seller.[676] While there are no specific requirements as to form or content, the buyer's declaration must at least make it clear that the seller no longer can count on the buyer's performance in respect of the sales contract concerned. In cases where the grounds for avoidance relate to fundamental non-conformity, the time frame for the avoidance declaration may extend beyond that which applies to the requisite notice under Article 39(1).[677]

If a buyer faced with a fundamental breach first elects to avoid after the goods have been delivered, he or she must, as regards late delivery, make his or her avoidance declaration within a reasonable time after learning that delivery has been made; in other cases, for example, involving non-conforming delivery, the avoidance notice must be given within a reasonable time after he or she learns of the breach or after the expiration of an additional performance period fixed in accordance with Article 47(1) or 48(2).[678]

A CISG buyer can 'rely' on a rightfully dispatched avoidance declaration, even if it does not reach the seller.[679] If a seller receives – but refuses to respect – the buyer's (rightful) declaration, the buyer may, in certain circumstances, be entitled to revoke it.[680]

3. Relationship to Cure; Avoidance as to Part

228. As discussed previously, a seller who effectively exercises his or her right to cure a non-conforming delivery might effectively limit the buyer's right to avoid by reason of fundamental breach.[681]

As a factor which works in a more buyer-friendly direction, the Convention contains special rules which extend the buyer's right to avoid in cases where the seller

---

676. Regarding Art. 26, *see supra*, No. 138.
677. *See* Schwenzer in Schlechtriem & Schwenzer, *Commentary* 4th ed. (2016), at 791–793. Regarding Art. 39(1) *see supra*, Nos 190 et seq.
678. Article 49, subpara. 2(a).
679. Regarding Art. 27 *see supra* No. 139.
680. Professor Schlechtriem persuasively argued that the matter of whether a declaration of avoidance is binding upon the declaring party is 'governed-but-not-settled' by the Convention and that the general CISG 'estoppel' principle can be used to 'settle' it: *see* Schlechtriem in Schlechtriem & Schwenzer, *Commentary* 2nd ed. (2005), at 314 f. *Accord* Müller-Chen in *Commentary* 4th ed. (2016), at 726 f. *See also* Lookofsky, *Understanding the CISG* 5th Worldwide ed. (2017), §6.8 with note 105, referring to the decision by the ad hoc arbitral tribunal award of 10 Nov. 2000, reported as CLOUT Case 999, and described in the related Danish Supreme Court decision available at http://cisgw3.law.pace.edu/cases/060503d1.html. In the dispute underlying these arbitral proceedings, a Danish seller (S) had supplied a large machine (to produce concrete slats for pig sties) to a Canadian buyer (B). After the failure by S to repair a serious non-conformity, B declared the contract avoided. When S then refused to acknowledge its fundamental breach, B revoked its avoidance declaration and pursued other remedies, including damages. In these circumstances, the arbitral tribunal held B entitled to revoke.
681. *Supra*, Nos 183 et seq. and 221 et seq.

delivers only a part of the goods or where only a part of the goods delivered conform with the contract: in such cases, the buyer may avoid as to such part if the breach is fundamental with respect to the part.[682]

4. Avoidance for Non-compliance with Nachfrist Notice

229. In the case of non-delivery by the seller, the Convention provides injured buyers with an alternative to avoidance for fundamental breach. Article 49(1)(b) provides that the buyer may declare the contract avoided:

> in case of non-delivery, if the seller does not deliver the goods within the additional period of time fixed by the buyer in accordance with paragraph (1) of Article 47 or declares that he will not deliver within the period so fixed.

As noted previously, a CISG buyer may have reason to doubt: (1) whether a delayed delivery will arrive, and/or (2) whether the existing (or an extended) delay is fundamental under Article 49(1)(a); for these reasons, CISG Article 47(1) gives the buyer confronted by a delay the right to fix a warning period (*Nachfrist*), that is, an additional, reasonable period of time,[683] so that after the expiration of that time period, the buyer need not speculate as to whether the delay has reached fundamental proportions. If the seller, after the expiration of the warning period, has not delivered the goods (or even before that, if the seller declares that he or she will not comply),[684] Article 49(1)(b) gives the buyer the right to avoid.

Note that, unlike the rule in Article 49(1)(a), which permits avoidance by the buyer for (any) fundamental breach by the seller, the rule in Article 49(1)(b) applies only in case of non-delivery.

5. Limitations Regarding Goods Delivered

230. If the buyer elects to avoid after the goods have been delivered, he or she must do so (as regards late delivery) within a reasonable time after learning that delivery has been made or (in other cases) within a reasonable time after learning of the breach.[685]

---

682. Regarding Art. 51(1), *see infra*, No. 233.
683. *See supra*, No. 220.
684. Regarding anticipatory breach, *see* generally *infra*, Nos 281 et seq.
685. *See* Art. 49, subparas (2)(a) and (2)(b)(i). *See*, e.g., Cour d'appel de Douai, France, 6 Feb. 2014, available at http://www.unilex.info/cisg/case/1998 (noting that according to case law, a two-year period is generally considered reasonable; in the case concerned, the lapse of thirteen months before buyer notified seller of its intent to avoid was deemed reasonable under Art. 49(2)(b), considering buyer's legitimate attempt to preserved the contract and the usefulness of the goods/machinery for continued business activity; however, eight years of use were held to deprive the buyer of the right to avoid under Art. 82). As regards the time for avoidance after a *Nachfrist* notice or a seller's request under Art. 48(2), *see* subparas 49(2)(b)(ii)–(iii). *See also supra*, Nos 220 and 229.

6. Consequences of Avoidance

231. If the buyer avoids the contract with justification, both parties are released from their contractual obligations, subject to liability for any damages which may be due. In addition, each party may claim restitution from the other party of whatever has been supplied or paid under the contract.[686]

J. Proportionate Reduction in Price

232. In cases involving the delivery of non-conforming goods, the buyer may be entitled to a restitutionary measure of monetary relief even where he or she is not entitled to avoid. Article 50 provides, *inter alia*:

> If the goods do not conform with the contract and whether or not the price has already been paid, the buyer may reduce the price in the same proportion as the value that the goods actually delivered had at the time of the delivery bears to the value that conforming goods would have had at that time.

The proportionate price reduction (*actio quanti minoris*) is a remedy well known in Civilian (but not in Common law) systems. The proportionate price reduction constitutes an alternative to avoidance for non-conformity under Article 49, although it is also available in cases where the buyer would not be entitled to avoid. In the case of avoidance, the buyer who rightfully returns (fundamentally) non-conforming goods is entitled to full restitution of the contract price, if previously paid;[687] in the case of a proportionate price reduction, where the buyer keeps the non-conforming goods (either because he cannot or will not avoid), the buyer is compensated for the quality-gap: he or she receives a reduction in the contract price proportional to the reduced value of the goods due to the defect.[688]

Note that if the seller successfully remedies a given non-conformity in accordance with Article 37 or 48, the buyer may not reduce the price.[689]

In cases where the delivered goods have no value at all, the price can be reduced to zero. The buyer retains this possibility even if the right to declare the contract avoided is lost due to lapse of time.[690]

---

686. Regarding Art. 81, *see infra*, Nos 315 et seq.

687. Regarding Art. 81(2), *see infra*, No. 317.

688. *See*, for example, OLG Graz (Austria), 9 Nov. 1995, CLOUT Case 175, available at www.cisg.law.pace.edu/cases/951109a3.html. *See also* J. Lookofsky, *Understanding the CISG* 5th ed. (2017), §6.13.

689. The same applies if the buyer refuses to accept performance by the seller in accordance with Art. 37 or 48: *see* Art. 50, second sentence, and *supra*, Nos 183 and 221.

690. Oberlandesgericht Koblenz, Germany, 14 Dec. 2006, CLOUT Case 724, abstract available at http://cisgw3.law.pace.edu/cases/061214g1.html#uab. Regarding declarations of avoidance under Art. 49 (2) *see supra*, No. 227. Regarding Art. 39, *see supra*, Nos 191 et seq.

When the proportionate reduction is available as a remedy (for non-conforming delivery), it often constitutes an alternative to an award of damages for breach,[691] and since the Convention basis of liability for breach is essentially strict,[692] the damages remedy will often be preferred.[693]

K. Partial Non-conformity and Remedies for Breach

233. Articles 46–50, discussed above, regulate the buyer's remedies for seller's breach, *inter alia*, the important rights to demand performance or to avoid the contract. Article 51 concerns the applicability of these provisions to certain situations where the seller performs, but only in part. According to paragraph (1) of Article 51:

> If the seller delivers only a part of the goods or if only a part of the goods delivered is in conformity with the contract, Articles 46 to 50 apply in respect of the part which is missing or which does not conform.

In some respects, Article 51(1) sets forth a rule which would seem hardly necessary to (re)state. If, for example, a seller delivers two-thirds of the quantity agreed, but fails to deliver one-third, the buyer's right to require performance under Article 46 would obviously apply only to the third not delivered; similar considerations would apply in the case of redelivery or repair.[694]

L. Avoidance: In Part or in Full

234. As regards avoidance, paragraph (1) of Article 51 represents an amplification of Article 49(1): the general rule for part-performance is avoidance in part.

Against this background, paragraph (2) of Article 51 restates the obvious:

> The buyer may declare the contract avoided in its entirety only if the failure to make delivery completely or in conformity with the contract amounts to a fundamental breach of the [entire] contract.

---

691. Regarding Arts 74 et seq., *see infra*, Nos 291 et seq. Note, however, that it may be possible to combine proportionate price reduction and damages claims, provided the claimant does not thereby claim 'double compensation' for the same items of loss: *see* Müller-Chen in Schlechtriem & Schwenzer, *Commentary* 4th ed. (2016), at 808.
692. *See supra*, No. 211. For an imaginative example illustrating the relationship between an award of damages and a proportionate reduction, *see* Honnold/Flechtner, *Uniform Law* 4th ed. (2009), at 444–445.
693. Although consequential damages are only available as damages under Art. 74, the Art. 50 formula may nonetheless prove advantageous in cases where the buyer accepts delivery in a falling market: *see* generally, Bergsten & Miller, 'The Remedy of Reduction in Price', *American Journal of Comparative Law* 27 (1979) 255.
694. *See supra*, Nos 214 et seq.

M. Delivery Before the Date Fixed

235. The seller must deliver the goods as required by the contract.[695] If the contract provides that the goods must be delivered on a fixed date or within a given period, delivery at an earlier date would, without more, constitute a breach. In this situation, Article 52(1) provides that the buyer may take delivery or refuse to take delivery. Assuming, however, that the breach is not fundamental,[696] a buyer who refuses delivery will have to accept redelivery when (later) made at the proper time.

N. Delivery of Excess Quantity

236. The buyer is not obligated to accept (or pay) for more than what he or she has agreed to accept. If the seller delivers more than that which is provided for in the contract, the buyer may refuse to take delivery of the excess quantity;[697] however, if the buyer takes delivery of all or part of the excess quantity, he or she must pay for it at the 'contract rate'.[698]

§4. Obligations of the Buyer and Seller's Remedies for Breach

I. Introduction

237. Chapter III of CISG Part III (Articles 53–65) defines the obligations of the buyer and provides the seller with a catalogue of remedies for the buyer's breach. Many of the specifically tailored rules in Chapter III of Part III must be read in conjunction with the General Provisions set forth previously in Chapter I of Part III,[699] as well as with the rules set forth in Chapter V (Provisions Common to the Obligations of the Seller and of the Buyer).[700]

II. Summary of Buyer's Obligations

238. The main obligations of the CISG buyer are summarized in Article 53:

> The buyer must pay the price for the goods and take delivery of them as required by the contract and this Convention.

695. Article 30, *supra*, No. 148.
696. Regarding Art. 49(1)(a), *see supra*, No. 226.
697. In certain circumstances, for example, where the contract and the excess quantity are shipped under a single negotiable bill of lading, the non-conforming tender of delivery may constitute a fundamental breach: *see* Honnold/Flechtner, *Uniform Law* 4th ed. (2009), at 459–460.
698. Article 52(2). Regarding possible complications in this connection, *see ibid.*, 460–461.
699. Regarding Arts 25–29, *see supra*, Nos 135 et seq.
700. Regarding Arts 71–88, *see infra*, Nos 281 et seq.

Payment of the price is clearly the buyer's main obligation under the contract and the Convention, but depending on the circumstances, a buyer's failure to 'take delivery' can also trigger one or more of the CISG remedies available to the seller in cases of buyer's breach.[701]

When fixing the price in an international sales contract, most parties also fix the currency of payment. In cases where the contract leaves a gap on this issue, some courts have looked to the currency of the place of payment (which is often the place where the seller's place of business is located),[702] whereas other courts have resolved the issue on the basis of the domestic law applicable by virtue of the rules of PIL.[703]

III. Payment of the Price

A. Introduction

239. Section I of Chapter III provides more detailed provisions regarding the payment of the price.

B. Steps to Enable Payment of the Price

240. Since payment of the price in an international context is likely to require that the buyer take 'special steps', Article 54 provides:

> The buyer's obligation to pay the price includes taking such steps and complying with such formalities as may be required under the contract or any laws and regulations to enable payment to be made.

If, for example, the contract requires payment by letter of credit, the buyer's failure to take steps to open the letter (and thus assure timely payment) will clearly constitute a breach, and that breach may well be 'fundamental'.[704] And, as discussed

---

701. Regarding a buyer's failure to take delivery as a fundamental breach, thus triggering the seller's right to avoid under Art. 64, *see infra*, No. 261.

702. *See*, for example, Oberlandesgericht Koblenz, Germany, 17 Sep. 1993, CLOUT Case 281, available at http://cisgw3.law.pace.edu/cases/930917g1.html. According to F. Ferrari & M. Torsello, *International Sales Law – CISG in a Nutshell* 2nd ed. (2018), at 298, the matter of the currency of payment is governed by the CISG, but not expressly settled in it. Therefore, under Art. 7(2), the matter is to be settled, if possible, 'in conformity with the general principles on which [the Convention] is based', in that the relevant general principle applicable can be drawn from Art. 57(1)(*a*).

703. *See*, for example, Tribunal cantonal du Valais, Switzerland, 27 Apr. 2007, CLOUT Case 934, available at http://cisgw3.law.pace.edu/cases/070427s1.html.

704. *See* (e.g.) Seoul Central District Court (Korea), 19 Dec. 2008, CLOUT Case 1283, available at https://www.uncitral.org/clout/clout/data/kor/clout_case_1283_leg-2992.html; Seoul High Court, 14 Oct. 2010, CLOUT Case 1278, available at https://www.uncitral.org/clout/clout/data/kor/clout_case_1278_leg-2994.html.

more fully below, the buyer's failure to perform his or her obligations under the contract or this Convention will entitle the seller to exercise the remedial rights set forth in section III of Chapter III.[705] For one thing, the seller may avoid the contract if the breach is fundamental; alternatively, the seller may issue a *Nachfrist* notice, which provides for an additional performance period and permits subsequent avoidance for the buyer's failure to comply.[706]

C. Contract with Open Price Term

241. As emphasized in connection with contract formation under Part II of the Convention, a CISG contract proposal does not qualify as an offer (capable of acceptance) unless it is sufficiently definite.[707] Under Article 14(1), a proposal is sufficiently definite if it (among other things) expressly or implicitly fixes or makes provision for determining the price.

This provision (in CISG Part II) should not be understood to mean that a proposal which does not fix (or make provision for determining) the price necessarily fails to meet the requirement of definiteness, especially if the circumstances indicate that parties concerned have (otherwise) indicated their intention to be bound,[708] but such a proposal must nonetheless be considered in conjunction with Article 55 (in CISG Part III), which provides as follows:

> Where a contract has been validly concluded but does not expressly or implicitly fix or make provision for determining the price, the parties are considered, in the absence of any indication to the contrary, to have impliedly made reference to the price generally charged at the time of the conclusion of the contract for such goods sold under comparable circumstances in the trade concerned.

Only a few courts have found occasion to apply the gap-filling rule in Article 55.[709] And although some see a contradiction between Articles 14(1) and 55, a Swiss appellate court has opined that the practical importance of this contradiction should not be exaggerated.[710] The relationship between the phrase 'validly concluded' and the definiteness requirement of Article 14(1) has, however, been the subject of considerable academic controversy, just as the interplay of Articles 14 and 55 has been described as 'one of the most difficult questions raised by the Convention'.[711]

---

705. *See* discussion *infra*, Nos 252 et seq.
706. Regarding Art. 64, *see infra*, Nos 261 et seq.
707. *See supra*, No. 102.
708. *Ibid.*
709. *See UNCITRAL Digest of CISG Case Law* (2016 ed.), Art. 55, available at https://uncitral.un.org/en/case_law/digests.
710. Cour d'appel civile du Tribunal Contonal de Vaud (Switzerland), 29 Feb. 2016, CLOUT Case 1772 (where the Court of Appeal, citing Arts 8(3) and 9, determined the price by virtue of the parties' past practices and subsequent conduct).
711. *UNCITRAL Digest of CISG Case Law* (2016 ed.), Art. 55, para. 1.

To take a concrete example: assume that A and B conclude a sales contract which leaves the price open, but that the contract nonetheless meets the requirements of Article 14(1), in that the circumstances suggest that both parties at the time of contracting intended to be bound.[712] Assume also that A has its place of business in CISG State X where sales contracts with such open price terms are invalid under domestic law, whereas B has its business in CISG State Y where such terms are valid. Now assume that B sues A in a court in State X (or Y), demanding that A pay the price generally charged for such goods and that the applicable PIL (PIL/conflict-of-laws) rules of that forum State as regards validity issues point to the domestic law of State X.[713] *Query*: should the forum court render a judgment in favour of A on the ground that the PIL rules of the forum point to the law of a State where open-price-term contracts are invalid under domestic law?

According to the view held by some CISG commentators, a court in this situation should hold the contract invalid (and refuse to enforce it). In reaching this conclusion, these commentators attach great weight to the CISG legislative history (*travaux préparatoires*), arguing that the CISG drafters intended that a contract like the one in this example was not validly concluded.[714]

According to the view held by other Convention commentators, however, a rule in State X which invalidates open-price-term agreements under domestic law should not be allowed to override the intent of the parties to a CISG contract who have agreed to be bound.[715] Although some reach this conclusion with reference to the CISG party-autonomy principle,[716] other commentators in this camp base their conclusion on their own interpretation of the CISG legislative history.[717]

To be sure: 'Interpretation based on discussions by a large legislative body is [arguably] more meaningful for decisions of broad issues of policy than for detailed applications.'[718] Then again, the legislative history on this Article 55 issue does at least serve to illustrate the complex nature of issues which relate to validity and the interface between the Convention and domestic law,[719] not to mention the fact that CISG disputes are often resolved by international arbitral tribunals which, under the

712. *See supra*, No. 102.

713. Note in this connection that modern PIL rules attach great weight to the parties' intentions with respect to the applicable law. Regarding the relationship between party autonomy and mandatory rules under the EU (Rome I) Regulation on the Law Applicable to Contractual Matters (2008), *see* J. Lookofsky, & K. Hertz, *EU-PIL: European Union Private International Law in Contract and Tort* 2nd ed. (2015), Ch. 3. Regarding resolution of this issue under the American *Restatement (Second) of Conflict of Laws*, *see* J. Lookofsky & K. Hertz, *Transnational Litigation and Commercial Arbitration* 4th ed. (2017), Ch. 3.3.2.

714. *See* Honnold/Flechtner, *supra* note 697, 209–210 and 468–471.

715. *See* F. Mohs in Schlechtriem & Schwenzer, *Commentary* 3rd ed. 2010, at 820. *See also* C. Witz, *Les premières applications jurisprudentielles du droit uniforme de la vente internationale* (Paris, 1995), at 61 f; J. Lookofsky, *Understanding the CISG* 5th Worldwide ed. (2017), §§3.3 and 4.13.

716. *See*, for example, Lookofsky at *ibid*. *See also* Landgericht Neubrandenburg, Germany, 3 Aug. 2005, available at http://cisgw3.law.pace.edu/cases/050803g1.html (according to Art. 6 CISG, parties entitled to exclude the requirements of Art. 14(1) sentence two).

717. *See* Mohs, *supra* note 715, at 820 with additional authorities cited in notes 40–41.

718. *See supra*, No. 76 with note 180 (quoting Honnold/Flechtner).

719. *See*, for example, *infra*, No. 308 (regarding Art. 79 and 'hardship').

lex arbitri applicable in some CISG Contracting States, are generally empowered to resolve commercial sales cases without resort to *any* PIL rules.[720]

These considerations notwithstanding, Article 55 has not been the source of much difficulty in CISG practice, primarily because the overwhelming majority of parties to CISG contracts fix (or provide for determination of) the price, but also because of increasing acceptance of open-price-term contracts under domestic laws.[721]

The domestic sales laws of all Scandinavian States regard open-price-term contracts as valid.[722] And during the period in which the Scandinavian States, due to their then-applicable Article 92 declarations, were 'not bound' by CISG Part II (including Article 14), Article 55 had obvious relevance for CISG contracts with one Scandinavian party,[723] whereas the position that Article 55 should apply *only* in cases where one party resided in a Scandinavian State (which made an Article 92 declaration) was hardly tenable.[724]

D. Price Fixed by Weight

242. Article 56 provides the following rule of CISG contract interpretation: if the price is fixed according to the weight of the goods, in case of doubt it is to be determined by the net weight.

E. Place of Payment – Jurisdiction

243. The terms of the contract between the parties concerned ordinarily determine the place of payment. As to cases where the contract is silent on this particular point, Article 57(1) provides:

> If the buyer is not bound to pay the price at any other particular place, he must pay it to the seller:

---

720. *See* J. Lookofsky & K. Hertz, *Transnational Litigation & Commercial Arbitration* 4th ed. (2017), Ch. 6.2.3. *See also UNCITRAL Digest of CISG Case Law* (2016 ed.), available at https://uncitral.un.org/en/case_law/digests, Art. 55, text with note 11: 'Arbitration case law also appears to indicate a willingness to give effect to contracts whose price was not specified by the parties, by reason, *inter alia*, of the needs of international trade.'

721. Unwillingness to accept open price terms was long the case under French domestic law. In applying the CISG, however, French courts have not maintained a 'hard-line' interpretation on this point: *see* Schlechtriem in Schlechtriem & Schwenzer, *Commentary* 2nd ed. (2005), at 192, n. 24; *see also* Mohs in *Commentary* 4th ed. (2016), at 844; *compare* Honnold/Flechtner, *Uniform Law for International Sales under the 1980 United Nations Convention* 4th ed. (2009), at 469 with note 8.

722. *See*, for example, regarding §6 of the Danish Sales Act (*Købeloven*) J. Lookofsky & V. Ulfbeck, *Køb: Dansk Indenlandsk Købsret* (Danish Domestic Sales Law) 5th ed. (2020), Ch. 4.2.c.

723. Regarding the Art. 92 declarations and their withdrawal, *see infra*, No. 333.

724. According to para. 2 of the *Secretariat Commentary* to Art. 51 of the 1978 Draft (an earlier version of CISG Art. 55) has effect only if one of the parties has his or her place of business in a Contracting State which has ratified or accepted CISG Part III, but not Part II, and if that State accepts open price contracts as valid, but nothing in CISG Art. 55 supports the conclusion that the applicability of this Part III rule depends on whether the parties concerned reside in States which have ratified Part II.

a. at the seller's place of business;[725] or
b. if the payment is to be made against the handing over of the goods or of documents, at the place where the handing over takes place.

The place of payment may be significant in an international context, *inter alia*, if currency export restrictions are involved.

244. As previously explained,[726] a connection exists in some legal systems between substantive contract law rules relating to the 'place of performance' of a party's obligation (e.g., the place of payment under CISG Article 57) and domestic rules of procedure which determine the juridical jurisdiction of national courts.[727]

As regards contractual actions brought against EU domiciliaries in EU Member State courts, however, (e.g.) an action brought in Germany by an Italian CISG seller against a German buyer in respect of the latter's failure to pay, the 'place of performance' under Article 7(1)(b) of the Brussels I Regulation – and thus the juridical jurisdiction of that German court – is to be determined 'autonomously' and without recourse to the CISG or other gap-filling substantive law rules.[728]

F. Time of Payment

245. The buyer is obligated to pay at the time designated in the contract.[729] For cases where the contract is silent on this point, Article 58(1) provides the general gap-filling rule:

> If the buyer is not bound to pay the price at any other specific time, he must pay it when the seller places either the goods or documents controlling their disposition at the buyer's disposal in accordance with the contract and this Convention. The seller may make such payment a condition for handing over the goods or documents.

---

725. According to Art. 57(2): 'The seller must bear any increase in the expenses incidental to payment which is caused by a change in his place of business subsequent to the conclusion of the contract.'
726. *See* generally *supra*, No. 158.
727. *See* (e.g.) Cour d'appel de Quebec, 12 Apr. 2011, available at http://unilex.info/cisg/case/1646 (court applied CISG to determine the place of performance of American buyer's obligation to pay price; established practice between parties that Quebec was place of performance; no place of payment established in accordance with Art. 57 CISG except buyer's practice, known to the seller, of paying price in Gaspesie, thus conferring jurisdiction on Canadian court).
728. *See* generally *supra*, No. 158 and *Car Trim v. KeySafety Systems*, Case C-381/08, decided 25 Feb. 2010 (autonomy of linking factors in Brussels Regulation rule (then numbered) Art. 5(1)(b) precludes application of rules of private international law of Member State where action is brought and substantive law which would be applicable thereunder). *See* J. Lookofsky & K. Hertz, *Transnational Litigation & Commercial Arbitration* 4th ed. (2017), pp. 89–105.
729. *See* Arts 53 (*supra*, No. 238) and 59 (*infra*, No. 250).

246. In a bilateral contract, and unless otherwise agreed, the parties are to exchange their performance obligations at the same point in time, that is (as Common lawyers put it): payment and delivery are 'constructive conditions concurrent'.[730] Since the seller in a CISG contract has no obligation to extend credit, the buyer must pay when the seller makes the goods available, either by placing the goods themselves or the documents controlling them at the buyer's disposal.[731] Conversely, the buyer need not pay until the goods (or controlling documents) are made available.[732]

G. Contracts Involving Carriage

247. In an international sales context, the contract will ordinarily (i.e., in the average case) 'involve' carriage of the goods (by an independent carrier).[733] For these ordinary cases, where the parties deal with each other at a distance, Article 58(2) provides the necessary modification to the 'construction conditions concurrent' rule in paragraph (1):

> If the contract involves carriage of the goods, the seller may dispatch the goods on terms whereby the goods, or documents controlling their disposition, will not be handed over to the buyer except against payment of the price.

So, in cases where the contract involves 'carriage' (by an independent carrier), Article 58(2) permits the seller to protect its interests while proceeding to dispatch the goods: absent contrary contractual provision, and at seller's election, the terms of carriage may provide that an exchange of goods (or documents) against payment will take place later, when the goods (or documents) are actually 'handed over' to the buyer.

248. Article 58 deals with the time, not the place for exchange. In the paragraph (2) situation, when the seller elects to ship under terms whereby the goods (or documents) are to be handed over to the buyer against payment, the CISG default rule calls for payment to be made where the handing over takes place.[734]

In many instances, however, the seller may not wish to ship under such terms without some assurance that the ultimate exchange will proceed as planned.[735] For

730. *Compare*, for example, s. 28 of the Sale of Goods Act (UK): unless otherwise agreed, delivery of the goods and payment of the price are concurrent conditions, that is, to say, the seller must be ready and willing to give possession of the goods to the buyer in exchange for the price, and the buyer must be ready and willing to pay the price in exchange for possession of the goods.
731. *Accord* Arrondissementsrechtbank Arnhem, 31 Jan. 2008, available at http://www.unilex.info/cisg/case/1340 (CISG contains no provision giving either party right to withhold performance, but case law and doctrine agree such a right can be inferred from Art. 58).
732. Regarding inspection of the goods, *see* para. (3) of Art. 58, discussed *infra*, No. 249.
733. Regarding seller's obligation to deliver under Art. 31, *see supra*, Nos 153 et seq.
734. *See* Art. 57(1)(b), *supra*, No. 243.
735. Paragraph (2) protects the seller against having to deliver without receiving payment; it does not protect, for example, against the risk of buyer's insolvency which may first become apparent when the goods arrive in buyer's State.

this reason, the contract will often require the buyer to arrange for the issuance of a letter of credit in the seller's favour; in this case, payment will be made – in exchange for documents – in the seller's locale, by the local (confirming) bank concerned.[736]

H. Buyer's Right to Inspect Before Payment

249. The buyer has of course no obligation to make (full) payment for goods which do not conform to the contract.[737] This explains why the buyer, before making payment (and accepting delivery), is entitled (though not obligated) to examine the goods.[738] Article 58(3) provides:

> The buyer is not bound to pay the price until he has had an opportunity to examine the goods, unless the procedures for delivery or payment agreed upon by the parties are inconsistent with his having such an opportunity.

In the Article 58(2) situation, when the seller elects to ship under terms whereby the goods (or documents) are to be handed over to the buyer against payment, the seller must preserve the buyer's right to inspect, for example, by arranging for buyer's access to the goods at the point of destination.[739]

The right of inspection under Article 58(3) is a supplementary (contract gap-filling) rule, so if the parties agree on other delivery or payment procedures which are inconsistent with that rule, the buyer has no right to inspect prior to payment. The payment clause 'cash against documents' is one example of such an agreement which is inconsistent with inspection prior to payment.[740]

A common arrangement, particularly suitable if the buyer is concerned that the seller might ship defective goods, is that the documents to be tendered by the seller in exchange for payment by letter of credit shall include a certificate of quality by an independent inspection agency.[741]

---

736. The CISG does not deal with letters of credit. As to whether the seller may require buyer to pay by letter of credit absent agreement, *see* Honnold/Flechtner, *Uniform Law for International Sales under the 1980 United Nations Convention* 4th ed. (2009), 479–480.
737. *See*, for example, Art. 50, *supra*, No. 232.
738. Contrast the *obligation* of the buyer to inspect within as short a period as possible as practicable *following* delivery under Art. 38: *see supra*, Nos 187 et seq.
739. In a German decision involving a large quantity of used shoes, the fact that the Ugandan buyer would have had to fly to Kenya in order to examine the goods at the place of delivery before transshipment to Uganda (and that such an examination might have triggered Kenyan custom duties) did not relieve the buyer of the duty to examine the goods in Kenya under Art. 38(3), a rule discussed *supra*, No. 189. *See* Landgericht Frankfurt, Germany, 11 Apr. 2005, CLOUT Case No. 775, available at http://cisgw3.law.pace.edu/cases/050411g1.html. For a commentary critical of this decision, *see* H. Flechtner, 'Funky Mussels, a Stolen Car, and Decrepit Used Shoes: Non-conforming Goods and Notice Thereof under the United Nations Sales Convention', *Boston University International Law Journal* 26(1) (2008), available at http://papers.ssrn.com/sol3/papers.cfm?abstract_id=1144182.
740. *See* F. Mohs in Schlechtriem & Schwenzer, *Commentary* 4th ed. (2016), at 886.
741. *See* Honnold/Flechtner, *supra* note 736, at 481.

I. Payment Due Without Request or Formality

250. According to some domestic rules, a party may not recover damages for delayed payment without first having made a formal demand (*mise en demeure*).[742]

There is no corresponding principle in the CISG. In fact, as Article 59 expressly confirms, the buyer must pay the price on the date fixed or determinable from the contract and this Convention without the need for any request or compliance with any formality on the part of the seller.

IV. Taking Delivery

251. Section II of Chapter III consists of but one provision: Article 60. This rule, which breaks down buyer's obligations as regards delivery into two main elements, provides:

> The buyer's obligation to take delivery consists:
>
> a. in doing all the acts which could reasonably be expected of him in order to enable the seller to make delivery; and
> b. in taking over the goods.

Paragraph (a) concerns preliminary acts. Sometimes, for example, it will be up to the buyer to arrange for carriage. In other cases, the buyer will need to designate the desired destination, so that the seller can arrange for timely shipment to the right place.

The buyer's obligation to take over the goods in paragraph (b) is significant, *inter alia*, where the seller's delivery obligation involves placing the goods at the buyer's disposal:[743] the buyer who fails to take over the goods in time will bear the risk of accidental loss or damage after that time.[744]

In cases involving carriage, the buyer's failure to take over the goods from the independent carrier concerned will constitute a breach, and the buyer can be held liable for the damages which result, for example, so as to provide the seller with compensation for extra costs payable to the carrier in this regard.

742. *See*, for example, J. Herbots, *The Belgian Law of Contracts*, para. 404, in *International Encyclopaedia of Contracts, Belgium* (2000).
743. *See* Art. 31, paras (b) and (c), *supra*, Nos 155 et seq.
744. Regarding Art. 69, *see infra*, Nos 275 et seq. Note, however, that the buyer may reject the goods in the event of a delay or non-conformity amounting to a fundamental breach of contract: F. Ferrari & M. Torsello, *International Sales Law – CISG in a Nutshell* 2nd ed. (2018), at 313. Under Art. 86(1), however, the buyer remains subject to the obligation to take such steps to preserve the goods as are reasonable in the circumstances: *see id.*, at 314.

V. Remedies for Breach of Contract by the Buyer

A. *Introduction*

252. Section III of Chapter III is entitled 'Remedies for breach of contract by the buyer'.

For every breach by the buyer of an enforceable CISG sales contract, there must be some remedy.[745] Article 61(1) summarizes the remedies which the Convention makes available to the seller for buyer's breach:

> If the buyer fails to perform any of his obligations under the contract or this Convention, the seller may:
>
> a. exercise the rights provided in Articles 62–65;
> b. claim damages as provided in Articles 74–77.

B. *Performance, Avoidance and Damages for Breach*

253. The seller's rights referred to in subparagraph (a) of Article 61(1), and detailed in Articles 62–65, concern the right to require (specific) performance and the right to avoid; subparagraph (b) refers to the rules in Chapter V of CISG Part III (Provisions Common to the Obligations of the Seller and of the Buyer), which concern the extent and measurement of damages for breach. Whether a given breach entitles a seller to relief within one or more of these three fundamental categories will generally depend both on the particular circumstances and on the applicable CISG rule(s).

C. *No-Fault Liability Based on Breach*

254. Significantly, Article 61(1) does more than merely summarize the various other CISG provisions regarding seller's remedies for buyer's breach. In fact,

745. *See* generally the Overview, *supra*, Nos 40 et seq.

Article 61(1) sets forth the very 'basis' of the CISG buyer's liability in damages; it is, in other words, the very source of the seller's right to claim damages for the buyer's breach.[746]

Since Articles 74–77 concern only the 'extent' of damages for breach (i.e., 'how much'), and since Article 61(1)(b) bluntly states that the seller may claim damages thus measured for *any* breach, it is clear that Article 61(1) represents a *no-fault* liability rule. So, assuming that the injured party has suffered some loss, the basis of Convention liability in damages is the breach itself.[747] The limited 'exemptions' made available to the buyer under Article 79 do not water Article 61 down to a fault rule based on culpable breach.[748]

D. Relationship among Remedies

255. As indicated previously, there is no mutual exclusivity as between the aggrieved seller's right to demand either specific performance or termination (on the one hand) and that seller's right to demand damages (on the other).[749] Article 61(2) confirms the point: the seller is not deprived of any right he may have to claim damages by exercising his or her right to other remedies.

E. No Grace Period in CISG Context

256. In some legal systems, where a buyer's failure to pay would otherwise permit the seller to avoid (terminate) the contract, the buyer may apply to a court for a delay of grace (*délai de grâce*) which, in effect, establishes a new payment date.[750] Under the Convention, however, avoidance is usually triggered by a fundamental breach.[751] Therefore, Article 61(3) provides that no period of grace may be granted to the buyer by a court or arbitral tribunal when the seller resorts to a remedy for breach of contract.

746. *See* A/CONF./97/5, para. 1 of the *Secretariat's Commentary* to Art. 57 of the 1978 Draft Convention.
747. Among the many cases citing Art. 61(1)(b) in this connection, *see* Bundesgerichtshof, Germany, 27 Nov. 2007, available at http://cisgw3.law.pace.edu/cases/071127g1.html (seller's damages claim for failure to perform held well-founded because buyer did not fulfil its contractual obligations to take delivery and to pay the purchase price: *Vertragspflichten zur Abnahme und Kaufpreiszahlung nicht erfüllt*). As regards the buyer's corresponding right to damages for seller's breach under Art. 45(1)(b), *see supra*, No. 211.
748. Regarding Art. 79, *see infra*, Nos 302 et seq.
749. *Supra*, No. 43.
750. *See also supra*, No. 213. Regarding, for example, the French domestic rules, *see* Treitel, *Remedies for Breach of Contract* (1988), at 323.
751. Regarding Art. 64(1)(a), *see infra*, Nos 261 et seq. Regarding the *Nachfrist* warning under Art. 64(1)(b), *see* Nos 263 et seq.

F. Specific Performance

1. Right to Require (Specific) Performance

257. If a CISG buyer fails to perform his or her promise to pay, to take delivery, etc., the Convention permits the seller to require that the buyer perform as promised. Article 62 provides:

> The seller may require the buyer to pay the price, take delivery or perform his other obligations, unless the seller has resorted to a remedy which is inconsistent with this requirement.

The seller may demand performance unless he or she has resorted to an inconsistent remedy. Avoidance is an inconsistent remedy in this context, since, by definition, a party who rightly avoids (terminates) a contract puts an end to both parties' right to demand specific relief.[752] Such an inconsistency would also exist (e.g.) in cases where the seller has fixed an additional period of time for performance under Article 63(2) or where the seller has sold goods which had to be preserved under Article 88.

2. Other Convention Limitations

258. In certain circumstances, other Convention provisions will affect the seller's right to compel the buyer's performance, for example, to take delivery or pay the price. Not only must the seller take appropriate steps to preserve goods in his or her possession;[753] if the goods are subject to rapid deterioration or their preservation would involve unreasonable expense, the seller who is otherwise bound to preserve the goods must also take reasonable measures to sell them.[754]

Arguably, the 'duty' which obligates a contracting party to mitigate could be interpreted as a general Convention principle,[755] particularly when combined with a Convention interpretation promoting the observance of good faith.[756] However, because the Convention version of the mitigation rule applies expressly as a limitation on the right to recover damages,[757] and because of the legislative history rejecting an amendment to expand the express scope of the mitigation rule,[758] there

752. *See supra*, No. 43.
753. Article 85: *infra*, No. 326.
754. Article 88(2): *infra*, No. 328. *See also* Mohs in Schlechtriem & Schwenzer, *Commentary* 4th ed. (2016), 913.
755. Regarding Art. 77, *see infra*, Nos 297 et seq.
756. *See* Honnold/Flechtner, *Uniform Law for International Sales under the 1980 United Nations Convention* 4th ed. (2009), 596–598. Regarding good faith under Art. 7, *see supra*, Nos 75 et seq.
757. Regarding Art. 77, *see infra*, Nos 297 et seq.
758. *See* S. Walt, *supra* No. 215 note 600, at 215–216. *Compare* Honnold/Flechtner, *supra* note 756, at 598–600 (challenging the meaning to be attached to rejection of this amendment).

is considerable support for the view denying the application of mitigation as a limitation of the right to claim performance.[759]

3. Specific Performance Limited by Forum Law

259. Article 61(1) is tied to Article 28.[760] Even if a court holds that, under the Convention remedial scheme, the seller can require that buyer performs his or her obligations, that court must also consider whether such specific relief would be available pursuant to its own domestic sales law, that is, the law of the forum State.[761] If specific relief is not so available, the forum court is not bound to require performance under the Convention. In particular, as regards Common law fora, Article 28 may assume significance in cases where the seller demands performance while still in possession of the goods.[762]

G. Nachfrist Warning, Fixing an Additional Performance Period

260. According to the general Convention rule, the CISG seller is entitled to avoid (terminate) only if the buyer's breach is fundamental.[763] However, in cases where the buyer does not pay or take delivery, the seller may also avoid if the buyer does not perform within an additional period of time (*Nachfrist*) fixed by the seller in accordance with paragraph (1) of Article 63.[764] This rule provides:

> The seller may fix an additional period of time of reasonable length for performance by the buyer of his obligations.

Once the buyer is late in performing, the seller may have reason to doubt whether the buyer will perform before the breach becomes truly serious, i.e., assumes the proportions of a 'substantial detriment' which would entitle the seller to avoid;[765] indeed, the seller may have reason to doubt how the Convention requirement of fundamental breach will be applied in a given case. For this reason, the CISG gives the seller the right to fix an additional period of time, after which the seller may avoid without having to consider whether the total delay has reached fundamental proportions.[766]

---

759. *See* A/CONF./97/5, para. 3 of the *Secretariat's Commentary* to Art. 73 of the 1978 Draft Convention and Walt, *ibid. Compare* Mohs, *supra* note 754 at 912 (arguing that Art. 77 might apply despite the legislative history of Art. 62).
760. *Supra*, Nos 140 et seq.
761. Regarding specific performance in Civil and Common law systems, *see* Treitel, *Remedies for Breach of Contract* (1988), Ch. 3.
762. *See* generally Kastely, 'The Right to Require Performance in International Sales', *Washington Law Review* 63 (1988) 607.
763. Article 64(1)(a): *infra*, No. 261.
764. Article 64(1)(b), *infra*, No. 263.
765. Regarding Art. 25, *see* generally *supra*, Nos 136 et seq. *Compare* also *supra*, No. 220.
766. Regarding Art. 64(1)(b), *see infra*, No. 263.

Once such a so-called *Nachfrist* notice is sent, the seller must await the buyer's reaction. During the period fixed, the seller may not resort to any remedy he or she might otherwise have by virtue of the breach.[767]

H. Avoidance

1. Seller's Right to Avoid for Buyer's Breach

261. The general Convention rule as regards putting an end to a CISG contract applies to sellers and buyers alike: avoidance requires a showing of a fundamental breach.[768] According to Article 64(1)(a):

> The seller may declare the contract avoided:
>
> a. if the failure by the buyer to perform any of his obligations under the contract or this Convention amounts to a fundamental breach of contract. ...

Under some domestic statutes of sale, time is (absent contrary agreement) assumed to be 'of the essence', in that any delay in performance (however brief) entitles the injured party to avoid (terminate) the contract, and the delay need not even relate to the buyer's main obligation to pay the price.[769] In international sales, however, Article 64(1)(a) follows the general Convention rule: seller can avoid only if buyer's failure to perform amounts to a fundamental breach. This applies to all of the buyer's obligations under the contract and the Convention, not only to the obligation to pay but also, for example, to an obligation to apply for a letter of credit or a bank guarantee to facilitate the payment of the price.[770] To take another such example: a French court has held that a buyer of goods for the manufacture of medical equipment who unlawfully refused to take delivery pursuant to Article 53 committed a fundamental breach under Article 64.[771]

Then again, the notion of fundamental breach under Article 25 is often interpreted restrictively in order to preserve the existence of the contract. For example, the Supreme Court of Poland has held that a buyer's failure to make a contractually agreed payment 'in advance' did not constitute a fundamental breach.[772] The seller

---

767. Article 63(2) provides: unless the seller has received notice from the buyer that he will not perform within the period so fixed, the seller may not, during that period, resort to any remedy for breach of contract. However, the seller is not deprived thereby of any right he may have to claim damages for delay in performance.

768. Regarding buyer's avoidance for seller's breach under Art. 49, *see supra*, Nos 225 et seq.

769. Regarding English law, *see*, for example, J. Lookofsky, *Consequential Damages in Comparative Context* (1989), at 126 with note 105, https://jura.ku.dk/jurabog.

770. Regarding Art. 54, *see supra*, No. 240.

771. *See* Tribunal de Commerce – Versailles (France), 12 Mar. 2010, available at http://www.unilex.info/cisg/case/1527.

772. Supreme Court of Poland, 28 Nov. 2013, http://www.unilex.info/cisg/case/1993, CLOUT Case 1598 (especially since buyer had not declared its unwillingness to pay; nor did buyer's failure to provide specification of goods constitute fundamental breach, as seller could have made the specification itself under Art. 65).

is, of course, entitled to expect payment on time.[773] If, however, the buyer tenders payment one or two days later than the contract date, or delays taking delivery for a few days, it is far from certain that the seller has thereby suffered a substantial deprivation under Article 25.[774] And even if the seller has suffered such a deprivation, he or she will only be entitled to avoid if the buyer (or a reasonable buyer) at the time of contracting had reason to know that such a breach would have this substantial effect.[775]

That said, even a brief delay by the buyer (to pay or take delivery) can amount to a fundamental breach in a situation where punctual performance is especially important for the seller, for example, if the goods are perishable or if the seller needs rapid access to storage or transport facilities.[776] By the same token, even the breach of an ancillary duty will sometimes be regarded as fundamental, that is, sufficiently serious to provide the seller with grounds to avoid.[777]

A seller who would require greater certainty than that provided by the CISG gap-filling regime (which generally conditions avoidance on a fundamental breach) is well advised to insist on a contract term which clearly spells out the remedial rights of the seller in the event the buyer, for example, fails to make payment on or before the date required by the contract.

2. Declaration of Avoidance

262. Article 64(1)(a) entitles the seller to declare the contract avoided. Such a declaration of avoidance is effective only if made by notice to the buyer.[778]

3. Avoidance for Non-compliance with Nachfrist Notice

263. As regards cases involving non-payment or a failure to take delivery, the Convention provides an injured seller with an alternative to avoidance by reason of fundamental breach. Article 64(1)(b) provides that the seller may declare the contract avoided:

773. *See* Arts 53 (*supra*, No. 238) and 58–59 (Nos 245 et seq.).
774. *See* Cour d'appel de Grenoble, France, 4 Feb. 1999, CLOUT Case 243, available at http://cisgw3.law.pace.edu/cases/990204f1.html (contract for sale of 860,000 litres of pure orange juice, delivery staggered over several months, delay in taking delivery of one shipment).
775. Regarding this Art. 25 requirement, *see supra*, Nos 136 et seq. *See*, for example, Cour d'appel de Grenoble, France, 4 Feb. 1999, *supra* (*l'acheteur ne pouvait pas comprendre qu'un retard de quelques jours à prendre livraison […] constituerait de sa part une contravention essentielle*).
776. *See UNCITRAL Digest of CISG Case Law* (2016 ed.), available at https://uncitral.un.org/en/case_law/digests, Art. 64.
777. *See*, for example, French Court of Appeal (Grenoble), 22 Feb. 1995, CLOUT Case 154, also reported in UNILEX (French seller sold jeans to American buyer with contract stipulating that jeans would be resold in South America; buyer's resale of goods in Spain and refusal to reveal true destination was fundamental breach giving seller right to avoid).
778. *See* Art. 26, *supra*, No. 138.

if the buyer does not, within the additional period of time fixed by the seller in accordance with paragraph (1) of Article 63, perform his obligation to pay the price or take delivery of the goods, or if he declares that he will not do so within the period so fixed.

In some situations, the seller may be in doubt as to whether a court would regard a given delay by the buyer as fundamental under Article 64(1)(a). To help deal with such situations, CISG Article 63(1) gives the seller the right to fix an additional period of time (*Nachfrist*), after which the seller may avoid without having to consider whether the delay in question has reached fundamental proportions.[779] And if the buyer does not make payment or take delivery within the additional period of time so fixed (or if buyer declares that he or she will not comply),[780] Article 64(1)(b) gives the seller the right to avoid.[781]

4. Limitations Regarding Goods Delivered

264. If the seller first elects to avoid after the buyer has paid the price, he or she must do so (as regards late performance) within a reasonable time after learning that performance has been made or (in other cases) within a reasonable time after learning of the breach.[782]

5. Consequences of Avoidance

265. If the seller avoids the contract with justification, both parties are released from their obligations under it, subject to any damages which may be due. In addition, each party may claim restitution from the other party of whatever has been supplied or paid under the contract.[783]

I. Seller's Right to Supply Specifications

266. Suppose a given buyer (B) would enter a binding contract to purchase goods (e.g., sweaters) even though (B), at the time of contracting, is as yet undecided about the precise specifications: sizes, colours, etc. In this case, the contract can provide that (B) will provide such specifications in due course. If (B) then fails to make such specification, either on the date agreed upon or within a reasonable

779. *See supra*, No. 136.
780. Regarding anticipatory breach generally, *see infra*, Nos 281 et seq.
781. *See*, for example, the award by the ICC Court of Arbitration (Paris), No. 7197/1992, CLOUT Case 104, abstract available at www.unilex.info/cisg/case/37 (buyer did not fulfil its obligation to open documentary credit within additional period of time granted by seller; seller *would* then *have been* entitled to avoid under Art. 64(1)(b) *if* it had given *notice of avoidance* pursuant to Art. 26).
782. *See* Art. 64, subparas (2)(a) and (2)(b)(i). As regards the time for avoidance after a *Nachfrist* notice, *see* subpara. 64(2)(b)(ii).
783. Regarding Art. 81, *see infra*, Nos 315 et seq.

time after receipt of the seller's request to do so, the Convention permits the seller to make the specification himself. According to Article 65(1):

> If under the contract the buyer is to specify the form, measurement or other features of the goods and he fails to make such specification either on the date agreed upon or within a reasonable time after receipt of a request from the seller, the seller may, without prejudice to any other rights he may have, make the specification himself in accordance with the requirements of the buyer that may be known to him.[784]

Article 65(1) can be seen as a supplement to Article 14(1), in that a proposal for concluding a contract can be sufficiently definite to constitute an offer if the offeror's proposal makes provision – for example, by means of subsequent specification – for determining (not only the quantity but also) the nature or quality of the goods.[785] Once the goods are so specified, the contract cannot be declared 'void for vagueness'.[786]

§5. Passing of Risk

I. Introduction

267. Chapter IV of CISG Part III (Articles 66–70) regulates the question of Passing of Risk, that is, the question of which party is to bear the risk in the event that the goods are accidentally damaged or lost.

It is a well-known fact of life that goods are sometimes damaged or destroyed by fire, storms, theft, vandalism, etc. During the period before the owner of the goods in question enters a contract to sell them to another, that owner is of course the only logical candidate to bear the risk of their accidental loss; so, if the goods are in fact lost during that period, the loss must 'lie where it falls', i.e., with the owner.

Nor will the mere fact that the owner enters an agreement to sell the goods to another ordinarily work to transfer the risk of accidental loss.[787] At some point in time, however – most often, when the CISG seller 'delivers' the goods in accordance with the contract between the parties and the Convention – the buyer must accept the fact that the risk of loss has passed to him or her.[788]

784. If the seller makes such a specification (following the buyer's failure to do so), Art. 65(2) requires that the seller inform the buyer of the details thereof and also fix a reasonable time within which the buyer may make a different specification. If the buyer then fails to make such a different specification, the specification made by the seller is binding.
785. Regarding Art. 14(1) *see supra*, No. 101.
786. Regarding Art. 14 (offer 'sufficiently definite if it indicates the goods'), *see supra*, No. 102.
787. For a limited exception, *see* Art. 68 (*infra*, No. 274).
788. Note that the fact that the seller or the buyer carries insurance designed to protect against the economic consequences of the risks discussed here does not obviate the need to determine which of the two parties actually carries the risk of a given loss. And the insured party must bear the burden of asserting a claim against the insurer, suffer some depletion of current assets while waiting for settlement, etc.

As with most other sales issues, the Convention provides a supplementary (gap-filling) set of rules designed for cases where the contract itself does not otherwise provide. And in fact, many international contracts of sale will expressly resolve the question of risk of loss allocation by the incorporation of a simple trade term; in such event, the Convention regime on this issue will be effectively displaced.[789]

II. Legal Effect of the Passing of Risk

268. By way of introduction, the Convention sets forth a basic proposition which helps define the legal effect of the passing of risk. Article 66 provides:

> Loss of or damage to the goods after the risk has passed to the buyer does not discharge him from his obligation to pay the price, unless the loss or damage is due to an act or omission of the seller.

The gap-filling determination of the precise point in time at which the risk passes from the seller to the buyer is, as we shall see, the main purpose of Chapter IV of CISG Part III. The simple message in Article 66 is that once the risk has in fact passed, in accordance with the contract and the Convention, the buyer must pay the price agreed for the goods, and this holds true even though the goods delivered are damaged beyond repair;[790] indeed, once the risk has passed, the buyer must pay even if the goods never arrive.

If, however, the loss or damage suffered in a given case is due to an act or omission of the *seller*, the buyer need not pay, even if the risk has passed in the technical sense.[791] Another way of stating this is that the ordinary rules regarding the passing of risk apply only to 'accidental' loss or damage: a term which covers both 'acts of God' and the acts of mortal third parties (thieves, vandals, etc.), but which does not cover the acts or omissions of the seller. In similar fashion, if the loss or damage is due to the *buyer's* own act or omission, he or she will be the one to bear this risk.

789. *See infra*, No. 269. *See also*, *supra*, No. 152.

790. *See*, e.g., Arbitration Court attached to the Hungarian Chamber of Commerce and Industry, Hungary, 10 Dec. 1996, CLOUT Case 163, available at www.cisg.law.pace.edu/cases/961210h1.html (when seller S placed quantity of caviar at disposal of buyer B as agreed; risk of loss passed to B, notwithstanding fact that international sanctions later imposed prevented B from taking possession; under Art. 66, B remained obligated to pay price, even though said event had rendered goods worthless).

791. *See* (e.g.) Oberlandesgericht Koblenz, Germany, 14 Dec. 2006, http://www.unilex.info/cisg/case/1165 (goods/bottles damaged due to inadequate packaging; risk should have passed when bottles handed over to carrier, but seller liable as damage due to seller's act).

III. Use of Trade Terms (CIF, C&F, FOB, FAS, CPT, CIP, Etc.)

269. Since most international sales involve carriage of goods (by independent carriers), the most important risk rules in the Convention are those which regulate the passing of risk in that context.[792]

But before we examine the content of these risk rules, we note that the parties to an international sale often derogate from or vary the effect of the CISG supplementary regime,[793] not least its provisions regarding the passing of risk. Indeed, many CISG contracts contain trade terms (Incoterms) designed to regulate the passing of risk in carriage cases: terms such as Cost, Insurance and Freight (CIF), Cost and Freight (C&F or CFR), Free on Board (FOB), Free Alongside Ship (FAS), Carriage Paid To (CPT), Carriage and Insurance Paid (CIP), etc.[794]

The International Chamber of Commerce (ICC) is a federation composed of merchant organizations from around the world.[795] Although the ICC did not invent trade terms such as CIF, FOB, etc., the ICC did in 1936 set forth a comprehensive set of definitions for the various trade terms then in use, and these 'Incoterms', which since then have been updated on a regular basis, are now widely recognized and in widespread use.[796]

In many instances, the parties refer expressly to a particular trade term as defined by the ICC, for example, by a reference to 'CIF (Incoterms)'. In these cases, the risk of loss question will be defined by the official Incoterms definition, simply because that definition has been incorporated into the contract by reference to the term.[797] But even if the contract merely refers to a common trade term, such as 'CIF' (without referring specifically to the Incoterms), the Incoterm definition of that term is likely to be held incorporated into the contract by virtue of its widespread trade usage.[798] American Federal Courts, for example, have interpreted the terms 'CIF' and 'CFR' in accordance with the definitions of those terms in Incoterms.[799]

792. Regarding Art. 67, *see infra*, Nos 271 et seq.
793. Regarding Art. 6, *see supra*, Nos 70 et seq.
794. *See*, e.g., the judgment of Tribunale di Appello di Lugano (Switzerland), 15 Jan. 1998, reported in UNILEX at http://www.unilex.info/cisg/case/368 (contract contained Incoterm 'CIF', so risk passed under that term when goods handed over to carrier); *see also infra* with note 797.
795. *See* www.internationalchamberofcommerce.com/.
796. The Incoterms are updated by the ICC at regular intervals (latest edn 2020). *See also supra*, No. 152.
797. *Compare* Tribunale di Appelo di Lugano (Switzerland), *supra* note 794. In this case, since contract contained the Incoterm 'CIF', the risk passed *under that contract term* when the goods were handed over to the carrier, so the court's reference to CISG Art. 67 seems out of place.
798. Regarding the incorporation of such usages under Art. 9, *see supra*, Nos 87 et seq.
799. *St. Paul Guardian Insurance Company et al. v. Neuromed Medical Systems & Support et al.* (D.C. New York), 26 Mar. 2002, CLOUT Case 447, available at http://cisgw3.law.pace.edu/cases/020326u1.html; *BP Oil International v. Empresa Estatal Petroleos de Ecuador*, US Court of Appeals (5th Circuit), 11 Jun. 2003, CLOUT Case 575, available at www.cisg.law.pace.edu/cases/030611u1.html.

In the case of traditional trade terms such as CIF, C&F (now CFR), as well as FOB, the risk passes to the buyer when the goods are actually put on board the vessel concerned.[800] Under more modern terms designed especially for containerized transport, such as CPT and CIP, the risk passes to the buyer at an even earlier point: at the time the goods are delivered into the custody of the first carrier.[801]

270. In practice, many international sales are documentary sales, whereby the seller hands the goods over to a carrier and receives, in exchange, a bill of lading (or equivalent). The bill of lading, together with other relevant shipping documents, is then tendered to the buyer (or to the buyer's bank)[802] in return for payment of the price. If the contract is a 'shipment' contract,[803] the holder of the bill of lading normally bears the risk of loss or damage from the time the goods are placed on board; in the case of a 'destination' contract,[804] the risk remains with the seller until the carrier arrives with the goods at the destination. Some systems characterize documentary sales as 'sales of commercial paper', but there is little doubt that the Convention applies to them,[805] although certain contractual gaps regarding documentary sales practices (including questions relating to payment against documents, insurance, etc.) will usually have to be filled in by the customs of the trade or by the otherwise applicable domestic law.

IV. Contracts Involving Carriage: The CISG Gap-Filling Rule

271. As already indicated, most international sales contracts involve carriage of the goods. For such cases, but only insofar as the contract does not itself contain an express trade term,[806] Article 67(1) of the CISG Convention provides the gap-filling rule:

> If the contract of sale involves carriage of the goods and the seller is not bound to hand them over at a particular place, the risk passes to the buyer when the

800. Or at least pass the 'ships rail'. Under the latest (2020) edition of Incoterms, the term 'FOB' is applicable for sea and inland waterway transport only (but not for multimodal sea transport in containers); FOB obligates the seller to load the goods on board the vessel nominated by the buyer and the risk passes when the goods are actually on board. The Incoterm 'CFR' – that is, Cost and Freight (named port of destination) – obligates the seller to pay the costs and freight (but not insurance) to the port of destination; the risk is transferred to the buyer once the goods are loaded on the vessel. 'CIF' (now used for maritime transport only) works the way same as CFR, except that the seller must also procure and pay for insurance.
801. 'CPT' – Carriage Paid To (named place of destination) – obligates the seller to pay for carriage; the risk transfers to buyer upon handing goods over to the first carrier. CIP – Carriage and Insurance Paid to (named place of destination) – is the containerized transport/multimodal equivalent of CIF: seller pays for carriage and insurance to the named destination point, but the risk passes when the goods are handed over to the first carrier.
802. For example, in a transaction financed by a letter of credit.
803. For example, a contract with a CIF, CFR, or FOB term.
804. That is, if the contract trade term is ex ship or free carrier point of destination.
805. *See* Schwenzer/Hachem in Schlechtriem & Schwenzer, *Commentary* 3rd ed. 2010, at 36.
806. *See supra*, Nos 269 et seq.

goods are handed over to the first carrier for transmission to the buyer in accordance with the contract of sale. If the seller is bound to hand the goods over to a carrier at a particular place, the risk does not pass to the buyer until the goods are handed over to the carrier at that place. The fact that the seller is authorized to retain documents controlling the disposition of the goods does not affect the passage of the risk.

In the great majority of sales contracts involving carriage of the goods, the seller is not bound to hand them over at any 'particular place',[807] and in these instances, the risk passes to the buyer when the goods are handed over to the first (independent) carrier.[808] So, in most carriage cases, transit risks fall on the buyer, and practical considerations accord with this general CISG rule: the buyer will often be in a better position to inspect goods damaged by transit-related risks and make claims against the carrier or insurer concerned.[809]

Goods are – as a rule – only considered as 'handed over to the first carrier' if that carrier is a third party (an 'independent' carrier).[810] If the seller delivers the goods to the buyer using means of transportation and personnel under his or her own control, the goods are not handed over to a carrier in the Article 67(1) sense;[811] in that case, Article 67(1) does not apply, and so the risk does not pass until the buyer actually 'takes over the goods'.[812]

If the seller transports the goods to an independent carrier, the risk does not pass to the buyer if the goods are damaged (e.g., due to the error of the seller's employee) before they are handed over to the carrier.[813]

If the seller arranges for carriage by two successive (independent) carriers, the risk usually passes when the goods are handed over to the first of these; however, if the seller is contractually bound to hand the goods over at the transhipment point, the risk passes first at that particular place.

---

807. According to information available as of this writing, no reported decisions involve the rule in the second sentence of Art. 67(1). *See also UNCITRAL CISG Case Digest* of Art. 69, para. 11 (2016 edition).

808. Absent proof that the parties had agreed on delivery at another location, a German court found that the risk passed to when the seller handed over pizza cartons to the first (independent) carrier. *See Amtsgericht* Duisburg 13 Apr. 2000, CLOUT Case No. 360, available online at http://cisgw3.law.pace.edu/cases/000413g1.html. Regarding the seller's delivery obligation, *see supra*, Nos 153 et seq. *Compare*, for example, FOB and similar shipment terms (discussed *supra*, No. 269), where the risk does not pass until the goods actually placed 'on board'.

809. *See* generally Honnold/Flechtner, *Uniform Law for International Sales under the 1980 United Nations Convention* 4th ed. (2009), at 519–520, noting that in the case of complex or high-technology equipment the contract may provide that the goods to be tested at their destination (e.g., by seller's experts, in cooperation with the buyer). This is, for example, the procedure set forth in the Nordic General Conditions for the supply of machinery and other mechanical, electrical and electronic equipment (NL); while obligating the seller to repair defects discovered in such tests, the NL Conditions do not reallocate the risk applicable pursuant to the delivery term which applies to the particular contract.

810. *See* Hager & Schmidt-Kessel in Schlechtriem & Schwenzer, *Commentary* 4th ed. (2016), at 971.

811. *See* Honnold/Flechtner, *supra* note 809, at 520, emphasizing that the term 'hand over' indicates a transfer of possession.

812. Or when the goods are placed at the buyer's disposal. Regarding Art. 69, *see infra*, Nos 275 et seq.

813. For an example, *see* Bundesgericht, Switzerland, 16 Dec. 2008, available at http://cisgw3.law.pace.edu/cases/081216s1.html.

272. Article 67(1) concludes with the observation that the seller's retention of documents controlling the disposition of the goods does not affect the passage of the risk. But if an express trade term (Incoterm) is included in a documentary sales contract,[814] that term, as opposed to the gap-filling rule in Article 67(1), will regulate the risk issue in the transaction concerned.[815]

V. Goods Not Identified to the Contract

273. In certain situations, a given buyer (B) will deserve some assurance that the goods which have been damaged or lost were actually the same goods which the seller (S) intended (B) to receive: for example, where the seller regularly ships large quantities of fungible goods to many buyers, buyer (B) should only bear the risk if it is clear that the goods damaged in a given shipment were the subject matter of the contract between (S) and (B). Therefore, Article 67(1) operates only with respect to 'identified' goods; the risk does not pass to the buyer unless and until the goods are clearly identified to the contract: by markings on the goods, by shipping documents, by notice given to the buyer or otherwise.[816] In sales involving the carriage of bulk goods, a particular buyer should only bear the risk as to his or her undivided share in the bulk if that share has somehow been identified to the contract in question.[817]

VI. Goods Sold in Transit

274. Article 68 deals with the special problem of goods which are sold while in transit. The main risk rule and its exception in this context are as follows:

> The risk in respect of goods sold in transit passes to the buyer from the time of the conclusion of the contract. However, if the circumstances so indicate, the risk is assumed by the buyer from the time the goods were handed over to the carrier who issued the documents embodying the contract of carriage. [...]

814. *See supra*, No. 269.
815. *See* J. Berman & M. Ladd, 'Risk of Loss or Damage in Documentary Transactions under the Convention on the International Sale of Goods', *Cornell International Law Journal* 21 (1988) 423, 427. *Compare* Honnold/Flechtner, *Uniform Law for International Sales under the 1980 United Nations Convention* 4th ed. (2009), at 406–407.
816. Article 67(2).
817. According to Professors Honnold & Flechtner (*supra* note 815, at 525), a buyer should not be held to have agreed to share loss involving an unidentified 'bulk' absent express contractual provision to the contrary. However, if (as in Honnold/Flechtner's example at *id.*) buyer A agrees to buy one-half of the oil in a given (identified) shipment, and the whole cargo is destroyed, it is hard to see why A should not impliedly be held to bear half the total risk, for in such event it is clear that the goods destroyed included those intended for A. *See also* Hager & Schmidt-Kessel, *supra* note 810, at 932 (in *accord* with the view taken here).

The first point to note in this connection is that the sales contract for goods sold in transit will often contain a trade term which itself allocates the risk of loss, thus displacing the CISG gap-filling rule.[818]

In the relatively few cases where courts have had occasion to cite Article 68, its contents have not been interpreted.[819] The gap-filling rule set forth in the first sentence, whereby the risk passes at the time of contracting, was apparently intended to protect buyers in developing countries,[820] but the rule has been criticized by Western experts as unworkable in most cases: where damage during transport results from an event difficult to pinpoint in time (e.g., water seepage, etc.);[821] the principle set forth in the second sentence (which passes the risk, retroactively, at the time the goods were handed over to the carrier) seems preferable,[822] but this exception governs only when (arguably vague) 'circumstances' so indicate.[823] In any event, the rule ensures that the seller will not profit by a failure to disclose events which would lead to the passing of risk.[824]

VII. Passage of Risk in Other (Non-carrier) Cases

275. Articles 67 and 68 both provide gap-filling rules in cases involving carriage of the goods. Article 69 provides the residual gap-filling rules, that is, for cases not covered by Articles 67 and 68. Article 69 provides as follows:

(1) In cases not within Articles 67 and 68, the risk passes to the buyer when he takes over the goods or, if he does not do so in due time, from the time when the goods are placed at his disposal and he commits a breach of contract by failing to take delivery.

(2) However, if the buyer is bound to take over the goods at a place other than a place of business of the seller, the risk passes when delivery is due and the buyer is aware of the fact that the goods are placed at his disposal at that place.

(3) If the contract relates to goods not then identified, the goods are considered not to be placed at the disposal of the buyer until they are clearly identified to the contract.

818. *See supra*, No. 269.
819. *See* the *UNCITRAL CISG Case Digest* of Art. 68.
820. *See* Honnold/Flechtner, *supra* note 815, at 410.
821. *See* Berman & Ladd, *supra* note 815, at 430.
822. This was originally the rule in the 1978 Draft Convention: *see* A/CONF./97/5, para. 1 of *Secretariat's Commentary* to Art. 80 (purely practical concerns).
823. *See* Berman & Ladd, *ibid.*, at 430, distinguishing between 'circumstances' and contract terms (the exception, like the rule, applies only where no trade term applies). *Compare* Honnold/Flechtner, *supra* note 815, at 529 (endorsement of insurance policy to buyer as 'circumstance').
824. The third sentence of Art. 68 provides: nevertheless, if at the time of the conclusion of the contract of sale the seller knew or ought to have known that the goods had been lost or damaged and did not disclose this to the buyer, the loss or damage is at the risk of the seller.

VIII. Buyer to Take Goods at Seller's Place of Business (Ex Works)

276. Because most international sales contracts involve carriage of the goods (Articles 67–68), the role of Article 69, which applies only in non-carriage cases, is very limited in practice.

Article 69(1) provides the gap-filling rule for cases *not* involving carriage, provided the buyer is *not* bound to take over the goods at a place *other than* the seller's place of business: where the buyer in a non-carriage case is obligated to take over the goods at *seller's place*, the risk generally passes when the buyer actually takes over the goods; if the buyer does not take over (available) goods on time, the risk passes at that point in time when the buyer commits this breach.[825] If the contract permits the buyer to collect the goods within a given period, the risk will not pass until the period has expired, even if the goods were held available during that period.[826]

IX. Buyer to Take Goods at Another Place

277. If the buyer is bound to take over the goods at a place *other than* the seller's place of business, for example, at a warehouse, the risk passes under Article 69(2) when delivery is due and the buyer is aware of the fact that the goods are placed at his or her disposal at that place. This seems to have been the situation where a Danish seller agreed to sell and deliver a mobile grain dryer to a buyer in Germany.[827]

In a somewhat different situation, also covered by the Article 69(2) rule, the contract may permit the buyer to collect the goods within a given period; if so, and provided the goods remain 'available', the risk may pass to the buyer before the period has expired.[828] In a German case, the parties entered an agreement for the manufacture and sale of furniture. According to the parties' prior practices, the seller would arrange for the storage of goods, as and when they were manufactured, in a warehouse for the buyer's account; the handing over would then take place in the warehouse. In this instance, however, the goods disappeared following the bankruptcy of the warehouse. Since the buyer had not been made aware that the goods had been placed at the buyer's disposal in the warehouse, the risk had not passed under Article 69(2), and so the buyer did not have to pay for them.[829]

---

825. Regarding Art. 60(b), *see supra*, No. 251.
826. *Accord*: A/CONF./97/5, paras 3–4 of *Secretariat's Commentary* to Art. 81 of the 1978 Draft Convention (noting that the seller is in the best position to protect the goods, etc.) and Honnold/Flechtner, *supra* note 815, at 534. In some domestic sales systems (e.g., in Denmark), a different default risk rule, more like the one in Art. 69(2), *infra* No. 277, applies.
827. *See* County Court of Randers (Denmark), 8 Jul. 2004, CLOUT Case 995, available at http://cisgw3.law.pace.edu/cases/040708d1.html. *See also* the case commentary by Henschel & Lookofsky at http://cisgw3.law.pace.edu/cisg/biblio/lookofsky10.html.
828. In this situation, the seller is arguably in no better position to protect against the loss. *See* A/CONF./97/5, paras 5–6 of *Secretariat's Commentary* to Art. 81 of the 1978 Draft Convention and *compare supra* note 826.
829. Oberlandesgericht Hamm (Germany), 23 Jun. 1998, CLOUT Case 338, available at http://cisgw3.law.pace.edu/cases/980623g1.html.

X. Identification Required

278. Like Article 67, Article 69 presupposes identification of the goods.[830] If the contract relates to goods not then identified, the goods are first considered to be placed at the disposal of the buyer when such identification takes place: by marking, notice, etc.[831]

XI. Seller's Fundamental Breach: Effect on Risk

279. 'If the seller has committed a fundamental breach of contract, Articles 67, 68 and 69 do not impair the remedies available to the buyer on account of the breach.'[832] So in this (fundamental breach) situation, the buyer can insist on the delivery of substitute goods,[833] or avoid the contract,[834] i.e., avail himself or herself of remedies which would not otherwise be available.[835] Nor would the fact that the buyer is unable to make restitution necessarily constitute a bar to avoidance in such a case.[836]

§6. Provisions Common to the Parties' Obligations

I. Introduction

280. Chapter V of CISG Part III (Articles 71–88) is entitled Provisions Common to the Obligations of the Seller and the Buyer. This chapter supplements both the General Provisions in Chapter I of Part III and the more specialized remedial rules in Chapters II and III. The provisions in Chapter V deal with such varied topics as anticipatory breach, damages for breach, liability exemptions, the effects of avoidance and the preservation of the goods.

---

830. *See supra*, No. 273.
831. *See* Art. 69(3) and *compare* Art. 67(2). The identification must, of course, accord with seller's rights and obligations under the contract.
832. Article 70.
833. Regarding Art. 46(2) *see supra*, No. 217.
834. Regarding Art. 49 *see supra*, Nos 225 et seq.
835. *See also* F. Ferrari & M. Torsello, *International Sales Law – CISG in a Nutshell* 2nd ed. (2018), at 328 (in this respect, Art. 70 shifts risk of accidental loss or damage back to seller).
836. Regarding Art. 82 *see infra*, Nos 318 et seq.

II. Anticipatory Breach and Instalment Contracts

A. Introduction

281. The Convention defines the point in time at which the seller and buyer are to perform their respective obligations.[837] Prior to this time, there can be no breach and thus no remedy for breach in the usual sense.

However, when one party clearly repudiates his or her obligation to perform, the other party can no longer be expected to remain ready to perform a one-sided deal; therefore, in domestic law, such injured party's duties are, at the minimum, considered discharged.[838] Even short of an outright repudiation, the serious possibility of one party's non-performance and the accompanying threat of injury to the other will, in certain circumstances, necessitate legal protection.[839]

Articles 71–73, collected in section I of Chapter V under the heading 'Anticipatory breach and instalment contracts', are designed to deal with this same problem in the international sales context, and the CISG solutions indeed resemble those of many domestic contract and sales laws. Depending on the circumstances, a party faced with prospective non-performance, the real possibility of a serious breach, may be entitled either to suspend his or her own performance (Article 71) and/or to avoid his or her own obligations altogether (Article 72). In addition, Article 73 provides a special (instalment contract) application of the avoidance rule.

B. Right to Suspend Performance: Generally

282. Article 71(1) sets forth the general rule which entitles a party to suspend his or her performance when faced with an anticipatory breach:

> A party may suspend the performance of his obligations if, after the conclusion of the contract, it becomes apparent that the other party will not perform a substantial part of his obligations as a result of:
>
> a. a serious deficiency in his ability to perform or in his creditworthiness; or
> b. his conduct in preparing to perform or in performing the contract.

As regards a (potentially injured) party's right to suspend performance, Article 71(1) requires that it become apparent (*il apparait*) that the other party will not perform a substantial part (*une partie essentielle*) of his or her obligations. Although these terms cannot be measured with mathematical precision, a comparison with the

837. Regarding Art. 33, *see supra*, No. 159; regarding Art. 58, *see supra*, No. 245.

838. *Compare*, for example (as regards American domestic law), E.A. Farnsworth, *Contracts* 4th ed. (2004), §8.20. A more difficult question is whether such a 'breach by anticipatory repudiation' gives the injured party an immediate action for damages. The CISG provides no clear answer: *see infra*, No. 286. Regarding American law, *see* Farnsworth at *ibid*.

839. Regarding domestic solutions *see* generally, Treitel, *Remedies for Breach of Contract* (1988), 379–381.

rules set forth in Article 72 indicates that the Convention makes it somewhat easier to suspend than to avoid: as regards the nature of the non-performance, a promisee's prospective failure to perform a substantial part of its obligations, although obviously significant, is presumably intended to denote something less than a fundamental breach;[840] as regards the degree of certainty, an 'apparent' non-performance is designed to indicate a slightly lesser probability than one which is 'clear'.[841]

Beyond this, Article 71(1) requires that the prospect of non-performance be the result of either: (a) a serious deficiency in the promisor's performance ability or creditworthiness or (b) his or her conduct in preparing to perform or in performing the contract.[842] Examples of deficiencies and conduct which courts have held to fulfil these criteria include a buyer's late payments in respect of other contracts between the same parties and a seller's demand that the buyer makes payments beyond those provided for in the contract.[843] Note, however, that only circumstances which first 'become apparent' after the conclusion of the contract concerned can entitle a party to suspend performance.[844]

840. *See* generally Fountoulakis in Schlechtriem & Schwenzer, *Commentary* 4th ed. (2016), at 1011–1013. *See*, for example, LG Berlin, 15 Sep. 1994, abstract available at www.unilex.info/cisg/case/218 (buyer could suspend performance when it became apparent that seller would not deliver conforming goods; non-performance under Art. 71(1) need not amount to a fundamental breach).

841. *Accord*: Honnold/Flechtner, *supra* note 815, at 551–552. Regarding the Art. 72 requirements, *see infra*, Nos 285 et seq.

842. *See*, e.g., International Court of Arbitration at the Belarusian Chamber of Commerce and Industry, 5 Jan. 2016, available at http://www.unilex.info/cisg/case/2138 (seller had not proved serious deficiency in buyer's creditworthiness or other circumstance established by Art. 71 as ground for suspension; nor had seller informed buyer of suspension, thus depriving buyer of opportunity to provide adequate assurance of performance of its prepayment obligations).

843. *See* Rechtbank van Koophandel, Hasselt (Belgium), 1 Mar. 1995, abstract available at www.unilex.info/cisg/case/269 (seller could suspend delivery of second order by reason of buyer's serious (seven-month) delay in payment of first order); Bundesgerichtshof, Germany, 27 Nov. 2007, abstract available at www.unilex.info/cisg/case/1345 (party unjustifiably insisting on payment of supplemental consulting fees gave implied indication that it would not perform); Rechtbank Arnhem, the Netherlands, 29 Jul. 2009, available at http://cisgw3.law.pace.edu/cases/090729n1.html (seller could suspend delivery of bus where payment on contracts for other busses outstanding); US District Court, Southern District of New York, US, 29 May 2009 (*Doolim Corp. v. R Doll, LLC*), available at http://cisgw3.law.pace.edu/cases/090529u1.html (defaults on earlier consignments, apparent that buyer would not pay under related contract).

844. *See* generally Fountoulakis, *supra* note 840, at 956–957 and, for example, Bundesgericht, Switzerland, 17 Jul. 2007, CLOUT Case 936, available at http://cisgw3.law.pace.edu/cases/070717s1.html#cx (seller not entitled to rely on Art. 71, since insufficient evidence that seller was unaware of buyer's poor financial condition before the contract between the parties was concluded).

C. Goods Dispatched: Stoppage in Transit

283. Under principles generally applicable under domestic law, a seller's rights in respect of buyer's prospective inability to perform include the right to 'stop' the (further) transit of goods already dispatched (shipped).[845] Article 71(2) contains the CISG version of this rule:

> 2. If the seller has already dispatched the goods before the grounds described in the preceding paragraph become evident, he may prevent the handing over of the goods to the buyer even though the buyer holds a document which entitles him to obtain them. […]

Paragraph (2) of Article 71 extends the just-discussed general protection against potential injury provided by paragraph (1), in that paragraph (2) is concerned with the special problem of the seller who has dispatched the goods before the indications of the buyer's prospective non-performance become manifest. The provision applies not only where the buyer holds a bill of lading or similar instrument but also where the sales contract extends credit until sometime after the buyer's receipt of the goods.[846]

In line with the general CISG principle that the Convention is concerned with the *inter partes* sales relationship,[847] Article 71(2) relates only to the rights in the goods as between the buyer and the seller.[848] The seller's right to effectuate stoppage vis-à-vis carriers and warehousemen will depend on the contract of carriage or bailment (and on the relevant domestic law), just as the rights which creditors or good-faith purchasers may have under the applicable domestic law remain unaffected by this Convention rule.[849]

D. Notice: Adequate Assurance of Performance

284. If one party rightly suspends its performance, whether before or after dispatch of the goods, that is, under Article 71, paragraph (1) or (2), that party must 'immediately' give notice of the suspension to the other party (B). In the event that the other party then provides an adequate assurance of its performance, the suspending party must then continue with its performance as originally agreed.[850]

845. *See* Fountoulakis, *id.*, at 1016 (citing similar provisions in American, English and Scandinavian law).
846. *See* A/CONF./97/5, para. 10 of *Secretariat's Commentary* to Art. 62 of the 1978 Draft Convention.
847. Regarding Art. 4, *see supra*, No. 64.
848. Article 71(2), second sentence.
849. *See* generally, Honnold/Flechtner, *supra* note 815, 556–557.
850. Article 71(3). *See also*, for example, Amtsgericht Frankfurt am Main (Germany), 31 Jan. 1991, CLOUT Case 51, available at www.cisg.law.pace.edu/cases/910131g1.html (seller's failure to give notice of suspension gave buyer right to recover damages for loss of profit suffered when seller interrupted delivery). *Compare* cisg-online.org, case 4318 (2019).

E. Right to Avoid for Prospective Fundamental Breach

285. Article 72(1) sets forth the general rule which entitles a party to avoid the contract when faced with an anticipatory breach:

> If prior to the date for performance of the contract it is clear that one of the parties will commit a fundamental breach of contract, the other party may declare the contract avoided.

As regards the right to declare the contract avoided, Article 72 requires that it be clear (*il et manifesté*) that the other party will commit a fundamental breach of contract.

As is logical, the requirements for avoidance under Article 72 (which effectively terminates the performance obligations of both parties)[851] are somewhat stricter than those associated with the right to suspend under Article 71.[852] In any event, the right to avoid under Article 72 should be exercised with special caution, particularly in light of the availability of suspension under Article 71: a party who fails to perform by virtue of an avoidance not justified under Article 72 will itself commit a (likely fundamental) breach.[853]

F. Damages for Prospective Fundamental Breach?

286. While Article 72(1) clearly gives the injured party the right to avoid in the face of an impending fundamental breach, the Convention contains no correspondingly specific rule as regards an 'immediate' action for damages in this situation, that is, an action brought before the date upon which the obligor's performance actually become due. It has, however, been suggested that Articles 75 and 76 would provide authority for such an action.[854] Since the right to claim damages under the Convention is based on a party's failure to perform its obligations,[855] it seems logical to allow an action based on prospective breach, in that a promise to perform in the future 'by implication includes an engagement not deliberately to compromise

---

851. *See supra*, No. 46 and *infra*, No. 315.
852. *See supra*, No. 282. *See also*, for example, OLG Düsseldorf (Germany), 14 Jan. 1994, CLOUT Case 130, available at http://cisgw3.law.pace.edu/cases/940114g1.html (seller had right to avoid second shoe contract since it had become 'clear' that buyer, who had not yet performed under prior contract, would not pay). *See also* US District Court, Southern District of New York, US, 29 May 2009 (*Doolim Corp. v. R Doll, LLC*), available at http://cisgw3.law.pace.edu/cases/090529u1.html (buyer's persistent failure to pay for garments ordered demonstrated that it was unable or unwilling to pay the price agreed, seller permissibly cancelled contract); Tribunal of International Commercial Arbitration at the Russian Federation Chamber of Commerce and Industry, the Russian Federation, 7 Jun. 1999, CLOUT Case No. 473, available at www.cisg.law.pace.edu/cases/990607r1.html#ua (seller refused to perform obligation as to 'exclusive' use of vessel, that is, for transporting only goods in question; anticipatory breach under Art. 72, buyer entitled to avoid).
853. *Accord* F. Ferrari & M. Torsello, *International Sales Law – CISG in a Nutshell* 2nd ed. (2018), at 460.
854. *See* Honnold/Flechtner, *supra* note 815, at 564.
855. *See* Arts 45 (*supra*, No. 209) and 61 (*supra*, No. 252).

the probability of performance'.[856] The CISG protects the expectation interest of the promisee in general,[857] and the promisee should be entitled that his or her performance expectation be protected against anticipatory repudiation as well.[858] Such a flexible interpretation of the rules on damages would also require that the promisee take steps to mitigate the loss occasioned by a promisor's prospective failure to perform.[859]

G. Notice. Adequate Assurance of Performance

287. As in the case of suspension of performance under Article 71, the party intending to declare the contract avoided under Article 72 must, if time permits, give reasonable notice to the other party in order to permit him or her to provide adequate assurance of his or her performance.

This rule does not apply, however, if the other party has declared that he or she will not perform his or her obligations,[860] in that such a repudiation itself makes the prospect of a forthcoming fundamental breach (abundantly) clear. The Convention does not prescribe the form the assurance must take, nor does Article 72(2) explain how long a party has to provide an otherwise adequate assurance – a fact which complicates coordination between Articles 71 and 72.[861]

H. Instalment Contracts: Avoidance for Fundamental Breach

288. Article 73 of the Convention provides a special set of rules applicable to sales contracts involving the delivery of goods by instalments. Depending on the circumstances, a breach by one party as regards a single instalment may serve to indicate a prospective non-performance of greater dimension and thus affect the other party's avoidance rights as regards the contract overall.

First, according to Article 73(1), if a seller's or buyer's failure to perform any of its obligations in respect of any instalment constitutes a fundamental breach of contract, the injured party may declare the contract avoided with respect to that instalment.

Beyond this, if the seller's or buyer's failure to perform its obligations in respect of a given instalment gives the injured party 'good grounds' to foresee a fundamental breach with respect to future instalments, that party may (within a reasonable

856. This was the Common law reasoning of Judge Learned Hand in *Equitable Trust Co. v. Western Pac. Ry.*, 244 F. 485, 502 (S.D.N.Y. 1917), aff'd., 250 F. 327 (2nd Cir.), cert. denied, 246 US 672 (1918).
857. Regarding Art. 74, *see infra*, No. 291.
858. This reasoning also underlies the American rule: *see* Farnsworth, *Contracts* 4th ed. (2004), para. 8.20.
859. *Accord*: A/CONF./97/5, para. 4 of *Secretariat's Commentary* to Art. 63 of the 1978 Draft Convention; Fountoulakis, *supra* note 840, at 971.
860. Article 72, paras (2)–(3).
861. For details on this point, *see* Honnold/Flechtner, *Uniform Law for International Sales under the 1980 United Nations Convention* 4th ed. (2009), at 565.

time thereafter) declare the entire contract avoided under Article 73(2). In an illustrative Swiss case, a German buyer contracted with a French seller for the delivery of 2–4 million litres of sunflower oil per month. Although the buyer paid for the first delivery, the seller did not ship the goods to Romania as agreed; since the seller's failure to perform with respect to this instalment gave the buyer good grounds to expect a fundamental breach of contract with respect to further instalments, the buyer was held entitled to avoid.[862] In another Article 73(2) decision, a German buyer, unsatisfied with the efforts of a Danish seller to obtain an additional discount from its Japanese supplier, refused to take delivery of a given instalment of motorcycles and also cancelled the bank guarantee previously issued in favour of the seller; given these circumstances, the Supreme Court of Denmark held that the Danish seller had been entitled to avoid the entire contract.[863]

Article 73(3) contains a special rule regarding buyer's instalment contract rights: a buyer who declares the contract avoided in respect of any delivery may, at the same time, declare it avoided in respect of deliveries already made or of future deliveries if, by reason of their interdependence, those deliveries could not be used for the purpose contemplated by the parties at the time of the conclusion of the contract.

III. Damages for Breach

A. *Introduction*

289. Section II of Chapter V supplements the remedial rules in Chapters II and III. Those chapters deal primarily with the remedies of specific performance and avoidance. Chapter V deals with provisions common to buyers and sellers alike, in particular with the important topic of damages for breach.

B. *CISG Liability: Basis, Extent and Exemptions*

290. Before proceeding with an examination of the damages rules in Chapter V, it should be remembered that Chapters II and III of CISG Part III also contain significant provisions as regards damages for breach. In particular, Articles 45(1) and 61(1) do more than merely catalogue the various CISG provisions regarding buyer's and seller's breach. These rules provide the *basis* of Convention liability; they are, in other words, the very sources of the buyer's and the seller's respective rights to claim damages for breach.[864]

According to Articles 45(1) and 61(1), if the seller or buyer fails to perform any of its obligations under the contract or this Convention, the other party may claim

862. Handelsgericht Zürich (Switzerland), 5 Feb. 1997, CLOUT Case 214, available at www.cisg.law.pace.edu/cases/970205s1.html.

863. Højesteret (Supreme Court), Denmark, 17 Oct. 2007, CLOUT Case No. 993, available at http://cisgw3.law.pace.edu/cases/071017d1.html.

864. Regarding these rules, *see supra*, Nos 211 and 254.

damages as provided in Articles 74–77. As indicated below, these latter articles concern only the extent or the measurement of damages, the question there being 'how much' compensation the injured party should receive. In other words, Articles 74–77 operate on the assumption that the breaching party is liable on the basis of either Article 45(1) or 61(1). And since Articles 45(1) and 61(1) allow the injured party to claim damages for any breach, the basis of Convention liability in damages is the breach itself; there is no requirement that the party claiming damages must establish a 'culpable' breach; i.e., these provisions clearly represent no-fault liability rules.[865]

Then again, the fact that the Convention operates on the basis of an essentially no-fault liability scheme does not mean that CISG liability is absolutely 'strict'. In certain exceptional circumstances, a non-performing promisor may be held exempt from liability in damages, provided such non-performance is attributable to unforeseeable and unavoidable circumstances, that is, the kind of 'impediments' often associated with a force majeure event.[866] For the present, however, it is sufficient to note that the possibility of such an exemption does not water down Convention liability to a regime based culpable breach.[867]

C. Expectation Protection: The General Rule

291. Article 74 sets forth the general principle by which the CISG measures liability for breach:

> Damages for breach of contract by one party consist of a sum equal to the loss, including loss of profit, suffered by the other party as a consequence of the breach. Such damages may not exceed the loss which the party in breach foresaw or ought to have foreseen at the time of the conclusion of the contract, in the light of the facts and matters of which he then knew or ought to have known, as a possible consequence of the breach of contract.

The basic CISG formula with respect to the measurement of damages is quite simple: damages for breach of contract are designed to compensate (and are thus measured by) the loss 'suffered by the other party as a consequence of breach'. Assuming that the plaintiff (the injured party) can establish such a causal ('as a consequence') connection between the defendant's breach and the plaintiff's loss,[868] the rule in Article 74 will tend to place that injured party in the position he or she would have enjoyed 'but for' the breach.

865. Furthermore, since the basis of Convention liability in damages is the breach itself, the breach concerned in this (damages) context need not be 'fundamental'. *Accord*: Müller-Chen in Schlechtriem & Schwenzer, *Commentary* 4th ed. (2016), at 729.

866. Regarding Art. 79, *see infra*, Nos 302 et seq.

867. *Accord* Müller-Chen, *ibid.*

868. That is, that the loss is a 'consequence' of the breach.

In this way, an award of damages under Article 74 provides the injured party with 'substitutionary' relief (i.e., a substitute for the promised performance), thus protecting that party's rightful expectation of full performance, that is, the so-called expectation interest.[869] Depending on the circumstances, a lesser/alternative measure of 'reliance interest' protection might also be awarded with reference to the Article 74 rule.[870]

The recovery of damages under Article 74 does not depend on the particular nature (kind) or category of loss for which compensation is claimed. For this reason, the provision can serve to compensate the kind of losses often classified as 'direct', as well as those classified as 'indirect' and/or 'incidental'. A buyer who elects to retain goods which do not conform to the contract may recover damages under Article 74 which compensate the difference between the value of the goods delivered and the value conforming goods would have had. Alternatively, such a CISG buyer might seek to recover compensation for reasonable expenses incurred in repairing the goods received, so as to make them conform to the promised quality.[871] Damages can also be awarded under Article 74 to compensate physical damage (injury) which non-conforming goods cause to the buyer's property.[872]

Depending on the circumstances, aggrieved buyers are sometimes also entitled to recover compensation for lost profits; as noted in the following, however, damages for lost profits are often limited or denied by reason of the 'foreseeability' rule in Article 74, as well as in cases where such losses are not proved with reasonable 'certainty'.[873] The mitigation rule in Article 77 can also pose a significant barrier to recovery in such cases.[874]

Sellers who suffer economic losses when their buyers do not perform as promised (e.g., by not paying for the goods and/or by not taking delivery on time) are of course entitled to similar protection under the general Article 74 rule.

---

869. *See*, for example, Treitel, *Remedies for Breach of Contract* (1988), 43 and 82.

870. Although the CISG contains no express provision with respect to the Common Law concept of the 'reliance interest' (a concept derived from the German 'negative interest'), the broadly formulated rule in Art. 74 may be read as comprising, *inter alia*, damages based on this form of protection *See* Honnold/Flechtner, *Uniform Law for International Sales under the 1980 United Nations Convention* 4th ed. (2009), 571–573. *Accord*: *Delchi Carrier, S.p.A. v. Rotorex Corp.*, 9 Sep. 1994, CLOUT Case 85 (Art. 74 'seeks to provide the injured party with the benefit of the bargain, including both its expectation interest and its reliance expenditures'); aff'd. in part and rev'd. in part, and remanded, 71 F.3d 1024 (2nd Cir. 1995), CLOUT Case 138, available at http://cisgw3.law.pace.edu/cases/951206u1.html#ua. *See* in this connection Eric Schneider, 'Consequential Damages in the International Sale of Goods: Analysis of Two Decisions', *Journal of Business Law* 16 (2005) 615.

871. Regarding this measurement (cost to cure defect) *see* A/CONF./97/5, paras 6–7 of *Secretariat's Commentary* to Art. 70 of the 1978 Draft Convention.

872. *See* Handelsgericht des Kantons Zürich, Switzerland, 26 Apr. 1995, CLOUT Case No. 196, abstract available at www.unilex.info/cisg/case/166 (while damages for death or personal injury caused by defective goods excluded from CISG scope, damages caused by leak of salted water to buyer's premises governed by CISG). As regards consequential loss which takes the form of damage to buyer's property (other than the goods themselves), the Convention may not supply the only relevant rule, in that some domestic systems regard liability for such product damage as grounded both in contract and in tort. Regarding Art. 5, *see supra*, Nos 66 et seq.

873. *See infra*, No. 293.

874. *See infra*, No. 297.

Note that Articles 75 and 76 (discussed below) provide specific (*lex specialis*) rules for measurement of 'direct' loss when an injured buyer or seller rightfully avoids the contract, for example, by reason of the other party's fundamental breach.[875] However, an award of damages representing the contract/cover price differential under Article 75 or 76 will not always be adequate to compensate the injured party's full expectation; in such cases, the general Article 74 rule remains available, for example, to provide supplementary compensation for 'incidental' expenditures incurred in connection with inspection, handling, storage and shipping (return) of goods which do not conform.[876]

An important more general point is that Article 74 is a default (gap-filling) rule which the parties can displace or vary in their contract.[877] The standard sales terms of many sellers, for example, exclude or limit the right of the buyer to claim damages suffered by reason of non-conformity,[878] but such limitations are of course only effective if they are accepted by both parties, so as to become 'incorporated' as part of the contract concerned.[879] The validity of such limitation clauses which do become part of the contract, if arguably unreasonable, can be challenged under the applicable domestic law.[880]

D. *Attorneys' Fees as Damages under Article 74?*

292. A special CISG question relating to the kinds of loss for which damages may be recovered, one which is of particular interest for those who litigate CISG claims before American courts, involves the relationship between Article 74 and the so-called American rule which applies in any civil (contract or tort) litigation in American (State and Federal) courts. Briefly stated, this rule provides that the losing party is generally *not* required to reimburse the winning party for its lawyers' fees.[881]

In breach of (sales) contract cases, this American rule on the allocation of lawyer's fees (which runs contrary to the *lex fori* rule applicable in Europe and elsewhere) might look like an exception to Article 74, that is, an exception to the general CISG principle of full expectation interest protection for all foreseeable loss which

875. Regarding Art. 75, *see infra*, No. 294; regarding Art. 76, *see infra*, No. 296. Avoidance usually requires a 'fundamental' breach: *see supra*, Nos 226 and 261.

876. *See* numerous cases cited in *UNCITRAL Digest of CISG Case Law* (2016 ed.), available at https://uncitral.un.org/en/case_law/digests, Art. 74, paras 21–24 and accompanying notes.

877. Regarding Art. 6 *see supra*, Nos 70 et seq.

878. While at the same time obligating the seller to repair or replace.

879. *See* (e.g.) Cour d'appel de Rouen (France), 3 Oct. 2013, available at http://www.unilex.info/cisg/case/1902 (seller's standard terms, including liability limitation, not accepted by buyer; buyer therefore entitled to full compensation under Art. 74, including damages for loss of reputation).

880. Regarding Art. 4 *see supra*, Nos 62 et seq.

881. As in Europe the losing party in an American litigation is usually required to pay the successful party's 'costs' (e.g., fees paid to the court), but in the US such costs do not generally include lawyers'/attorneys' fees. The principle has been modified in certain instances by 'fee-shifting' statutes, but *no* fee-shifting remains the general 'American rule'. *See*, for example, *Alyeska Pipeline Service Co. v. Wilderness Society*, 421 US 240 (1975) and *Buckhannon Board and Care Home, Inc. v. West Virginia Dept. of Health and Human Resources*, 532 US 598 (2001).

flows from the breach,[882] but the American rule is in fact a 'procedural' (as opposed to a substantive) rule.[883] And since the CISG Convention is 'about contracts' (and not about procedure), the question of whether the losing party in a CISG-related litigation is required to reimburse the winning party for its lawyers' fees is rightly regarded as 'not governed' by Article 74 (or any other CISG rule); rather, this question is best resolved in accordance with the procedural rules of the forum concerned,[884] at least in cases where the contract between the parties does not otherwise provide.[885] For this and other good reasons, the US Court of Appeals in the *Zapata* case rightly held that Article 74 does not provide authority for a special (CISG) exception to the general American rule,[886] and post-*Zapata* American precedent does not alter that view.[887]

E. Foreseeability and Certainty as Limitations

293. A major component of Article 74 is the 'foreseeability' limitation: CISG damages may not exceed the loss which the breaching party foresaw or ought to

---

882. *Accord* E.A. Farnsworth, *Contracts* 4th ed. (2004), para. 12.8.
883. Domestic rules which determine whether (or under what circumstances) lawyers' fees are to be 'shifted' (borne by the losing party) are regarded as procedural rules in many CISG jurisdictions. *See* generally, H. Flechtner, 'Recovering Attorneys' Fees as Damages under the UN Sales Convention (CISG): The Role of Case Law in the New International Commercial Practice', with *Comments on Zapata Hermanos v. Hearthside Baking*, 22 *Northwestern Journal of International Law & Business* 121 (2002), also available at www.cisg.law.pace.edu/cisg/biblio/flechtner4.html#iv.
884. For a clear and succinct elaboration of this position, *see* Honnold/Flechtner, *Uniform Law for International Sales under the 1980 United Nations Convention* 4th ed. (2009), at 578–581. *Compare* Schwenzer in Schlechtriem & Schwenzer, *Commentary* 4th ed. (2016), at 1068–1069.
885. *Accord* (on this freedom-of-contract point): Schwenzer in *Commentary* at *ibid.*
886. *Zapata Hermanos Sucesores, S.A. v. Hearthside Baking Co., Inc.*, etc., US Court of Appeals (7th Cir.), 19 Nov. 2002, available at http://cisgw3.law.pace.edu/cisg/wais/db/cases2/021119u1.html, reversing 2001 US Dist. LEXIS 15191 and 2001 WL 1000927 (N.D. Ill), also in CISGW3. *See* H. Flechtner & J. Lookofsky, 'Viva Zapata! American Procedure and CISG Substance in a US Circuit Court of Appeal', *Vindobona Journal of International Commercial Law and Arbitration* 7 (2003) 93, also available at www.cisg.law.pace.edu/cisg/biblio/flechtner5.html; H. Flechtner & J. Lookofsky, 'Zapata Retold: Attorneys' Fees Are (Still) Not Governed by the CISG', *Journal of Law and Commerce* 26(1) (2007), also available at http://papers.ssrn.com/sol3/papers.cfm?abstract_id=1334299 (arguing, once again, that relegating to domestic law the question of recovering attorney fees incurred during litigation over a CISG transaction reflects the likely view of the *Convention's drafters* that the recovery of such fees is a 'procedural' matter beyond the intended field of a substantive sales law treaty; CISG Advisory Council Opinion No. 6, while agreeing with the Flechtner/Lookofsky result, objects to and rejects that reasoning). For another contrary view (critical of the result in *Zapata*) *see* J. Felemegas, 'An Interpretation of Article 74 CISG by the US Circuit Court of Appeals', *Pace International Law Review* 15 (2003), also available at http://cisgw3.law.pace.edu/cisg/biblio/felemegas4.html. On 16 Jun. 2003, the US Supreme Court denied the plaintiff's/Zapata's petition for *certiorari* (third-instance review).
887. *See* Gillette & Walt, *UN Convention in Theory and Practice* 2nd ed. (2016), at 354–355, providing a careful analysis of *Stemcor USA, Inc. v. Miracero, A.A. de C.V.*, U.S. District Court (S.D.N.Y.) 30 Sep. 2014.

have foreseen as a consequence of the breach of contract.[888] Foreseeability under the Convention is measured at the time of the conclusion of the contract in the light of the facts and matters of which the breaching party then knew or ought to have known, the underlying idea being that the parties, at that point in time, should be able to calculate the risks and potential liability which they assume by agreement.[889]

On its face, the test in Article 74 seems quite liberal (pro-plaintiff), requiring only that the injured party's loss be foreseeable (as opposed to actually foreseen) by the defendant (as opposed to by both parties) as a 'possible' (as opposed to a likely) consequence of breach.[890] A Dutch court, for example, has held that a seller doing business in the Czech Republic could reasonably have foreseen that its Dutch buyer's customers would demand that buyer pay them compensation for the difference between the contract price agreed upon between the buyer and its customers and the higher price which those customers, as a consequence of seller's breach, paid for cover purchases.[891] Similarly, if a given seller (S) fails to deliver goods which (S) knew were meant to be resold at retail, the buyer (B) is entitled to recover the profit it ordinarily would earn by such resale, provided (B) can provide the evidence necessary to prove its loss.[892] An American court, in yet another application of the rule, has held that a German seller of a production system could not reasonably foresee that its breach would cause its American buyer to acquire an entirely new warehouse to store the system.[893]

Plaintiffs seeking compensation for loss under Article 74 are also likely to face other significant barriers, not least as regards claims for lost profits, and this is the requirement that such losses be proved with a sufficient degree of 'certainty'. Although it seems clear that the party making a damages claim under Article 74

888. The CISG 'foreseeability' rule can be traced back, *inter alia*, to the classic English case of *Hadley v. Baxendale*: 9 Ex. 341, 156 Eng. Rep. 145 (1854); *compare* American *Restatement Second of Contracts*, para. 351; *accord* Stoll & Gruber in Schlechtriem & Schwenzer, *Commentary* 2nd ed. (2005), at 749 with note 26, and Schwenzer in the 4th (2016) ed. of that work at 1058.

889. *Accord* Stoll/Gruber, *ibid.*, at 747.

890. *See*, for example, Swiss Supreme Court (Schweizerisches Bundesgericht), 28 Oct. 1998, CLOUT Case 248, available at http://cisgw3.law.pace.edu/cases/981028s1.html (German sellers delivered frozen meat containing excessive fat to Swiss buyer; buyer's loss of clientele was foreseeable consequence of breach, particularly since buyer was wholesale dealer in sensitive market and had no alternative by which it could meet obligations to its buyers).

891. Rechtbank Arnhem, the Netherlands, 1 Mar. 2006, available at http://cisgw3.law.pace.edu/cases/060301n1.html.

892. Bundesgericht, Switzerland, 17 Dec. 2009, available at http://www.unilex.info/cisg/case/1578 (Convention does not expressly solve issue of what evidence necessary to establish lost profit; could be resolved in accordance with otherwise applicable law or according to the canon that lost profit be established with 'reasonable certainty'; adhering to first approach and applying Swiss law, Supreme Court rejected buyer's claim, as buyer failed to exhibit retail contract with its final customer).

893. US District Court, Southern District of New York, US, 23 Aug. 2006 (*TeeVee Tunes, Inc. et al v. Gerhard Schubert GmbH*), available at http://cisgw3.law.pace.edu/cases/060823u1.html (unforeseeable that buyer would have to look for entirely new facility in event of malfunction in seller's system).

bears the 'burden' of establishing (proving) that it has suffered a given loss,[894] several courts have held the standard of proof and the weight to be given evidence when determining damages is governed by domestic procedural and evidentiary law (i.e., *lex fori* and not the Convention).[895] Some CISG commentators, however, have taken a contrary view,[896] and their argument – that the degree of certainty required to prove a given loss is a matter 'governed' by the Convention – seems tenable, in that corresponding certainty issues are regarded as substantive contract law issues in many domestic systems.[897] Arguably, the CISG general principle of 'reasonableness' leads to the conclusion that (only) 'reasonable certainty' is required,[898] and that solution matches the domestic criteria now applicable in some jurisdictions.[899]

A related but more specific (and so far more theoretical) question which has been debated by scholars in this connection is whether Article 74 provides authority for damages calculated on the basis of 'loss of a chance'.[900] Another controversial issue, potentially relevant in at least some jurisdictions, relates to the relationship

---

894. *See* cases cited in *UNCITRAL Digest of CISG Case Law* (2016 ed.), available at https://uncitral.un.org/en/case_law/digests, Art. 74, para. 36.

895. *See ibid.*, para. 37 and, e.g., Bundesgericht, Switzerland, 17 Dec. 2009, *supra*, note 892. *See also*, for example, Handelsgericht Zürich (Switzerland), 5 Feb. 1997, available at www.cisg.law.pace.edu/cases/970205s1.html CLOUT Case 214 (although currency losses can be damages under Art. 74, claim for damages in this case was not granted because, pursuant to general principle of Swiss tort law, damages for future losses can only be awarded when amount can at least be estimated). *Compare*, for example, LG Düsseldorf (Germany), 5 Mar. 1996, abstract available at www.unilex.info/cisg/case/246 (German buyer denied damages for lost profit caused by Italian seller's non-delivery; buyer failed to provide 'sufficient evidence' that customers were not interested in any other type of shoes). For an example of a compromise verdict, *see* Rechtbank van Koophandel, Hasselt (Belgium), 2 May 1995, abstract available at www.unilex.info/cisg/case/263 (court determined Chilean seller's lost profits *ex aequo et bono*, taking into account probability of cover sale at price significantly lower than price agreed in contract with Belgian buyer).

Domestic evidentiary standards always require some degree of certainty. In American courts, for example, the standards of proof applicable to a lost profits claim lie well beyond the usual burdens of persuasion, but due to a relaxation of the certainty requirement, only 'reasonable certainty' is now required. Outside the Common law realm, lost profits may be more difficult to prove, not only because some courts insist on greater certainty but also because plaintiffs in, for example, Scandinavian or Civilian systems sometimes seem less willing than their American counterparts to produce confidential business accounts in court. *See* J. Lookofsky, 'Consequential Damages in CISG Context', *Pace International Law Review* 19 (2007) 63 at 67, also available at http://digitalcommons.pace.edu/pilr/vol19/iss1/5/.

896. *See* Schwenzer, *supra* note 888, at 1026 (arguing that allowing different domestic rules on the standard of proof would undermine uniform Convention interpretation and application). *Compare* Stoll & Gruber, *supra* note 888, at 759 (noting that the CISG does not lay down what degree of probability applies, but arguing that the judge should be 'convinced' that the profit would actually have been made).

897. *See* generally, as regards American and English law, E.A. Farnsworth, *Contracts* 4th ed. (2004), para. 12.15.

898. *See* Schwenzer at *ibid.*

899. For example, under American law: *see* Farnsworth, *ibid.* ('reasonable certainty' is the standard reflected in the *Restatement (Second) of Contracts*). *See also supra* note 895.

900. *Compare UNIDROIT Principles of International Commercial Contracts*, Art. 7.4.3, requiring: (1) that damages be proved with 'reasonable certainty', and allowing (2) compensation for 'value of lost chance' – a concept persuasively supported for application in the CISG context by D. Saidov, 'Standards of Proving Loss and Determining the Amount of Damages', *Journal of Contract Law* 22 (2006), at 51, but flatly rejected by Stoll & Gruber, *supra* note 888, at 759; *compare* Schwenzer, *supra* note 888, at 1073.

between the foreseeability limitation in Article 74 and certain domestic rules designed to prevent compensation for 'disproportionate' loss.[901]

As explained more fully in the following, compensation for profits lost is sometimes held precluded or restricted by application of the mitigation rule in Article 77.[902]

F. The Contract/Cover Differential

294. The Convention contains two specific rules which measure damages for direct loss in situations where an injured buyer or seller exercises the right to avoid the sales contract (for fundamental breach, etc.).[903] The first of these practical provisions, Article 75, provides:

> If the contract is avoided and if, in a reasonable manner and within a reasonable time after avoidance, the buyer has bought goods in replacement or the seller has resold the goods, the party claiming damages may recover the difference between the contract price and the price in the substitute transaction as well as any further damages recoverable under Article 74.

Both buyers and sellers can elect to measure damages by the 'contract/cover differential' as expressed in this general CISG rule. Where the seller's delayed or defective delivery constitutes a fundamental breach, the buyer may avoid the contract and (within a reasonable time thereafter) arrange for a reasonable substitute transaction,[904] and a court can then measure damages by the difference in price, as well as any further (e.g., incidental) damages recoverable under Article 74.[905]

---

901. §351(3) of the American *Restatement (Second) of Contracts* provides: 'A court may limit damages for foreseeable loss by excluding recovery for loss of profits, by allowing recovery only for loss incurred in reliance, or otherwise if it concludes that in the circumstances justice so requires in order to avoid disproportionate compensation.' Regarding matters 'governed-but-not-settled' under Art. 7, *see supra*, Nos 75 et seq. For an argument that the CISG rules on damages might be supplemented by generally applicable 'safety-valve' provisions such as those in Danish and Swedish statutory law which operate to deny 'unreasonably burdensome' compensation in civil actions grounded in contract or tort, *see* J. Lookofsky, 'Consequential Damages in CISG Context', *supra* note 895.
902. *See infra*, No. 297.
903. *See supra*, Nos 226 and 261.
904. *See*, for example, OLG Hamburg (Germany), 28 Feb. 1997, CLOUT Case 277 available at www.cisg.law.pace.edu/cases/970228g1.html (buyer's cover purchase at price three times higher than contract price (in volatile market, two weeks after seller's non-performance) held reasonable).
905. *See supra*, Nos 291 et seq. *See*, for example, the award of the ICC Court of Arbitration (Paris), No. 8128/1995, available at www.cisg.law.pace.edu/cases/958128i1.html (cover transaction reasonable if buyer acted as prudent and careful businessman; goods bought in replacement should be of same kind and quality, but small differences allowed; short period in which buyer had to cover so as to make timely delivery to third party justified cover price higher than market price). *Compare*, for example, Højesteret, Denmark, 17 Oct. 2007, CLOUT Case 993, available at http://cisgw3.law.pace.edu/cases/071017d1.html (selling goods in limited market in situation where larger market readily available not resale in 'reasonable manner').

Technically speaking, there is no CISG duty to 'cover', but a buyer who, after avoiding a given sale, makes no reasonable effort to procure substitute goods by reasonable means may later be barred from compensation for loss which he or she, by such inaction, failed to mitigate.[906] In this way, the buyer's recovery even for direct loss is limited by the broadly recognized general principle of 'substitution'[907] and thus (more specifically) by an implied obligation to cover.[908]

Similar principles apply in the wake of the buyer's fundamental breach. If the seller elects to avoid, for example, because of the buyer's failure to pay, and if, within a reasonable time thereafter, the seller resells the goods concerned, he or she may recover the contract-cover price differential,[909] as well as any further damages recoverable under Article 74.[910] Assuming the second transaction is (as discussed below) rightly regarded as a 'substitute' for the first, there will be little or no loss if the cover price obtained equals or exceeds the price which the first buyer failed to pay.

G. No Cover if Seller's Supply Exceeds Demand

295. A party cannot demand compensation for any loss which could have been prevented by cover.[911] However, not all loss is preventable by cover.

In particular, a seller's own supply may sometimes exceed his or her own demand. In such market conditions,[912] the seller cannot 'cover' buyer's breach, simply because a subsequent sale of the same goods to another buyer is not a 'substitute' for the first transaction: in this situation, there is no causal relationship between buyer's breach and seller's subsequent sale.[913] For this reason, the loss suffered in such a situation is rightly regarded as unavoidable, and the Article 75 contract/cover differential is therefore inadequate to put the 'lost-volume seller' in as good

906. *See infra*, No. 297. *See also* Hof van Beroep Antwerp, Belgium, 24 Apr. 2006, abstract available at www.unilex.info/cisg/case/1152 (seller's resale not within reasonable time after notification of avoidance, but seller could recover difference between the unpaid invoices and the income from the resale (Art. 75 CISG), since buyer failed to prove higher price if resale had been timely).

907. Regarding this principle under American domestic law, *see* E.A. Farnsworth, 'Legal Remedies for Breach of Contract', *Columbia Law Review* 70 (1970) 1145, 1188.

908. To minimize his or her 'loss on this bargain' and maximize his or her 'cost avoided', the buyer must cover his or her loss by securing a substitute. Regarding this terminology under American domestic contract law, *see* generally E.A. Farnsworth, *Contracts* 4th ed. (2004), §12.9.

909. *See*, for example, L.G. Krefeld (Germany), 28 Apr. 1993, abstract available at www.unilex.info/cisg/case/85 (shoe seller who rightfully avoided awarded damages for difference between contract price and price in substitute transaction with a second buyer, as well as for difference between contract price and current value of goods with respect to shoes not resold; damages also for attorney's fees incurred to declare contract avoided, interest paid for loans necessitated by buyer's breach and loss suffered from devaluation of Italian Lira since the date buyer's payment due).

910. *See*, for example, the decision by LG Berlin (Germany), 30 Sep. 1992, available at www.cisg.law.pace.edu/cases/920930g1.html. Also 'incidental' damages, such as the administrative costs of cover, are recoverable under the Art. 74 rule: *see supra*, Nos 291 et seq.

911. Neither party can recover for reasonably 'avoidable' loss: regarding Art. 77, *see infra*, No. 297.

912. 'You have always to ask yourself, "what market."' *See* Farnsworth, *Contracts* 4th ed. (2004), §12.12 with note 36, quoting Lord Dunedin in *Charrington & Co. v. Wooder* [1914] A.C. 71, 74.

913. *See* Farnsworth at *ibid.*

a position as performance would have done.[914] In these circumstances, the profit lost by reason of buyer's breach is best described as a direct loss,[915] which can only be recovered by damages under Article 74, thus protecting the 'lost-volume' seller's justifiable expectation.[916] Domestic sales law has long recognized this kind of expectation protection,[917] just as several scholars have long argued that the CISG lost-volume seller's case for recovery is equally strong.[918] Fortunately, this position also now has persuasive CISG case law (precedent) to support it.[919]

H. The Contract/Market Differential

296. As an alternative to the contract/cover differential, a more abstract measure of damages available to a party electing to avoid is set forth in Article 76. If there is a current (i.e., market) price for the goods concerned,[920] the party claiming damages may, if he or she has not covered by purchase or resale under Article 75, recover the difference between the price fixed by the contract and such current price at the time of avoidance. In addition, the injured party may recover further damages under Article 74.[921]

Conversely, an injured CISG seller or buyer who has in fact entered a substitute (cover) transaction cannot claim market-price damages under Article 76.[922]

Unlike the avoidance analogues of certain domestic laws, the Convention does not make a formal distinction between rejected and accepted goods.[923] If, however, the party claiming damages has avoided the contract after taking over the goods, the current price at the time of such taking over shall be applied instead of the current price at the time of avoidance.[924]

914. The American domestic sales law rule is in *accord*: *see* UCC §2-708(2).
915. Although the CISG does not distinguish between various forms of loss as such, it may be noted that the loss suffered relates not to 'collateral transactions' but rather to the value of the breached transaction itself; *accord*: Farnsworth *supra*, §12.0.
916. *See supra*, No. 291.
917. Regarding American sales law and UCC, §2-708(2), *see* White and Summers, *Uniform Commercial Code* 6th ed. (2010), §8-9.
918. *See* Lookofsky, *Understanding the CISG* 5th Worldwide ed. (2017), §6.28 with *Illustration 6h*. *Accord*: Schwenzer in Schlechtriem & Schwenzer, *Commentary* 4th ed. (2016), at 1093.
919. *See* Oberster Gerichtshof, 28 Apr. 2000, CLOUT Case 427, abstract available at www.unilex.info/cisg/case/481 (seller's failure to enter cover transaction not breach of 'obligation' to mitigate under Art. 77 (*infra*, No. 297); seller, who would have lost profit even if goods 'resold' to third person, entitled to recover difference between contract price and cost of manufacturing under Art. 74).
920. According to Art. 76(2), the 'current price' is the price prevailing at the place where delivery of the goods should have been made or, if there is no current price at that place, the price at such other place serves as a reasonable substitute, making due allowance for differences in the cost of transporting the goods.
921. Article 76(1), first sentence.
922. According to Art. 76(1), the market-price formula is available only if the avoiding party 'has not made a purchase or resale under Art. 75'.
923. *Compare* the American UCC scheme described by H. Flechtner, 'Remedies under the New International Sales Convention: The Perspective from Article 2 of the UCC', *Journal of Law and Commerce* 8 (1998) 53.
924. Article 76(1), second sentence.

I. Mitigation: No Recovery for Avoidable Loss

297. Under the CISG, as is also the case under most domestic laws, a plaintiff cannot recover for harms that he or she could have avoided by reasonable action. Within the Convention context, Article 77 applies:

> A party who relies on a breach of contract must take such measures as are reasonable in the circumstances to mitigate the loss, including loss of profit, resulting from the breach. If he fails to take such measures, the party in breach may claim a reduction in the damages in the amount by which the loss should have been mitigated.

There is no Convention 'duty' to mitigate as such.[925] However, a party who fails to take reasonable measures to mitigate loss cannot recover for the loss which could have been mitigated, and the principle should apply even as regards a prospective failure to perform: once a party has reason to know that performance by the other party will not be forthcoming, he or she is expected to take such affirmative steps as are appropriate in the circumstances to avoid loss.[926] And as in domestic law, so under the CISG: the avoidability principle determines the point in time at which we calculate the contract-cover and contract-market price differentials.[927]

Losses otherwise recoverable under the more general Article 74 rule are limited by the mitigation principle.[928] If, for example, the seller delays delivery of goods intended to serve as a key ingredient or tool in buyer's production, and the buyer makes no reasonable efforts to secure a substitute, any profits lost will not have been suffered solely 'in consequence' of seller's breach. Of course, the extent of avoidability will depend on the buyer's ingenuity, experience and financial resources (ability to obtain credit quickly, etc.), and what is 'reasonable' mitigation will depend on the court's evaluation of the concrete case.[929]

925. *Compare* Internationales Schiedsgericht der Bundeskammer der gewerblichen Wirtschaft – Wien (Vienna), Austria, arbitral award of 15 Jun. 1994, CLOUT Case 94, available at www.cisg.law.pace.edu/cases/940615a4.html (holding that CISG seller had right – and presumably also 'duty' – to make cover sale under Art. 77).

926. *See*, for example, Tribunal of International Commercial Arbitration at the Ukraine Chamber of Commerce and Trade, Ukraine, 2005 (Arbitral award No. 48), translation available at http://cisgw3.law.pace.edu/cases/050000u5.html (damages for loss of profit not awarded where loss easily avoidable by cover purchases).

927. *See supra*, Nos 294 and 296. *See also*, for example, OLG Hamburg (Germany), 28 Feb. 1997, CLOUT Case 277 available at www.cisg.law.pace.edu/cases/970228g1.html (buyer's cover purchase at price three times higher than contract price (in volatile market, two weeks after seller's non-performance) consistent with obligation to mitigate under Art. 77).

928. *See*, e.g., Bundesgericht, Switzerland, 17 Dec. 2009, available at http://www.unilex.info/cisg/case/1578 (buyer refused to buy watches in replacement from seller's exclusive Ukrainian distributor, thus failing to mitigate loss as required by Art. 77).

929. *See* OLG Hamburg, *ibid. See also*, for example, Amtsgericht München (Germany), 23 Jun. 1995, abstract at www.unilex.info/cisg/case/147 (chemical for production of pharmaceuticals; when German buyer's customers complained of non-conformity, Italian seller agreed to cure in Italy; cure delayed, buyer secured costlier cure in Germany; buyer, who had not previously informed seller of customer's urgent need, had not breached its 'duty to mitigate'). *Compare* German Supreme Court (BGH) of 25 Jun. 1997, NJW 1997, 3311–3313, abstract at www.unilex.info/cisg/case/257 (citing

298. Sometimes, a given buyer's loss may seem (at least partly) caused by his or her own pre-breach, negligent act.[930] And although CISG Article 77 was designed mainly to regulate post-breach mitigation, the Convention does not expressly bar recognition of the pre-breach (prevention) aspect of avoidability and might even impliedly authorize such recognition.[931] For example, where the harm caused by a CISG seller's delayed delivery of a simple standard part is extensively aggravated by the fact that buyer keeps no such spare parts on hand, such a failure to take precautionary measures, if judged unreasonable, might prevent or limit the recovery of compensation (for an 'avoidable' loss).[932]

299. A somewhat analogous scenario arose in a case decided by the highest German court in 2012 where a German seller delivered clay to a Dutch buyer for use in potato grading. The clay delivered had been extracted from a pit, which, as the seller knew, had been previously contaminated with dioxin, thus leading to contamination of the potatoes produced by the buyer and a loss for which the seller was clearly liable. The damages payable to the buyer were reduced, however, since the buyer had marketed the potatoes without first conducting a test to ensure that they were not contaminated. Since both parties had thus contributed to causation of the loss, the court took the actions of both into account by reference to Article 7(2) and to the general principles said to underlie Article 77, as well as Article 80.[933]

J. Interest

300. Section III of Chapter V contains a single – and deceptively simple – provision which deals with the controversial subject of interest. Article 78 provides:

> If a party fails to pay the price or any other sum that is in arrears, the other party is entitled to interest on it, without prejudice to any claim for damages recoverable under Article 74.

Arts 74 and 77 in denying CISG buyer's right to recover expenses incurred in adapting its equipment to process defective metal, as such expenses unreasonable in relation to the purchase price).

930. For a discussion comparing American and Scandinavian domestic law on this issue, *see* J. Lookofsky, *Consequential Damages in Comparative Context* (1989), at 166 et seq., https://jura.ku.dk/jurabog.

931. Regarding protection of the expectation interest under Art. 74 *see supra*, No. 291. To support recognition of the pre-breach (prevention) aspect of avoidability, one might regard the right to recover compensation for loss suffered 'as a consequence of breach' as expressing a general CISG principle (regarding this aspect of Art. 7(2) *see supra*, Nos 78–80).

932. *See* Lookofsky, *Understanding the CISG* 5th ed. (2017), §6.17 at 146 f. with notes 236–237. In the absence of reported cases directly on point, various commentators have taken differing positions on this issue: *see*, for example, Stoll in Schlechtriem, *Commentary* 1st ed. (1998), at 587 (requirement to counteract potentially harmful consequences of impending or threatened breach); *but compare* Stoll/Gruber in the 2nd ed. (2005) of *Commentary* at 788 (obligation to mitigate even before loss arises); *compare* also Schwenzer in the 4th (2016) ed. of the *Commentary* at 1108 (no general duty to take preventive measures for possible breach).

933. *See* Bundesgerichtshof (Germany), 26 Sep. 2012, available at http://www.unilex.info/cisg/case/1684; regarding this aspect of Art. 7(2) *see supra*, Nos 78–80; regarding Art. 80 *see infra*, No. 313.

301. Some domestic systems take the view that interest is a component of damages;[934] others do not.[935] In most countries, interest (however conceived) is at least compensable; in others, it is not.[936]

Article 78 appears to resolve some, but not all aspects of these conflicting views. Although Article 78 sets forth a general obligation for the breaching party to pay interest, an award of interest under Article 78 might be unenforceable in those fora where the applicable domestic law prohibits interest payments.[937]

According to Article 78, a claim for interest is without prejudice to a claim for damages, so an injured party may claim damages or interest or both. Since interest is designed, *inter alia*, to compensate lost use of capital, and since compensation for that kind of loss may also be awarded as damages, an injured party may be left with a choice between Articles 74 and 78 in this particular respect. In exceptional circumstances, where a party cannot claim damages by virtue of an Article 79 exemption,[938] a claim under Article 78 would obviously be preferred.[939] Conversely, damages might be preferred in cases where the injured party has reason to doubt that an award of interest under Article 78 would be enforced.

Since the Convention does not determine the *rate* of interest, a clear majority of national courts have settled this particular matter on the basis of domestic law,[940]

934. Representing compensation for the lost use of capital.
935. In Scandinavia, where a distinction between damages and interest is made, interest is awardable without proof of economic loss.
936. In those countries where interest is forbidden, the mere *mention* of interest in the agreement might render it invalid. Regarding arbitration agreements in this context, *see* Hunter & Triebel, 'Awarding Interest in International Arbitration', *Journal of International Arbitration* 6 (1989) 1, 8 with note 4.
937. P. Schlechtriem, *Uniform Sales Law: The UN-Convention on Contracts for the International Sale of Goods* (1986), at 100 n. 414 ([t]o the extent applicable domestic law prohibits interest payments, Article 78 would, of course, be unenforceable). *Compare* F. Ferrari, 'Uniform Application and Interest Rates under the 1980 Vienna Sales Convention', *Georgia Journal of International and Comparative Law* 24 (1995) 467 with note 64; T.S. Twibell, 'Implementation of the United Nations Convention on Contracts for the International Sale of Goods (CISG) under Shari'a Law: Will Article 78 of the CISG Be Enforced When the Forum Is an Islamic State?', *International Legal Perspectives* 9 (1997) 25–92, 87 (in light of Art. 6 and despite prohibition of *riba* in Shari'a, 'likely that an Islamic forum will enforce Art. 78'). *Compare* C. Brunner and M. Feit, 'Article 78 [Interest on Sums in Arrears]', in *Commentary on the UN Sales Law (CISG)* (Brunner & Gottlieb eds, 2019), at 555 (in States which prohibit payment of interest, e.g., States with Islamic legal systems, interest rate would be nil, but recourse can be taken to credit costs, which in these States correspond functionally to interest rates).
938. *See infra*, Nos 302 et seq.
939. *See*, e.g., International Court of Arbitration of Chamber of Industry and Commerce of Russian Federation, 13 May 2008, available at http://www.unilex.info/cisg/case/1492 (payment of interest for delayed return of price held due notwithstanding exempting event, also citing UNIDROIT Principles of International Commercial Contracts, Art. 7.4.9).
940. *See* cases cited in *UNCITRAL Digest of CISG Case Law* (2016 ed.), Art. 78, para. 13, available at https://uncitral.un.org/en/case_law/digests. *See also* F. Ferrari & M. Torsello, *International Sales Law – CISG in a Nutshell* 2nd ed. (2018), at 379 (tendency to apply *lex contractus*, i.e., law that would be applicable to contract if not subject to CISG).

provided of course that the parties have not themselves settled the matter in the particular contract concerned. Some courts and arbitrators, however, have filled contractual gaps with respect to the rate of interest by means of Convention-based criteria, not least the (arguably) general CISG principle of 'full compensation'.[941]

Although the most common applications of Article 78 relate to situations where a seller claims interest (and/or damages) as a remedy for buyer's failure to pay the price, Article 78 also expressly authorizes an award of interest for 'any other sum that is in arrears',[942] and a US Federal Court has rightly cited CISG Article 78 as authority for awarding prejudgment interest to an Italian buyer who suffered various losses (profits, etc.) attributed to an American seller's failure to deliver conforming goods.[943] This decision accords with the reported decisions on this issue rendered by nearly all other national courts and international arbitral tribunals,[944] as well as with the opinion expressed by the majority of CISG commentators.[945]

941. *See* generally *UNCITRAL Digest of CISG Case Law, ibid.*, paras 10–15. *Accord* Audit, *Vente internationale*, No. 180 (interest rate must be determined under the Convention itself). For one much-discussed example of the minority approach, *see* Internationales Schiedsgericht der Bundeskammer der gewerblichen Wirtschaft – Wien, award No. SCH-4366, 15 Jun. 1994, CLOUT Case 93, available at www.uncitral.org/uncitral/en/case_law/abstracts.html.

942. Among other sums in arrears, Art. 78 seems broad enough to cover the situation where buyer rightfully avoids, but seller delays refunding the price. However, Art. 84(1) contains a special rule on this particular point: *see* the UNILEX report of OLG München (Germany), 8 Feb. 1995, No. 7 U 1720/94 (buyer entitled to interest on sum to be refunded) and LG Landshut (Germany), 5 Apr. 1995, abstract available at www.unilex.info/cisg/case/121 (interest on price under awarded under Art. 84(1) from date of payment, interest under Art. 78 on amount awarded as damages under Art. 74).

943. This although the 'sum in arrears' first became liquidated at the time of the judgment: *see Delchi Carrier S.p.A. v. Rotorex Corp.*, 1994 WESTLAW 495787 (N.D.N.Y.), CLOUT Case 85, aff'd. in part and rev'd. in part, and remanded, 71 F.3d 1024 (2nd Cir. 1995), CLOUT Case 138 (District Court held plaintiff entitled to prejudgment interest at the US treasury bill rate pursuant to Art. 78 – a holding not contested on appeal). *See also* US District Court, 15 Apr. 2009, *San Lucio, S.r.l. et al. v. Import & Storage Services, LLC et al.*, available at http://www.unilex.info/cisg/case/1438.

944. For an illustration of the overwhelming majority view, *see* Kantonsgericht des Kantons Zug, Switzerland, 21 Oct. 1999, CLOUT Case No. 328, abstract available at www.unilex.info/cisg/case/412 (buyer granted interest on sums accruing from time damages were due); Handelsgericht des Kantons Zürich, Switzerland, 5 Feb. 1997, CLOUT Case 214, available at www.cisg.law.pace.edu/cases/970205s1.html (interest to be paid on claim for damages, belongs to 'any other sum that is in arrears' which party fails to pay; interest on damage claim to be paid starting on maturity date); Arbitration – International Chamber of Commerce No. 7585, 1992, CLOUT Case 301 available at www.unilex.info/cisg/case/134 (seller entitled to interest from date on which buyer had to pay, that is, date of acceptance test and expected date of installation); Cour d'appel, Grenoble, France, 26 Apr. 1995, CLOUT Case 152, available at www.cisg.law.pace.edu/cases/950426f2.html (interest starts to accrue on date replacement goods handed over to buyer); Amtsgericht Nordhorn, Germany, 14 Jun. 1994, abstract available at www.unilex.info/cisg/case/114 (seller entitled to recover interest accruing from dates on which different payments had fallen due); Tribunal commercial Namur, Belgium, 15 Jan. 2002, available at http://cisgw3.law.pace.edu/cases/020115b1.html (balance of the sale price (90%) due from 1 Oct. 1999, buyer ordered to pay interest calculated on EUR 339,528.49 at legal rate from 1 Oct. 1999); CLOUT Case 432, Landgericht Stendal, Germany, 10 Dec. 2000, available at www.cisg.law.pace.edu/cases/001012g1.html (no date for payment of purchase price fixed, interest due after buyer had opportunity to examine goods). Only one published CISG decision would seem to express the contrary view: *see* Supreme Court of Denmark, 17 Oct. 2007, CLOUT Case 993, available at http://cisgw3.law.pace.edu/cases/071017d1.html.

945. *See*, for example, C. Brunner and M. Feit, 'Article 78 [Interest on Sums in Arrears]', in *Commentary on the UN Sales Law (CISG)* (Brunner & Gottlieb eds, 2019), at 553; Bacher in Schlechtriem

K. Liability Exemptions for Failure to Perform

1. Introduction

302. Section IV of CISG Chapter V, headed 'Exemptions', deals with the kinds of problems often discussed in domestic law under such labels as impossibility (or impracticability) of performance and force majeure. Section IV consists of only two articles, the most important being Article 79.

Article 79 represents a limited exception to the CISG no-fault liability starting point set forth in Articles 45(1) and 61(1).[946] Taken together, these provisions constitute the CISG regime which determines when the obligor (seller or buyer) is liable for a failure to perform as promised.

According to the case law statistics compiled by UNCITRAL, Article 79 has been invoked with some frequency in litigation, but only with limited success. In five cases, a seller successfully claimed exemption for a failure to perform, but in at least twenty-seven other cases, a seller's claim of exemption was denied; buyers have been granted an exemption under Article 79 four times, but in at least fourteen other cases, their claims have been denied.[947] Since these statistics only take account of cases where non-performing parties (or their lawyers) felt their exemption claim was so strong that litigation was worth undertaking, the clear implication of the outcome of the reported cases is that such exemptions are very difficult to achieve.

Article 79 contains five paragraphs. The main exemptions rule, set forth in Article 79(1), provides:

> A party is not liable for a failure to perform any of his obligations if he proves that the failure was due to an impediment beyond his control and that he could not reasonably be expected to have taken the impediment into account at the time of the conclusion of the contract or to have avoided or overcome it or its consequences.

Note, by way of introduction, that an exemption – if granted to a given CISG obligor – only exempts that party from liability (in damages); Article 79 does not, in other words, prevent the obligee from exercising any other right under this Convention, such as the right to avoid.[948]

& Schwenzer, *Commentary* 4th ed. (2016), at 1113; Lookofsky, *Understanding the CISG* 5th Worldwide ed. (2017), §6.18; J. Ramberg & J. Herre, *Internationella köplagen* 3rd ed. (2009), 14.1.2. The majority view *accords* with the CISG principle of 'full compensation' expressed in Art. 74 (*see supra*, No. 291) as well as the *lex mercatoria* view expressed in the Comment to Art. 7.4.10 of the *UNIDROIT Principles on International Commercial Contracts* 4th ed. (2016) (declaring it 'only natural' that the aggrieved party be compensated with interest on damages as of the date of the harm). *Compare* Honnold/Flechtner, *Uniform Law for International Sales under the 1980 United Nations Convention* 4th ed. (2009), at 608 (maintaining that the requirement of 'sum' in arrears refers, not to damages awarded, but only to 'money' payable under parties' contract).

946. *See supra*, Nos 211 and 254.

947. *See UNCITRAL Digest of CISG Case Law* (2016 ed.), Art. 79, para. 7, available at https://uncitral.un.org/en/case_law/digests.

948. Regarding Art. 79(5) *see infra*, No. 312.

2. Freedom of Contract and the Gap-Filling Rule

303. Before proceeding to analyse various key aspects of Article 79, it should be emphasized that Article 79 is a default (gap-filling) rule, and that it is not uncommon that the liability of a given seller or buyer for non-performance is regulated by the express terms of the parties' agreement.[949] And although it is rare that the express terms of a given sales contract provide for 'absolute' liability (i.e., for any breach, without exception), many international sales contracts contain a so-called force majeure clause.[950] Clauses limiting the seller's liability for non-performance to instances of negligent breach are also quite common, especially when coupled with an obligation to repair or replace.[951]

For the many cases where the contract leaves a gap on the force majeure question, or where the contract simply provides that a party is not liable in the event of 'force majeure' (without further specification),[952] Article 79 works to fill the contractual gap.

3. Requirements for Exemption and the Burden of Proof

304. As explained more fully in the following, a liability exemption will not be granted under Article 79 unless the obligor's non-performance was due to an unforeseeable and unavoidable impediment which lay beyond the obligor's control. Although it is possible to break down (and list) these requirements in various ways, they will – with a view towards establishing an easily accessible overview – be presented in the following under three main heads.[953] An important common element as regards the satisfaction of each of these individual elements/requirements is that the burden of proof lies with the non-performing obligor. According to the clear weight of academic authority and CISG case law, the party who seeks an exemption remains liable, pursuant to Articles 45(1) and 61(1),[954] *unless he* (the non-performing obligor) *proves* that all the requirements set forth in Article 79 are fulfilled. This 'reversed' burden of proof, whereby courts and arbitrators interpret the

949. *See* Art. 6, *supra*, Nos 70 et seq.

950. *See*, for example, Tribunal of Int'l Commercial Arbitration at the Russian Federation Chamber of Commerce, 17 Oct. 1995, CLOUT Case 142, available at http://cisgw3.law.pace.edu/cases/951017r1.html (contract between parties gave exhaustive list of force majeure circumstances discharging them from liability for non-performance; buyer's lack of foreign currency not included on list). *See also* Int'l Commercial Arbitration Court at the Ukrainian Chamber of Commerce and Industry, Ukraine, 23 Jan. 2012, available at http://www.unilex.info/cisg/case/1876 (contract contained provisions on force majeure other than those in Art. 79; applying Art. 6, tribunal held these express provisions should prevail over Art. 79(1)).

951. Such limitations (and agreed remedies), if reasonable, are likely to be valid pursuant to the applicable domestic law: *see supra*, Nos 63 and 79.

952. *See*, for example, OLG Hamburg (Germany), 28 Feb. 1997, available at www.cisg.law.pace.edu/cases/970228g1.html (seller not exempt from liability: neither under clause in seller's standard terms expressly exempting it from liability by reason of 'force majeure' nor by reason of Art. 79; seller's risk includes non-delivery caused by its supplier).

953. *See infra*, Nos 305, 306 and 307.

954. *See supra*, Nos 211 and 254.

'if' in Article 79(1) to mean 'unless', itself represents a formidable barrier to the party who seeks an Article 79 exemption.

305. The first requirement for the achievement of an exemption under Article 79 is that the non-performing party must demonstrate the existence of an 'impediment beyond his control'.

The Convention does not define the word 'impediment' (*empêchement*), and the legislative history casts little clear light on its intended meaning or scope. Judging by the ordinary meaning of words, an impediment is an obstacle, something which 'gets in the way'.

The most typical obstacles to a CISG obligor's performance are likely to lead to delay or non-delivery (or in the case of buyer's breach non-payment), but a few CISG commentators realized early on that certain impediments might also 'get in the way' of a seller's obligation to deliver conforming goods.[955] In 1999, the Supreme Court of Germany (*Bundesgerichtshof*) rendered a landmark decision which lent clear and convincing support to this expansive (inclusive) reading of Article 79,[956] thus countering the views of jurists from Common law systems who (still) maintain that Article 79 should never apply to cases of non-conformity.[957]

Of course, the fact that we define a given obstacle as a potential impediment to performance does not mean that a non-performing party who is disadvantaged by that impediment automatically qualifies for an Article 79 exemption. Indeed, as the German Supreme Court took pains to emphasize in its landmark 1999 decision, a party can never be granted an Article 79 exemption unless he proves that the impediment in question lies 'beyond his control', and because the possibility of assuring that the goods in question do conform will nearly always lie *within* the seller's sphere of control, the beyond-control requirement itself severely reduces the possibility of exempting a given seller from liability for non-conformity.[958] So

955. *See* generally, J. Lookofsky, 'Fault and No-Fault in Danish, American and International Sales Law. The Reception of the 1980 United Nations Sales Convention', *Scandinavian Studies in Law* 27 (1983) 109, 135, also available at www.cisgw3.law.pace.edu/cisg/biblio/lookofsky4.html. Regarding more recent domestic legislation in Finland, Norway and Sweden (but not Denmark) patterned on Art. 79, *see* J. Lookofsky, *Consequential Damages in Comparative Context* (1989), at 101–102 with notes 146–149, https://jura.ku.dk/jurabog. *See also* Stoll & Gruber in Schlechtriem & Schwenzer, *Commentary* 2nd English ed. (2005), at 810 with note 24, and Schwenzer in the 4th (2016) ed. of the same work at 1132 with note 22 (both correctly referring, *inter alia*, to Lookofsky's concurring view in *Consequential Damages* (*id.*), at 282, but inaccurately citing Lookofsky for the proposition that 'application of Art 79 is excluded because of the lack of foreseeability of any defect').

956. *See* Bundesgerichtshof (Germany), 23 Mar. 1999, CLOUT Case No. 271, full text at https://www.uncitral.org/clout/clout/data/deu/clout_case_271_leg-1494.html.

957. *See*, for example, Honnold/Flechtner, *Uniform Law for International Sales under the 1980 United Nations Convention* 4th ed. (2009), at 616–621 (contending that the Art. 79 exemption cannot apply to defective performance). According to American domestic sales law, a seller is strictly liable for non-conforming goods, so – at least within that (UCC) system – no 'state-of-the-art' exemption applies: *see*, for example, *Spartanburg County School District Seven v. National Gypsum Co.*, 842 F. 2nd 1292 (4th Cir. 1988).

958. For one thing, since a party should always be deemed to be 'in control' of his or her own business and financial condition in general, internal 'excuses' connected with business operations (poor quality control, etc.) or financial management are never 'beyond' that party's control. Moreover, as the

although a lower French court (in a 1998 decision) granted a 'good-faith' CISG seller a liability exemption for failure to supply conforming goods,[959] it seems unlikely that other courts would find this French precedent persuasive, especially since its *ratio decidendi* was clearly refuted just one year later by the highest German court.

The exemption rule in Article 79 is clearly most relevant as regards the seller's liability for delayed delivery or non-delivery and the buyer's liability for delayed payment or non-payment. Even in these instances, however, the beyond-control requirement has proved extremely difficult to satisfy. To take one example of considerable practical importance, difficulties in delivery or payment due to financial or organizational problems (and the like) are not considered to be impediments beyond an obligor's control;[960] on the contrary, such impediments belong to the non-performing party's own general 'sphere (area) of risk',[961] and the CISG case law provides numerous concrete examples on this particular point.[962]

306. In addition to the difficulties posed by the beyond-control requirement to a would-be exemptee, the non-performing party who seeks an Article 79 exemption must also demonstrate that he or she could not reasonably be expected to have taken the impediment in question 'into account' at the time of the conclusion of the contract. This is the so-called foreseeability requirement, and it too constitutes a key element in the exemptions equation and the overall Convention allocation of risk.[963]

Bundesgerichtshof put it in 1999: since Art. 79 does not alter the basic CISG allocation of risk, the seller must assure that his supplier provides defect-free goods. For this reason, the CISG buyer need not distinguish between cases where the seller is the manufacturer and cases where the seller obtains the goods from others; nor should the risk of non-conformity depend on whether the defect is 'discoverable' by inspection or not. *See* the BGH decision cited *supra* and P. Schlechtriem, 'Uniform Sales Law in the Decisions of the Bundesgerichtshof', available at www.cisg.law.pace.edu/cisg/biblio/schlechtriem3.html (this BGH decision demonstrates that 'control' within meaning of Art. 79(1) includes 'economic risk control').

959. Tribunal de Commerce de Besançon, France, 19 Jan. 1998, abstract available at www.unilex.info/cisg/case/416 (seller's failure to perform held due to impediment 'beyond its control' since the goods manufactured by third party and no evidence that seller had acted in bad faith).

960. *See*, e.g., Audencia Provincial de Valladolid (section 1), Spain, 6 Apr. 2015, available at http://www.unilex.info/cisg/case/1951 (problems encountered with members of cooperatives outside scope of Art. 79, as such circumstance within seller's control, organization and system of production).

961. *See* (as regards delayed delivery) the arbitral award rendered by Schiedsgericht der Handelskammer – Hamburg (Germany), 21 Mar. 1996, CLOUT Case 166 (difficulties in delivery due to seller's financial problems or to financial problems of seller's supplier, even when connected to act of public authority in supplier's country, not considered impediment beyond seller's control but rather belonging to seller's area of risk). *See also* generally J. Lookofsky, *Understanding the CISG* 5th Worldwide ed. (2017), §§6.19 and 6.32.

962. *See* cases cited in *UNCITRAL Digest of CISG Case Law* (2016 ed.), Art. 79, para. 15 with notes 68–75.

963. *See*, e.g., Audencia Provincial de Valladolid (section 1), Spain, 6 Apr. 2015, *supra* note 962 (considering high volatility in pine kernel market, reduction in production not event that could not be expected or avoided; seller might have protected itself from that risk by contract terms reflecting market features.).

Indeed, since virtually all potential impediments to performance are foreseeable to some degree, this particular Article 79 element has (as originally predicted by UNCITRAL) proved very difficult for the breaching CISG promisor to prove.[964] To take one example: a German seller of a car which proved to be stolen failed to convince a German court of the unforeseeability of that contingency, especially since the car's low price, mileage and registration all served to document disparities which should have led the seller to entertain doubts about the car's ownership.[965]

The party damaged by a foreseeable contingency, such as increased cost, will, of course, be entitled to protection if the contract in question contains a force majeure clause which reallocates that particular risk.[966] But assuming the parties' contract is silent on the issue of an increase in seller's cost or a decrease in buyer's value, the obligor's inability to make a profit on a particular contract is not likely to lead to a liability exemption under the CISG. This is because price fluctuations, for example, a significant drop in the market price of frozen berries, are generally foreseeable;[967] put another way, merchants who buy or sell goods at fixed prices are themselves in the 'business' of assuming this kind of commercial risk.

Granted, at some (extreme) point, we might reach what jurists trained in Civil law systems sometimes call the 'sacrifice threshold', that is, the economic force majeure borderline where a court or arbitral might exempt an oppressed obligor from liability for non-performance under Article 79, but such highly exceptional cases serve to underscore the general CISG liability rule.

In one example from CISG case law which illustrates this point, a French buyer argued for an exemption when its client (a truck manufacturer) significantly reduced the price it would pay for goods (crankcases) which the buyer had purchased under a long-term contract with a Swiss seller-manufacturer.[968] In refusing to grant an exemption, the French Court of Appeal noted that such a development was foreseeable, not least in a long-term contract like the one in question. Since the final customer's reduction of the repurchase price was foreseeable at the time of contracting, it was up to the buyer, in its contract with its own supplier, to provide for mechanisms of renegotiation in the case of changes of circumstances, in particular by inclusion of a 'hardship' clause in that contract. Having failed to so protect itself by contract, the buyer was held to bear the risk of the contingency concerned.

This example also illustrates the fact that the possibility of achieving an exemption under Article 79 by reason of changed economic circumstances is tightly connected to (some would even say identical with) the issue of changed economic

964. *See* A/CONF./97/5, para. 5 of *Secretariat's Commentary* to Art. 65 of the 1978 Draft Convention.

965. *See* Oberlandesgericht München, 5 Mar. 2008, available at http://unilex.info/cisg/case/1342.

966. For a comparison of the corresponding principle in American and Scandinavian law, *see* J. Lookofsky, *Consequential Damages in Comparative Context* (1989), https://jura.ku.dk/jurabog, at 78 et seq.

967. *See* Rechtbank van Koophandel, Hasselt (Belgium), 2 May 1995, English abstract available at http://www.unilex.info/cisg/case/263 (significant drop in market price of frozen raspberries after conclusion of contract not 'force majeure' exempting the buyer for non-performance under Art. 79; price fluctuations are foreseeable events in international trade which do not render performance impossible but result in economic loss well within normal risk of commercial activities). *Compare* (regarding analogues in American and Scandinavian law) J. Lookofsky, *ibid.*, Part 3.2.3.

968. Cour d'appel Colmar, France, 12 Jun. 2001, CLOUT Case 480, available at http://cisgw3.law.pace.edu/cases/010612f1.html.

circumstances due to 'hardship' – this even though the relief granted in a hardship situation can, depending on the applicable rule of law, comprise a duty on the part of the obligee to renegotiate or (in the event of failed negotiations) a court-imposed contractual adjustment. Since hardship relief of this kind is obviously very different from the kind of relief expressly authorized by Article 79, and since such hardship relief might be held available under non-CISG (e.g., domestic) rules of law and/or by virtue of an 'expansive' interpretation of Article 79(1), it seems most appropriate to explore the possibility of relief by virtue hardship under a separate heading.[969]

307. Returning for the moment to the more generally applicable conditions for a CISG exemption from liability, Article 79(1) requires that the non-performing party demonstrate that he or she could not reasonably be expected to have 'avoided or overcome' the impediment or its consequences. This is yet another requirement which represents an imposing barrier to a would-be exemptee, particularly in the common case of generically defined obligations.

Suppose, for example, that the seller's obligation is to deliver coal or wood, and that this obligation to deliver is not limited by contract to any particular source of supply. The fact that the seller's own intended source of supply (at the time of contracting) later 'dries up' will not exempt that seller from liability under Article 79(1), in that a seller can usually avoid breach simply by securing an alternative (although perhaps more expensive) source of supply; so, under this assumption – that is, that performance remains practicable (as opposed to impossible) – the seller remains liable for breach.[970] Following a similar line, a German court refused to exempt a French seller of tomatoes for its failure to deliver to a German buyer when heavy rainfalls damaged much of the tomato crop in France, causing an increase in market prices as regards those tomatoes which remained: because the entire French tomato crop had not been destroyed, the seller's performance was still possible; that is, the reduced availability of supplies as well as their increased cost were impediments that seller could indeed overcome.[971] It should in this connection be noted that some CISG courts and commentators prefer to classify those who supply CISG sellers with goods or raw materials as 'TPs' within the ambit of Article 79, paragraph (2).[972]

A much-discussed – but rarely liability-exempting – contingency is a given party's own (internal) financial inability to perform, that is, insolvency and the like. Even if such a contingency were best classified as an 'unavoidable impediment',[973]

969. *See* discussion *infra*, No. 308.

970. *Accord*: A/CONF./97/5, para. 5 of *Secretariat's Commentary* to Art. 65 of the 1978 Draft Convention (party required to provide commercially reasonable substitute). *See also* Example 65b at *ibid.* (delivery of replacement machine tools) and OLG Hamburg (Germany), 28 Feb. 1997, available at www.cisg.law.pace.edu/cases/970228g1.html (seller not exempt from liability under Art. 79 nor under clause in seller's standard terms expressly exempting it from liability by reason of 'force majeure'; seller's risk includes non-delivery caused by its supplier; seller only exempt from liability if impossible to find goods of similar quality on market).

971. Oberlandesgericht Hamburg, Germany, 4 Jul. 1997, abstract available at http://www.unilex.info/cisg/case/438.

972. This, however, would not change the outcome in such cases. *See infra*, No. 309.

973. *See* A/CONF./97/5, para. 10 of the *Secretariat's Commentary* to Art. 65 of the 1978 Draft Convention (probably not an impediment). *Compare supra*, No. 306.

a party's inability to finance his or her own performance should not lead to an exemption under Article 79(1), in that such a contingency is one which a (commercial) seller or buyer should reasonably foresee; put another way, a party who voluntarily makes a promise to sell or buy goods is generally regarded as having assumed the risk of not being able to finance performance as promised.[974]

However, an unanticipated and highly unusual (and thus not reasonably foreseeable) imposition of exchange controls by public authorities might lead to a liability exemption for the buyer,[975] but only if such an obligor can prove (not only that the particular impediment in question was unforeseeable but also) that the impediment could not reasonably be overcome, for example, by arranging for payment by alternative means.[976]

4. Hardship: Governed by CISG or by Domestic Rules?

308. As already indicated,[977] a difficult question may arise as to the relationship between the more typical (force majeure-type) impediments clearly covered by the exemptions rule in CISG Article 79 and situations which fall under the arguably separate heading of 'hardship', as that term is typically understood in domestic systems and also within the field of international commercial law. As defined in the UNIDROIT Principles (4th ed. 2016), Article 6.2.2:

> There is hardship where the occurrence of events fundamentally alters the equilibrium of the contract either because the cost of a party's performance has increased or because the value of the performance a party receives has diminished, and (a) the events occur or become known to the disadvantaged party after the conclusion of the contract; (b) the events could not reasonably have

974. *See*, for example, the arbitral award rendered by Schiedsgericht der Handelskammer, Hamburg (Germany), 21 Mar. 1996, available at www.cisg.law.pace.edu/cases/960321g1.html (difficulties in delivery due to financial problems of seller or seller's supplier, even if connected to act of public authority, not impediment beyond seller's control; rather part of seller's area of risk). *Compare* (regarding American law) *Restatement 2nd of Contracts*, para. 261, Comment e; *see also* J. Lookofsky, *Consequential Damages in Comparative Context* (1989), https://jura.ku.dk/jurabog, at 90–91.

975. *See*, for example, the award rendered by the ICC Court of Arbitration (Paris), No. 7197/1992, CLOUT Case 104, available at www.cisg.law.pace.edu/cases/927197i1.html (suspension of payment of foreign debts ordered by Bulgarian Government not 'force majeure' contingency which prevented buyer from opening documentary credit; buyer did not prove failure to open credit was consequence of [due to] suspension; in any case, suspension had already been declared at time of conclusion of contract and was therefore an 'impediment' which buyer could reasonably have foreseen).

976. *Accord*: A/CONF./97/5, para. 10 of *Secretariat's Commentary* to Art. 65 of the 1978 Draft Convention. In this case, avoidability presumes the availability of alternative measures consistent with the contractual obligation assumed: if the contract requires payment from a particular source, the impediment would not be avoidable by alternative means.

977. *See supra*, No. 307.

> been taken into account by the disadvantaged party at the time of the conclusion of the contract; (c) the events are beyond the control of the disadvantaged party; and (d) the risk of the events was not assumed by the disadvantaged party.[978]

For situations which qualify as hardship under this definition, the UNIDROIT Principles make the following remedial relief available to the disadvantaged obligor:

> In case of hardship the disadvantaged party is entitled to request renegotiations. […] Upon failure to reach agreement either party may resort to the court. If the court finds hardship it may, if reasonable, terminate the contract [or] adapt the contract with a view to restoring its equilibrium.[979]

Given the obvious affinity between situations (scenarios) which might be categorized not only as hardship (under the UNIDROIT Principles and/or domestic law) but also as 'economic force majeure' under CISG Article 79, some would argue that the disadvantaged obligor in such a situation might have a choice: either to seek relief for hardship or to seek relief under Article 79.[980]

Until recently, there was little (significant) CISG case law on this complex subject,[981] but scholars had nonetheless seen good reason to explore and debate various possible means of dealing with hardship situations within the CISG international sales context.

Some of these scholars (following traditions in Common law systems where relief for hardship is *never* granted in the absence of express contractual provision)

---

978. *UNIDROIT Principles of International Commercial Contracts* (2016), Art. 6.2.2 (*Definition of Hardship*).

979. *See* UNIDROIT Principles Art. 6.2.3 (*Effects of hardship*), the full version of which provides as follows: (1) In case of hardship the disadvantaged party is entitled to request renegotiations. The request shall be made without undue delay and shall indicate the grounds on which it is based. (2) The request for renegotiation does not in itself entitle the disadvantaged party to withhold performance. (3) Upon failure to reach agreement within a reasonable time either party may resort to the court. (4) If the court finds hardship it may, if reasonable (a) terminate the contract at a date and on terms to be fixed; or (b) adapt the contract with a view to restoring its equilibrium.

980. *See* (regarding hardship and force majeure) *UNIDROIT Principles of International Commercial Contracts* 4th ed. (2016), Art. 6.2.2 (*Definition of Hardship*), Comment 6, explaining that in situations which can, at the same time, be considered as cases of hardship *and* force majeure (Art. 7.1.7), it is for the party affected to decide which remedy to pursue.

981. *See* (e.g.) the decision by Tribunale Civile di Monza 14 Jan. 1993, CLOUT Case 54, noted in the CISG *Case Digest* of Art. 79 (2016 ed.), section headed 'Treatment of Particular Impediments: Change in the Cost of Performance or the Value of the Goods'. *See also* the English translation available at http://cisgw3.law.pace.edu/cisg/wais/db/cases2/930114i3.html. *See also* J. Lookofsky, 'Walking the Tightrope Between CISG Article 7 and Domestic Law', *Journal of Law & Commerce* 25 (2006).

proposed exclusive use of the black-letter formula of Article 79 to 'settle' the hardship question, so that the only relief (if any) available to a CISG obligor disadvantaged by economic dislocation would be a difficult-to-obtain liability exemption under Article 79.[982]

A second group of scholars have preferred to regard hardship as a 'matter' which is 'governed' but not 'settled' by the CISG but which nonetheless can be settled on the basis of good faith and other CISG general principles, including unwritten principles which might be said to lie between the lines of Article 79.[983]

A third position, differing in principle from both these (purely CISG) solutions, would allow the CISG and other (domestic or international) rule-sets to coexist, such that the exemption rule in Article 79 might, depending on the concrete circumstances, be supplemented by more flexible rules designed to regulate hardship.[984] The justification for this approach lies in the fact that the remedies traditionally associated with force majeure and hardship are fundamentally different, just as the 'force majeure' rule in Article 79 and hardship have different functions.[985]

982. *See* generally H. Flechtner, 'The Exemption Provisions of the Sales Convention, Including Comments on "Hardship" Doctrine and the 19 Jun. 2009 Decision of the Belgian Cassation Court', *Belgrade Law Review* 3 (2011), 84–101, also available at http://cisgw3.law.pace.edu/cisg/biblio/flechtner10.html (2009 decision by Belgian Court of Cassation, holding that CISG incorporates, as part of its general principles, the 'hardship' provisions of the UNIDROIT Principles, distorts the meaning of the CISG and threatens its political legitimacy).

983. *See*, for example, CISG Advisory Council Opinion No. 7, Exemption of Liability for Damages Under Art. 79 of the CISG, Comments 35, 40 (2007), available at http://www.cisgac.com/cisgac-opinion-no7/ (infer from obligation to interpret Convention in good faith a duty imposed upon the parties to renegotiate); *compare* (more hesitant) Stoll & Gruber in Schlechtriem & Schwenzer, *Commentary* 2nd English ed. (2005), 824–825; *compare also* Schwenzer in the 4th ed. (2016) of the same work at 1151 (suggesting possible recourse to Art. 6.2.3(2) of the UNIDROIT Principles). *But compare* (adjusting positions expressed in its Opinion No. 7, *supra*) CISG Advisory Council Opinion No. 20 (2020), available at http:// http://cisgac.com/opinion-no20-hardship-under-the-cisg/.

984. *See* J. Lookofsky, 'Impediments and Hardship in International Sales', *International Review of Law & Economics* 25 (2005), 434, available at www.cisg.law.pace.edu/cisg/biblio/lookofsky17.html; J. Lookofsky, 'Walking the Tightrope Between CISG Article 7 and Domestic Law', *Journal of Law & Commerce* 25 (2006), 87–105, available at www.cisg.law.pace.edu/cisg/biblio/lookofsky16.html; J. Lookofsky, 'Not Running Wild with the CISG', *Journal of Law & Commerce* 29 (2011), also available at https://jlc.law.pitt.edu/ojs/index.php/jlc/article/view/27/27. *Accord* C. Brunner, 'Article 79 [Impediment Excusing a Party From Damages]', in *Commentary on the UN Sales Law (CISG)* (Brunner & Gottlieb eds, 2019), at 580 (if impediment amounts to fundamental equivalency distortion, courts should allow UNIDROIT Principles Art. 6.2.3 to supplement Art. 79, thus allowing aggrieved party to request renegotiations, with possible judicial adaptation or termination). Note that the solution advocated by Lookofsky and Brunner does *not* entail use the UNIDROIT rule to help fill an '*internal* (CISG) gap' or to 'interpret' the black letter of CISG Art. 79. *See infra*, note 989.

985. This is confirmed by the fact that the CISG is (generally) not concerned with rules of validity (*see* Art. 4), whereas hardship can rightly be regarded as a 'validity-related' conception: a blood relative of other validity-based defences to (sales) contract enforcement which courts regularly use to police contracts for unfairness. Therefore, some arbiters faced with the issue might see good reason to opt for rule-concurrence (as opposed to pre-emption), for example, in situations where the applicable domestic law provides authority for the censorship and/or modification of contract terms which – though perhaps fair when originally agreed to – have become unreasonable. *See* Lookofsky, 'Walking the Tightrope', *supra* note 984, at 100–101.

In 2009, the Supreme Court of Belgium (*Cour de cassation*) was faced with a situation where a CISG seller had refused to deliver due to a post-contractual 70% increase in costs. When the buyer refused to renegotiate the price, the seller sued for the difference between the contract price and the increase in cost. As it turned out, the highest Belgian court opted for a solution essentially in line with the second approach outlined above.[986] Holding that there was a 'gap' in the CISG Convention concerning the issue of *adapting* the terms of the contract in this situation, the court – referring, *inter alia*, to the UNIDROIT Principles on hardship – filled that gap pursuant to CISG Article 7(2),[987] in particular by authorizing the adaptation of the contractual terms pursuant to the general CISG principle of good faith and requiring the buyer to pay an additional 450,000 beyond the original price.[988]

This Cour de cassation decision, and especially its underlying reasoning, has been severely criticized.[989] More recently, however, the highest court in France lent some support to the Belgian position.[990] Whether courts in other countries will follow these controversial Belgian and French leads, or whether they will prefer one of the other hardship solutions outlined above,[991] remains an open question.

5. Non-performance Due to Failure of TP

309. Paragraph (2) of CISG Article 79 deals with the situation where a party's failure to perform is 'due to the failure by a TP whom he has engaged to perform the whole or a part of the contract'.

In this situation, the party claiming the exemption is exempt from liability only if:

(a) he is exempt under the preceding paragraph; and

986. *See* text *supra* with note 983.

987. As convincingly argued by F. Ferrari & M. Torsello, *International Sales Law-CISG in a Nutshell* 2nd ed. (2018), at 405, this conclusion by the Belgian court rests on the untenable premise that the UNIDROIT Principles can be considered general principles upon which the CISG is based under the gap-filling rule in Art. 7(2); *accord* Flechtner, *supra* note 982. Regarding the UNIDROIT Principles on Hardship, *see* text *supra* with notes 978 ff.

988. Hof van Cassatie/Cour de Cassation, Belgium, 19 Jun. 2009; (Supreme Court), available at http://cisgw3.law.pace.edu/cases/090619b1.html.

989. For a commentary highly critical of the Belgian decision, *see* H. Flechtner, 'The Exemption Provisions of the Sales Convention, Including Comments on "Hardship" Doctrine and the 19 June 2009 Decision of the Belgian Cassation Court', *Belgrade Law Review* 3 (2011), 84–101, also available at http://cisgw3.law.pace.edu/cisg/biblio/flechtner10.html. *See also* J. Lookofsky, 'Not Running Wild with the CISG', *Journal of Law & Commerce* 29 (2011), also available at http://papers.ssrn.com/sol3/papers.cfm?abstract_id=2376353; *see also* F. Ferrari & M. Torsello, *supra* note 987, at 403 ff.

990. *See* Cour de Cassation (France) 17 Feb. 2015, available at http://www.unilex.info/cisg/case/1999 (upholding lower court ruling that seller in this particular case failed to demonstrate increased cost of performance or existence of situation whose occurrence profoundly altered the balance of the contract, thus constituting hardship). For a critique of the hardship dicta in this French decision *see* Gillette & Walt, *UN Convention Theory and Practice* 2nd ed. (2016), at 308–309.

991. *See* text *supra* with notes 982–985.

(b) the person whom he has so engaged would be so exempt if the provisions of that paragraph were applied to him or her.

The first point to be noted is that the rule in paragraph (2), by virtue of its own express terms, only covers situations where a party has 'engaged [a third person] to perform the whole or a part of [that party's obligations under] the contract'. In the absence of an express contractual provision on point, the question of whether one contracting party (e.g., the seller: S) enjoys the right to 'delegate' to an independent TP any of the contractual duties which S has incurred vis-à-vis the other contracting party (in this case, the buyer: B) is likely to be governed by domestic law.[992] Assuming that such delegation is possible, Article 79(2) would seem to comprise a situation like this:

> S, after entering a sales contract with B, and before breaching any obligation thereby incurred, engages an independent third person (TP) to perform (some or all of) the duties which S has undertaken vis-à-vis B; S then fails to perform his obligation (to make timely and conforming delivery) to B, after which S claims a liability exemption, arguing that S's failure to perform is due to TP's failure to perform its obligations to S.

Read against this background, it is easy to understand why Article 79(2) has become one of the more misunderstood and controversial CISG provisions. Indeed, one might wonder why any special rule was needed to cover this particular kind of excuse. One explanation is the fear that, given the kind of scenario just described, some might lend a sympathetic ear to S' argument that the conduct of an independent TP lies 'beyond [S's] control', thus giving rise to an exemption under the general rule in Article 79(1).[993] Fortunately, this fear has proved to be largely unfounded: since the possibility that such a TP might fail to perform must almost always be 'foreseeable' by S, the appointment of such a TP could hardly lead to a reallocation of the usual S-B contractual risk, that is, an unwarranted adjustment of the general CISG liability scheme.

That said, significant disagreement remains as to the proper scope of the rule, and the provision's legislative history, i.e., the 'chaotic discussions' which preceded the adoption of Article 79(2) in Vienna, hardly helps to clear things up.[994] For although many have argued that the TPs referred to in paragraph (2) should not be interpreted to include 'general suppliers' of the goods or of raw materials,[995] there is also prominent authority to the contrary.[996]

---

992. Regarding, for example, the general American (domestic law) rule, *see* Farnsworth, *Contracts* 4th ed. (2004), para. 11.10.

993. *Compare* Stoll's interpretation of the legislative history in Schlechtriem, *Commentary* 1st English ed. (1998), at 615.

994. *See* Schlechtriem in 15/16 Juristen Zeitung, 13 Aug. 1999; also in English at http://cisgw3.law.pace.edu/cases/990324g1.html#ce.

995. *See* Honnold/Flechtner, *Uniform Law for International Sales under the 1980 United Nations Convention* 4th ed. (2009), at 634–636; Lookofsky, *Understanding the CISG* 5th Worldwide ed. (2017),

In those cases where the 'double force majeure'[997] solution set forth in paragraph (2) applies, S must prove: (a) that she could not herself foresee or avoid the alleged impediment to performance; and (b) that the impediment was unforeseeable and avoidable by TP. In other words, in those cases where a party's excuse is deemed due to the failure of a TP who falls within paragraph (2), it should be even more difficult for the non-performing party (seller or buyer) to obtain an exemption than if the situation were judged (solely) in accordance with the rule in paragraph (1).[998] Then again, since most courts construe the general rule in paragraph (1) as a very narrow (safety-valve) provision,[999] the possibility of differing interpretations of the scope of the phrase TP in paragraph (2) need not lead courts and arbitrators to different results in exemption cases falling within the overall ambit of Article 79.

6. Duration of Exemption

310. The exemption provided in Article 79 has effect only during the period during which the impediment exists.[1000] Therefore, when a temporary impediment to performance abates, the non-performing party becomes liable once again. However, since Article 79 does not prevent the other party from exercising any right other than to claim damages,[1001] a serious delay by one party will entitle the other party to avoid, that is, to put an end to the contract by reason of a fundamental breach.[1002]

7. Notice of Impediment

311. The party who fails to perform must give notice to the other party of the impediment and its effects on his or her ability to perform.

If the notice is not received by the other party within a reasonable time after the party who fails to perform knew or ought to have known of the impediment, he or

---

§6.19, at 154–155; CISG Advisory Council Opinion No. 7, Exemption of Liability for Damages Under Art. 79 of the CISG (2007), Comment 24, available at http://www.cisgac.com/cisgac-opinion-no7/.

996. *See* generally, Schlechtriem, *supra* note 994, text at notes 15–16 (much to be said in favour of considering suppliers and their suppliers as third parties under Art. 79(2)). *Compare* the award of the ICC Court of Arbitration (Paris), No. 8128/1995, available at www.cisg.law.pace.edu/cases/958128i1.html (seller not exempted pursuant to Art. 79(2); non-delivery caused by seller's supplier held 'part of seller's risk').

997. Regarding this epithet, *see* CISG Advisory Council Opinion No. 7, Exemption of Liability for Damages Under Art. 79 of the CISG (2007), Comment 15, available at http://www.cisgac.com/cisgac-opinion-no7/.

998. *See* Comment 24 in CISG Advisory Council Opinion No. 7, Exemption of Liability for Damages under Art. 79 of the CISG (2007), available at http://www.cisgac.com/cisgac-opinion-no7/.

999. *See supra*, Nos 305–307.

1000. Article 79(3).

1001. Article 79(5).

1002. *See*, for example, regarding buyer's right to avoid, *supra*, No. 226.

she is liable for damages resulting from such non-receipt.[1003] The requirement that the notice be received (to take effect) represents a reversal of the general CISG transmission-risk rule.[1004]

8. Exemption Applies Only as Regards Damages

312. Article 79(5) states that nothing in Article 79 prevents a party from exercising any right other than to claim damages under this Convention. In other words, an exemption – if granted due to the fulfilment of the requirements set forth in Article 79(1) – only serves to exempt the obligor from liability in damages.

The effect of an impediment on avoidance has already been noted.[1005] As regards specific performance, it should be noted that Article 28, and the forum law to which it refers, will usually serve to insulate a non-performing party from a demand that he or she performs (deliver or pay) notwithstanding the fact that performance as agreed is physically impossible.[1006] An Article 79 exemption does not preclude a claim to interest,[1007] just as a party who receives non-conforming goods remains entitled to a proportionate reduction in price.[1008] In a controversial 2009 decision, the highest Belgian court held that a party to a CISG contract disadvantaged by 'hardship' (changed circumstances that fundamentally disturb the contractual balance) was entitled to demand that the other party renegotiate the terms contract concerned.[1009]

9. Non-performance Caused by Other Party

313. Article 80 sets forth a seemingly simple rule:

> A party [to a CISG contract] may not rely on a failure of the other party to perform, to the extent that such failure was caused by the first party's own act or omission.

Judging by its placement in section IV (on 'Exemptions'), as well its drafting history,[1010] it would seem that Article 80 was intended to serve as an adjunct to the

1003. Article 79(4). Such liability extends also to cases where a party intends to perform by furnishing a commercially reasonable substitute: *see* A/CONF./97/5, para. 16 of *Secretariat's Commentary* to Art. 65 of the 1978 Draft Convention.

1004. *See* Art. 27, *supra*, No. 139.

1005. *Supra*, No. 310.

1006. *See supra*, Nos 140 et seq.

1007. *Supra*, No. 300.

1008. *Supra*, No. 232.

1009. *See* Hof van Cassatie/Cour de Cassation, Belgium, 19 Jun. 2009, available at http://cisgw3.law.pace.edu/cases/090619b1.html, also discussed *supra*, No. 308.

1010. *See* H. Flechtner, 'The Exemption Provisions of the Sales Convention, Including Comments on "Hardship" Doctrine and the 19 June 2009 Decision of the Belgian Cassation Court', *Belgrade Law Review* 3 (2011), 84–101, also available at http://cisgw3.law.pace.edu/cisg/biblio/flechtner10.html, noting that Art. 80 was a late addition to the Convention, considered unnecessary by some

exemptions rule in Article 79, hereunder Article 79(5).[1011] For example, a buyer whose own conduct frustrates performance by the seller cannot rightfully claim access to remedies – such as damages, specific performance or avoidance – which might otherwise be available. Although some Convention drafters felt Article 80 was hardly needed to reach such an obviously reasonable result, they saw no harm in stating the obvious.[1012]

Beyond this, some courts and arbitrators have used Article 80 as a tool for sorting out the parties' rights when both sides have allegedly failed to perform their obligations,[1013] just as a significant number of decisions have applied Article 80 to deny a remedy to a party whose own breach caused the other side to refuse to perform.[1014] In a related application, an arbitral tribunal in China exempted a Chinese seller of metallic silicon of liability for non-delivery to a buyer in Hong Kong, *inter alia*, by reason of conduct which the tribunal characterized as the 'buyer's blackmail'.[1015] Note in this connection that Article 80 (when applicable) eliminates not only a party's right to claim damages but also that party's right to avoid the contract – this is in contrast with Article 79, which operates solely as an exemption of liability in damages.[1016]

With arguably dubious justification, a German Court of Appeals has applied Article 80 in a case where a seller refused to deliver certain goods due to the buyer's failure to pay for previous shipments.[1017] Denying the buyer's right to claim damages in this situation, the court reasoned that the buyer could not rely on the seller's failure to perform, since that failure was caused by the buyer's own omission. Although the outcome (no damages) seems correct, the decision might better have been based on CISG rules which were specifically designed to apply in a situation like this.[1018]

---

delegates to the 1980 Vienna Diplomatic Conference, although the majority seemed to feel that there might be some value and, at any rate, no danger in stating the obvious. *See also* Honnold /Flechtner, *Uniform Law for International Sales under the 1980 United Nations Convention* 4th ed. (2009), at 644–645.

1011. *See supra*, No. 312.

1012. Honnold/Flechtner, *supra* note 1010.

1013. *See* (e.g.) Bundesgerichtshof (Germany), 26 Sep. 2012, available at http://www.unilex.info/cisg/case/1684, also discussed *supra* under No. 299.

1014. *See UNCITRAL Digest of CISG Case Law*, Art. 80, available at https://uncitral.un.org/en/case_law/digests.

1015. China International Economic and Trade Arbitration Commission, People's Republic of China, 9 Jan. 2008, available at http://cisgw3.law.pace.edu/cases/080109c1.html. Note that the issue of whether Hong Kong is a CISG Contracting State (discussed *infra* in No. 334) did not arise in this case, presumably as the parties had expressly opted in to the CISG.

1016. Honnold/Flechtner, *supra* note 1010, at 644; UNCITRAL Digest, *supra*, para. 7.

1017. Oberlandesgericht München, Germany, 9 Jul. 1997, CLOUT Case 273, available atwww.cisg.law.pace.edu/cases/970709g1.html.

1018. *See* Professor Flechtner's elaboration in Honnold/Flechtner, *Uniform Law for International Sales under the 1980 United Nations Convention* 4th ed. (2009), at 648, citing Arts 64(1)(a) and 71–73.

IV. Effects of Avoidance

A. *Introduction*

314. Section V of Chapter V provides a series of rules regarding the effects of avoidance. The provisions of this section are common to the obligations of both parties.

B. *Release from Obligation*

315. The primary effect of (total) avoidance is to relieve both parties of their obligations to perform; that is, the seller need not deliver the goods, and the buyer need not pay.[1019]

Partial avoidance of the contract, for example, where the buyer avoids with respect to a portion of the goods not delivered,[1020] releases both parties from their obligations as to the part of the contract avoided: (in the example) the seller is released from the obligation to deliver the portion concerned, and the buyer need not pay for that portion.

C. *Damages for Breach, Arbitration Clauses, Etc.*

316. Although avoidance of the contract releases both parties from their performance obligations, it does not eliminate all rights and obligations which arose out of the contract.

For one thing, as provided in Article 81(1), avoidance does not affect claims for any damages which may be due.[1021] Thus, though the party in breach need not deliver or pay under an avoided contract, that party remains liable for any loss suffered by the other party as a consequence of the breach.[1022] Nor does avoidance affect any provision of the contract for the settlement of disputes,[1023] such as an arbitration clause, choice-of-forum clause or a contractual provision governing the applicable law.[1024] The same applies as regards any other provision of the contract

1019. Article 81(1).
1020. *See* Art. 51(1). *See also* Art. 73(1) regarding avoidance with respect to a particular instalment.
1021. *See* Art. 81(1) and, for example, Tribunale di Appello di Lugano (Switzerland), 15 Jan. 1998, available at www.cisg.law.pace.edu/cases/980115s1.html.
1022. *See* Art. 74, *supra*, No. 291. Regarding the breaching party's continuing obligation to pay damages *see*, for example, LG Landshut (Germany), 5 Apr. 1995, available at www.cisg.law.pace.edu/cases/950405g1.html.
1023. Article 81(1), second sentence.
1024. In the case of an international sales contract, such a clause might designate the CISG as the applicable law and/or point to the domestic law which regulates contract validity, etc. *See supra*, Nos 70 et seq.

governing the rights and obligations of the parties upon the avoidance of the contract, for example, a clause providing for liquidated damages in the event of non-performance. However, the question of whether such clauses remain binding might also depend on their validity, and validity is always a question for the applicable domestic law.[1025]

Article 81 provides a non-exhaustive list of obligations which continue even after avoidance. The duty of the buyer to take steps to preserve goods which he or she intends to reject constitutes an example of such an obligation not extinguished by avoidance.[1026]

D. Restitution

317. Restitution is another effect of avoidance. According to Article 81(2), a party who has performed the contract either wholly or in part may claim restitution from the other party of whatever the first party has supplied or paid under the contract. If both parties are bound to make restitution, they must do so concurrently.[1027] In principle, the party in breach will bear the reasonable expenses which both parties incur in relation to making restitution for goods or sums received prior to avoidance; as regards the non-breaching party's expenses, the breaching party is liable in damages for such losses as a consequence of the breach.[1028]

The Convention rules on restitution regulate only *inter partes* rights.[1029] In a bankruptcy situation, the Convention rules on restitution may be thwarted by local rules which create third-party property rights or priorities in goods or sums delivered, etc.[1030]

1025. Regarding Art. 4, *see supra*, No. 63.

1026. *See* generally *infra*, No. 327.

1027. *See*, for example, LG Landshut (Germany), 5 Apr. 1995, available at www.cisg.law.pace.edu/cases/950405g1.html (contract validly avoided by buyer; both parties bound to make restitution concurrently: when buyer placed non-conforming goods at seller's disposal, seller obliged to retake goods and refund price paid).

1028. Article 74, *supra*, No. 291. As always, damages are limited by the mitigation principle: *see* Art. 77, *supra*, No. 297.

1029. *See* Art. 4, *supra*, Nos 62 et seq. *See also*, e.g., Tribunale d'Appello Ticino, Switzerland, 20 Apr. 2016, CLOUT Case 1771 (contractual repayment obligation under Art. 81(2) has no effect on ownership of goods); US District Court, Northern District of Illinois, US, 28 Mar. 2002 (*Usinor Industeel v. Leeco Steel Products, Inc.*), CLOUT Case 613, available at http://cisgw3.law.pace.edu/cases/020328u1.html (avoiding seller's rights trumped by third-party creditor under applicable national law notwithstanding retention-of-title clause). *Compare* Federal Court of Australia, Australia, 28 Apr. 1995 CLOUT Case No. 308, available at www.cisg.law.pace.edu/cases/950428a2.html (retention-of-title clause valid under applicable national law; no third party with claim superior to seller's claim).

1030. *See* A/CONF./97/5, para. 10 of *Secretariat's Commentary* to Art. 66 of the 1978 Draft Convention.

E. Buyer's Obligation to Return Goods in Condition Received

318. It follows from the general CISG restitution rule that a seller who has delivered the goods either wholly or in part may, if the buyer avoids the contract, claim restitution from the buyer of the goods supplied.[1031] Article 82(1) sets forth a corollary of the general rule: the buyer loses the right to declare the contract avoided if it is impossible for him or her to make restitution of the goods substantially in the condition in which he or she received them.[1032] Applying this principle, the highest court in France has held that the buyer of a machine lost its right to avoid the contract since, instead of returning the machine when the defect was discovered, the buyer had continued to use it for a long period of time, thereby precluding its restitution in substantially the condition in which it had been received.[1033]

Similar considerations would apply in a case where the buyer demands that the seller performs *in natura* by redelivering substitute (conforming) goods:[1034] the buyer loses the right to demand such redelivery if he or she cannot return the goods first delivered in the condition in which they were received.[1035]

F. Exceptions to the Return-of-Goods Rule

319. The general rule (that the buyer loses the right to avoid and to demand redelivery if he or she cannot return the goods in the condition received) is subject to three exceptions.

320. First, the buyer need not return goods substantially in the condition received if the impossibility of making such restitution is not due to the buyer's act or omission.[1036] Under this exception, the buyer is relieved of his or her duty to make restitution not only where the deterioration of the goods is attributable to the seller[1037] but also where the goods are lost or damaged due to force majeure or the act of a third party.[1038] It has been suggested, however, that this limitation relieves the buyer of the duty to make restitution only in cases where he or she has exercised reasonable care in protecting the goods.[1039]

1031. Article 81, *supra*, No. 317. Regarding the place where restitution should be effected, *see* F. Ferrari & M. Torsello, *International Sales Law – CISG in a Nutshell* 2nd ed. (2018), at 447 ff.
1032. *See*, e.g., Tribunale di Modena, Italy, 19 Feb. 2014, English abstract available at http://www.unilex.info/cisg/case/1956 (buyer had used and processed all goods supplied by seller, therefore unable to make restitution as required by Art. 82, buyer not entitled to terminate/avoid).
1033. Cour de cassation, France, 3 Nov. 2009, CLOUT Case 1025, available at http://cisgw3.law.pace.edu/cases/091103f1.html.
1034. Regarding Art. 46(2), *see supra*, No. 217.
1035. Article 82(1).
1036. Article 82(2)(a).
1037. As where the goods delivered contain a foreign chemical causing them to decompose.
1038. *See* UNCITRAL Case Digest of Art. 82 (2016 ed.), available at https://uncitral.un.org/en/case_law/digests.
1039. *See* Honnold/Flechtner, *Uniform Law for International Sales under the 1980 United Nations Convention* 4th ed. (2009), at 663, applying the principle set forth in Art. 86(1). *See also infra*, No. 327.

321. Second, according to Article 82(2)(b), the buyer need not return goods in the condition received if the goods (or – as is more likely – part of the goods) have perished or deteriorated as a result of the examination provided for in Article 38.[1040]

322. Finally, the buyer need not return the goods in the condition received if the goods or part of the goods have been sold in the normal course of business or have been consumed or transformed by the buyer in the course of normal use before he or she discovered or ought to have discovered the lack of conformity.[1041] In this case, however, the buyer must account to the seller for all benefits derived by such sale or consumption.[1042]

G. Retention of Other Remedies Notwithstanding

323. Even though a buyer may have lost the right to declare the contract avoided or to require the seller to deliver substitute goods, all other remedies under the contract and the Convention are retained nonetheless.[1043] In particular, the buyer retains the right to claim damages for breach;[1044] in the case of non-conforming goods, the buyer may instead advance a claim for a proportionate reduction in price.[1045]

H. Accounting for Interest and Other Benefits Received

324. The Convention adopts a corollary to the restitutionary principle which is generally accepted in domestic systems of law: to avoid unjust enrichment, a party who is required to make restitution must also account for benefits received in the interim.

Thus, if the seller is bound to refund the price, he or she must also pay interest on it, from the date on which the price was paid.[1046] The Convention does not set

1040. For an extension of this principle, *see* German Supreme Court (BGH), 25 Jun. 1997, CLOUT Case 235, available at www.cisg.law.pace.edu/cases/970625g2.html (buyer who processed goods (stainless steel wire) unable to make restitution in condition received, but buyer did not lose right to avoid, as non-conformity only discoverable upon processing, which – in this case – had actually augmented value of goods). Regarding Art. 38, *see supra*, No. 187.

1041. Article 82(2)(c).

1042. Regarding Art. 84(2), *see infra*, No. 324.

1043. Article 83.

1044. Regarding Arts 74 et seq., *see supra*, Nos 290 et seq.

1045. *See*, for example, Oberlandesgericht Stuttgart, Germany, 12 Mar. 2001 available on the Internet at http://cisgw3.law.pace.edu/cases/010312g1.html (avoidance unjustified as non-conformity not fundamental breach, but buyer permitted to reduce price). Regarding Art. 50, *see supra*, No. 232.

1046. Article 84(1).

forth the rate of interest, thus leaving the calculation to domestic law.[1047] The interest calculation may vary in cases where the party claiming restitution is not the party in breach.[1048]

The benefits-received principle applies to the buyer as well: if the buyer must make restitution of the goods or in whole or part, he or she must account to the seller for all benefits derived from the goods or part of them.[1049] The buyer must also account to the seller for all benefits derived in cases where it is impossible to make restitution of all or part of the goods substantially in the condition received, but where the buyer nevertheless has declared the contract avoided or required the seller to deliver substitute goods.[1050]

V. Preservation of the Goods

A. Introduction

325. Sometimes, one party will be in control of goods on the other party's behalf. Section VI of Chapter V, concerning the duty to preserve the goods in such cases, provides rules designed to prevent waste and minimize loss.

B. Seller's Duty to Preserve Goods on Buyer's Behalf

326. The first of these rules is set forth in Article 85. If the buyer is in delay in taking delivery of the goods and, even though the risk of loss may have passed, the seller is either in possession of the goods or otherwise able to control their disposition,[1051] the seller must take such steps as are reasonable in the circumstances to preserve them; the same applies where payment of the price and delivery of the goods are to be made concurrently, and the buyer fails to pay the price.[1052]

In either case, in exchange for fulfilling his or her duty to preserve the goods, the seller in possession acquires a right of retention akin to a 'mechanic's lien', in that he or she is entitled to retain the goods until reimbursement of reasonable expenses by the buyer.[1053]

1047. Regarding Art. 78, *see supra*, Nos 300 et seq.

1048. If the seller is bound to refund the price paid because he or she has committed a fundamental breach, it may be more appropriate to calculate interest on the basis of buyer's loss (Art. 74) rather than on the restitutionary approach set forth in Art. 84(1): *see* Honnold/Flechtner, *Uniform Law for International Sales under the 1980 United Nations Convention* 4th ed. (2009), at 673 and (as regards cross-claims) *ibid.*, at 675–676.

1049. Article 84(2)(a).

1050. Article 84(2)(b). *See also* Art. 82(2), *supra*, Nos 319 et seq.

1051. The seller may be in possession even after the risk has passed: regarding Art. 69, *see supra*, No. 275. Similarly, the seller may retain documents controlling disposition after the risk has passed: regarding Art. 67, *see supra*, No. 271.

1052. Article 85 has been cited in relatively few decisions, most of which have focused on the seller's right to reimbursement for the expenses of preserving the goods. *See* the UNCITRAL Digest of Case Law (2016 ed.), Art. 85, available at https://uncitral.un.org/en/case_law/digests.

1053. Article 85, second sentence. Regarding the possible sale of goods retained, *see infra*, No. 328.

C. Buyer's Duty to Preserve Goods on Seller's Behalf

327. A similar, albeit reverse situation arises in cases where the buyer has received the goods but intends to exercise his or her right to reject them (either with a view towards avoiding the contract or requiring the seller to redeliver). In such cases, according to Article 86, paragraph (1), the buyer must take such steps as are reasonable in the circumstances to preserve the goods. In return for such efforts, the buyer in possession acquires a right of retention, i.e., a right to retain the goods until reimbursement by the seller of reasonable expenses incurred.[1054]

According to Article 86, paragraph (2) if goods dispatched to the buyer have been placed at his or her disposal at their destination, and the buyer exercises the right to reject them, he or she must take possession of them on behalf of the seller, provided that this can be done without payment of the price and without unreasonable inconvenience or unreasonable expense. This provision does not apply if the seller or a person authorized to take charge of the goods on the seller's behalf is present at the destination. If the buyer takes possession of the goods under this paragraph, the buyer's rights and obligations are governed by Article 86, paragraph (1).

D. Deposit in Warehouse; Sale of Goods Preserved

328. Depending on the circumstances, a party bound to preserve the goods in accordance Article 85 or 86[1055] may be entitled to deposit them in a warehouse (Article 87) or sell them by appropriate means (Article 88). As regards the first alternative, deposit in a warehouse of a TP at the expense of the other party is permitted, provided the expense incurred is not unreasonable.[1056]

The second alternative applies when there has been an unreasonable delay by the other party in taking possession of the goods or in taking them back or in paying the price or the cost of preservation; in that situation, the party in possession may sell them by any appropriate means provided that reasonable notice of the intention to sell has been given to the other party.[1057] If, however, the goods are subject to rapid deterioration or their preservation would involve unreasonable expense, a party who is bound to preserve the goods in accordance with Article 85 or 86 *must* take reasonable measures to sell them. To the extent possible, he or she must give notice to the other party of the intention to sell.[1058]

1054. Article 86(1), second sentence. Article 86 has been cited or involved in a small number of decisions. Most of those decisions have focused on a buyer's claim for the recovery of expenses of preserving goods that it wished to reject. *See* the UNCITRAL Digest of Case Law (2016 ed.), Art. 86, available at https://uncitral.un.org/en/case_law/digests.

1055. Regarding Arts 85 and 86, *see supra*, Nos 326 et seq.

1056. Article 87.

1057. Article 88(1). *See*, e.g., Republic of Korea, Commercial Arbitration Board, 8 Aug. 2012, CLOUT Case 1768 (buyer's resale in accord with Art. 88).

1058. Article 88(2).

A party selling the goods, either by right or by reason of duty, has the right to retain out of the proceeds of sale an amount equal to the reasonable expenses of preserving the goods and of selling them. That party must then account to the other party for the balance.[1059]

1059. Article 88(3).

Chapter 6. Final Convention Provisions

§1. Overview

329. Part IV of the Convention is entitled Final Provisions. These provisions constitute the Convention's 'public international law' framework, *inter alia*, the rules regarding Convention ratifications, reservations, entry into force, etc.

§2. Signature, Ratification, Entry into Force

330. As is common for treaties entered into under the auspices of the United Nations (UN), the Secretary General of the UN was designated as the 'depository' for the CISG.[1060] The Convention was opened for signature at the concluding meeting of the CISG Conference and remained open for signature until 30 September 1981.[1061] Instruments of ratification, acceptance, approval and accession (adherence) were thereafter deposited with the Secretary General.

By 11 December 1986, eleven States had deposited instruments of adherence, and – as among these States – the Convention entered into force on 1 January 1988.[1062] The list of ratifications continues to grow (more than ninety Contracting States as of July 2021);[1063] in the case of each new State, the Convention enters into force one year after the deposit of its instrument of adherence.[1064]

§3. Relationship to the 1955 Hague Convention

331. According to Article 90, the CISG does not prevail over any international agreement which has already been or may be entered into and which contains provisions concerning the matters governed by the CISG.[1065] In limited circumstances, this provision may be significant for those (relatively few) States which, prior to ratifying the CISG, had already ratified the 1955 Hague Convention on the Law Applicable to International Sale of Goods.[1066]

As noted with respect to the provisions which regulate the CISG sphere of application, those States which have ratified both the 1955 Convention and the CISG will

1060. Article 89.
1061. Article 91(1).
1062. That is, one year after the deposit of the tenth instrument of adherence. *See* Art. 99(1).
1063. *See* the Appendix, *infra*. For the current list, *see* https://uncitral.un.org/en/texts/salegoods/conventions/sale_of_goods/cisg/status.
1064. Article 99(2).
1065. Provided that the parties have their places of business in States which are parties to such agreement. *See* generally Schlechtnem in Schwenzer & Hachem in Schlechtnem & Schwenzer, *Commentary* 4th ed. (2016), 1245–1251.
1066. Belgium, Denmark, Finland, France, Italy, Norway, Sweden and Switzerland have ratified both Conventions. Niger, which has ratified the 1955 Convention, has not (as of July 2021) ratified the CISG.

utilize the 1955 treaty when applying CISG Article 1(1)(b),[1067] that is, to determine when the rules of PIL lead to the application of the law of a CISG Contracting State.[1068] In this respect, the two treaties work in tandem. As regards the application of CISG Article 1(1)(a), the relationship between the CISG and the 1955 Convention seems somewhat less clear.[1069] Although Article 1(1)(a) makes the CISG generally applicable without recourse to the rules of PIL,[1070] the 1980 CISG does not, according to Article 90, prevail over the 1955 Convention to the extent that the older treaty contains provisions concerning the matters governed by the CISG. The potential for conflict seems limited, however; when the CISG would apply by virtue of Article 1(1)(a), the 'seller's law' rule in Article 3 in the 1955 Convention would usually lead to the application of the CISG as well. In a few limited situations – for example, where a sales contract calls for delivery in a non-CISG State, and a problem arises as to the rules regarding inspection and notification in that State – the two conventions might lead to different results; presumably, in such a situation, the 1955 Convention would prevail.[1071] A primary goal of the 1986 revision of the 1955 Convention is to eliminate such potential conflicts with the CISG.[1072]

§4. Reservations

I. Introduction

332. Part IV of the Convention contains provisions concerning the right of signatory States to make certain specified declarations (reservations) to specified articles and/or parts of the CISG.

No reservations are permitted except those expressly authorized in Part IV.[1073]

Among the more significant reservations permitted include the right of a State to declare that it will be bound only by the Convention's Part II (Contract Formation) or Part III (Sale of Goods) rules; the right of States having closely related legal rules not to apply the CISG as between them; the right of a State to declare that it will not be bound by the PIL rule in subparagraph (1)(b) of Article 1; and a rule which

1067. Assuming, at least, that the State concerned has not made a declaration pursuant to Art. 95 which limits the applicability of Art. 1(1)(b). *See supra*, Nos 54–55 and *infra*, No. 336.

1068. *Supra*, No. 54.

1069. *See* generally, P. Winship, 'Private International Law and the U.N. Sales Convention', *Cornell International Law Journal* 21 (1988) 487, also at https://scholarship.law.cornell.edu/cgi/viewcontent.cgi?article=1201&context=cilj.

1070. *See supra*, No. 53.

1071. Under Art. 4 of the 1955 Convention, the law applicable to inspection and notification is the place of delivery.

1072. The 1986 Convention (which is not in effect as of this writing) states that it 'shall not prejudice' the application of the CISG. *See* generally, P. Winship, 'The Scope of the Vienna Convention on International Sales Contracts', in *International Sales* (Galston & Smit eds, 1984), also available at https://www.cisg.law.pace.edu/cisg/biblio/winship5.html, at 1–43 and Honnold/Flechtner, *Uniform Law for International Sales under the 1980 United Nations Convention* 4th ed. (2009), 695–698. Regarding other potential Art. 90 conflicts *see* Schlechtnem, Schwenzer & Hachem, *supra* note 1065.

1073. *See* Art. 98.

permits a State to recognize only sales contracts and modifications if in writing. These reservations are discussed in greater detail below.

II. Article 92 Declarations

333. Surely, the most far-reaching reservation permitted is that contained in Article 92, whereby a CISG Contracting State may declare at the time of adherence that it will not be bound by Part II of this Convention (Contract Formation), or that it will not be bound by Part III (Sale of Goods).

An Article 92 reservation with respect to CISG Part II was made by each of the Scandinavian States (Denmark, Finland, Norway and Sweden) when they originally ratified the Convention,[1074] because – at that point in time – they found certain Part II rules regarding sales contract formation to be unacceptable from a Scandinavian point of view.[1075] As indicated below, these Scandinavian reservations were later *withdrawn*, and no other States have made Article 92 reservations with respect to CISG Part II or Part III.

The effect of the *formerly applicable* (e.g.) Danish reservation with respect to CISG Part II was that Denmark was not to be considered a Contracting State within paragraph (1) of Article 1 in respect of matters governed by CISG Part II.[1076] So, as regards a sales contract made between Danish and non-Danish parties in 1998, i.e., when Denmark's Article 92 reservation was still in effect, the CISG Part II rules could not apply by virtue of Article 1(1)(a), because – as regards CISG Part II – Denmark was not then a Contracting State.

However, under Article 1(1)(b), the CISG also applies where the rules of PIL lead to the application of the law of a Contracting State,[1077] and depending on the circumstances, this rule could serve to activate CISG Part II in a Scandinavian State, i.e., notwithstanding that State's Article 92 reservation.[1078] In 1998, this academic analysis was confirmed by the Danish High Court of Appeals.[1079]

1074. Note that Iceland, a 'Nordic' State which ratified the CISG in 2001, did *not* make an Art. 92 declaration.

1075. Two main arguments were advanced by those Scandinavian jurists who advocated that reservations be made with respect to CISG Part II: first, as regards the revocability of offers, the Part II rules were said to be unduly influenced by the corresponding Common law rules: in particular, the right to revoke a CISG offer was perceived as something foreign to Scandinavian law. Second, it was feared that CISG Part II – which regulates only contract formation, but not contract validity – might create uncertainty as to whether a valid sales contract had been made. Neither argument seems convincing upon closer analysis: *see* J. Lookofsky, 'Alive and Well in Scandinavia: CISG Part II', *Journal of Law & Commerce* 18 (1999) 289.

1076. Article 92(2).

1077. *See supra*, No. 54.

1078. *See* J. Lookofsky, 'Alive and Well in Scandinavia: CISG Part II', *Journal of Law & Commerce* 18 (1999) 289.

1079. Eastern Appellate Court, Denmark, 23 Apr. 1998, CLOUT Case 309, available at http://cisgw3.law.pace.edu/cases/980423d1.html. Regarding this decision (reported in Danish in *Ugeskrift for Retsvæsen* 1998 at 1092), *see* J. Lookofsky, 'Alive and Well in Scandinavia: CISG Part II', *Journal of Law & Commerce* 18 (1999) 289–299. *Compare* Oberlandesgericht Rostock, 27 Jul. 1995, CLOUT Case 228, available at http://cisgw3.law.pace.edu/cases/950727g1.html (CISG Part II not

With the passage of time, an increasing number of Scandinavian commentators came to regard the Article 92 declarations originally made by the Scandinavian States as ill-advised and counterproductive.[1080] These commentators, with subsequent support provided by non-Scandinavian commentators, as well as the ICC, urged that the Article 92 reservations be withdrawn.[1081] Finally, during the period 2012–2014, common sense prevailed, and the governments of Denmark, Finland, Sweden and Norway officially *withdrew* their respective Article 92 declarations, as authorized by CISG Article 97(4).[1082]

III. Contracting States with Territorial Units

334. In most States operating under a federal system, the central government is empowered with the treaty-making power to bind the entire federation to the CISG. The effect of the U.S. ratification, for example, is to bind all fifty territorial units (states) within the US.

In a few States, such as Australia and Canada, the federal government does not have this power.[1083] Article 93 permits such States, upon ratification, to declare that the CISG is to extend to only some, but not all of its territorial units. Australia, Canada, Denmark and New Zealand have made declarations pursuant to Article 93. So, even if the place of business of a party is located in one of these States, this

---

applied in dispute between Danish seller and German buyer, as relevant German PIL rules (1980 Rome Convention) pointed to law of Danish seller).

The notion that CISG Part II might sometimes apply in spite of an Art. 92 reservation was suggested in 1987 by Evans in Bianca & Bonell in their *Commentary* at 643. In 1989, when Denmark ratified the Convention subject to Art. 92, Lookofsky expressed the view that even Scandinavian courts should consider themselves bound (by Art. 1) to apply CISG Part II in cases where the 1(1)(b) rule pointed to the law of a CISG State which had not made such a reservation: *see* 'Loose Ends and Contorts in International Sales: Problems in the Harmonization of Private Law Rules', *American Journal of Comparative Law* 39 (1991) 405. In 1995, a prominent German commentator concurred, arguing that only this interpretation of Art. 92 could advance the goal of uniform Convention application: *see* Schlechtriem in Schlechtriem & Schwenzer, *Commentary* 2nd English ed. (2005), 926; *see also* Schlechtriem/Hachem in the 4th (2016) of this work at 1254 with note 5.

1080. *See*, for example, Lookofsky, *supra*.

1081. *See* generally J. Lookofsky, 'The Rise and Fall of Article 92', in *Festschrift für Ulrich Magnus* (Mankowski & Wurmnest eds, 2014), 243–254.

1082. According to this provision: 'Any State which makes a declaration under this Convention may withdraw it at any time by a formal notification in writing addressed to the depositary. Such withdrawal is to take effect on the first day of the month following the expiration of six months after the date of the receipt of the notification by the depositary.' The only remaining practical concern in this connection relates to the rather remote possibility that litigation could still arise in relation to a CISG contract between a Scandinavian and a non-Scandinavian party which was concluded at a point in time when the Scandinavian Art. 92 declarations applied, in which case domestic law could displace CISG Part II, unless the applicable PIL rules were to point to the law of the non-Scandinavian party.

1083. *See* P. Winship, 'The Scope of the Vienna Convention on International Sales Contracts', in *International Sales* (Galston & Smit eds, 1984), also available at https://www.cisg.law.pace.edu/cisg/biblio/winship5.html, at 1–45 and Ziegel in *Canadian Business Law Journal* 12 (1986/1987) 366.

place of business is considered not to be in a Contracting State unless it is in a territorial unit to which the Convention extends.[1084]

A special situation exists with respect to Hong Kong. China ratified the CISG on 1 December 1986. Prior to the retrocession of Hong Kong to China on 1 July 1997, the Convention did not apply to Hong Kong. After the retrocession (under which Hong Kong is now considered a Special Administrative Zone of China with a different legal system), China deposited with the Secretary General of the United Nations a declaration announcing the conventions to which China was a party and which thereafter should apply to Hong Kong, but the CISG was not on this list. In two cases, decided in 2009 and 2010, each involving a seller in Hong Kong and a buyer in China, Chinese courts denied application of Convention on the ground that the parties were not located in different countries.[1085] Courts elsewhere are divided as to whether China's declaration satisfies the requirements to constitute an Article 93(1) declaration.[1086]

IV. States Having Closely Related Legal Rules

335. The Scandinavian States (Denmark, Finland, Norway and Sweden) all wished to join the international community in ratifying the CISG. As regards inter-Scandinavian sales, however, these States did not wish to replace their (then) essentially uniform sales laws with the new CISG regime. Article 94 made it possible for the Scandinavian States, at the time of their CISG ratifications (1987–1989), to declare that the Convention is not to apply to contracts of sale or to their formation

1084. Article 93(3).

1085. *See* Shenzhen Municipal Intermediate People's Court, China, 30 Mar. 2009, CLOUT Case 1706; Zheniang Provincial High People's Court (China), 15 Dec. 2010, CLOUT Case 1778 (noting that after the return of Hong Kong to China, the Convention could not be considered applicable in Hong Kong).

1086. *See* C. Gillette, & S. Walt, *The UN Convention on Contracts for the International Sale of Goods* (2016), 34–36; *see also UNCITRAL Digest of CISG Case Law* (2016 ed.), Art. 93. Decisions supporting the view that Hong Kong is a Contracting State include: US District Court, *CNA International, Inc. v. Guangdong Kelon Electronical Holdings et al.*, 3 Sep. 2008, at http://www.unilex.info/cisg/case/1637 (document deposited by Government of China with UN Secretary General regarding which international conventions apply to Hong Kong but without reference to the CISG should not qualify as Art. 93 declaration); US District Court, 19 Aug. 2010, *Electrocraft Arkansas, Inc. v. Super Electric Motors, Ltd, U.S. District Court, ED of Arkansas*, available at http://cisgw3.law.pace.edu/cases/100819u1.html#ce and 13 Dec. 2009, available at http://www.unilex.info/cisg/case/1490 (citing *CNA International v. Guangdon Kelon, supra*). Decisions supporting the contrary view include: Cour de Cassation (France), 2 Apr. 2008, available at http://www.unilex.info/cisg/case/1304 and http://cisgw3.law.pace.edu/cases/080402f1.html#uab (holding that French Court of Appeal legally justified in declining to apply CISG); Federal Court of Australia, 24 Oct. 2008, *Hannaford v. Australian Farmlink Pty Ltd*, CLOUT Case 958, also available at http://cisgw3.law.pace.edu/cases/081024a2.html (China has not yet taken necessary steps to make Hong Kong a Contracting State); US District Court, 17 Dec. 2009, *Innotex Precision Limited v. Horei, Inc., et al.*, available at http://www.unilex.info/cisg/case/1489 (China's intention was to exclude CISG's application to the territory of Hong Kong); US District Court E.D. Texas, 20 Oct. 2010, *America's Collectibles Network, Inc. v. Timlly et al*, available at http://www.unilex.info/cisg/case/1563 (citing Cour de Cassation).

where the parties have their places of business in those States.[1087] At the time of its CISG ratification (2001), Iceland made a similar declaration.[1088]

The Article 94 declarations presupposed and indeed required that the Scandinavian States at the time of their ratifications had essentially similar legal rules on matters governed by the CISG Convention. And while it is still true that the Scandinavian rules are similar with regard to the rules which govern contract formation (the Contracts Acts), subsequent statutory amendments to some, but not all, of the Scandinavian domestic sales statutes (the Sales Acts) now give the Scandinavian States good reason to question whether all these States (still) all have the kind of closely related sales law rules required by Article 94.[1089]

V. PIL: Article 1(1)(b) and Article 95

336. The CISG applies to contracts for the sale of goods between parties having their places of business in different States. More specifically, according to the two main rules of applicability in Article 1(1), the Convention applies: (a) when these States are both CISG Contracting States and (b) when the rules of PIL lead to the application of the law of a (single) Contracting State.[1090] This latter rule proved controversial and led to the declaration set forth in Article 95 whereby a State may declare upon ratification that it will not be bound by subparagraph (1)(b) of Article 1. States which have ratified the CISG subject to this reservation include China, the Czech Republic, Saint Vincent and the Grenadines, Singapore, Slovakia and the US.

So if, for example, a seller in the US sells to a buyer in State X, a non-Contracting State, Article 95 means that the US courts are not bound to apply the Convention rules, i.e., even if the relevant rules of PIL lead to the application of US law (i.e., the law of a CISG Contracting State).[1091] And so in this situation, assuming the relevant conflict-of-laws rule points to the seller's (American) law, an American court would likely apply domestic American law, that is, the UCC as enacted in the American state concerned.

Also, courts in Contracting States which have not made an Article 95 declaration will sometimes need to consider the effect of that declaration when deciding cases

1087. As regards the Scandinavian Art. 92 declarations, *see supra*, No. 333.

1088. According to this declaration, 'the Convention will not apply to contracts of sale or to their formation where the parties have their places of business in Denmark, Finland, Iceland, Norway or Sweden'.

1089. The relevant (and rather controversial) provisions in the revised Sales Acts now effective in Finland, Norway and Sweden – but *not* in Denmark – limit the seller's liability for 'indirect loss' to cases where the breach can be attributed to the seller's fault. Given this significant disparity between Danish domestic sales law and the domestic sales law of Finland, Norway and Sweden, several Scandinavian commentators have suggested that the Art. 94 declarations should be withdrawn. *See also* Brunner & Gottlieb, 'Article 94 [Applicability to Contracting States Having the Same or Closely Related Legal Rules]', in *Commentary on the UN Sales Law (CISG)* (Brunner & Gottlieb eds, 2019), at 641 (whether or not their respective legal provisions are same or closely related is determined by the States themselves).

1090. *See* generally *supra*, Nos 52 et seq.

1091. In the US, private international law is usually governed by local (state) law. *See* J. Lookofsky & K. Hertz, *Transnational Litigation and Commercial Arbitration* 4th ed. (2017), Ch. 3.3.1.

involving a party who resides in an Article 95 declaration State. Courts in a Contracting State which has not made an Article 95 declaration (e.g., Germany) should not apply Article 1(1)(b) in respect of any Contracting State that has made an Article 95 declaration (e.g., US) when the conflict-of-laws rules of the forum point to the law of the declaring State.[1092]

Given the number of variables (parties' places of business, situs of forum court, applicable PIL), the number of possible permutations involving Article 1(1)(b) and the Article 95 reservation is large, just as the application of these rules can be highly complex and the resulting outcomes difficult to predict.[1093]

VI. Preservation of Formal Requirements

337. As discussed previously, Article 11 dispenses with the formal requirement, posed by some domestic laws, that sales contracts be concluded in or evidenced by writing;[1094] similarly, CISG Part II contains no writing requirements with respect to the constituent parts of the contract (the offer and the acceptance), and Article 29 dispenses with writing requirements as regards contract modification.[1095]

But because some States still attach importance to writing requirements, Article 12 of the CISG provides that the various Convention rules which permit non-written contracts, modifications, etc., do not apply where any party has his or her place of business in a Contracting State which has made a declaration under Article 96.[1096] Argentina, Armenia, Belarus, Chile, Paraguay, the Russian Federation, Ukraine and Vietnam have all made such (currently effective) declarations.

CISG case law and scholarly writing reveal differing opinions as to the situation when only one of the parties to a CISG contract has its place of business in a CISG

1092. Upon ratifying the Convention, the Government of Germany declared that it would not apply Art. 1(1)(b) in respect of any State that had made an Art. 95 declaration. This German 'declaration', while not expressly authorized by CISG Part IV, can be viewed as a statement interpreting the concept of a 'Contracting State' in Art. 1(1)(b) so as to exclude States which have made Art. 95 declarations. *See*: P. Schlechtriem, 'Uniform Sales Law – The Experience with Uniform Sales Laws in the Federal Republic of Germany', *Juridisk Tidsskrift vid Stockholms Universitet* (1992), https://cisgw3.law.pace.edu/cisg/biblio/schlech2.html, 6–7.

1093. *See* generally, P. Winship, 'The Scope of the Vienna Convention on International Sales Contracts', in *International Sales* (Galston & Smit eds, 1984), also available at https://www.cisg.law.pace.edu/cisg/biblio/winship5.html, at 1–26 et seq. and the appendix thereto; *see also* Flechtner & Brand, 'Opting in to the CISG', in *A Tribute to Joseph M. Lookofsky* (Andersen & Henschel eds, 2015), 102 ff., discussing, *inter alia*, the US District Court's decision in *FPM Financial Services, LLC v. Redline Products*, 17 Sep. 2013, available at http://cisgw3.law.pace.edu/cases/130917u1.html.

1094. *See supra*, Nos 92–93.

1095. *See* Art. 29(1) which allows a contract of sale to be modified or terminated by the 'mere agreement' of the parties, subject to the exception in Art. 29(2). *See supra*, Nos 142–146.

1096. *See supra*, Nos 94 et seq.

State which has made an Article 96 declaration, for example, where an oral sales contract is concluded between one party doing business in Argentina and the other in the United States.[1097]

According to the majority view, the fact that Argentina has made an Article 96 reservation does not (itself) mean that such a transaction is subject to a writing requirement. Rather, the resolution of that issue will depend on a choice-of-law analysis.[1098] So if the PIL principles applied by the forum court (or arbitral tribunal) lead to the application of Argentine law, then the writing requirements of Argentine domestic sales law will apply. If, however, the relevant PIL rules lead to the application of American law, then the CISG freedom-from-formal-requirements rule in Article 11 will apply.[1099]

Consistent with this view, a Hungarian court has held that a Hungarian buyer who accepted the oral offer of a German seller was bound under the CISG, notwithstanding the fact that Hungary had made a (then-applicable) declaration under Article 96.[1100]

There is, however, significant case law supporting the view that the formal writing requirements of an Article 96 declaring State apply even if the applicable PIL rule does not point to the domestic law of that declaring State.[1101]

1097. *See* H. Flechtner, 'The Several Texts of the CISG in a Decentralized System: Challenges to the Uniformity Principle in Article 7(1)', *Journal of Law and Commerce* 17 (1998) 187–217, also available at www.cisgw3.law.pace.edu/cisg/biblio/flecht1.html.

1098. *Accord* Schwenzer/Hachem in Schlechtriem & Schwenzer, *Commentary* 4th ed. (2016), at 1264.

1099. *See UNCITRAL Digest of CISG Case Law* (2016), Art. 96, text with note 16. *See also* Ferrari & M. Torsello, *International Sales Law – CISG in a Nutshell* 2nd ed. (2018), at 172, citing Rechtbank Rotterdam, Netherlands, 12 Jul. 2001 http://cisgw3.law.pace.edu/cases/010712n1.html. *Accord* Brunner & Krisztina Balogh, 'Article 96 [Declaration Regarding the Written Form]', in *Commentary on the UN Sales Law (CISG)* (Brunner/Benjamin/Gottlieb eds, 2019), 644.

Compare Honnold/Flechtner, *Uniform Law* 4th ed. (2009), 188–191 (generally in favour of PIL analysis, but arguing that an Art. 12 derogation should also apply when applicable PIL principles point to domestic law of State which has a formal writing requirement, even though that State has not made an Art. 96 declaration). Applying Flechtner's view to the example set forth in the text, the transaction might be subject to the American Statute of Frauds (UCC, paras 2–201, which requires certain sales transactions to be in writing), even though the US, by not making an Art. 96 declaration, in effect declared its willingness to forego that writing requirement in CISG international sales. *Accord Forestal Guarani S.A. v. Daros International, Inc.*, 21 Jul. 2010, available at http://www.unilex.info/cisg/case/1537 (court must conduct choice-of-law analysis on the basis of PIL principles to determine which State's domestic law governs contract formation, and then apply that law to party's claim), cited with approval by Gillette & Walt, *CISG Theory & Practice* (2016), at 85–86.

1100. *See* Metropolitan Court of Budapest, 24 Mar. 1992, CLOUT Case 52, available at http://cisgw3.law.pace.edu/cases/920324h1.html.

1101. *See* cases cited in *UNCITRAL Digest of CISG Case Law* (2016), Art. 96, text with note 17. *Compare* Honnold/Flechtner, *supra* note 1099.

§5. Relationship to ULF/ULIS

338. A State which adheres to the CISG Convention and which is a party to the 1964 ULF Convention and/or the 1964 ULIS Convention shall at the same time denounce, as the case may be, either or both these Conventions.[1102]

§6. Contract Formation: Entry into Force

339. According to Article 100(1), the CISG applies to the formation of a contract only when the proposal for concluding the contract is made on or after the date when the Convention enters into force in respect of the Contracting States referred to in subparagraph (1)(a) or the Contracting State referred to in subparagraph (1)(b) of Article 1.

According to Article 100(2), the CISG applies only to contracts concluded on or after the date when the Convention enters into force in respect of the Contracting States referred to in subparagraph (1)(a) or the Contracting State referred to in subparagraph (1)(b) of Article 1.

§7. Six Authentic Texts

340. The CISG Convention – 101 articles in all – was done at Vienna, on 11 April 1980 in a single original, of which the Arabic, Chinese, English, French, Russian and Spanish texts are equally authentic.

1102. Article 99(3). *See also supra*, No. 11.

Appendix

CISG Ratifications (as of 1 July 2021) and date on which Convention entered or enters into force:

State	*Effective*
Albania	1 June 2010
Argentina	1 January 1988
Armenia	1 January 2010
Australia	1 April 1989
Austria	1 January 1989
Azerbaijan	1 June 2017
Bahrain	1 October 2014
Belarus	1 November 1990
Belgium	1 November 1997
Benin	1 August 2010
Bosnia-Herzegovina	6 March 1992
Brazil	1 April 2014
Bulgaria	1 August 1991
Burundi	1 October 1999
Cameroon	11 October 2017
Canada	1 March 1991
Chile	1 March 1991
China	1 January 1988
Columbia	1 August 2002
Congo, Republic of	1 July 2015
Costa Rica	1 August 2018
Croatia	8 October 1991
Cuba	1 December 1995
Cyprus	1 April 2006

The Czech Republic	1 January 1993
Denmark	1 March 1990
The Dominican Republic	1 July 2011
Ecuador	1 February 1993
Egypt	1 January 1988
El Salvador	1 December 2007
Estonia	1 October 1994
Fiji	1 July 2018
Finland	1 January 1989
France	1 January 1988
Gabon	1 January 2006
Georgia	1 September 1995
Germany	1 January 1991
Greece	1 February 1999
Guatemala	1 January 2021
Guinea	1 February 1993
Guyana	1 October 2015
Honduras	1 November 2003
Hungary	1 January 1988
Iceland	1 June 2002
Iraq	1 January 1991
Israel	1 February 2003
Italy	1 January 1988
Japan	1 August 2009
Korea, Democratic People's Republic	1 April 2020
Korea, South	1 March 2005
Kyrgyzstan	1 June 2000
Latvia	1 August 1998
Laos	1 October 2020
Lebanon	1 December 2009
Lesotho	1 January 1988
Liberia	1 October 2006
Liechtenstein	1 May 2020
Lithuania	1 February 1996
Luxembourg	1 February 1998
Macedonia	1 December 1991

Madagascar	1 October 2015
Mauritania	1 September 2000
Mexico	1 January 1989
Moldova	1 November 1995
Mongolia	1 January 1999
Montenegro	3 June 2006
The Netherlands	1 January 1992
New Zealand	1 October 1995
Norway	1 August 1989
Palestine, State of	1 January 2018
Paraguay	1 February 2007
Peru	1 April 2000
Poland	1 June 1996
Portugal	1 October 2021
Romania	1 June 1992
The Russian Federation	1 September 1991
Saint Vincent and the Grenadines	1 October 2001
Saint Marino	1 March 2013
Serbia	27 April 1992
Singapore	1 March 1996
Slovakia	1 January 1993
Slovenia	25 June 1991
Spain	1 August 1991
Sweden	1 January 1989
Switzerland	1 March 1991
Syria	1 January 1988
Turkey	1 August 2011
Uganda	1 March 1993
Ukraine	1 February 1991
United States of America	1 January 1988
Uruguay	1 February 2000
Uzbekistan	1 December 1997
Vietnam	1 January 2017
Zambia	1 January 1988

Selected Bibliography

Note: The full texts of more than 1,500 CISG-related articles, including many of those listed in this Selected Bibliography, are freely available online at: cisg.law-.pace.edu

Andersen, C. 'Reasonable Time in Article 39(1) of the CISG – Is Article 39(1) Truly a Uniform Provision?'. *1999 Review of the CISG* (1998).

Andersen, C. 'Good Faith? Good Grief!'. *International Trade and Business Law Review* 17 (2014): 310.

Baily, J. 'Facing the Truth: Seeing the Convention on Contracts for the International Sale of Goods as an Obstacle to a Uniform Law of International Sales'. *Cornell International Law Journal* 32 (1999): 273.

Basedow, J. 'Towards a Universal Doctrine of Breach of Contract: The Impact of the CISG'. *International Review of Law and Economics* 25 (2005): 487.

Bergsten, E. & A. Miller. 'The Remedy of Reduction in Price'. *American Journal of Comparative Law* 27 (1979) 255.

Berman, J. & M. Ladd. 'Risk of Loss or Damage in Documentary Transactions under the Convention on the International Sale of Goods'. *Cornell International Law Journal* 21 (1988): 423.

Berman, P. 'The Inevitable Legal Pluralism Within Universal Harmonization Regimes: The Case of the CISG'. *Uniform Law Review* 21(1) (2016).

Bianca, C. & M. Bonell. *Commentary on the International Sales Law* (1987).

Bonell, M. 'The CISG and the UNIDROIT Principles of International Commercial Contracts: Two Complementary Instruments'. *International Law Review of Wuhan University* 10 (2008–2009): 100.

Bridge, M. 'A Law for International Sales'. *Hong Kong Law Journal* 37 (2007): 17.

Bridge, M. 'Good Faith, the Common Law, and the CISG'. *Uniform Law Review* 22 (2017): 98.

Brunner, C. & Gottlieb, B. (eds), *Commentary on the UN Sales Law (CISG)* (2019).

De Ly, F. 'Sources of International Sales Law: An Eclectic Model'. *Journal of Law and Commerce* 25(1) (2006).

Farnsworth, E.A. *Contracts* 4th ed. (2004).

Farnsworth, E.A. 'Formation of Contract'. In *International Sales*, Galston & Smit eds (1984).

Farnsworth, E.A. 'Legal Remedies for Breach of Contract'. *Columbia Law Review* 70 (1970): 1145.

Ferrari, F. 'Autonomous Interpretation Versus Homeward Trend Versus Outward Trend in CISG case law'. *Uniform Law Review* 22 (2017): 244.

Selected Bibliography

Ferrari, F. 'Uniform Interpretation of the 1980 Uniform Sales Law'. *Georgia Journal of International and Comparative Law* 24 (1994):183.

Ferrari, F. 'Uniform Application and Interest Rates under the 1980 Vienna Sales Convention'. *Georgia Journal of International and Comparative Law* 24 (1995): 467.

Ferrari, F. 'Specific Topics of the CISG in the Light of Judicial Application and Scholarly Writing'. *Preadviezen Uitgebracht Voor de Vereniging Voor Burgerlijk Recht* 10 (1995), also in *Journal of Law & Commerce* 15 (1995).

Ferrari, F. 'What Sources of Law for Contracts for the International Sale of Goods? Why One Has to Look Beyond the CISG'. *International Review of Law and Economics* 25 (2005): 314.

Ferrari, F. 'Remarks Concerning the Implementation of the CISG by the Courts (The Seller's Performance and Article 35)'. *Journal of Law and Commerce* 25 (2005–2006): 223.

Ferrari, F. 'Fundamental Breach of Contract under the UN Sales Convention: 25 Years of Article 25 CISG'. *Journal of Law and Commerce* 25 (2005–2006): 489.

Ferrari, F. & Torsello, M., *International Sales Law-CISG in a Nutshell* 2nd ed. (2018).

Flechtner, H. 'Remedies under the New International Sales Convention: The Perspective from Article 2 of the U.C.C.'. *Journal of Law and Commerce* 8 (1988): 53.

Flechtner, H. 'Another CISG Case in the U.S. Courts: Pitfalls for the Practitioner and the Potential for Regionalized Interpretations'. *Journal of Law & Commerce* 15 (1995): 127.

Flechtner, H. 'The Several Texts of the CISG in a Decentralized System: Observations on Translations, Reservations and Other Challenges to the Uniformity Principle in Article 7(1)'. *Journal of Law & Commerce* 17 (1998): 187.

Flechtner, H. 'Buyers' Remedies in General and Buyers' Performance-Oriented Remedies'. *Journal of Law and Commerce* 25 (2005–2006).

Flechtner, H. 'Article 79 of the United Nations Convention on Contracts for the International Sale of Goods (CISG) as Rorschach Test: The Homeward Trend and Exemption for Delivering Non-conforming Goods'. *Pace International Law Review* 19 (2007).

Flechtner, H. 'Funky Mussels, a Stolen Car, and Decrepit Used Shoes: Non-conforming Goods and Notice Thereof under the United Nations Sales Convention ("CISG")'. *Boston University International Law Journal* 26(1) (2008).

Flechtner, H. 'The Exemption Provisions of the Sales Convention, Including Comments on "Hardship" Doctrine and the 19 June 2009 Decision of the Belgian Cassation Court'. *Belgrade Law Review* 84(3) (2011), also available at http://cisgw3.law.pace.edu/cisg/biblio/flechtner10.html.

Flechtner, H. & Brand, R. 'Opting in to the CISG: Avoiding the *Redline Products* Problem'. Chapter 5 in *A Tribute to Joseph M. Lookofsky* (2015).

Flechtner, H. (& Honnold, J), *Uniform Law for International Sales* 4th ed. (2009). Also cited as Honnold/Flechtner.

Flechtner, H. & Lookofsky, J. 'Viva Zapata! American Procedure and CISG Substance in a U.S. Circuit Court of Appeal'. *Vindobona Journal of International Commercial Law and Arbitration* 7 (2003): 93.

Flechtner, H. & Lookofsky, J. 'Zapata Retold: Attorneys' Fees Are (Still) Not Governed by the CISG'. *Journal of Law and Commerce* 26 (2007).

Gillette, C. 'The Political Economy of International Sale Law'. *International Review of Law and Economics* 25 (2005): 446.

Gillette, C. & Walt, S. *Sales Law, Domestic and International* 3rd ed. (2016).

Gillette, C. & Walt, S. *The UN Convention on Contracts for the International Sale of Goods. Theory and Practice* 2nd ed. (2016).

Gruber, P. 'Legislative Intention and the CISG'. In *CISG Methodology*, Janssen & Meyer eds (2009).

Henschel, R. 'Conformity of Goods in International Sales Governed by CISG Article 35: Caveat Venditor, Caveat Emptor and Contract Law as Background Law and as a Competing Set of Rules'. *Nordic Journal of Commercial Law*, 1 (2004).

Henschel, R. *The Conformity of Goods in International Sales* (2005).

Honnold, J. *Documentary History of the 1980 Uniform Law for International Sales* (1989).

Honnold, J. *Uniform Law for International Sales*, edited by H. Flechtner. 4th ed. (2009). Also cited as Honnold/Flechtner.

Janssen, A. & Spilker, M. 'The Application of the CISG in the World of International Commercial Arbitration', *Rabels Zeitschrift fuer auslaendisches und internationales Privatrecht* 77(1) (2013): 131–157.

Kastely, A. 'The Right to Require Performance in International Sales'. *Washington Law Review* 63 (1988): 607.

Kritzer, A. *International Contract Manual: Guide to Practical Application of the United Nations Convention on Contracts for the International Sale of Goods* (1994).

Lookofsky, J. 'CISG Foreign Case Law: How Much Regard Should We Have?'. In *The Draft UNCITRAL Digest and Beyond: Cases, Analysis and Unresolved Issues*, Ferrari/Flechtner/Brand eds (2004).

Lookofsky, J. 'Cator Can't Compete: Caveat Emptor under CISG Article 35(3)?', Chapter 10 In *The CISG Convention and Domestic Contract Law. Harmony, Cross-Inspiration or Discord?,* Lookofsky & Andersen eds (2014).

Lookofsky, J. *Consequential Damages in Comparative Context* (1989), https://jura.ku.dk/jurabog.

Lookofsky J. 'Fault and No-Fault in Danish, American and International Sales Law. The Reception of the 1980 United Nations Sales Convention'. *Scandinavian Studies in Law* 27 (1983): 109.

Lookofsky, J. 'Loose Ends and Contorts in International Sales: Problems in the Harmonization of Private Law Rules'. *American Journal of Comparative Law* 39 (1991), also at http://cisgw3.law.pace.edu/cisg/biblio/lookofsky6.html.

Lookofsky, J. 'International Sales Contracts: A Scandinavian View'. In *Suum Cuique* Blume, Tamm, Vindeløv eds (1993).

Lookofsky, J. 'Alive and Well in Scandinavia: CISG Part II'. *Journal of Law & Commerce* 18 (1999): 289–299.

Lookofsky, J. 'Remedies for Breach under the CISG'. In *Commercial Damages*, Knapp ed., Chapter 43 (2011).

Selected Bibliography

Lookofsky, J., 'The Rise and Fall of Article 92'. In *Festschrift für Ulrich Magnus*, Mankowski & Wurmnest eds (2014).

Lookofsky, J. 'In Dubio Pro Conventione? Some Thoughts about Opt-outs, Computer Programs and Pre-emption under the 1980 Vienna Sales Convention CISG'. *Duke Journal of Comparative and International Law* 13 (2003).

Lookofsky, J. & Hertz, K. *Transnational Litigation and Commercial Arbitration* 4th ed. (2017).

Lookofsky, J. & Hertz, K. *EU-PIL* 2nd ed. (2015).

Lookofsky, J. 'Impediments and Hardship in International Sales'. *International Review of Law & Economics* 25 (2005).

Lookofsky, J. & H. Flechtner. 'Nominating Manfred Forberich: The Worst CISG Decision in 25 Years?'. *Vindobona Journal of International Commercial Law and Arbitration* 9 (2005): 199.

Lookofsky, J. 'Walking the Tightrope Between CISG Article 7 and Domestic Law'. *Journal of Law & Commerce* 25 (2006): 87.

Lookofsky, J. 'Tooling Up for Warranties with the CISG Case Digest'. *CILE Studies. The CISG and the Business Lawyer: The UNCITRAL Digest as a Contract Drafting Tool* 4 (2008).

Lookofsky, J. 'Consequential Damages in CISG Context'. *Pace International Law Review* 19 (2007).

Lookofsky, J. & H. Flechtner. 'Zapata Revisited: Attorneys' Fees Are (Still) Not Covered by the CISG'. *Journal of Law and Commerce* 26(1) (2006–2007).

Lookofsky, J. *Understanding the CISG* 5th Worldwide ed. (2017).

Lookofsky, J. 'Not Running Wild with the CISG'. *Journal of Law & Commerce* 29 (2011), also available at http://papers.ssrn.com/sol3/papers.cfm?abstract_id=2376353.

Lookofsky, J. 'The CISG in Denmark and Danish Courts'. *Nordic Journal of International Law* 80 (2011): 295.

Magnus, U. 'CISG and Set-Off'. Chapter 12 In *A Tribute to Joseph M. Lookofsky*, Andersen & Henschel eds (2015).

Magnus, U. 'The Remedy of Avoidance of Contract under CISG: General Remarks and Special Cases'. *Journal of Law and Commerce* 25 (2005–2006): 423.

Nicholas, B. 'Force Majeure & Frustration'. *American Journal of Comparative Law* 27 (1979): 231.

Saidov, D. 'Standards of Proving Loss and Determining the Amount of Damages'. *Journal of Contract Law* 22 (2006): 27.

Schlechtriem, P. 'The Sellers Obligations under the United Nations Convention on Contracts for the International Sale of Goods'. In *International Sales*, Galston & Smite eds (1984).

Schlechtriem, P. 'Uniform Sales Law – The Experience with Uniform Sales Laws in the Federal Republic of Germany'. *Juridisk Tidskrift vid Stockholms Universitet* (1991–1992).

Schlechtriem, P. 'Opting out of Merger and Form Clauses under the CISG – Second Thoughts on TeeVee Toons, Inc. & Steve Gottlieb, Inc. v. Gerhard Schubert GmbH'. In *Sharing International Law Across National Boundaries: Festschrift for Albert H. Kritzer on the Occasion of his Eightieth Birthday*, Andersen & Schroeter eds (2008), 416.

Schlechtriem, P. & Schwenzer, I. *Commentary on the UN Convention on the International Sale of Goods (CISG)* 4th ed. Schwenzer ed. (2016).

Schroeter, U., 'Contract Validity and the CISG', 22 *Uniform Law Review* 47 (2017).

Schroeter, U. 'The Cross-Border Freedom of Form Principle Under Reservation: The Role of Articles 12 and 96 CISG in Theory and Practice'. *Journal of Law and Commerce* 33 (2014): 81.

Schroeter, U. 'Defining the Borders of Uniform International Contract Law: The CISG and Remedies for Innocent, Negligent, or Fraudulent Misrepresentation'. *Villanova Law Review* 58 (2013): 553.

Schroeter, U. 'A Time-Limit Running Wild? Article 39(2) CISG and Domestic Limitation Periods'. In *A Tribute to Joseph M. Lookofsky*, Andersen & Henschel eds (2015): 335–362.

Secretariat Commentary to 1978 UNCITRAL Draft Convention, A/CONF. 97/5.

Treitel, G. *Remedies for Breach of Contract* (1988).

UNCITRAL. *Digest of Case Law on the United Nations Convention on the International Sales of Goods* (2016), available at https://uncitral.un.org/en/case_law/digests.

Walt, S. 'For Specific Performance under the United Nations Sales Convention'. *Texas International Law Journal* 26 (1981): 211.

Walt, S. 'The CISG's Expansion Bias: A Comment on Franco Ferrari'. *International Review of Law and Economics* 25 (2005): 342.

White, J. & R. Summers. *Handbook of the Law under the Uniform Commercial Code* 6th ed. (2010).

Winship, P. 'The Scope of the Vienna Convention on International Sales Contracts'. In *International Sales*, Galston & Smit eds (1984).

Winship, P. 'Private International Law and the U.N. Sales Convention'. *Cornell International Law Journal* 21 (1988): 487.

Witz, C. *Les premières applications jurisprudentielles du droit uniforme de la vente international* (1995).

Ziegel, J. 'The Remedial Provisions in the Vienna Sales Convention: Some Common Law Perspectives'. In *International Sales*, Galston & Smit eds (1984).

Selected Bibliography

Index

The numbers here refer to paragraph numbers

Index

Index

Index

Made in the USA
Monee, IL
22 August 2023

41478578R00140